West of Fiction

West of Fiction

edited by Leah Flater, Aritha van Herk,
Rudy Wiebe

NeWest Press
Edmonton

Canadian Cataloguing in Publication Data

Main entry under title

West of fiction

ISBN 0-920316-62-X (cloth), 0-920316-64-6 (paperback)

1. Short stories, Canadian (English) - Canada, Western.*
I. Flater, Leah.   II. Van Herk, Aritha, 1954-   III. Wiebe Rudy, 1934-
PS8329.5.W48W48   C813'.01089712   C83-091214-2
PR9197.32.W48

Book design: May Chung
Cover illustration: Margaret Reece
Printing and binding: Friesen Printers, Altona, Manitoba
Financial assistance: Alberta Culture
                     The Canada Council

NeWest Publishers Ltd.
#204, 8631 - 109 Street
Edmonton, Alberta
Canada   T6G 1E8

Acknowledgements

For permission to reprint copyrighted material, grateful acknowledgement is made to the following:

George Bowering for "A Short Story", ECW Press for "Deer Trails in Tzityonyana" by Leon Rooke, Hurtig Publishers Ltd. for "The Darkness Inside the Mountain" by Rudy Wiebe from *Alberta/A Celebration* by Rudy Wiebe, Harry Savage, and Tom Radford, Ed Kleiman for "The Immortals", Henry Kreisel for "The Travelling Nude", Margaret Laurence for "A Bird in the House", Jake MacDonald for "Becoming", Macmillan of Canada, A Division of Gage Publishing Ltd. for "The Plague Children" from *The Barclay Family Theatre* by Jack Hodgins, and for "Old MacLachlin Had a Farm" from *Jake and the Kid* by W.O. Mitchell, Fredelle Bruser Maynard for "A Jewish Christmas", McClelland and Stewart for "One's a Heifer" from *The Lamp at Noon* by Sinclair Ross, Ken Mitchell for "The Great Electrical Revolution", from *Everyone Gets Something Here* published by MacMillan of Canada, Farley Mowat for "Walk Well, My Brother", Alice Munro for "Forgiveness in Families", Oberon Books for "Manitou Motors" from *Scars* by W.P. Kinsella, and for "The Skating Party" from *The Skating Party* by Merna Summers, Oolichan Books for "Under the I" by Edna Alford, Press Gang Publishers for "The Lost Gold Mine" from *Daughters of Copper Woman* by Anne Cameron, Brenda Riches for "Gall", Helen J. Rosta for "Midsummer Feast", Jane Rule for "A Television Drama", Sam Selvon for "Ralphie at the Races", Kathryn Sinclair for "The Long Wind", Fred Stenson for "Teeth", Audrey Thomas for "Xanadu", Turnstone Press for "Truda" by Sandra Birdsell, University of British Columbia for "We Have to Sit Opposite" by Ethel Wilson, W.D. Valgardson for "Saturday Climbing", Aritha van Herk for "Never Sisters", Wilfred Watson for "The Lice".

Contents

West of Fiction

W.D. Valgardson

Old Masters

W.D. (William Dempsey) Valgardson (1939-) was born in Winnipeg and raised near Gimli, Manitoba. He now lives on Vancouver Island and is head of the creative writing program at the University of Victoria. He has published three collections of short stories: *Bloodflowers* (1973), *God is Not a Fish Inspector* (1975) and *Red Dust* (1979); a book of poems, *In the Gutting Shed* (1976), and his first novel, *Gentle Sinners*, won the Books in Canada Best First Novel of the Year Award for 1981. Several of his short stories have been made into films, including "God is Not a Fish Inspector," "The Peddlar," and "Capital".

SATURDAY CLIMBING

W.D. Valgardson

Sixty feet up the cliff, the toe of his climbing boot resting on a ledge no wider than a dime, two fingers curled around a nubbin of rock, Barry was suddenly afraid that he would fall. "Rope," he called.

At the foot of the cliff, his daughter let out the golden line of rope that joined them. As Barry felt the rope go slack, he raised his right knee and pressed his toe into a shallow depression. Grunting with the strain, he stood up on his right leg, then paused, uncertain of his next move.

The cliff had proven to be deceptive. The conglomerate, with its rough, gravel-like surface, had looked easy. Close to the base, there were large handholds, so that at first the climbing was little more difficult than walking up stairs. Then, unexpectedly, the surfaces smoothed; the places where he could get a secure hold were spread farther and farther apart. At the same time, the numerous cracks dwindled until there was no place to set any protection. Unable to go back because of his pride, he had continued on until he now found himself dangerously far above his last piton. If he fell, he would drop twenty-five feet to the piton, then twenty-five feet past it before his rope came taut and held him. There was, because of the elasticity of the rope, a chance that he would ground out.

The thought flitted through his mind that it would be like falling from the top of a six-story building. Tensing his fingers, he straightened his elbow and leaned back from the rock so that he could search for his next hold. Above him, there was a half-inch ledge. He reached up, got a good grip, then lifted his left leg higher than he had ever imagined he could and set his foot on a rough patch that would provide the necessary friction to hold his weight.

He had been scared many times but never like this. Never before had he been this close to paralysis, to a sensation of letting go so that the tension and the fear would be over. The way he felt, he imagined, was the way a wounded animal felt when it finally gave up fleeing and allowed itself to be killed.

Six inches from his left hand there was a vertical crack that seemed hardly wider than a fingernail. Cautiously, he explored it with his fingers. Just within his reach it widened slightly. He ran his hand over his rack and unsnapped the smallest chock nut. He forced the aluminum wedge deep into the crack. From the wedge there hung a wire loop and from that a carabiner. Catching hold of the rope tied to his harness, he lifted it up, forced open the spring-loaded gate of the carabiner and fitted the rope into the aluminum oval.

Once the gate snapped shut, he sighed with relief. The chock nut, the wire loop, the carabiner, the rope, fragile as they looked, would hold ten times his weight. If he wanted to, he could let go and simply hang in space.

"You all right?" his daughter called. "Yeah," he lied. "Just resting."

His voice sounded faint and breathy. He was glad she could not see his momentary weakness. He could not control the trembling of his legs. The muscle of his right arm jerked spasmodically. Ever since his wife had left him, he had tried to compensate by providing unhesitating leadership for his daughter. He did his best to keep life simple and uncomplicated. It was, he thought, the way to provide security.

He glanced down. Among the scattered gray boulders, Moira's red hair gleamed like a burnished cap.

"You're doing fine," she hollered. The crosscurrents of air that played over the cliff face blurred her voice, making it seem farther away than it really was. To hear what she said, he had to strain toward the sound. "You've got another twenty feet to a big ledge. You can do it easy."

He was grateful for her confidence. Before they had started climbing, there had crept into his daughter's voice a constant note of disparagement and disappointment. The times he had managed to overcome his own insecurity and had asked her what was the matter, she had turned her back on him, answering, "Nothing," with a tightly controlled voice.

Bewildered, he had sought the advice of women at work who had teen-age daughters. They had been no help. Behind their competent, efficient professional selves, they too, he realized, were just as confused as he was. In desperation, he had gone so far as to pose the question of the relationship of fathers and daughters to his class. He had not been prepared for the reaction he got. From every corner of the room came cries of bitter disappointment and resentment.

As he had left the classroom, one student had called to him. He had stopped to wait for her. She had frizzy dark hair, wore long dresses that might have come from a western movie set, a rainbow assortment of beads and a nose ring. She always talked as if she was thinking in some exotic language and was translating it badly. She was the only student he'd ever had who insisted on analyzing *War and Peace* by consulting the *I Ching*.

"The caged bird proves nothing but the power of the captor," she had intoned.

For a moment, he suffered vertigo, and the cliff seemed to sway as if in an earthquake. He pressed his forehead to the cool stone and shut his eyes. Inside his flesh, his bones trembled.

Taking up rock-climbing had been an act of desperation. All the past activities Moira and he had done together—going to foreign films, visiting Seattle, beachcombing—she dismissed with a contemptuous shrug of her shoulders. At one time, they had played chess nearly every day. Lately, she pretended she had never seen the game. When he had noticed an advertisement for rock-climbing, he remembered that she had spoken admiringly of classmates who had hiked the West Coast Trail. He had registered them and paid their fees. Then he informed her.

He hoped she would be pleased. Instead, she was incensed that he had committed her to something without her consent. He knew she was right to be angry but he was too frantic to care. Over the previous month, she had come home late a number of times. Each time, the sweet-sour smell of marijuana clung to her, and her pupils seemed unnaturally large. He had not dared to accuse her of smoking dope. If he was wrong, she would never forgive him for being unjust. Being right frightened him even more. If she said, "That's right, I'm smoking dope, six joints a day, and sniffing coke and participating in orgies," he didn't know what he would do. Ranting and raving had ceased to work. Reasoning with her had no effect. He felt utterly helpless.

By emphasizing that the money was spent and there was no refund, he won the argument over rock-climbing. However, he took the car to the first class while she took her bike. She went prepared to sneer at everything, but once she saw her classmates, her attitude changed. Instead of Moira being isolated by her youth, Barry was isolated because of his age. Of the fifteen members, eleven were under twenty. The instructor still didn't need to shave more than once a week.

By the time the three hours were over and he realized that

rock-climbing wasn't going to be rough hiking, it was too late to back out. There were only three girls in the class. In return for the attention of one-third of the young men, Moira was prepared to scale the Himalayas.

Barry began with an attitude that was typical of someone raised on the Prairies. Anything over three feet was a substantial elevation. During the second class, he was expected to climb vertical cliffs. He gave some thought to dropping out of the class but realized that, after the fuss he had made about the fees, he would look like a dreadful hypocrite.

Gradually, as a dozen Saturdays passed, what had seemed impossible was reduced to the merely difficult. Cliffs that had looked flat and smooth as polished marble became a series of problems and solutions. The names of the unfamiliar equipment became a part of his vocabulary. Young men in climbing boots frequented his backyard and kitchen. To his relief, Moira accepted him enough to spend an occasional hour practising knot-tying with him.

This weekend there had been no class. In an attempt to heal a rift caused by an argument over her going away to college—she was two years ahead of herself in school and, therefore, in spite of being in grade 12 was only 16—he had offered to go climbing with her. To his surprise, she'd accepted.

"Climbing," he called.

"Climb on," Moira answered.

He stepped up, away from the safety of his perch. His life, he realized, was in her hands. If he fell, she was his protection.

The thought of giving her so much responsibility was like the prick of a thorn. In all other things, he had been trying to keep her from rushing headlong into taking on too much responsibility at once. The result had been a long series of disagreements. She did not have the decency to let one dispute finish before she began another. Sometimes three or four overlapped.

On Fridays, when he went to the faculty club, he ordered double brandies and brooded over whether he shouldn't have insisted on Sunday school in a good fundamentalist church all the past years. His colleagues, the majority of whom were the epitome of liberal tolerance about most things, when they talked about their teenage children reverted to wistful fantasies about convents and boarding schools in inaccessible locations.

The weekend past, Moira had wanted to go to an all-night party with a boy he just vaguely recognized as having drifted through the house two or three times. Barry was dumbfounded. At the same age, he'd had to have his girlfriends in before midnight. If he had kept a girl out all night, her father would have met them with a shotgun.

"Good girls," he said, quoting something he'd heard in adolescence, "don't stay out all night."

"Good fathers," she shot back, "don't think the worst of their daughters."

That afternoon was filled with slamming doors, weeping and raised voices. He found himself fighting so hard against her staying out all night that he compromised on three o'clock and afterward, when he had calmed down, wondered how it had happened. He had been determined to start with a deadline of midnight and let himself be persuaded to accept one o'clock. Although Moira claimed not to remember the chess moves, he had the distinct feeling that he'd been checkmated.

The final blow had been her insistence on going away to college. They had the money, he admitted. It just wasn't sensible, at sixteen, to travel 2,000 miles to attend a school when the local university was every bit as good, even if it did have him on the faculty. He suspected the choice had more to do with her all-night-party boy than with academic excellence.

Now, as he worked his way up toward the large ledge where he was to set up a belay station, it was as if Barry were in danger of being pulled backward by the sheer weight of his memories. It was with a sense of relief that he heaved himself onto the ledge. He paused to catch his breath, then anchored himself to a boulder.

"On belay," he shouted down, giving Moira the signal that he was ready.

His daughter, eighty feet below, seemed so small that Barry felt he could lift her into his arms. She looked no larger than she had been when, at three, she had eaten a bottle of aspirin. He had scooped her up and run with her four blocks to the hospital. After that desperate race and the struggle to hold her down—it had taken both him and a nurse to control her flailing limbs while the doctor had pumped her stomach— he was acutely aware of how tenuous her life was, of how much he would suffer if he lost her. For a long time afterward, he thought of her as being intricately constructed of fragile paper.

"Climbing," Moira answered.

"Climb on," he shouted.

From time to time, she paused to pull loose the chock nuts and pitons her father had left behind. These, since they would be needed later, she clipped to a sling that hung over her shoulder. Once, when she deviated from the route her father had taken, she became stuck at an overhang. Not having dealt with the obstacle himself, Barry could not help and had to leave her to find her own solution.

The climb seemed agonizingly slow, as if it would never be completed. Then, when it was over, and his daughter, grinning, breathless, was climbing over the edge, it was as if hardly any time had passed.

They sat side by side, sipping orange juice, their feet dangling in space.

"I thought you were in trouble," Moira said.

"I thought you were too," he replied, matching his weakness with hers. Then, ashamed, he admitted, "I gripped."

Moira twisted about. Her red hair was snugged at the back with a rubber band. Being outside had sprinkled her nose with light freckles.

She studied the cliff face. It rose another hundred feet. There was a crack that ran more than halfway, then a small series of outcrops. He tried to see the route they should take, but the last ten or fifteen feet seemed impossible.

"I'd come home for Christmas," she said in a rush, "and classes are out in April. It's not as if it was such a long time to be away."

She had caught him unawares, and none of his carefully prepared arguments were at hand.

"It's just so unexpected," was all that he could manage.

"I've got to leave sometime."

The house will be so empty, he wanted to say. How will I get used to being alone? It is as if you lost your first tooth only last year. As if I took you to kindergarten six months ago. You're barely rid of your braces.

She lifted her index finger and rubbed the side of her nose. She had done it as long as he could remember. It was her signal that she was going to impart a confidence or confess a wrongdoing—that she liked some boy in her class, that she had got a detention or spent all her allowance before the end of the week and needed more money.

"I'm not innocent, you know.'

He wondered what she meant by that but was afraid to ask.

"I mean," she continued, "Vic Hi's a big school. You hear a lot. Everybody's on the Pill. The dope's there if you want it. There's lots of opportunity."

He was tempted to let loose his anxiety in a lecture, but the memory of the frizzy-haired student in his class stopped him. She had stood on one foot all the time they were talking, the sole of her left sandal pressed to her right knee. She had passed her hand before his face in an affected arc. He'd heard her father was a prominent lawyer in the East but found it hard to believe.

She had talked in aphorisms and riddles, then a silence had fallen between them. He'd wondered why she had bothered to call after him, what she had really wanted to say. He had left her but, after a few steps, glanced back. She had given up her storklike stance and was standing with feet together, shoulders slumped, her face slack beneath her gaudy makeup. For the first time, he had seen how much younger she was than he had thought. If he had not known better, he'd have said she was a lost child.

Just then, she had seen him watching her. Immediately, she had drawn up her shoulders, flung back her head, given an exaggerated sway of her hips and pranced away. That had been the last time he'd seen her. She had never come back to his class, and one day a yellow drop-slip with her name on it had appeared in his mailbox.

"I want to lead this pitch," Moira said.

Barry was startled. She had never led. Always before she'd been second or third on a rope.

"I was thinking of rappeling down," he answered. "I can't see a clear route up."

"There," she said. "There and there and there." She jabbed her fingertip at a series of holds.

"But where would you set your protection?"

Her hand wove a series of stitches in the air. "There. Up there. To the side. Back across. Up about six feet."

His fear for her was not without reason. The climbing, after seeming so dangerous at first, had begun to lose its aura of hazard. They all fell from time to time, but their ropes kept them from suffering more than bruised knees and elbows. Then, one of the climbers who was leading had ignored instructions and, overconfident, had put in only one piece of protection. He placed it improperly, and when he slipped and fell, his weight jerked it loose. For a moment, no one had been able to move, then those who were not belaying or climbing had run toward the boy who lay sprawled on his back. Bright red blood seeped from his nose and ear.

"Jackets," Barry had demanded. Red Cross training that he'd not thought about in years came back with an intense clarity. "Every piece of clothing you can spare. We mustn't let him get cold."

They all had moved automatically, clumsily, unable to think. Having done as he instructed, they all stood stupefied. Their faces were shocked white beneath their tans.

He sent two of the students racing down the hill for help.

For an hour, they huddled in a ragged circle around the boy whose hair was paler than the sun-drenched grass and whose skin might have been molded from wax. He slipped in and out of consciousness. Each time his eyes shut, they all tensed, afraid that he had died. But then, he would groan or let out his breath harshly, and the moment would pass. Someone, Barry had not noticed who, had started collecting gear. One, and then another, began to pack. They moved slowly, silently, as if any noise would disturb the delicate balance between life and death.

Grounded out. That was what they called it. Because his safety had not been properly set, he had grounded out. Barry remembered that the air force had been like that too. Pilots never failed. They washed out. They never died. They bought it. *Grounded out.* The semantics covered up the fear.

Now, for a moment, it was as if, once again, he could hear the sharp startled cry; see the backward arc, the body, falling without grace or beauty, the rope writhing and twisting, the red-shirted boy settling in a cloud of unexpected dust.

"Ron," Barry protested, surprising himself at remembering the boy's name.

"Do you think I'd be so careless?"

It was asked in a tone that allowed no argument.

Stiffly, he stood up and tested his belay.

Don't climb, he thought, *it's too dangerous. Let us go back the way we came and find somewhere that'll always be safe.* But even as he thought it, he knew that it was impossible.

Once again, it was as if he were standing before the frizzy-haired girl, watching her long green nails sweep slowly before his face. At the time, he had not wanted to understand. "The world seeks balance," she'd said. "Extremism begets extremism."

"On belay," he said.

"Climbing," Moira replied.

His daughter, easily, with the supreme confidence of youth, grasped a handhold and pulled herself onto a flake. Smoothly, she worked her way up one side of the crack, straddled it and crossed over.

Below her, her father, ever watchful, full of fear, smoothly payed out the rope, determined to give her all the slack she needed while, at the same time, keeping his hands tensed, ready to lock shut, ready to absorb the shock of any fall.

■

Fred Stenson

Dale Hannaford

Fred Stenson (1951-   ) grew up on a mixed farm near Pincher Creek, Alberta, and now lives in Calgary. He has been a creative writing instructor in the penitentiaries at Drumheller and Bowden, and has worked as a researcher and script-writer for numerous documentary and dramatic films. He has published stories in *Chatelaine, The Canadian Review,* and *Saturday Night;* his novel *Lonesome Hero* (1974) was a finalist in the Search for an Alberta Novelist Competition, and won the CAA's Silver Medal for Literature in 1975. "Teeth" was first published in *Edmonton Magazine* (1981).

TEETH

Fred Stenson

Sixteen minutes and seven seconds are gone in the third period of this hockey game. We are behind four to three. The score might suggest to some that we have had a titanic struggle here, but we have not. Of the seven goals scored, five went in accidently off skates and legs. Our goalie slipped and fell on one of the other two.

If the technicians who are steadily creeping into this game ever equip players with a device for clocking average speed (an innovation I suspect and dread), this would show up as a far slower than average game. It's Tuesday night, not long after Christmas, and all around me I see that fatigued, glassy look that tells me that the rest of the players, like myself, are lapsing into a low energy coma. At the end of the game, they might have to move all this meat off the bench with a stock prod.

They say that some people play this game for fun. I personally can't imagine it and suspect this of being something cooked up by the owners and the press. I do have a foggy recollection of thirteen-year-old kids flailing away on corner lots in the freezing cold for reasons other than money or coercion, but I also know that I was never one of them.

My parents gave me no choice in the matter. They drove me to the rink late at night or at dawn and counted themselves the finest parents in the land for doing so. The fact that I didn't like hockey was unimportant. I was taught to believe that it was something you did whether you liked it or not—like school and community clean-up. For some parents, it's religion or music lessons; but my parents wanted neither Christian nor concert musician. They wanted a big, mean pro-hockey player who would wish them toothless Happy Birthdays during the Hockey-Night-in-Canada intermissions of their autumn years.

"Burns! Go on! C'mon, get the hell out there!"

Amazing. For a moment, I totally forgot where I was. All the hockey rinks and benches of my life merged into one and I didn't know whether I was twelve, eighteen or twenty-five—a bantam, a Junior or an NHLer.

I am an NHLer of course. And I am on our toasty warm

home bench. The man yelling at me is Chip, our manager, all crimson with rage. And, he is yelling because my line didn't go on when the other line came off. For many seconds, there has been no one on the ice but our goalie and six members of the other team.

One of them shoots. Carrasco, our goalie, gets a leg on it. Another one shoots. He stops that too. We are all cheering now, like mad; but, still, NOT ONE OF OUR PLAYERS CLIMBS OVER THE BOARDS TO PLAY!

"Goddamn you, Burns! Get out there before I break your leg!"

There is a blood vessel on Chip's forehead big and beating like an exposed heart. I climb over the boards and my linemates follow. Just in time to see the third rebound come off our goalie, Carrasco's pad right onto the stick of one of the five players buzzing around his net. The stick flicks, Carrasco dives; but the puck pops over him and into the net. The red light goes on just as we, the cavalry, arrive.

Fishing the puck out of the net, I look through the eye aperture of Carrasco's mask. He has drawn stitch marks on the plastic each time it saved him from a killing blast to the face. The mask looks like a railway map of southern Britain. From a distance this motif is ghoulish, but from this close, I can see Ronnie's eyes behind. They are red, watery and scared.

"Where were you guys?" he croaks, a dribble of water running out the bottom of the mask onto his padded chest.

I hand him the puck. "A souvenir, Ronnie. You were terrific." I whack him on the pads and skate to centre ice.

Later, after losing the game 5-3, we sit in the dressing room. We grunt orchestrally. A few tubas, a bassoon; I am more of a French Horn. There is no mood to this music, happy or sad; it is just there. Heavy, heartless breathing in a thought vacuum.

Again I slip quietly off to the ice-bound years of my adolescence. I was on the verge of rebelling, of telling my parents to varnish my hockey stick because it was my last. I was thinking about joining a tribe of travelling potters. I was about to do all that when a scout appeared after one of our play-off games. He took me to the best restaurant in town and told me to order as much of whatever I liked. While I ate, he mentioned several multi-digit money figures and I felt a sudden urge to take my hockey a little more seriously.

But, lately, something has gone wrong. I can't concentrate, not even on money. I just drift off. I start seeing the fifteen-year-old girls who hung around our hockey practices. I can see their faces and my memory has edited out every zit. The shy way they used to lurk in the shadows when we came out of the locker room with our hockey bags over our shoulders. I can hear them giggling, but I can't hear my own manager when he's screaming, "Go on, Burns! For the sake of sweet Jesus, go on!"

Chip enters and slams the door. His hair is sticking up valiantly from its sea of grease. His cheeks are flaming and he brings the smell of whisky in to do battle with the robust aroma of sweat. He stomps up and down between us, his every movement ferocious.

"You guys stunk out there, tonight!" he shouts at last, relieving the tension.

Smitty Smith, the cornerman on my line, wrinkles up his often-smashed nose and gives an attempt at a loud sniff which winds up being a thunderous snort. "Still do." he says, laughing and snorting. "Smell," he adds for the slow ones.

Chip whirls, his coat tails winding up like a propeller. "Who said that?"

"I did, coach," says Smitty.

Poor Smitty, or should I say lucky Smitty, because, surely hockey is keeping him out of an institution for the criminally stupid. He is regular cannon fodder for Chip's post-game rages. Chip walks up to him and levels a finger at the still snorting nose.

"Remember when I told this team that the next time we got scored on because of a slow line change, some lard asses were going to find themselves in the minor leagues!"

"No." Chip chooses to ignore this.

"Your line, Smith, was scored on tonight when you weren't even on the goddam ice!"

"But, Burnsy..."

"Screw Burnsy!" I can't say I care for the sound of this. "It was your line and I might just decide to put all three of you idiots down for awhile. Maybe down there you could remember how to play hockey!"

This is a fairly idle threat. Obviously Chip would love to send most of us to the minor leagues and would except for the total lack of better players there to bring up.

"I'm telling you guys this team's on the verge of shake-up!

Nobody's job is secure as long as we keep losing. There's three things wrong with you: No hustle! No brains! No speed! And NO GUTS!!"

"That's four." Smitty grins with happy idiocy, not a tooth in his giant head. He is so proud of his deduction.

The effect on Chip is quite fascinating. He begins to sag slowly like a pin-punctured inflatable couch. Frowning at the floor, he mutters in a vague monotone; something about the plane we have to catch to Montreal in the morning. He finishes by saying, "If we play like this against Montreal . . ." But his voice tails off into silence before he can entirely tell us what we're in for. He shuffles to the door, still sagging. Smitty really can't help himself; he has to give the old coach just one more helping hand.

"They'll kill us," he offers cheerfully.

Chip is at the door by now, with his hand draped on the knob. Hearing Smitty, he finds one last nerve of fury, yet unexploded. He swings around. His eyes travel the bench on which we sit. His eyes meeting ours. I wouldn't be surprised if there are tiny cross hairs in the middle of his vision. When his eyes reach mine, they stop. His mind pushes the button marked torpedo.

"Burns. In my office after you shower."

When I step into Chip's office a half hour later, he is gnawing on one of his hands. A lonely cannibal. I feel something for him close akin to sympathy: disgust, I think. If Chip's stomach was a garbage bag, you wouldn't want to carry anything wet or heavy in it.

"You took your sweet time."

"Heavy dirt and grime."

I move a dog-eared scouting file off a chair and sit. Chip waits deliberately hoping the suspense will fill me with regret for my many wrongdoings.

"You're not putting out, Burns."

"I'm the team's highest scorer."

"Look, Burnsy," 'Burnsy' means an appeal to my sporting side. Chip is still under the impression I have one. "You could do a hell of a lot more for this team. You're a great little hockey player when you want to be. You were a first-round draft pick."

"Fire the scout."

"But, cripes, just sitting there during a line change."

"I think it was my inner ear acting up again."

"Okay, alright. Water under the bridge." Such is Chip's obsession with this game, I'm sure he sees ice on the water and kids with great potential playing shinny on the ice.

He looks up, past my head, at a yellowing photograph of his last winning team; juniors he coached to a national final.

"You could lead this team out of the doldrums." His voice has taken on that misty monotone again, as if he was talking from the cockpit of a time machine. "We wouldn't have to be in the cellar if you played your best game. Take charge. Like Bobby Clarke. The players look up to you." He pauses, frowns, takes a bite out of his hand and glares at me crazily. "They look up to you and you infect the whole bunch of them with a lack of desire!"

I feel this is a bit strong. I try to instil in them a sensible lack of hope.

"Don't you ever want to be on the all-star team, Burns?"

The answer to this question is 'No' but I won't break Chip's heart by telling him. The all-star game is sixty minutes of hockey I presently have the luxury of taking or leaving.

"The point is this, Burns; if you don't start putting out, I'm going to trade you."

I shrug.

Chip looks heavenward and grasps the air. Maybe God is lowering him a ladder.

"This rotten damn game! I can remember juniors I coached; big kids, tough as nails, crying their eyes out because they didn't get drafted. And you. Big fat contract. Commercials. Endorsements. And you couldn't care less if we trade you."

Chip rips open the bottom drawer of his desk and pulls out a whisky bottle. He spins off the top and it bounds across the carpet. He drains off a couple of inches from the neck of the bottle and scrapes his hand viciously across his mouth. His eyes are those of a cornered pig.

"What about me? What the hell do I do when I get fired off this tail-end team?"

Perhaps Chip could sell endorsements for ulcer milk:

'It was the third period of the game. We were behind and stinking the place out. It would be our sixth loss in a row and I could already hear the management baying for my blood. I can tell you, my ulcers were giving me hell. I reached for the mickey of rye in the inside pocket of my sports jacket; but my wife had taken it out and replaced it with a bottle of

Abdomal, the Ulcer Milk. My first thought was, I'll break
that bitch's face; but when that Abdomal got down there and
started to soothe . . .'
   "Get out of my sight, Burns! You make me sick."

A speedy jaunt in my Porsche and I am home to my
luxurious two bedroom condo by the river. The kitchen·
faucet exudes a thin stream of boiling hot water which in
former times was a simple drip. The dirty socks, the
Kentucky Fried Chicken bones, the cones of cigar ash on the
carpet, the beer bottles lying on their sides...
   I had a cleaning lady once. She clucked her tongue and said
How disgusting! A monkey wouldn't live like this and you a
big shot hockey player too! As a helping hand to a better life,
she stole my liquor.
   In the midst of all this filth, I sit in almost abject misery. If
I was someone else looking in I would sneer. How dare you
be abjectly miserable with a salary the size of yours, I'd say.
And all I could say back at me would be a lot of whining
about too many practices and road trips, about our grueling
schedule. I would also plead my peculiar belief about the
women of this world.
   According to the popular myth, there are a million women
in this land who are dying to take care of and slip between the
satin sheets with me, a national sporting hero. I believe in
this ghostly battalion of beauties with a kind of desperate
fervour. I do my best to keep myself attractive for them. For
instance, all thirty-two of my teeth are still straight and solid
in their gums—a rarity if not a total exception among hockey
players.
   My secret is regular brushing, flossing and a total
avoidance of anything resembling a fight, an elbow or a high
stick. It was once said of me by a smart-ass reporter that I
could go into the corners with fresh eggs in my hockey pants
and never break a one. So what? It's true.
   But where are these women? This is the greatest mystery of
my life. Maybe they are in bed with my toothless teammates
but I doubt it. I have a feeling that they are already married to
lawyers and carpenters and accountants and that they limit
their goings-on with pro athletes to a sly lusting after our
brutishness in front of the colour TV Saturday night. Oh,
please. Just one of you. Come to me!
   But really, as I sit here in my bathrobe, sipping an orange
juice past my perfect, mint-flavoured teeth—my jock strap

drying on a chair between me and the national news—I look at my purple shins, the scars on my knees and ask, who in their right mind would be interested in this body?

Less than twenty hours later, the gate swings open and the Montreal Forum ice gleams ahead of me under the TV lights. Yes, for the first time all year, we are going to be displaying our talents on National TV. At last, our Moms and Dads across the land will have the opportunity of watching their favourite sons being thrashed by one of the nation's most powerful hockey machines.

We emerge to a chorus of jeers and boos from the rabid Forum fans. Our team name is the Bisons.

That name always seemed like a prophetic and fitting title for our team. I devised my own little cheer from it to motivate me across dull spots in the play. It goes like this:

> Go Bisons go!
> Big, stupid and slow;
> Onward to'rd extinction,
> Go Bisons go!

The game begins and before it is a minute old, the Canadians' star right winger has picked the puck from Steve Burke's skates, gone in alone on our goalie Carrasco and popped the puck past his internationally famous weak spot: low, to the stick side.

Soon after, we take a penalty and the Canadians have us all hemmed in our own end again. It looks like just a matter of time until they bang another one in. I'm staying out of trouble by the blue line. It's safe and quiet there and a nice, short skate to centre ice after the goal.

All of a sudden one of our defencemen takes a wild swipe at the puck, connects and knocks it rolling up the ice. The Montreal defencemen have all closed in on our net for the kill and, as a result, I am the closest person to the puck by about twenty yards. I skate for it and have perhaps the cleanest breakaway of my life.

I try hard to concentrate. I haven't scored a goal in six games and Chip may just be getting serious about trading me. A new team might mean pressure, extra practices, or, God forbid, the playoffs.

The goalie is coming out to meet me. I should really deke and go around him, but I might screw up and lose the puck if I did. Better to shoot now. I pick a spot in the right corner and fire. Somehow I fan. I get practically no wood on the shot at all, but the goalie, seeing what I was planning to do, moved to cover the right hand corner. This opens up a little hole between his legs and, through that hole, my meagre shot trickles. It has just enough momentum tò get over the goal line into the net. The period ends 1-1.

During the intermission, Chip tries to tell us that the Canadians aren't that tough. We'll take 'em boys, he says. This is such a good one that several of us cannot stifle laughter.

Halfway through the second period, pucks start streaming past Carrasco's stick side. Every time we make a big effort to stop this shelling, we take a penalty and they pot another one. After the fifth goal, Carrasco comes skating over to the bench like a man possessed. He tries to open the door into the bench but Chip holds it shut from the other side.

"What's wrong with you? You're not hurt."

"Lemme in." Carrasco whimpers. "I saw it again."

He jerks his helmet off. His face is white. A drop of sweat jiggles crazily on the point of his chin. "I saw the ghost again. He had on a white uniform. He skated in on me laughing. His teeth were all black. He slapped the puck and it went right through me! Right in one side and out the other!"

"You stop talking like a nut and get the hell back out there!"

Bond, our captain, leans over. "Jeez, coach, let him come out. He won't stop nothing like this. It's a mental problem."

"You're damn right he's got a mental problem. He can't stop a G.D. thing on his stick side. That's the problem!"

Carrasco stops yanking on the door. He throws his goalie stick up into the crowd and climbs over the boards. He beats his way past Chip and runs on his skates down the alley to the dressing room.

"Fart!" screams Chip. "No one else in this league has half the crazy bastards I do. Bordeaux get in there."

Bordeaux is our back-up goalie, a fuzz-faced kid from Montreal. His home town is the very last place on earth he ever wanted to appear—on TV yet—playing behind a cheesecloth outfit like the Bisons. But fear drives him to brilliance and the second period ends without further scoring. 5-1 Canadians.

In the third period, I score again. If the TV colour man was to discuss my goal after the game, he might describe it this way:

"Burns was parked out in front of the net jostling with a defenceman and keeping up a constant stream of chatter. 'Watch it, you bastard, you almost got me in the eye. Hey, ref, this guy's trying to hack my head off here!' All of a sudden a defenceman on Burns' team winds up for a slapper from the point. It comes in like a bullet and, well, nobody could jump higher on skates than Burns when he thought he was going to get hit by the puck. So, there it was, the puck doing about a hundred and Burns up in the air this high; the puck hits his skate blade, whango! and its right in the net. Heck, I must have seen Burns score five goals that way over the years."

But, the colour man won't be discussing my goal as it only serves to make the Habs mad. They come storming back scoring on poor Bordeaux almost at will. Soon, the Montreal crowd are cheering wildly every time the kid stops a dribbler.

Then, it happens. Steve Burke, who has been on the ice for every Montreal goal, goes nuts. He boards the Canadians' super-star right winger so hard a pane of plexi-glass falls out into the crowd. The super-star drops as if shot and does not move.

The rest is axiomatic. Two of the Montreal players go for Burke with sticks up and threatening. One of our boys goes in to even up the odds. The referees race over to try and prevent total war. Fat chance. The super-star still isn't moving. His eyes are closed. He may be dead. All the Montreal players come storming off the bench which means that all our players must storm off the bench too.

I am on the bench and would love to stay here. But it isn't done. All these things are as pre-ordained as the order of events at a Vatican high mass. I file dutifully onto the ice with my gloves held by the gauntlets and skate around the perimeter of the six fights now in progress, trying to look as unmenacing as possible.

The super-star is up now. Unhurt, and forgotten. The crowd that was gasping in fear for his career seconds ago is now too busy watching the fight to notice him up and skating off the ice. Right now, he's unimportant. One fight is busy spawning another. Oathes wing hither and thither in need of bilingual translation. Fans are up on their feet, clinging to the plexi-glass and crying for blood.

In the midst of all this bloddy hubbub, it happens again. I begin to drift. I drift down the thousand or so benches I have sat on and pick up not a sliver. I drift right back to Buffalo Flats, the Alberta small town where I was allowed to live for a few years before I had to move on to bigger centres and better coaches. I am with a girl I had forgotten existed. Her name is Paulette. We're thirteen and we're in the dark beside the rink. She is letting me put my hand up under her heavy woolen sweater. It is the first time I have ever done this. It is freezing cold out. One of my ears is totally numb, but I don't own a hat. Hats are sissy. It's so cold that Paulette is afraid we might freeze solid. I think one part of me is already afflicted, but I don't tell her this. She may be able to feel the evidence anyway. She is most worried about freezing solid because it would mean that we would be found as we are with my hand up her sweater. I am more worried about dying.

I am so far gone, so absorbed in these philosophical matters, with Paulette and her sweater, that I hardly notice the kid who races over to me, screeches to a halt in a spray of ice and grabs hold of my sweater. I hardly see his pimply, writhing face, his madman eyes. I hardly hear the stream of abuse from his toothless mouth. While I am in Paulette's sweater, he is trying to pull mine over my head. Unable to do this and frustrated to total insanity by the faraway, seraphic smile on my face, he lowers his head and drives the top of his helmet into my mouth.

This, I feel.

Suddenly, Paulette is gone. Her sweater. Buffalo Flats. All banished back to the foreign past. The crazy kid is gone somewhere too. Dragged off by a referee or maybe by one of my teammates. I am back in the Forum. Standing at centre ice. I look down at the red dot and it is getting redder by the second, dyed by a stream from my mouth. A quick lick tells me that one of my two perfect, well-flossed and brushed front teeth is no longer occupying its traditional place in my healthy gum. I don't remember swallowing it. Slowly, I skate around the ice looking. It's got to be here somewhere. Teeth don't just vanish.

Then, I am corralled by our trainer and two of our players. I keep telling them I must find my tooth, but they are pushing me along toward the gate, like a senile granny on wheels.

On the narrow bench in the dressing room. Mouth wadded full of cotton batting. The muffled roar of the crowd as the game peters out to its lopsided conclusion.

The game ends. The team trudges in. Chip follows, raving about a shake-up. I am not around to be raved at, however. I am off in the near future this time, rather than the distant past that I so often visit. In this near future, there are sticks but they are all embedded in weenies or the soft belly of an ice cream bar. There are pucks too, of bacon. Body checks come annually at the doctor's office and he always announces that you are in great physical condition. Afterwards you go home to your pad, an old fashioned, but modest and clean apartment. Meeker is someone more meek than someone else.

Somehow, every time I lick up under my swollen lip, I am reminded of this near future and the many sources from which money can come. Money, unlike teeth, can be replenished. A missing tooth is a hole in your head for life.

■

Kathryn Sinclair

Kathryn Sinclair (1940-   ) was born in Stouffeville, Ontario.
She has lived in Saskatchewan, studied Fine Arts at the
University of Manitoba and lived and worked in Iowa. She
presently resides on an acreage near Devon, Alberta where she
breeds cats, goats and chickens. Her story, "The Golden Dragon",
was published in *Rubaboo 2* (1963); in 1981 she was selected
to attend the Clarion Science Fiction Writers' Workshop at
Michigan State University, where she was the only Canadian
writer present. She has published poetry, articles in
Harrowsmith, and "The Long Wind" originally appeared in *Isaac
Asimov's Science Fiction Magazine* (June 1982).

THE LONG WIND

Kathryn Sinclair

There was a long wind blowing. Scheer banked and curved, coming up into the current of the maelstrom, her wings cracking and booming with the stress. Up again and over. Now down, and . . . ah, there! She could feel the flow around her, hear the wind sizzle and crack just beyond the tips of her wings, but she hung in the peaceful knot of air that she knew had been there.

Below her, Rask mounted the steps of the roaring currents. She watched him with admiration tinged with disgust, cocking her head to keep him in view as she gently adjusted, curled, and lifted to stay in the tranquil eddy. Rask had skill. His control in the turbulent upper reaches was almost as good as hers. The strong muscles of his wings corded and flexed with strain. He slid up and across, then balanced and glided to another updraft. He worked his way closer.

It was really a shame, she thought, admiring the way he shifted and balanced, the way his golden hair clung sleekly to his body, the magnificent spread of his wings. It was really a shame that he irritated her so much. He had spoken before the Council for her; it was only the protection of her mother that had delayed the decision. If she did not earn a position on the Council of the Ara soon, he would again petition for a mindbond with her, and she would have little to say in the ruling they made.

She pictured herself going through the breeding ritual with him, but the real Rask, the one she knew in her mind, superimposed himself on the magnificent spectacle which he displayed, and she shook her head and turned her mind back to her windriding. Rask was an impressive sight, but Scheer would no more mate with him than with the zin they hunted for food.

The wind shifted suddenly, curling around in a giant eddy several miles long, and Scheer dipped and sorted the wind currents until she reached another quiet spot. She liked to come up here, to look up and wonder what lay beyond the limits to which the Ara could fly. Above her the sky stretched, purple deepening to black at the horizon. The sun had set. Overhead flared the aurora, rippling in curtains of rose and emerald. A few stars flickered through the lurid display. The stars! They beckoned to her. She was sure that they were more than just lights hanging in the sky. The Ara said that they were isci, swimming across the deepness of the heavens. As the Ara could not fly too far down, so they were not meant to fly too far up. But Scheer felt that they were wrong. The stars moved in patterns. Isci did not move in patterns. If she could just convince more of the Ara . . .

"Hello, Scheer." The voice came soft and crawling into her consciousness. Rask! In her star-gazing she had forgotten him. He hung in the eddy with her, his sharp face split in a grin, his body curled into a suggestive posture beneath the steady beat and balance of his wings. She turned her head away in disgust.

He ran a claw invitingly along the underside of one of her wings. She twisted from him with revulsion at the familiar gesture, folded her wings flat to her body and dropped.

As she fell, she was buffeted by the fierce crosswinds that tore the breath from her mouth and ripped at her tightly clenched body. She knew the danger, and so did Rask. He circled above her, a diminishing speck. But she had practiced this maneuver many times, glorying in the sudden pull of gravity, the tremendous force of the atmosphere tearing at her, the danger. There was a point at which the pull of the planet would start to be counteracted by the drag of the rapidly thickening air. It was at this point that the downward plunge could be controlled. But if she miscalculated, she would be unable to pull out of the dive without injuring herself, perhaps fatally.

A few more seconds and she could start to open her wings, a little at a time, gliding downward now rather than falling, gradually opening them until their lift counteracted the pull of gravity. Her descent slowed, until she hovered and glanced around her. She had gone through Silver layer and through White and was in the glow layer beneath. Below her lay the billowing surface of Yellow. Rask was left far above. She was alone again.

She circled for a while in the solitude, combing down her rumpled silver fur which had been stirred up by her precipitous fall, and working through her string of curse words. No star-watching now! When she felt sufficiently composed, she banked in a lazy arc and began to search for a corridor. She flew along swirling pillars of cloud, arching up out of Yellow to catch and tear in the silver strands of the fast moving White above. Scheer slid up the tangled skein of one of the columns, through an opening in the cloud layer and turned in the direction of Arahome.

Ara Council was in session. Voices hissed and babbled, airsacks boomed and wings snapped. Scheer appeared before them again for questioning.

"Your father was a Diver. Your mother is a Diver. It is an honourable profession. Why then do you waste your time *windriding*?" Councillor Meere was short of temper and patience today, and he put the greatest amount of scorn upon the word.

"I do windride, but it is not to waste time. I do more. I windride to study the stars." Scheer tried to keep the pleading note out of her voice.

"Ah, the heavenward isci," hissed councillor Droon. "The fantasy of the bubbleheads and shiftless, who do not wish to contribute to the well-being of the Ara." His voice dropped to a whisper. "Why do you ascend to 'study' these unattainable isci when the Ara have great need of those which can be caught below us by Divers?"

"With the council's pardon, I do not think that the stars are isci but are something else. . . ."

"Enough!" boomed Droon. "I will hear no more of this. Your mother will speak for you, if there is anything more to be said. She has earned her place on council."

Scheer obediently dropped below and out of the council ball as her mother's quiet voice hummed in the buzz of other voices. As a Diver, Mahr was well respected on council, but Scheer had no illusions that she could be protected by that respect forever.

Diving was a skill which few had mastered and the dangers were immense. But it would be a way to prove herself, and unless she did, she could not speak in the council nor direct her own affairs.

The discussion in council grew louder. Elder Droon finally brought an end to it by bringing his wings together with a thunderclap. Scheer hoped that this meant the meeting was coming to an end. Droon's son's wife was in labour in the sunward sector of White layer, and Droon wished to be there for the dropping. If he could touch the child as soon as the father caught it, and help unfold its wings, it would have a propitious start in life. Scheer didn't think that Droon wanted to drag things out. Which meant that there was a good chance they would leave the problem of Scheer's windriding for another day.

On the far side of the council drifted Rask. The looks he cast towards her were full of meaning, but she knew that he didn't dare make any improper gestures in full view of the council. She was safe enough.

She had to solve the problem soon. Rask was only the symptom. Until she proved herself among the Ara by taking a productive occupation, she would be in a precarious position. She had no say on council. Survival among the Ara depended on keeping the birthrate at a constant level, and Scheer had now come of breeding age. The Ara's numbers were small enough that she could not refuse to take liaison with any that the council might select. It was just that *she* wished to make the choice, even if it was to be Rask, not some limp-winged old darkfur on the council.

She realized that Rask had moved nearer, and was keeping pace with her at the closest limits that decency allowed. One wingspan closer and he would be guilty of a grave indiscretion before council. Of course, Rask would never make that error. She fumed at her inability to cope with him in a more direct manner.

The council started to disperse. From the east, the prevailing wind brought scents to her nostrils, the freshness of a storm, the electricity. Now she and her mother could go hunting. To the west, the streams of zin would be thick today.

It had been good hunting. Scheer withdrew the string of airsacks from the body of one of the zin and twined the glistening, pearly bubbles around her head. She and her mother had found a large pack of them fleeing downwind from the violence of the storm, the semi-transparent creatures sculling with their many arms in the top layer of Yellow. It was a bit deeper than Scheer liked to go, but her mother had insisted. *She will make a Diver of me yet*, Scheer thought.

Mahr circled nearby, the zin tied in a long string behind her, clutched in her claws. She didn't seem to notice the drag. Scheer again admired the toughness and strength of her mother. The years had not weakened the power of her wings and her fur still gleamed a bright silver, scarcely darkened yet with age. She had been alone since her mate, Scheer's father, had not returned from a dive. Scheer had been very young then, but the memory of her mother's grief, her own sense of loss and betrayal was still strong within her. The dive had taken her father, yet her mother returned to the depths again and again to bring up the rich meer and the isci that the Ara needed. Scheer wanted nothing to do with it. She would be a windrider, follow the stars, discover what no Ara had before her.

Mahr had taught Scheer the mechanics of the dive. It was not enough to have mastery of the downward pull of the world beneath them, not enough to have strong wings and good control in the deadly crosscurrents that swirled below. The body had to be trained to switch from the nose-breathing of the upper levels to the inflated airsack, which gave the Ara breath for an extended dive.

They had come to the lowest levels of normal breathing on this hunt, the upper layers of Yellow. Beneath Yellow was the boundary below which no one went without training and practice. Scheer could feel her body labour for breath even here, feel the instinctive urge of the airsack to take over the function of breathing, of her nostrils to close. She fought it.

Her mother's eyes showed concern. "Tomorrow we will go deeper yet, and bring back the meer which I feel are below us now. For today, you have had enough." Mahr's voice was a soft whisper in the roar of the wind around them.

"I do not wish to go deeper, Mother. You know that I have no love for the dive."

"You will go deeper. I am weary of turning aside proposals for your welfare in council. It is time you bargained for yourself. I cannot forever protect you. Tomorrow we will dive." Her mother suddenly released the stored-up power of her wings and rose swiftly out of sight into White. Scheer followed.

The long wind blew with more violence today, tearing with insane fury across the outer edge of Scheer's world. It was all she could do to keep control as it ripped and tore around her. The aurora stretched from one horizon to the other, rippling with color, cracking with sound. The points of light she longed to see were completely hidden. If she had any sense, she thought, she would go back down and submit to her mother's will, dive for the meer and isci and establish her place on council. But she wouldn't go, couldn't face the dark depths, and the darker memories of her father. He hadn't come back.

She balanced and wavered in the current, swept along with the violent speed of the wind. It would be a long way back to

Arahome. Already the mental trail was fading. She had found no stable eddies to drift in, and the main wind moved with far greater speed than the lower levels. It startled her to suddenly find Rask blowing along beside her, just out of wingtip reach.

"Your mother searches for you, Scheer." His lazy voice barely reached her over the constant roar of the wind.

"Let her, and may you search elsewhere yourself." She curled a claw derisively at him, and then looked away.

His voice held more amusement. "Do you run from that which she has chosen for you? You do not honour the memory of your father."

She stiffened with anger. How dare he probe so accurately to her inner feelings! How dare he! It was as if he already held the mindbond with her. She turned upon him with all the scorn she could muster. "Go back to your zin-chasing, Rask. I do not seek confidence with you. You intrude upon my space."

He recoiled a little, but his face still showed more humour than dismay. It was as if he felt that he had already won, that the council had decided in his favour. Scheer's anger flared higher. She slashed at him with her wingtips, and when he drew back further, she dropped as she had before. Down she sped, exhilarated as always by the fall, the controlled slowdown, the pullout . . . and found that Rask had dropped with her and was pulling out just below.

Scheer hissed with rage. Her wings cracked as she wheeled over into a steep dive and slid away down a long canyon of billowing white. Rask was a strong flier and she didn't think she could escape him that way, but she had the advantage of more maneuverability. Perhaps she could lose the pest if she took advantage of the many tunnels and canyons of White. She drove forward with strong wingthrusts until she had picked up speed, and then angled suddenly and shot up a chimney that appeared to her left. Rask was right behind her, she could hear his booming laughter. He actually thought that she was playing! She hissed again and swerved suddenly to the right, finding a small tunnel that she could barely clear with her wingtips. It would be dangerous to drag a wing in the viscous material of White layer going this speed. She had to cup her wings slightly to slip through, but she was so enraged that the thought of the danger was a small thing. He dared! He dared!

She dropped suddenly down a chimney that opened beneath her. Rask hurtled by overhead, unable to check himself in time, and Scheer felt a thrill of triumph. She would show him, she'd lose him completely. As the chimney opened onto the glow layer beneath White, she spread her wings again and slid along White's lower surface, looking for an updraft. There! She entered the stream of air which boiled up through White and let it lift her at tremendous speed, the walls blurring by. There was relief, breathlessness, residual anger, the ebbing of the sharp edge of fear that she had balanced on, as she had overflown at this dangerous level.

And then, from a side corridor, there was a flash of gold. Rask! Moving tremendously fast! He saw her too late, tried to swerve, a wingtip dragged deep into the cloud, and almost faster than she could see, he was tumbling down and out of sight into the foaming whiteness below.

Her wings grabbed the air frantically as she slowed to a stop. She was numb with panic. Rask! Rask! She turned mentally and searched for Arahome. Dimly, her mind could see it, but it was far away, the long wind had swept them too far. She sent a scream for help along the mental trail toward the Home, and then circled slowly down through the heavy white to the glow layer beneath.

He was nowhere to be seen. He hadn't been able to pull out. Below her Yellow swirled and whispered, lightning flickering evilly from billow to curl. Below Yellow lay Copper, where only the divers went. She circled frantically. Rask!

She started down, hardly aware that she was doing so, adjusting as she dropped, as her mother had taught her. Deep breaths, pumping pressure into the airsack. She felt it fill, felt the mechanism of her body slowly change as it compressed and stored air, reacting to the increase in pressure. Her nostrils closed.

She was through Yellow, deeper than she had ever gone with her mother. She hesitated. The glow layer was dark, the light from the sun hardly penetrated the many layers of clouds. Below her, Copper, gleaming and dangerous. It curled and swirled seductively, the air heavy with its electric menace. Down there was Rask. If he had survived the fall, if the crosscurrents hadn't torn his wings, if his airsack had time to expand, he would be through Copper and down to Brown, where she would need her second eyes, where the air was so thick that things crawled upon it and the Ara could not fly, where the drag from the world below and the pressure from above was so great that it pulled out the strength and held the diver down until the airsack emptied and the diver died. As her father had.

Scheer circled indecisively. Perhaps it would be best to wait for the help that would come in answer to her call. But he would never last that long.

She curved into a cautious circle and began to descend, down into Copper. The drag on her wings became extreme and she found that a gradual sloping fall, using her wings as little as possible, took the least of her energy. Down. Copper rose around her. There were no openings here, no chimneys or corridors. The currents roiled through it, the butter-smooth, lazy-looking, curls of cloud slammed into her. She fought to keep upright, to continue her angle of descent. Blue discharges of lightning ran along her wings and bounced off the ends. The noise numbed her. Her airsack laboured to keep her breathing steady.

A cluster of meer twirled by in a seductively swirling current, their heads glowing faintly, their vestigial wings paddling briskly. Over and behind her fear she noted the numbers. The hunting would be good here.

Her wings ached. Copper must end soon. She could hardly see as the darkness deepened. It opened beneath her. Another glow layer, but the light here was dimmed to the point of blackness. Her second eyes opened, and she could see again, but just barely. Below her was a strange dimness that she knew was Brown. The Ara believed there were other layers below Brown. Certain animals had been seen coming up from beneath, but no Ara could live in Brown.

Scheer hung in the viscous air, searching though the dimness. Rask! Where was he? Her heart had slowed, the laboured beating was loud in her ears; her airsack strained, keeping her lungs filled. She dropped lower, and slid over the surface of Brown. In the lightning flashes she could see isci in huge clusters, crawling in it. Now and then the tough back of one would appear, and then spiral back down, many stubby legs in a continuous whirl beneath the oval body.

Brown was thick. She had never encountered anything like it, and to be told about it was not the same as seeing it. She slid lower, fighting through the thickness, reaching out, touching it . . . there was no division between the glow layer and the starting of Brown layer, just a slow increase in thickness. No boundary like the upper levels. She swam through the glow layer over Brown, swam like a meer.

And then she saw him. Rask! He lay half submerged in Brown, moving slowly with the languid, deadly pull of the current. She hung over him. He was dead. His wings had been torn from him in the fall and he had not had time to inflate his airsack. His dead eyes, the light eyes, looked up towards Copper. His magnificent golden fur moved slowly, slowly in a stately dance around his body. A group of isci were hovering, tugging at it.

Scheer curled. She tried to remember what about him had so repelled her and she could not. She tried to think of what he had done to her that was so wrong and she could not. She tried to think of her anger but it was gone. He was just . . . dead, like her father. She hung motionless for some time until a tightness in her airsack made her pull back in a sudden realization of where she was.

She had dived! She looked to all sides, her head moving in slow motion in the heaviness. Darkness was all around. She could feel the many layers above pressing down. Suddenly, she felt that she was smothering and tried to gasp for breath, but the instincts of her body, her labouring airsack, would not let her. She tried to fly, but her wings could not move. She jerked and twisted, clawed at Brown, felt herself slowly falling. Her light eyes opened in terror, opened to total blackness spiked with blinding flashes of lightning. Her panic increased. She was smothering! She was sinking! She was being crushed! She scrambled and flailed. Her wings would not beat. She would die.

Scheer wasn't sure when it was that she came to the realization that there were strong claws holding her, lifting her. With great effort she closed her light eyes, turned and saw her mother and three other Ara. They grasped and lifted her slowly, so slowly out of Brown, up into the glow layer and gradually up toward Copper. By twos as their labouring wings quickly tired, Scheer hanging limp between them like a baby. To open her own wings would have hampered them further. Slowly they inched upward, using their wings like oars. Scheer knew what it was costing them, she could see their struggles.

The air in her airsack was running low and she could feel her lungs start to labour. She held down the panic that threatened to edge up again and forced herself to stillness. Up they inched, through Copper, swimming blind in the oily current, feeling their way around the violent whirlpools.

Her second eyes closed, her light eyes could finally see again. They came into the glow layer. Above them billowed the curls and crevasses of Yellow. They moved faster now, but Scheer knew they were approaching their limits of strength. As they rose up through Yellow, Scheer shook them away, her own wings unfolded, and they moved with increasing speed up through the glow layer and found an updraft which whipped them up through the welcome billows of White. They were breathing normally again, Scheer in long gasps as if she would never get enough air. She gasped and shudded as her body switched over from her airsack. It had been very close.

A corridor opened before them, and they turned and winged toward Arahome. Scheer flew beside her mother. Mahr looked worn and tired.

"He miscalculated a turn in White. He was chasing me, his wing caught and . . ."

Mahr sighed. "What a price to pay for arrogance."

"I tried to follow, to save him, but I was not fast enough."

"You did what you could, but it was foolhardy to try the dive. You did not have experience enough. We were lucky we did not lose you too."

"I never wished for such a thing to happen." Scheer shivered.

"I know, I know." Her mother was silent, and Scheer knew she was thinking of her lost mate.

And then they could see Arahome.

The long wind was still blowing. Sheer climbed up through the buffeting winds and settled into a gentle eddy. The sky glow was dim and the stars shone clear tonight. Her mind reached out to them; she held the patterns of all the brightest ones to be seen. And her favourite ones, the ones that moved, she looked for them. There were patterns, and behind the patterns, reasons.

She had spent several days in council explaining her thoughts to the elders, stringing luminous zin bubbles to illustrate the patterns her mind saw. Now that she was a Diver, she was member of Council, and the elders listened to her. And they gave her young Ara to train.

She watched the slow movement of one star across the pattern of the others. She knew she was right, knew that she would discover the secrets. Near her in the calm current circled another Ara, one of the recently mature. His eyes glowed as he followed the stars in the sky. They had glowed the same way when she had shown him the zin bubble patterns. He watched the lights, lost in them, rapt as she was.

And soon other of the young Ara would follow them. She had seen the interest in their eyes. Soon there would be others with her, riding in the long wind.

■

Ken Mitchell

Ken Mitchell (1940-   ) was born and grew up in Moose Jaw, Saskatchewan. He now teaches Canadian literature and creative writing at the University of Regina. He has published several novels, *Wandering Rafferty* (1972), *The Meadowlark Connection* (1975), and *The Con Man* (1979). "The Great Electrical Revolution" comes from a collection of short stories, *Everyone Gets Something Here* (1977). He has written widely for the stage, including the "country opera" *Cruel Tears* (1975), *Davin: The Politician* (1979), and *The Laughin' Jack Rivers Show* (1983). Mitchell also wrote the script for the feature film *The Hounds of Notre Dame* (1981).

THE GREAT ELECTRICAL REVOLUTION

Ken Mitchell

I was only a little guy in 1937, but I can still remember Grandad being out of work. Nobody had any money to pay him and as he said, there wasn't much future in brick-laying as a charity. So mostly he just sat around in his suite above the hardware store, listening to his radio. We *all* listened to it when there was nothing else to do, which was most of the time unless you happened to be going to school like me. Grandad stuck right there through it all—soap operas, weather reports and quiz shows—unless he got a bit of cash from somewhere. Then he and Uncle Fred would go downtown to the beer parlour at the King William Hotel.

Grandad and Grandma came from the old country long before I was born. When they arrived in Moose Jaw, all they had was three children: Uncle Fred, Aunt Thecla, and my Dad; a truck full of working clothes; and a twenty-six pound post mall for putting up fences to keep "rogues" off Grandad's land. Rogues meant capitalists, Orangemen, cattle rustlers and Indians. All the way out on the train from Montreal, he glared out the Pullman window at the endless flat, saying to his family:

"I came here for land, b'Christ, and none of 'em's goin' to sly it on me."

He had sworn to carve a mighty estate from the raw Saskatchewan prairie, although he had never so much as picked up a garden hoe in his life before leaving Dublin.

So when he stepped off the train at the C.P.R. station in Moose Jaw, it looked like he was thinking of tearing it down and seeding the site to oats. It was two o'clock in the morning, but he kept striding up and down the lobby of the station, dressed in his good wool suit with the vest, as cocky as a bantam rooster in a chicken run. My Dad and Uncle Fred and Aunt Thecla sat on the trunk, while Grandma nagged at him to go and find them a place to stay. (It was only later they realized he was afraid to step outside the station.) He finally quit strutting long enough to get a porter to carry their trunk to a hotel down the street.

The next morning they went to the government land office

to secure their homestead. Then Grandad rented a democrat and took my Dad and Uncle Fred out to see the land they had come half-way around the world to find. Grandma and Aunt Thecla were told to stay in the hotel room and thank the Blessed Virgin for deliverance. They were still offering their prayers some three hours later, when Grandad burst into the room, his eyes wild and his face pale and quivering.

"Sweet Jesus Christ!" he shouted at them. "There's too much of it! There's just too damn much of it out there." He ran around the room several times in circles, knocking against the walls. "Miles and miles of nothing but miles and miles!" He collapsed onto one of the beds, and lay staring at the ceiling.

"It 'ud drive us all witless in a week," he moaned.

The two boys came in and told the story of the expedition. Grandad had started out fine, perhaps just a little nervous. But the further they went from the town, the more agitated and wild-eyed he got. Soon he stopped urging the horse along and asked it to stop. They were barely ten miles from town when they turned around and came back, with Uncle Fred driving. Grandad could only crouch on the floor of the democrat, trying to hide from the enormous sky, and whispering hoarsely at Fred to go faster. He'd come four thousand miles to the wide open spaces—only to discover he suffered from agoraphobia.

That was his last real excursion onto the open prairie. He gave up forever the idea of a farm of his own. (He did make one special trip to Mortlach in 1928 to fix Aunt Thecla's chimney, but that was a family favour. Even then Uncle Fred had to drive him in an enclosed Ford sedan in the middle of the night, with newspapers taped to the windows so he couldn't see out.) There was nothing left for him to do but take up his old trade of brick-laying in the town of Moose Jaw, where there were trees and tall buildings to protect him from the vastness. Maybe it was a fortunate turn of fate; certainly he prospered from then until the Depression hit, about the time I was born.

Yet—Grandad always felt guilty about not settling on the land. Maybe it was his conscience that prompted him to send my Dad out to work for a cattle rancher in the hills, the day after he turned eighteen. Another point: he married Aunt Thecla off to a Lutheran wheat farmer at Mortlach who actually threshed about five hundred acres of wheat every fall. Uncle Fred was the eldest and closer to Grandad (he had worked with him as an apprentice brick-layer before they immigrated) so he stayed in town and lived in the suite above the hardware store.

I don't remember much about my father's cattle ranch, except whirls of dust and skinny animals dragging themselves from one side of the range to the other. Finally there were no more cattle, and no money to buy more, and nothing to feed them if we *did* buy them, except wild foxtails and Russian thistles. So we moved into Moose Jaw with Grandad and Grandma, and went on relief. It was better than the ranch where there was nothing to do but watch tumbleweeds roll through the yard. We would have had to travel into town every week to collect the salted fish and government pork, anyway. Grandad was very happy to have us, because when my Dad went down to the railway yard to get our ration, he collected Grandad's too. My Dad never complained about waiting in line for the handout, but Grandad would've starved to death first. "The Goddamned government drives us all to the edge," he would say. "Then they want us to queue up for the Goddamned swill they're poisoning us with."

That was when we spent so much time listening to Grandad's radio. It came in a monstrous slab of black walnut cabinet he had swindled, so he thought, from a secondhand dealer on River Street. An incandescent green bulb glowed in the centre to show when the tubes were warming up. There was a row of knobs with elaborate-looking initials and a dial with the names of cities like Tokyo, Madrid, and Chicago. Try as we might on long winter evenings to tune the needle into those stations and hear a play in Japanese or Russian, all we ever got was CHMJ Moose Jaw, The Buckle of the Wheat Belt. Even so, I spent hours lying on the floor, tracing the floral patterns on the cloth-covered speaker while I listened to another world of mystery and fascination.

When the time came that Grandad could find no more bricks to lay, he set a kitchen chair in front of the radio and stayed there, not moving except to go to the King William with Uncle Fred. My Dad managed to get a job with the city, gravelling streets for forty cents a day. But things grew worse. The Moose Jaw Light and Power Company came around one day in the fall of 1937 and cut off our electricity for non-payment. It was hard on Grandad not to have his radio. Not only did he have nothing to do, but he had to spend all his time thinking about it. He stared out the parlour window, which looked over the alley running behind the hardware store. There was a grand view of the back of the Rainbow Laundry.

That was what he was doing the day of his discovery, just before Christmas. Uncle Fred and my Dad were arguing about who caused the Depression—R.B. Bennett or the C.P.R. Suddenly Grandad turned from the window. There was a new and strange look on his face.

"Where does that wire go?" he said

"Wire?" said Uncle Fred, looking absent-mindedly around the room. He patted his pockets looking for a wire.

"What wire?" my Dad said.

Grandad nodded toward the window. "This wire running right past the window."

He pointed to a double strand of power line that ran from a pole in the back alley to the side of our building. It was a lead-in for the hardware store.

"Holy Moses Cousin Harry. Isn't that a sight now!" Grandad said, grinning like a crazy man.

"You're crazy," Uncle Fred told him. "You can't never get a tap off that line there. They'd find you out in nothing flat."

Grandma, who always heard everything that was said, called from the kitchen: "Father, don't you go and do some foolishness will have us all electrinated."

"By Jayzuz," he muttered. He never paid any attention to a word she said. "Cut off *my* power, will they?"

That night, after they made me go to bed, I listened to him and Uncle Fred banging and scraping as they bored a hole through the parlour wall. My Dad wouldn't have anything to do with it and took my mother to the free movie at the co-op. He said Grandad was descending to the level of the Moose Jaw Light and Power Company.

Actually, Grandad knew quite a bit about electricity. He had known for a long time how to jump a wire from one side of the meter around to the other, to cheat the power company. I had often watched him under the meter, stretched out from his tip-toes at the top of a broken stepladder, yelling at Grandma to lift the Goddamned Holy Candle a little higher so he could see what the Christ he was doing.

The next day, Grandad and Uncle Fred were acting like a couple of kids, snorting and giggling and jabbing each other in the ribs. They were waiting for the King William beer parlour to open so they could go down and tell their friends about Grandad's revenge on the power company. They spent the day like heroes down there, telling over and over how Grandad had spied the lead-in, and how they had bored the hole in the wall, and how justice had finally descended on the capitalist leeches. The two of them showed up at home for supper, but as soon as they ate they headed back to the King William where everybody was buying them free beer.

Grandma didn't seem to think much of their efforts, although now that she had electricity again, she could spend the evenings doing her housework if she wanted to. The cord came through the hole in the wall, across the parlour to the hall and the kitchen. Other cords were attached which led to the two bedrooms. Grandma muttered when she had to sweep around the black tangle of wires and sockets. With six of us living in the tiny suite, someone was forever tripping on one of the cords and knocking things over.

But we lived with all that because Grandad was happy again. We might *all* have lived happily if Grandad and Uncle Fred could have kept quiet about their revenge on the power company.

One night about a week later we were in the parlour listening to Fibber Magee and Molly when someone knocked at the door. It was Mrs. Pizak, who lived next door in a tiny room.

"Goot evening," she said, looking around. "I see your power has turnt beck on."

"Ha," Grandad said, "We turned it on *for* 'em. Damned rogues."

"Come in and sit down and listen to the show with us," Grandma said. Mrs. Pizak kept looking at the black wires running back and forth across the parlour, and at Grandad's radio. You could tell she wasn't listening to the show.

"Dey shut off my power, too, she said. "I alvays like listen to the Shut-In program. Now my radio isn't work."

"Hmmm," Grandad said, trying to hear Fibber and the Old-Timer. Grandma and my Dad watched him, not listening to the radio any more either. Finally he couldn't stand it.

"All right, Fred," he said. "Go and get the brace and bit."

They bored a hole through one of the bedroom walls into Mrs. Pizak's cubicle. From then on, she was on Grandad's power grid, too. It didn't take long for everybody else in the block to find out about the free power, and they all wanted to hook up. There were two floors of suites above the hardware store, and soon the walls and ceiling of Grandad's suite were as full of holes as a colander, with wires running in all directions. For the price of a bottle of whiskey, people could run their lights twenty-four hours a day if they wanted. By Christmas Day, even those who *paid* their bills had given notice to the power company. It was a beautiful Christmas in a bad year—and Grandad and Uncle Fred liked to take a lot of credit for it. Which everyone gave them. There was a lot of celebration up and down the halls, where they always seemed to show up as guests of honour. There was a funny feeling running through the block, like being in a state of siege, or a revolution, with Uncle Fred and my Grandad leading it.

One late afternoon just before New Year's, I was lying on the floor of the front parlour, reading a secondhand Book of Knowledge I had gotten for Christmas. Grandma and my mother were knitting socks, and all three of us were listening vaguely to Major Bowes' amateur show. Suddenly, out of the corner of my eye, I thought I saw Grandad's radio move. I blinked and stared at it, but the big console just sat there talking about Geritol. I turned a page. Again, it seemed to move in a jerk.

"Grandma," I said. "The radio—"

She looked up from her knitting, already not believing a word I might have to say. I gave up, and glared at the offending machine. While I watched, it slid at least six inches across the parlour floor.

"Grandma!" I screamed. "The radio's moving! All by itself!"

She looked calmly at the radio, then the tangle of wires spread across the floor, and out the front parlour window.

"Larry-boy, you'd best run and fetch your grandfather. He's over at McBrides'. Number eight."

McBrides' suite was down the gloomy hall and across. I dashed down the corridor and pounded frantically at the door. Someone opened it the width of a crack.

"Is my Grandad in there?" I squeaked. Grandad stepped out into the hall with a glass in his hand, closing the door behind him.

"What is it, Larry?"

"Grandma says for you to come quick. The radio! There's something—"

"My radio!" Grandad was not a large man, but he had the energy of a buzz-saw. He started walking back up the hall, broke into a trot, then a steady gallop, holding has glass of whiskey out in front at arm's length so it wouldn't spill. He burst through the door and skidded to a stop in front of the radio, which sat there, perfectly normal except that it stood maybe a foot to the left of the chair.

"By the Holy toe-nails of Moses—what is it?"

Grandma looked up ominously and jerked her chin toward the window. Her quiet firmness usually managed to calm him, but now, in two fantastic bounds, Grandad stood in front of the window, looking out.

"Larry," he said, glaring outside, "fetch your Uncle Fred." I tore off down the hall again to number eight and brought Uncle Fred back to the suite. The two women were still knitting on the other side of the room. Grandma was doing her stitches calmly enough, but my mother's needles clattered like telegraph keys, and she was throwing terrified glances around the room.

"Have a gawk at this, will you, Fred?"

Uncle Fred and I crowded around him to see out. There, on a pole only twenty feet from our parlour window, practically facing us eye-to-eye, was a lineman from the power company. He was replacing broken glass insulators; God knows why he was doing it in the dead of winter. Obviously, he hadn't noticed our home-made lead-in, or he would have been knocking at the door. We could only pray he wouldn't look at the wire too closely. Once, he lifted his eyes toward the lighted window where we all stood gaping out at him in the growing darkness. He grinned at us, and raised his hand in a salute. He must have thought we were admiring his work.

"Wave back!" Grandad ordered. The three of us waved frantically at the lineman, to make him think we appreciated his efforts, although Grandad was muttering some very ugly things about the man's ancestry.

Finally, to our relief, the lineman finished his work and got ready to come down the pole. He reached out his hand for support—and my heart stopped beating as his weight hung on the contraband wire. Behind me, I could hear the radio slide another foot across the parlour floor. The lineman stared at the wire he held. He tugged experimentally, his eyes following it up to the hole through our wall. He looked at Grandad and Uncle Fred and me standing there in the lit-up window, with our crazy horror-struck grins and our arms frozen above our heads in grotesque waves. Understanding spread slowly across his face.

He scrambled around to the opposite side of the pole and braced himself to give a mighty pull on our line. Simultaneously, Grandad leaped into action, grabbing the wire on our side of the wall. He wrapped it around his hands, and braced his feet against the baseboard. The lineman gave his first vicious yank, and it almost jerked Grandad smack against the wall. I remember thinking what a powerful man the lineman must be to do that to my Grandad.

"Fred, you feather-brained idiot!" he shouted. "Get over here and haul on this line before the black-hearted son of a bitch pulls me through the wall."

Uncle Fred ran to the wire just in time, as the man on the pole gave another, mightier heave. At the window, I could see the lineman stiffen with rage and determination. The slender wire sawed back and forth through the hole in the wall for at least ten minutes, first one side, and then the other, getting advantage. The curses on our side got very loud and bitter. I couldn't hear the lineman, of course, but I could see him—with his mouth twisted in an awful snarl, throwing absolutely terrible looks at me in the window, and heaving on the line. I know he wasn't praying to St. Jude.

Grandad's cursing would subside periodically when Grandma warned: "Now, now, father, not in front of the boy." Then she would go back to her knitting and pretend the whole affair wasn't happening, as Grandad's blasphemies would soar to monumental heights.

That lineman must have been in extra-good condition, because our side very quickly began to play out. Grandad screamed at Grandma and my mother, and even at me, to throw ourselves on the line and help. But the women refused to leave their knitting, and they wouldn't let me be corrupted. I couldn't leave my viewpoint at the window, anyway.

Grandad and uncle Fred kept losing footage until the huge radio had scraped all the way across the floor and stood at their backs, hampering their efforts.

"Larry!" Grandad shouted. "Is he weakenin' any?"

He wanted desperately for me to say yes, but it was useless. "It doesn't look like it," I said. Grandad burst out in a froth of curses I'd never heard before. A fresh attack on the line pulled his knuckles to the wall and barked them badly. He looked tired and beaten. All the slack in the line was taken up and he was against the wall, his head twisted, looking at me. A light flared up in his eyes.

"All right, Fred," he said. "If he wants the Goddamned thing so bad—let him have it!" They both jumped back—and nothing happened.

I could see the lineman, completely unaware of his impending disaster, literally winding himself up for an all-out assault on our wire. I wanted out of human kindness to shout a warning at him. But it was too late. With an incredible backward lunge, he disappeared from sight behind the power pole.

A shattering explosion of wild noises blasted my senses, like a bomb had fallen in Grandad's suite. Every appliance and electric light that Grandma owned flew into the parlour, bounding off the walls and smashing against each other. A table lamp from the bedroom caromed off Uncle Fred's knee. The radio collided against the wall and was ripped off its wire. Sparking and flashing like lightning, all of Grandma's things hurled themselves against the parlour walls, popping like a string of firecrackers as the cords went zipping through the hole. A silence fell—like a breath of air to a drowning man. The late afternoon darkness settled through the room.

"Sweet Jesus Christ!"Grandad said. Then there came a second uproar: a bloodcurdling barrage of bangs and shouts, as our neighbours recovered from seeing their lamps, radios, irons and toasters leap from their tables and collect in ruined piles of junk around the "free power" holes in their walls. Uncle Fred turned white as a sheet.

I looked out the window. The lineman sat on the ground at the foot of his pole, dazed. He looked up at me with one more hate-filled glare, then deliberately snipped our wire with a pair of cutters. He taped up the end and marched away into the night.

Grandad stood in the midst of the ruined parlour, trying in the darkness to examine his beloved radio for damage. Grandma sat in her rocking chair, knitting socks and refusing to acknowledge the disaster.

It was Grandad who finally broke the silence. "Well! They're lucky," he said. "It's just damned lucky for them they didn't scratch my radio."

•

Farley Mowat

Farley Mowat (1921-   ) was born in Belleville, Ontario, and has lived in Saskatchewan and the Canadian Arctic and Newfoundland; he now divides his time between homes in Ontario and Nova Scotia. His many books include *People of the Deer* (1952), *Lost in the Barrens* (1956) which won the Governor General's award for juvenile literature, *The Dog Who Wouldn't Be* (1957), *Owls in the Family* (1961) and *The Boat Who Wouldn't Float* (1969) which won the Leacock Medal for Humour. A number of his stories have been made into films, including *Never Cry Wolf* and *A Whale For the Killing.* "Walk Well, My Brother" was published in his collection of Arctic stories *The Snow Walker* (1975). His personal response to his experience of World War II is *And No Birds Sang* (1979).

"WALK WELL, MY BROTHER"

Farley Mowat

When Charlie Lavery first went north just after the war, he was twenty-six years old and case hardened by nearly a hundred bombing missions over Europe. He was very much of the new elite who believed that any challenge, whether by man or nature, could be dealt with by good machines in the hands of skilled men. During the following five years, flying charter jobs in almost every part of the artic from Hudson Bay to the Alaska border, he had found no reason to alter this belief. But through his familiarity with arctic skies and his ability to drive trackless lines across them had become considerable, he remained a stranger to the land below. The monochromatic wilderness of rock and tundra, snow and ice, existed outside his experience and comprehension, as did the native people whose world this was.

One mid-August day in 1951 he was piloting a warsurplus Anson above the drowned tundra plains south of Queen Maud Gulf, homeward bound to his base at Yellowknife after a flight almost to the limit of the aircraft's range. The twin engines thundered steadily and his alert ears caught no hint of warning from them. When the machine betrayed his trust, it did so with shattering abruptness. Before he could touch the throttles, the starboard engine was dead and the port one coughing in staccato bursts. Then came silence— replaced almost instantly by a rising scream of wind as the plane nosed steeply down toward the shining circlet of a pond.

It was too small a pond and the plane had too little altitude. As Lavery frantically pumped the flap hydraulics, the floats smashed into the rippled water. The Anson careened wickedly for a few yards and came to a crunching stop against the frost-shattered rocks along the shore.

Lavery barely glanced at his woman passenger, who had been thrown into a corner of the cabin by the impact. He scrambled past her, flung open the door and jumped down to find himself standing knee deep in frigid water. Both floats had been so badly holed that they had filled and now rested on the rocky bottom.

The woman crawled to the door and Lavery looked up into

an oval, warmly tinted face framed in long black hair. He groped for a few Eskimo words he knew:

"*Tingmeak . . . tokoiyo . . .* smashed to hell! No fly! Understand?"

As she stared back uncomprehending, a spasm of anger shook him. What a fool he'd been to take her aboard at all . . . now she was a bloody albatross around his neck.

Four hours earlier he had landed in a bay on the Gulf coast to set out a cache of aviation gas for a prospecting company. No white men lived in that part of the world and Lavery had considered it a lucky accident to find an Eskimo tent pitched there. The two men who had run out to watch him land had been a godsend, helping to unload the drums, float them to tideline and roll them up the beach well above the storm line.

He had given each of them a handful of chocolate bars in payment for their work and had been about to head back for Yellowknife when the younger Eskimo touched his arm and pointed to the tent. Lavery had no desire to visit that squat skin cone hugging the rocks a hundred yards away and it was not the Eskimo's gentle persistence that prevailed on him—it was the thought that these Huskies might have a few white fox pelts to trade.

There were no fox pelts in the tent. Instead there was a woman lying on some caribou hides. *Nuliak*—wife—was the only word Lavery could understand of the Eskimo's urgent attempt at explanation.

The tent stank of seal oil and it was with revulsion that Lavery looked more closely at the woman. She was young and not bad looking—for a Husky—but her cheeks were flushed a sullen red by fever and a trickle of blood had dried at the corner of her mouth. Her dark eyes were fixed upon him with grave intensity. He shook his head and turned away.

T.B. . . . sooner or later all the Huskies got it . . . bound to the filthy way they lived. It would be no kindness to fly her out to the little hospital at Yellowknife already stuffed with dying Indians. She'd be better off to die at home . . .

Lavery was halfway back to the Anson before the younger Eskimo caught up with him. In his hands he held two walrus tusks, and the pilot saw they were of exceptional quality.

Ah, what the hell . . . no skin off my ass. I'm deadheading anyhow . . .

"*Eeema.* Okay, I'll take your *nuliak*. But make it snappy. *Dwoee, dwoee!*"

While Lavery fired up the engines, the men carried the woman, wrapped in caribou-skin robes, and placed her in the cabin. The younger Eskimo pointed at her, shouting her name: Konala. Lavery nodded and waved them away. As he pulled clear of the beach he caught a glimpse of them standing in the slipstream, as immobile as rocks. Then the plane was airborne, swinging around on course for the long haul home.

Barely two hours later he again looked into the eyes of the woman called Konala . . . wishing he had never seen or heard of her.

She smiled tentatively but Lavery ignored her and pushed past into the cabin to begin sorting through the oddments which had accumulated during his years of arctic flying. He found a rusty .22 rifle and half a box of shells, a torn sleeping bag, an axe and four cans of pork and beans. This, together with a small box of matches and a pocket knife in his stylish cotton flying jacket, comprised a survival outfit whose poverty testified to his contempt for the world that normally lay far below his aircraft.

Shoving the gear into a packsack he waded ashore. Slowly Konala followed, carrying her caribou robes and a large sealskin pouch. With mounting irritation Lavery saw that she was able to move without much difficulty. Swinging the lead to get a free plane ride, he thought. He turned on her.

"The party's over, lady! Your smart-assed boy friend's got you into a proper mess—him and his goddamn walrus tusks!"

The words meant nothing to Konala but the tone was clear enough. She walked a few yards off, opened her pouch, took out a fishing line and began carefully unwinding it. Lavery turned his back on her and made his way to a ledge of rock where he sat down to consider the situation.

A thin tongue of fear was flickering in the back of his mind. Just what the hell *was* he going to do? The proper drill would be to stick with the Anson and wait until a search plane found him . . . except he hadn't kept to his flight plan. He had said he intended to fly west down the coast to Bathurst before angling southwest to Yellowknife . . . instead he'd flown a direct course from the cache, to save an hour's fuel. Not so bright maybe, considering his radio was out of kilter. There wasn't a chance in a million they'd look for him this far off-course. Come to that, he didn't even know exactly where he was . . . fifty miles or so north of the Back River lakes would be a good guess. There were so damn few landmarks in this godforsaken country . . . Well, so he wasn't going to be picked up . . . that left Shanks' mare, as the Limeys would say . . . but which way to go?

He spread out a tattered aeronautical chart on the knees of his neat cotton pants. Yellowknife, four hundred miles to the southwest, was out of the question . . . The arctic coast couldn't be more than a hundred and fifty miles away but there was nobody there except a scattering of Huskies . . . How about Baker Lake? He scaled off the airline distance with thumb and forefinger, ignoring the innumerable lakes and rivers across the route. About two hundred miles. He was pretty fit . . . should be able to manage twenty miles a day . . . ten days, and presto.

Movement caught his eye and he looked up. Konala, a child-like figure in her bulky deerskin clothes, had waded out to stand on the submerged tail of a float. Bent almost double, she was swinging a length of line around her head. She let the weighted hook fly so that it sailed through the air to strike the surface a hundred feet from shore.

Well, there was no way she could walk to Baker. She'd have to stay put until he could bring help. His anger surged up again . . . Fishing, for God's sake! What in Jesus' sweet name did she think she was going to catch in that lousy little pond?

He began to check his gear. Lord, no *compass* . . . and the sun was no use this time of year. He'd never bothered to buy one of the pocket kind . . . no need for it . . . but there was a magnetic compass in the instrument panel of the old crate . . .

Lavery hurried back to the Anson, found some tools and went to work. He was too preoccupied to notice Konala haul in her line and deftly slip a fine char off the hook. He did not see her take her curved woman's knife and slice two thick fillets from the fish. The first he knew of her success was when she appeared at the open cabin door. She was so small that her head barely reached the opening. With one hand she held a fillet up to him while with the other she pushed raw pink flesh into her mouth, pantomiming to show him how good it was.

"Jesus, no!" He was revolted and waved her away. "Eat it yourself . . . you animal!"

Obediently Konala disappeared from the doorway. Making her way ashore she scraped together a pile of dry lichens then struck a light with flint and steel. The moss smoked and began to glow. She covered it with dwarf willow twigs, then spread pieces of the fish on two flat rocks angled toward the rising flames. When Lavery descended from the plane with the compass in his hand his appetite woke with a rush at the sight and smell of roasting fish. But he did not go near the fire. Instead he retreated to the rocks where he had left his gear and dug out a can of beans. He gashed his thumb trying to open the can with his pocket knife.

Picking up the axe, he pounded the can until it split. Raging against this wasteland that had trapped him, and the fate that had stripped him of his wings, he furiously shovelled the cold mess into his mouth and choked it down.

Konala sat watching him intently. When he had finished she rose to her feet, pointed northward and asked, *"Peehuktuk?* We walk?"

Lavery's resentment exploded. Thrusting his arms through the straps of the packsack, he heaved it and the sleeping bag into position then picked up the rifle and pointed with it to the southwest.

"You're goddamn right!" he shouted. "Me—*owunga peechuktuk* that way! *Eeetpeet*—you bloody well stay here!"

Without waiting to see if she had understood, he began to climb the slope of a sandy esker that rose to the south of the pond. Near the crest he paused and looked back. Konala was squatting by the tiny fire seemingly unaware that he was deserting her. He felt a momentary twinge of guilt, but shrugged it off . . . no way she could make it with him to Baker, and she had her deerskins to keep her warm. As for food, well, Huskies could eat anything . . . she'd make out. He turned and his long, ungainly figure passed over the skyline.

With a chill of dismay he looked out across the tundra rolling to a measureless horizon ahead of him—a curving emptiness more intimidating than anything he had seen in the high skies. The tongue of fear began to flicker again but he resolutely shut his mind to it and stumbled forward into that sweep of space, his heavy flight boots slipping on rocks and sucking in the muskeg, the straps of the packsack already cutting into his shoulders through the thin cotton jacket.

There is no way of knowing what Konala was thinking as she saw him go. She might have believed he was going hunting, since that would have been the natural thing for a man to do under the circumstances. But in all likelihood she guessed what he intended—otherwise, how to explain the fact that ten days later and nearly sixty miles to the south of the downed plane, the sick woman trudged wearily across a waste of sodden muskeg to climb a gravel ridge and halt beside the unconscious body of Charlie Lavery?

Squatting beside him she used her curved knife to cut away the useless remnants of his leather boots, then wrapped his torn and bloody feet in compresses of wet sphagnum moss. Slipping off her parka, she spread it over his tattered jacket to protect him from the flies. Her fingers on his emaciated and insect-bitten flesh were tender and sure. Later she built a fire, and when Lavery opened his eyes it was to find himself under a rude skin shelter with a can of fish broth being pressed lightly against his lips.

There was a hiatus in his mind. Anxiously he raised himself to see if the aircraft was still on the pond, but there was no pond and no old Anson . . . only that same stunning expanse of empty plains. With a sickening lurch, memory began to function. The seemingly endless days of his journey flooded back upon him: filled with roaring clouds of mosquitoes and flies; with a mounting, driving hunger; the agony of lacerated feet and the misery of rain-swept hours lying shelterless in a frigid void. He remembered his matches getting soaked when he tried to ford the first of a succession of rivers that forever deflected his course toward the west. He remembered losing the .22 cartridges when the box turned to mush after a rain. Above all, he remembered the unbearable sense of loneliness that grew until he began to panic, throwing away first the useless gun, then the sodden sleeping bag, the axe . . . and finally sent him, in a heart-bursting spasm of desperation, toward a stony ridge that seemed to undulate serpent-like on the otherwise shapeless face of a world that had lost all form and substance.

Konala's face came into focus as she nudged the tin against his lips. She was smiling and Lavery found himself smiling weakly back at this woman who not so long before had roused his contempt and anger.

They camped on the nameless ridge for a week while Lavery recovered some of his strength. At first he could hardly bear to leave the shelter because of the pain in his feet. But Konala seemed always on the move: gathering willow twigs for fires, collecting and cooking food, cutting and sewing a new pair of boots for Lavery from the hides she had brought with her. She appeared tireless, but that was an illusion. Her body was driven to its many tasks only at great cost.

Time had telescoped itself so that Lavery would wake from sleep with shaking hands, hearing the engines of the Anson fail. It would seem to him that the plane had crashed only a few minutes earlier. It would seem that the terrible ordeal of his march south was about to begin again and he would feel a sick return of panic. When this happened, he would desperately fix his thoughts on Konala for she was the one comforting reality in all this alien world.

He thought about her a great deal, but she was an enigma to him. Sick as she was, how had she managed to follow him across those sodden plains and broken rock ridges . . . how had she managed to keep alive in such a country?

After Konala gave him the completed skin boots carefully lined with cotton grass, he began to find answers to some of these questions. He was able to hobble far enough from camp to watch her set sinew snares for gaudy ground squirrels she called *hikik*, scoop suckers from a nearby stream with her bare hands, outrun snow geese that were still flightless after the late-summer moult, and dig succulent lemmings from their peat bog burrows. Watching her, Lavery slowly came to understand that what had seemed to him a lifeless desert was in fact a land generous in its support of those who knew its nature.

Still, the most puzzling question remained unanswered. Why had Konala not stayed in the relative safety of the aircraft or else travelled north to seek her own people? What had impelled her to follow him . . . to rescue a man of another race who had abandoned her?

Toward the end of their stay on the ridge, the sun was beginning to dip well below the horizon at night—a warning that summer was coming to an end. One day Konala again pointed north and, with a grin, she waddled duck-like a few paces in that direction. The joke at the expense of Lavery's splayed and painful feet did not annoy him. He laughed and limped after her to show his willingness to follow wherever she might lead.

When they broke camp, Konala insisted on carrying what was left of Lavery's gear along with her own pouch and the roll of caribou hides which was both shelter and bedding for them. As they trekked northward she broke into song—a high and plaintive chant without much melody which seemed as much part of the land as the fluting of curlews.

When Lavery tried to find out what the song was all about, she seemed oddly reticent and all he could gather was that she was expressing kinship for someone or for some thing beyond his ken. He did not understand that she was joining her voice to the voice of the land and to the spirits of the land.

Retracing their path under Konala's tutelage became a journey of discovery. Lavery was forever being surprised at how different the tundra had now become from the dreadful void he had trudged across not long since.

He discovered it was full of birds ranging from tiny longspurs whose muted colouring made them almost invisible, to great saffron-breasted hawks circling high above the bogs and lakes. Konala also drew his attention to the endless diversity of tundra plants, from livid orange lichens to azure flowers whose blooms were so tiny he had to kneel to see them clearly.

Once Konala motioned him to crawl beside her to the crest of an esker. In the valley beyond, a family of white wolves was lazily hunting lemmings in a patch of sedge a hundred feet away. The nearness of the big beasts made Laveryy uneasy until Konala boldly stood up and called to the wolves in their own language. They drew together then, facing her in a half circle, and answered with a long, lilting chorus before trotting away in single file.

Late one afternoon they at last caught sight of a splash of brilliant colour in the distance. Lavery's heartbeat quickened and he pushed forward without regard for his injured feet. The yellow-painted Anson *might* have been spotted by a search plane during their absence . . . rescue by his own kind might still be possible. But when the man and woman descended the esker to the shore of the pond, they found the Anson exactly as they had left it. There had been no human visitors.

Bitterly disappointed, Lavery climbed into the cockpit, seated himself behind the controls and slumped into black depression. Konala's intention of travelling northward to rejoin her own people on the coast now loomed as an ordeal whose outcome would probably be death during the first winter storm . . . if they could last that long. Their worn clothing and almost hairless robes were already barely adequate to keep the cold at bay. Food was getting harder to find as the birds left, the small animals begasn to dig in and the fish ran back to the sea. And what about fuel when the weather really began to turn against them?

Lavery was sullen and silent that evening as they ate their boiled fish, but Konala remained cheerful. She kept repeating the word *tuktu*—caribou—as she vainly tried to make him understand that soon they would have the wherewithal to continue the journey north.

As the night wind began to rise he ignored the skin shelter which Konala had erected and, taking one of the robes, climbed back into the plane and rolled himself up on the icy mental floor. During the next few days he spent most of his time in the Anson, sometimes fiddling with the knobs of the useless radio, but for the most part morosely staring through the plexiglass windscreen at a landscape which seemed to grow increasingly bleak as the first frosts greyed the tundra flowers and browned the windswept sedges.

Early one morning an unfamiliar sound brought him out of a chilled, nightmarish sleep. It was a muffled, subdued noise as of waves rolling in on a distant shore. For one heart-stopping instant he thought it was the beat of an aircraft engine, then he heard Konala's exultant cry.

"*Tuktoraikayai*—the deer have come!"

From the window of the dead machine Lavery looked out upon a miracle of life. An undulating mass of antlered animals was pouring out of the north. It rolled steadily toward the pond, split, and began enveloping it. The rumble resolved itself into a rattling cadence of hooves on rock and gravel. As the animals swept past, the stench of barnyard grew strong even inside the plane. Although in the days when he had flown high above them Lavery had often seen skeins of migrating caribou laced across the arctic plains like a pattern of beaded threads, he could hardly credit what he now beheld . . . the land inundated under a veritable flood of life. His depression began to dissipate as he felt himself being drawn into and becoming almost a part of that living river.

While he stared, awe-struck and incredulous, Konala went to work. Some days earlier she had armed herself with a spear, its shaft made from a paddle she had found in the Anson and its double-edged blade filed out of a piece of steel broken from the tip of the plane's anchor. With this in hand she was now scurrying about on the edge of the herd. The press was so great that individual deer could not avoid her. A snorting buck leapt high as the spear drove into him just behind the ribs. His dying leap carried him onto the backs of some of his neighbors, and as he slid off and disappeared into the ruck, Konala's blade thrust into another victim. She chose the fattest beasts and those with the best hides.

When the tide of caribou finally thinned, there was much work for Konala's knife. She skinned, scraped and staked out several prime hides destined for the making of clothes and sleeping robes, then turned her attention to a small mountain of meat and began slicing it into paper-thin sheets which she draped over dwarf willow bushed. When dry this would make light, imperishable food fit to sustain a man and a woman—one injured and the other sick—who must undertake a long, demanding journey.

Revitalized by the living ambience of the great herd, Lavery came to help her. She glanced up at him and her face was radiant. She cut off a piece of brisket and held it out to him, grinning delightedly when he took it and tore off a piece with his teeth. It was his idea to make a stove out of two emply oil cans upon which the fat which Konala had gathered could be rendered into white cakes that would provide food *and* fuel in the times ahead.

Several days of brisk, clear weather followed. While the meat dried on the bushes, Konala laboured on, cutting and stitching clothing for them both. She worked herself so hard that her cheeks again showed the flame of fever and her rasping cough grew worse. When Lavery tried to make her take things a little easier she became impatient with him. Konala knew what she knew.

Finally on a day in mid-September she decided they were ready. With Lavery limping at her side, she turned her back on the white men's fine machine and set out to find her people.

The skies darkened and cold gales began sweeping gusts of snow across the bogs whose surfaces were already crusting with ice crystals. One day a sleet storm forced them into early camp. Konala had left the little travel tent to gather willows for the fire and Lavery was dozing when he heard her cry of warning through the shrilling of the wind.

There was no mistaking the urgency in her voice. Snatching up the spear he limped from the tent to see Konala running across a narrow valley. Behind her, looming immense and forbidding in the leaden light, was one of the great brown bears of the barrenlands.

Seeing Lavery poised on the slope above her, Konala swerved away, even though this brought her closer to the bear. It took a moment for Lavery to realize that she was attempting to distract the beast, then he raised the spear and flung himself down the slope, shouting and cursing at the top of his lungs.

The bear's interest in the woman shifted to the surprising spectacle Lavery presented. It sat up on its massive haunches and peered doubtfully at him through the veil of sleet.

When he was a scant few yards from the bear, Lavery tripped and fell, rolling helplessly among the rocks to fetch up on his back staring upward into that huge, square face. The bear looked back impassively then snorted, dropped on all fours and shambled off.

The meeting with the bear crystallized the changes which had been taking place in Lavery. Clad in caribou-skin clothing, a dark beard ringing his cheeks, and his hair **hanging** free to his shoulders, he had acquired a look of litheness and vigour—and of watchfulness. No longer was he an alien in an inimical land. He was a man now in his own right, able to make his way in an elder world.

In Konala's company he knew a unity that he had previously felt only with members of his bombing crew. The weeks they had spent together had eroded the barrier of language and he was beginning to understand much about her that had earlier baffled him. Yet the core of the enigma remained for he had not found the answer to the question that had haunted him since she brought life back to his body on that distant southern ridge.

For some time they had been descending an already frozen and snow-covered river which Konala had given him to understand would lead them to the coast. But with each passing day, Konala had been growing weaker even as Lavery regained his strength. At night, when she supposed him to be asleep, she sometimes moaned softly, and during the day she could walk only for short distances between paroxysms of coughing and left blood stains in the new snow at her feet.

When the first real blizzard struck them, it was Lavery who set up the travel tent and lit the fire of lichens and caribou fat upon which to simmer some dried deer meet. Konala lay under their sleeping robes while he prepared the meal, and when he turned to her he saw how the lines of pain around he mouth had deepened into crevices. He came close and held a tin of warm soup to her dry lips. She drank a mouthful then lay back, her dark eyes glittering too brightly in the meagre firelight. He looked deep into them and read the confirmation of his fear.

Keeping her eyes on his, she took a new pair of skin boots from under the robes and slowly stroked them, feeling the infinitely fine stitching which would keep them waterproof. After a time she reached out and placed them in his lap. Then she spoke, slowly and carefully so he would be sure to understand.

"They are not very good boots but they might carry you to the camps of my people. They might help you return to your own land . . . Walk well in them . . . my brother."

Later that night the gale rose to a crescendo. The cold drove into the tent and, ignoring the faint flicker of the fire, pierced through the thick caribou robes wrapped about Konala and entered into her.

When the storm had blown itself out, Lavery buried her under a cairn of rocks on the high banks of the nameless river. As he made his way northward in the days that followed, his feet finding their own sure way, he no longer pondered the question which had lain in his mind through so many weeks . . . for he could still hear the answer she had made and would forever hear it: Walk well . . . my brother . . .

■

Fredelle Bruser Maynard

Sidney Tabak

Fredelle Bruser Maynard (1922-   ) was born and grew up on the Canadian prairie; she moved to the United States in 1943 to take a doctoral degree at Harvard, later taught at Radcliffe and Wellesley Colleges. She now lives in Toronto as a free-lance writer of books and articles on education, child care, and family life. The author of *Guiding Your Child to a More Creative Life*, she is best known for her memoir of a prairie childhood, *Raisins and Almonds* (1972) from which "Jewish Christmas" is taken.

JEWISH CHRISTMAS

Fredelle Bruser Maynard

CHRISTMAS, when I was young, was the season of bitterness. Lights beckoned and tinsel shone, store windows glowed with mysterious promise, but I knew the brilliance was not for me. Being Jewish, I had long grown accustomed to isolation and difference. Difference was in my bones and blood, and in the pattern of my separate life. My parents were conspicuously unlike other children's parents in our predominantly Norwegian community. Where my school-mates were surrounded by blond giants appropriate to a village called Birch Hills, my family suggested still the Russian plains from which they had emigrated years before. My handsome father was a big man, but big without any suggestion of physical strength or agility; one could not imagine him at the wheel of a tractor. In a town that was all wheat and cattle, he seemed the one man wholly devoted to urban pursuits: he operated a general store. Instead of the native costume—overalls and mackinaws—he wore city suits and pearl-grey spats. In winter he was splendid in a plushy chinchilla coat with velvet collar, his black curly hair an extension of the high Astrakhan hat which he had brought from the Ukraine. I was proud of his good looks, and yet uneasy about their distinctly oriental flavor.

My mother's difference was of another sort. Her beauty was not so much foreign as timeless. My friends had slender young Scandinavian mothers, light of foot and blue of eye; my mother was short and heavyset, but with a face of classic proportions. Years later I found her in the portraits of Ingres and Corot—face a delicate oval, brown velvet eyes, brown silk hair centrally parted and drawn back in a lustrous coil— but in those days I saw only that she too was different. As for my grandparents, they were utterly unlike the benevolent, apple-cheeked characters who presided over happy families in my favourite stories. (Evidently all those happy families were gentile.) My grandmother had no fringed shawl, no steel-rimmed glasses. (She read, if at all, with the help of a magnifying glass from Woolworth's.) Ignorant, apparently, of her natural role as gentle occupant of the rocking chair, she was ignorant too of the world outside her apartment in

remote Winnipeg. She had brought Odessa with her, and—
on my rare visits—she smiled lovingly, uncomprehendingly,
across an ocean of time and space. Even more unreal was my
grandfather, a black cap and a long beard bent over the
Talmud. I felt for him a kind of amused tenderness, but I was
glad that my schoolmates could not see him.

At home we spoke another language—Yiddish or
Russian—and ate rich foods whose spicy odours bore no
resemblance to the neighbour's cooking. We did not go to
church or belong to clubs or, it seemed, take any meaningful
part in the life of the town. Our social roots went, not down
into the foreign soil on which fate had deposited us, but
outwards, in delicate, sensitive connections, to other Jewish
families in other lonely prairie towns. Sundays, they
congregated around our table, these strangers who were
brothers; I saw that they too ate knishes and spoke with
faintly foreign voices, but I could not feel for them or for their
silent swarthy children the kinship I knew I owed to all those
who had been, like us, both chosen and abandoned.

All year I walked in the shadow of difference; but at
Christmas above all, I tasted it sour on my tongue. There was
no room at the tree. "You have Hanukkah," my father
reminded me. "That is *our* holiday." I knew the story, of
course—how, over two thousand years ago, my people had
triumphed over the enemies of their faith, and how a single
jar of holy oil had miraculously burned eight days and nights
in the temple of the Lord. I thought of my father lighting
each night another candle in the *menorah*, my mother and I
beside him as he recited the ancient prayer: "Blessed are
Thou, O Lord our God, ruler of the universe, who has
sanctified us by thy commandments and commanded us to
kindle the light of Hanukkah." Yes, we had our miracle too.
But how could it stand against the glamour of Christmas?
What was *gelt*, the traditional gift coins, to a sled packed
with surprises? What was Judas Maccabaeus the liberator
compared with the Christ child in the manger? To my sense
of exclusion was added a sense of shame. "You *killed*
Christ!" said the boys on the playground. "*You* killed him!"
I knew none of the facts behind this awful accusation, but I
was afraid to ask. I was even afraid to raise my voice in the
chorus of "Come All Ye Faithful" lest I be struck down for
my unfaithfulness by my own God, the wrathful Jehovah.
With all the passion of my child's heart I longed for a
younger, more compassionate deity with flowing robe and

silken hair. Reluctant conscript to a doomed army, I longed to change sides. I longed for Christmas.

Although my father was in all things else the soul of indulgence, in this one matter he stood firm as Moses. "You cannot have a tree, *herzele*. You shouldn't even want to sing the carols. You are a Jew." I turned the words over in my mind and on my tongue. What was it, to be a Jew in Birch Hills, Saskatchewan? Though my father spoke of Jewishness as a special distinction, as far as I could see it was an inheritance without a kingdom, a check on a bank that had failed. Being Jewish was mostly not doing things other people did—not eating pork, not going to Sunday school, not entering, even playfully, into childhood romances, because the only boys around were *goyishe* boys. I remember, when I was five or six, falling in love with Edward Prince of Wales. Of the many arguments with which Mama might have dampened my ardour, she chose surely the most extraordinary. "You can't marry him. He isn't Jewish." And of course, finally, definitely, most crushing of all, being Jewish meant not celebrating Christ's birth. My parents allowed me to attend Christmas parties, but they made it clear that I must receive no gifts. How I envied the white and gold Norwegians! Their Lutheran church was not glamorous, but it was less frighteningly strange than the synagogue I had visited in Winnipeg, and in the Lutheran church, each December, joy came upon the midnight clear.

It was the Lutheran church and its annual concert which brought me closest to Christmas. Here there was always a tree, a jolly Santa Claus, and a program of songs and recitations. As the town's most accomplished elocutionist, I was regularly invited to perform. Usually my offering was comic or purely secular—*Santa's Mistake, The Night Before Christmas*, a scene from *A Christmas Carol*. But I had also memorized for such occasions a sweetly pious narrative about the housewife who, blindly absorbed in cleaning her house for the Lord's arrival, turns away a beggar and finds she has rebuffed the Saviour himself. Oddly enough, my recital of this vitally un-Jewish material gave my parents no pain. My father, indeed, kept in his safe-deposit box along with other valuables a letter in which the Lutheran minister spoke gratefully of my last Christmas performance. "Through her great gift, your little Freidele has led many to Jesus." Though Papa seemed untroubled by considerations of whether this was a proper role for a Jewish child, reciting

The Visit made me profoundly uneasy. And I suppose it was this feeling, combined with a natural disinclination to stand unbidden at the feast, which led me, the year I was seven, to rebel.

We were baking in the steamy kitchen, my mother and I— or rather she was baking while I watched, fascinated as always, the miracle of the strudel. First, the warm ball of dough, no larger than my mother's hand. Slap, punch, bang—again and again she lifted the dough and smacked it down on the board. Then came the moment I loved. Over the kitchen table, obliterating its patterned oilcloth, came a damask cloth; and over this in turn a cloud of flour. Beside it stood my mother, her hair bound in muslin, her hands and arms powdered with flour. She paused a moment. Then, like a dancer about to execute a particularly difficult pirouette, she tossed the dough high in the air, catching it with a little stretching motion and tossing again until the ball was ball no longer but an almost transparent rectangle. The strudel was as large as the tablecloth now. *"Unter Freidele's vigele Ligt eyn groys veys tsigele,"* she sang. "Under Freidele's little bed A white goat lays his silken head." *Tsigele iz geforen handlen Rozinkes mit mandlen . . . "* For some reason that song, with its gay fantastic images of the white goat shopping for raisins and almonds, always made me sad. But then my father swung open the storm door and stood, stamping and jingling his galoshes' buckles, on the icy mat.

"Boris, look how you track in the snow!"

Already flakes and stars were turning into muddy puddles. Still booted and icy-cheeked he swept us up—a kiss on the back of Mama's neck, the only spot not dedicated to strudel, and a hug for me.

"You know what? I have just now seen the preacher. Reverend Pederson, he wants you should recite at the Christmas concert."

I bent over the bowl of almonds and snapped the nut-cracker.

"I should tell him it's all right, you'll speak a piece?"

No answer.

"Sweetheart—dear one—you'll do it?"

Suddenly the words burst out. "No, Papa! I don't want to!"

My father was astonished. "But why not? What is it with you?"

"I hate those concerts!" All at once my grievances swarmed

up in an angry cloud. "I never have any fun! And everybody else gets presents and Santa Claus never calls out 'Freidele Bruser'! They all know I'm Jewish!"

Papa was incredulous. "But, little daughter, always you've had a good time! Presents! What presents? A bag of candy, an orange? Tell me, is there a child in town with such toys as you have? What should you want with Santa Claus?"

It was true. My friends had tin tea sets and dolls with sawdust bodies and crude Celluloid smiles. I had an Eaton Beauty with real hair and delicate jointed body, two French dolls with rosy bisque faces and—new this last Hanukkah—Rachel, my baby doll. She was the marvel of the town: exquisite china head, overlarge and shaped like a real infant's, tiny wrinkled hands, legs convincingly bowed. I had a lace and taffeta doll bassinet, a handmade cradle, a full set of rattan doll furniture, a teddy bear from Germany and real porcelain dishes from England. What *did* I want with Santa Claus? I didn't know. I burst into tears.

Papa was frantic now. What was fame and the applause of the Lutherans compared to his child's tears? Still bundled in his overcoat he knelt on the kitchen floor and hugged me to him, rocking and crooning. "Don't cry, my child, don't cry. You don't want to go, you don't have to. I tell them you have a sore throat, you can't come."

"Boris, wait. Listen to me." For the first time since my outburst, Mama spoke. She laid down the rolling pin, draped the strudel dough delicately over the table, and wiped her hands on her apron. "What kind of a fuss? You go or you don't go, it's not such a big thing. But so close to Christmas you shouldn't let them down. The one time we sit with them in the church and such joy you give them. Freidele, look at me . . . " I snuffled loudly and obeyed, not without some satisfaction in the thought of the pathetic picture I made. "Go this one time, for my sake. You'll see, it won't be so bad. And if you don't like it—pffff, no more! All right? Now, come help with the raisins."

On the night of the concert we gathered in the kitchen again, this time for the ritual of the bath. Papa set up the big tin tub on chairs next to the black iron stove. Then, while he heated pails of water and sloshed them into the tub, Mama set out my clothes. Everything about this moment contrived to make me feel pampered, special. I was lifted in and out of the steamy water, patted dry with thick towels, powdered from neck to toes with Mama's best scented talcum. Then came my "reciting outfit." My friends in Birch Hills had party dresses mail-ordered from Eaton's—crackly taffeta or shiny rayon satin weighted with lace or flounces, and worn with long white stockings drawn up over long woolen underwear. My dress was Mama's own composition, a poem in palest peach crepe de chine created from remnants of her bridal trousseau. Simple and flounceless, it fell from my shoulders in a myriad of tiny pleats no wider than my thumbnail; on the low-slung sash hung a cluster of silk rosebuds. Regulation drop-seat underwear being unthinkable under such a costume, Mama had devised a snug little apricot chemise which made me, in a world of wool, feel excitingly naked.

When at last I stood on the church dais, the Christmas tree glittering and shimmering behind me, it was with the familiar feeling of strangeness. I looked out over the audience-congregation, grateful for the myopia that made faces indistinguishable, and began:

A letter came on Christmas morn
In which the Lord did say
"Behold my star shines in the east
And I shall come today.
Make bright thy hearth . . . "

The words tripped on without thought or effort. I knew by heart every nuance and gesture, down to the modest curtsey and the properly solemn pace with which I returned to my seat. There I huddled into the lining of Papa's coat, hardly hearing the "Beautiful, beautiful!" which accompanied his hug. For this was the dreaded moment. All around me, children twitched and whispered. Santa had come.

"Olaf Swenson!" Olaf tripped over a row of booted feet, leapt down the aisle and embraced an enormous package. "Ellen Njaa! Fern Dahl! Peter Bjorkstrom!" There was a regular procession now, all jubilant. Everywhere in the hall children laughed, shouted, rejoiced with their friends. "What did you get?" "Look at mine!" In the seat next to me, Gunnar Olsen ripped through layers of tissue: "I got it! I got it!" His little sister wrestled with the contents of a red net stocking. A tin whistle rolled to my feet and I turned away, ignoring her breathless efforts to retrieve it.

And then—suddenly, incredibly, the miracle came. "Freidele Bruser!" For me, too, the star had shone. I looked up at my mother. A mistake surely. But she smiled and urged me to my feet. "Go on, look, he calls you!" It was true. Santa was actually coming to meet me. My gift, I saw, was not wrapped—and it could be no mistake. It was a doll, a doll just like Rachel, but dressed in christening gown and cap. "Oh Mama, look! He's brought me a doll! A twin for Rachel! She's just the right size for Rachel's clothes. I can take them both for walks in the carriage. They can have matching outfits . . ." I was in an ecstasy of plans.

Mama did not seem to be listening. She lifted the hem of the gown. "How do you like her dress? Look, see the petticoat?"

"They're beautiful!" I hugged the doll rapturously. "Oh, Mama, I *love* her! I'm going to call her Ingrid. Ingrid and Rachel . . ."

During the long walk home Mama was strangely quiet. Usually I held my parents' hands and swung between them. But now I stepped carefully, clutching Ingrid.

"You had a good time, yes?" Papa's breath frosted the night.

"Mmmmmmmm." I rubbed my warm cheek against Ingrid's cold one. "It was just like a real Christmas. I got the best present of anybody. Look, Papa—did you see Ingrid's funny little cross face? It's just like Rachel's. I can't wait to get her home and see them side by side in the crib."

In the front hall, I shook the snow from Ingrid's lace bonnet. "A hot cup of cocoa maybe?" Papa was already taking the milk from the icebox. "No, no, I want to get the twins ready for bed!" I broke from my mother's embrace. The stairs seemed longer than usual. In my arms Ingrid was cold and still, a snow princess. I could dress her in Rachel's flannel gown, that would be the thing . . . The dolls and animals watched glassy-eyed as I knelt by the cradle. It rocked at my touch, oddly light. I flung back the blankets. Empty. Of course.

Sitting on the cold floor, the doll heavy in my lap, I wept for Christmas. Nothing had changed then, after all. For Jews there was no Santa Claus; I understood that. But my parents . . . *Why* had they dressed Rachel?

From the kitchen below came the mingled aromas of hot chocolate and buttery popcorn. My mother called softly. "Let them call," I said to Ingrid-Rachel. "I don't care!" The face of the Christmas doll was round and blank under her cap; her dress was wet with my tears. Brushing them away, I heard my father enter the room. He made no move to touch me or lift me up. I turned and saw his face tender and sad like that of a Chagall violinist. "Mama worked every night on the clothes," he said. "Yesterday even, knitting booties."

Stiff-fingered, trembling, I plucked at the sleeve of the christening gown. It was indeed a miracle—a wisp of batiste but as richly overlaid with embroidery as a coronation robe. For the first time I examined Rachel's new clothes—the lace insets and lace overlays, the French knots and scalloped edges, the rows of hemstitching through which tiny ribbons ran like fairy silk. The petticoat was tucked and pleated. Even the little diaper showed an edge of hand crochet. There were booties and mittens and a ravishing cap.

"Freidele, dear one, my heart," my father whispered. "We did not think. We could not know. Mama dressed Rachel in the new clothes, you should be happy with the others. We so much love you."

Outside my window, where the Christmas snow lay deep and crisp and even, I heard the shouts of neighbours returning from the concert. "Joy to the world!" they sang.

>Let earth receive her King!
>Let every heart prepare Him room
>And heaven and nature sing . . .

It seemed to me, at that moment, that I too was a part of the song. I wrapped Rachel warmly in her shawl and took my father's hand.

■

W.P. Kinsella

W.P. (William Patrick) Kinsella (1935-   ) was born in Edmonton and did not attend school until grade five because he lived in an isolated area of the Alberta bush. For the past four years he has lived in Calgary, Alberta and taught writing at the University of Calgary. He has published four collections of stories about Silas Ermineskin and his friends: *Dance Me Outside* (1977), *Scars* (1978), *Born Indian* (1981), and *The Mocassin Telegraph* (1983). His original short story, "Shoeless Joe Jackson Comes to Iowa" was published in a collection of stories of that name in 1980, then expanded into a novel, *Shoeless Joe*, which won the Houghton Mifflin Literary Fellowship award in 1982 and the Books In Canada First Novel Award in 1983.

MANITOU MOTORS

W.P. Kinsella

Merton Wolfchild always been kind of a hero of mine. The year I was ten or eleven they held the Alberta Golden Gloves Championships in the Camrose High School Auditorium. In them days, boxers from our reserve, The Hobbema Boxing Club, was known all over the province as really good fighters, and Merton Wolfchild was the best of them.

He weren't very tall but he was built solid and move quick as a cat. Merton's skin was the colour of new cowboy boots and just as shiny. His eyes be set real wide apart and he say that makes him able to see real good from sideways. He always got one piece of black hair that keep falling down over his face like a shoelace. Boy, the final bout of the 150 lb. fighters was the best I ever seen. The RCMP guys from Wetaskiwin have their own boxing club and Merton he fought a Constable Pike. That Constable Pike don't look near so scary wearing nothing but blue boxing shorts and gloves, as he do all decked up in his uniform and carry a gun.

Merton close up one of Constable Pike's eyes in the first round and about halfway through the second he knock him right on the seat of his pants. Boy, I stand up and cheer for Merton loud as my voice will go, until a lady in a red mackinaw who sit in front of me turn around and say, "Try not to yell so loud in my ear, kid." In the third round, Merton he knock out that Constable Pike. Hit him with a right on the chin and boy his head hit the floor of the ring like a sack of feed thrown into an empty wagon box. His RCMP friends have to carry the Constable back to his corner.

There be a big celebration down to the bar of the Coronation Hotel in Camrose that night and Merton sure be a hero around the reserve for a while. He got presented with a big trophy with a gold boxer about six inches high on it, and it used to sit around the table at Wolfchild's cabin until it got all dusty: then the little kids played with it, and finally it just disappeared.

Merton never boxed no more that I know of except to fight in the Alice Hotel bar once in a while or out in the yard at Blue Quills Dance Hall at Hobbema after everybody got drunked up some, even though everybody say he could of been one of those professional boxers if he'd wanted to. Couple of years later he moved over to Camrose to live, that be thirty or so miles from the reserve. I heard he married with a white girl and be selling cars up there.

I wish I'd never heard that. Cause when my friend Norman Scar work all winter in the lumber camp and save his money to buy a car, it is me who suggests that we should go to Camrose and find Merton Wolfchild. I figure that if anybody not going to cheat us it be another Indian. Indians have a bad time buying cars. White salesmen always seem to cheat them one way or another.

Once I walk around Honest Ernie's Used Car Lot in Wetaskiwin and I hear a couple of salesmen say about a '57 Dodge with big fenders that painted pink and black and got white seats and a monkey on a stick in the back window: "That's a wahoo special." And sure enough a couple of weeks later I seen the car around the reserve, but not for long. Pretty quick the transmission and most everything else go on it and it been sit for a long time in a slough down a ways from our cabins.

Bunch of us pile in Louis Coyote's pickup truck and drive up to Camrose. There's me and Norman Scar, my friend Frank Fence-post, my girlfriend Sadie One-wound, Frank's girlfriend Connie Bigcharles, Norman's sister Julie, and two or three other guys who ride in the back of the truck after the cab be all full.

Camrose ain't all that much bigger than Wetaskiwin so it's not that hard to drive around the used car lots until we find one that got an Indian salesman. The sign say, Manitou Motors, easy credit, no down payments, and it got a picture of a tall Indian girl wear only a tiny bathing suit and a red-and-white war bonnet. It sure look like a big business to us as we pull the truck up to the curb. There be rows and rows of light bulbs in red, yellow and blue, and between the rows of bulbs is lines of plastic triangles in bright colours that blow in the wind and make noise like a whole lot of guys snapping their fingers. There must be thirty cars on the lot all shiny and fresh washed.

Merton spot us right away and he come down to meet us, shake our hands and say hello to us in Cree. Norman Scar be pretty shy with strangers so I have to tell Merton that it is my friend who wants to buy a car.

Merton Wolfchild sure ain't the way I remember him from back when he used to box. He put on lots of weight and some of it hang over his belt quite a ways. He got on a white shirt, black pants and some pretty old cowboy boots. He have a wide brown belt with a big square buckle have a picture of a bottle of Lethbridge Pale Ale on it.

"You guys just make yourself at home," he say, and wave his hand around the lot. "When you find something you like, let me know and I let you take it out for a ride." It easy to see that Merton's nose been busted a couple of times and he got a pretty bad scar on one cheek. I don't remember none of that from when I knew him before.

Frank Fence-post, him and Connie Bigcharles be climb in and out of cars like they look for something. It look like they maybe gonna try for set a record for sit in every car on the lot in maybe ten minutes.

"I used to watch you box," I tell Merton.

"Yeah?" he say, and give me a big smile. "Those were the days."

"I seen you the time you knocked out Constable Pike. I cheered so loud for you I didn't have no voice for a couple of days."

"You know something, Norman," he says to me, "that Constable Pike guy is still trying to get even on me. He be stationed up here now and he come around the lot give me tickets for no safety stickers on my cars, and he always digging up some new regulations that he say I broke some time or other."

"I'm Silas Ermineskin," I tell him just to straighten things out. But at least he remembered the name of the guy who want to buy the car.

"You must be Paul's kid maybe. You got a real pretty sister . . . Elaine? or . . . "

"Illianna," I say. "She's married with a white man and lives in Calgary."

"Too bad, I kind of had my eye on her one time. Well, I married with a white girl. We got four kids."

"This is sure a fancy car lot you got here."

"Yeah, well I think it's kind of nice. It make me a good living."

Merton talk like he own it but I see by the license on the wall of his office that it be some other name listed as own Manitou Motors Ltd.

"So Constable Pike still trying to get even for get beat up by you?"

"Yes, sir, I'm gonna have to punch him out again one of

these days," and Merton smack one fist into his other hand and laugh real loud.

Most everybody but Norman and Julie has followed us up to the office. Merton take a cigarette package out of his shirt pocket and pass them around to everybody.

"After your friend decide on a car we all have us a drink to celebrate," he say. "How much money has your friend got to spend?"

"$800," I tell him.

"Well for that I can get him one really good car, Norman," he say and slap my shoulder. "Us Hobbema Indians got to stick together. I sure glad you came to me instead of to some white bugger that rip you off."

Up at the front of the lot Merton is got built a little platform that have a nice sports car sit up on it, have a sign on the windshield say, Special of the Day, just like the Gold Nugget Cafe in Wetaskiwin have a grilled cheese sandwich and cole slaw for 99 cents. Frank and Connie and Norman all be up on that platform and have the hood up on the car. Now if there is one thing Frank be really good at it is start up a car without have no keys. We hear the motor go back-fire a couple of times and then start up. Connie Bigcharles who sit behind the steering wheel get all excited and put the car into gear and it be drive off across the country except that the back wheels catch on the edge of the platform and the car just sit there like it going down a really steep hill. They be awful lucky that they don't kill Frank or even Eddy Crier who was stand in front of the platform and have to jump like hell to get out of the way in time.

I figure that that sure ain't very smart thing to do especially when a Golden Glove Champion owns that car. I figure that Merton probably gonna pound those guys good. But he just have a big laugh about it, once he see that the car ain't hurt none. He gets all us guys down front and we lift that little car back up where it should be.

"Hey, partner," Merton say to Frank, "you let me start up the cars around here, okay?"

Norman come up to me real quiet and he look at the ground. "I seen one that I like, Silas," and he pointed over to where his sister Julie is stand beside a yellow-and-black Ford 4-door, got no hub caps and a pretty bad scratch along one fender. "You asks him for me how much it is?"

"My friend like the yellow Ford over there," I tell Merton. "How much you charge him for it?"

Merton make a sad face. "That one be a thousand bucks,"
he says, but then he stop and scratch his head and that
shoelace of hair fall down over his face. "Seeing as you guys
are brothers and all, and seeing as how you cheered for me
when I whipped Constable Pike, I sell it to youse guys for
$795, and I throw in the license plates."

Norman shake happy and kick some gravel around.

"First though, we want to drive it around," I say.

"I can see you got a good business head, Norman," Merton
say to me. "You guys come on inside the office and we fix up
the papers so's you can test drive it."

I introduce everybody around again and make sure that he
know that Norman is Norman and I's Silas. The office is
pretty tiny. Just a couple of desks, four or five chairs and
heater. It be built out of cedar and smell good to the nose.

Merton he take a long time fill out forms and stuff, and he
have to cross out a lot and he have a hard time spell an easy
name like Norman Scar. Finally he get Norman to sign in
about five places and he have Norman leave with him his
$800, just to be sure we don't run off to Montana with the
car, he say with a big laugh. When all that is done Merton say
we be able to test drive the car, but first Merton pull out a
whiskey bottle from the desk drawer, take a big drink, then he
pass the bottle around to each of us. We thank him for the
drink.

"What are friends for?" he say, and pass cigarettes around
again.

Frank, he already got the car started when we got out there
with the keys. But Merton he still in a good mood and say,
"Take it for a spin around town but be careful that Constable
Pike don't give you no tickets." He's had a couple more
drinks from the bottle and starting to feel pretty good.

Norman Scar and me is the only ones who got drivers'
licences, so Norman drive us off down the street after all
nine of us get settled in the car. "Why don't we head up to
Edmonton," Frank say. "The sales guy don't say when we
have to be back. We make a party up there and come back
tomorrow or the next day?" Norman probably go along with
that but I tell them we just test the car. We can go anyplace we
want after it been bought.

The car seem to me to run pretty rough. After a while I get
Norman to let me drive it. It got a standard transmission and
the clutch don't catch until it all the way out, and I think a
couple of cogs be broken off second gear. The steering be

pretty loose too. But Norman says he likes the colour of the car and the soft red seat covers and say he thinks he buy it.

I run it up to about 50 mph and it just about shimmy me right off the road but Norman ain't about to change his mind.

I notice that it's running pretty hot, so as we pull up in front of the car lot I give the clutch a pretty good kick and stall the motor. Then just like I figure, when I turn the key it don't start. I argue a little with Norman and tell him to try some other cars first before he buy this one and he finally agree with me.

Merton come down to meet us flipping his hair out of his eyes and smiling.

"I don't think we buy this one, Mr. Wolfchild." I tell him. "Maybe we'd like to look at the white Chevy over there."

"That one's too expensive for you," Merton say, and he scratch his head real hard. "I tell you what I do. I throw in a radio, and a tape deck, and hell, what are friends for, I'll even give you a couple of tapes. Take them right out of my own collection. I mean after all you guys are from my home town."

Norman just about to say okay, but I butt in. "This ain't a very good car, Mr. Wolfchild. I been working on engines down to the Technical School at Wetaskiwin for most of two years now, and I can tell there's lots of things wrong with this car."

"Five tapes, and that's my final offer. Two Merle Haggard, a Waylon Jennings, one each of Dolly Parton and Donna Fargo."

"The car don't even start no more and I think the clutch has gone out."

"It was okay when you took it out. Besides there ain't nothing else on the lot that you guys can afford. And why don't you let the buyer talk for himself," and he kind of elbow me out of the way. "Tell you what I do, and this is final," he say to Norman, "I give you one of them big chrome feet to put where your gas pedal is. Costs $12 wholesale at Midland Auto Supply. How about it Silas?"

He'd of had himself a deal if he hadn't mixed up the names again, cause Norman had his mouth all shaped to say yes.

"No, sir. I don't think so. I think we look around some more," Norman say in a small whisper.

Well, Merton step back and kind of take up a pose like he used to when he was a boxer. "Look, kid, I thought you understood. You bought the car. We made a deal in there a while ago. You got yourself a car. Now I'll still throw in the extras I promised, but you own the car, okay? Once you sign a deal there's no backing out of it."

"But he just signed it to test drive it," I say.

"Who asked you?" Merton say to me in a real nasty voice, and I see he got his fists clenched.

Boy I sure don't know what to do. We all just stand around for a while until Merton flip that hair out of his eyes and say he going to round up the tapes and chrome gas pedal and all. He put the radio and tape deck in the trunk, say we can get it hooked up by somebody who knows how.

We all try for a while to start that Ford up but even Frank can't get it going. "It be okay in an hour or so," Merton say. "It just run a little hot is all."

We sit around in Louis Coyote's pickup, smoke cigarettes and try to figure what to do. I tell Norman I sure is sorry for suggest we come here.

Then I start thinking about Constable Pike and I tell everybody about the idea I have, but they sure don't think much of it, cause us Indians the less we have to do with the RCMP guys the happier it makes both us and them.

There be a thunderstorm blowing up and all of a sudden it got dark and windy as the inside of a nose. Them flags snap loud and there be lots of dirt blow around the streets.

Nobody wants to use my idea so I let them all go and sit in Norman's car and I take my girlfriend Sadie One-wound and the truck and drive over to the RCMP headquarters.

Constable Pike seem a lot bigger that I remember him. He got red face like a polished apple and his boots slap loud on the floor when he walk.

"I'll come down and investigate," he say to me after I explain what has happened, "but I can't promise anything. Your friend Norman could take the company to court and probably get his money back but he'd have to go to a lot of trouble to do that. That's what men like Burge and Wolfchild count on."

"Who's this guy Burge?"

"He owns Manitou Motors. Merton Wolfchild married his daughter. Guess Burge figures it's better to have him working there than to support his daughter and all those kids of Merton's."

While we been in the RCMP office it rained real hard with thunder and lightning, but by the time we got over there, us in the truck and Constable Pike in his black-and-white car, only a few drops be fall and the sun start to come out again.

The windows of the Ford be fogged up tight and the only way we can tell there is people in there is by the cigarette smoke coming out of the vent window.

"How much did you say he charged you for that car?" the Constable ask.

"$800," I tell him.

"It's worth about $250 at the very most. No wonder he was trying to buy you off with a tape deck and other junk."

Merton come march down from his office and meet us about the middle of the car lot. "So what you gonna pick on me about today?" he say to Constable Pike.

"Boys here claim they only wanted to test drive the car."

"They're just sore cause it don't run as good as they thought. I sell my cars as-is-here-is. No refunds. No weaseling out of a deal."

"I suppose the car's got a safety sticker. You know it's illegal to sell a car without one."

"I got the papers someplace."

"I suggest you go find them. And I think we should test the tires. It's illegal to sell a car with less than 1/8 inch of tread on the tires."

"You gonna put me in jail for selling bald tires? That be about your speed. You make it damn hard for a poor Indian to make a living."

Merton get uglier as he go along but Constable Pike keep pretty cool. While I been away this Mr. Burge fellow is turn up. He look about 60 and wear a baggy grey suit, and have a lean face that come to a sharp point like a fox.

"Maybe you should give back the money," he say a couple of times. "We don't want no more trouble with cops." But he just hang around on the edge of things like an animal waiting for something to die.

They argue for a while more. It don't look like we gonna get that money back. Then Constable Pike get out his book and say he gonna write out tickets for no safety stickers and thin tires and he start to look around the lot at the other cars, saying he might as well check all of them while he here.

Merton jump about a foot off the ground. "You put me out of business," he yell. "No stinking cop gonna do that to me."

Merton he make a fist and raise up his hand to hit Constable Pike but before any of us know for sure what happened Merton be sitting on the seat of his pants in the wet gravel, feel with one hand at his chin, and look around like somebody asked him a real hard question.

Things move pretty quick after that. Mr. Burge he get the money from Merton's back pocket and give it to Norman, and then he get the papers from inside the office and tear them up for everybody to see. He say a lot of nice things to Constable Pike, and say that him and Merton promise to be good from now on if the Constable don't charge Merton with trying to hit him. I notice though that he never once look in Constable Pike's face while he saying all this.

We all head for the pickup truck, figure the sooner we get out of town the better. Louis Coyote's pickup ain't got no safety sticker and all four tires be so thin that a good healthy mosquito bite them into a blow-out.

Constable Pike is taking down numbers off all the cars on the lot.

Mr. Burge is yell loud at Merton for getting caught at do something bad.

"But they were Indians," Merton is say, spread his arms real wide. "I don't figure for them to make no trouble. You just can't trust anybody no more."

■

Merna Summers

Jean Richards

Merna Summers (1933-) was born in Mannville, Alberta and is presently living in Edmonton. She was a reporter for the *Edmonton Journal* for several years and has done free-lance journalism and writing for educational television and radio. She won the Katherine Anne Porter Prize for her story "Threshing Time" in 1979. She has published two collections of short stories: *The Skating Party* (1974) and *Calling Home* (1982).

THE SKATING PARTY

Merna Summers

Our house looked down on the lake. From the east windows you could see it: a long sickle of blue, its banks hung with willow. Beyond was a wooded ridge which, like all such ridges in our part of the country, ran from northeast to southwest.

In another part of the world, both lake and ridge would have had names. Here, only people had names. I was Maida; my father was Will, my mother was Winnie. Take us all together and we were the Singletons. The Will Singletons, that is, as opposed to the Dan Singletons, who were my grandparents and dead, or Nathan Singleton, who was my uncle and lived in the city.

In the books I read, lakes and hills had names, and so did ponds and houses. Their names made them more real to me, of greater importance, than the hills and lakes and sloughs that I saw every day. I was eleven years old before I learned that the hill on which our house was built had once had a name. It was called Stone Man Hill. My parents had never thought to tell me that.

It was my uncle, Nathan Singleton, who told me. Uncle Nathan was a bachelor. He had been a teacher before he came to Willow Bunch, but he had wanted to be a farmer. He had farmed for a few years when he was a young man, on a quarter that was now part of our farm. His quarter was just south of what had been my grandfather's home place, and was now ours. But then he had moved to the city and become a teacher again.

In some ways it seemed as if he had never really left Willow Bunch. He spent all his holidays at our place, taking walks with me, talking to my mother, helping my father with such chores as he hadn't lost the knack of performing. Our home was his home. I found it hard to imagine him as I knew he must be in his classroom: wearing a suit, chalk dust on his sleeve, putting seat work on the blackboard. He didn't even talk like a teacher.

Uncle Nathan was older than my father, quite a lot older, but he didn't seem so to me. In some ways he seemed younger, for he told me things and my father did not. Not that my father was either silent or unloving. He talked as much as anybody, and he was fond of some people—me included—and showed it. What he did not give away was information.

Some children are sensitive: an eye and an ear and a taking-in of subtleties. I wasn't like that. I wanted to be told. I wanted to know how things really were and how people really acted. Sometimes it seemed to me that collecting the facts was uphill work. I persisted because it was important for me to have them. I wanted to know who to praise and who to blame. Until I was in my mid-teens, that didn't seem to me to be too much to ask.

Perhaps my father had a reluctance to look at things too closely himself. He wanted to like people, and he may have found it easier to do if he kept them a little out of focus. Besides that, he believed that life was something that children should be protected from knowing about for as long as possible.

I got most of my information from my mother. She believed that knowledge *was* protection: that children had a right to know and parents had an obligation to teach. She didn't know all there was to know, but what she did know she intended to pass on to me.

I knew this because I heard her say so one night after I had gone to bed. Uncle Nathan, who was at the farm for the weekend, saw things my mother's way. "What you don't know *can* hurt you," he said. "Especially what you don't know about yourself."

So my mother and my uncle talked to me, both as a sort of innoculation against life and because, I now believe, both of them liked to talk anyway. I was always willing to listen. My father listened too. He might feel that my mother told me too much, but his conviction wasn't strong enough to stop her.

It was Uncle Nathan, talking for pleasure, not policy, who gave me the pleasure of knowing that I lived in a place with a name. Stone Man Hill was so named, he said, because long ago there had existed on the slopes below our house the shape of a man, outlined in fieldstones.

"He was big," Uncle Nathan said. "Maybe fifteen yards, head to foot."

It was a summer afternoon. I was eleven. My father, in from the fields for coffee, was sitting at the kitchen table. His eyelashes were sooty with field dust. My mother was perched on a kitchen stool by the cupboard, picking over berries.

"He must have been quite a sight," my father said.

I walked to the east window of the kitchen and looked out, trying to imagine our hillside field of brome as unbroken prairie sod, trying to picture what a stone man would look like stretched out among the buffalo beans and gopher holes, his face to the sky.

"You get me a writing pad and I'll show you what he looked like," Uncle Nathan said.

I got the pad and Uncle Nathan sat down at the table opposite my father. I sat beside him, watching as he began to trace a series of dots. His hand worked quickly, as if the dots were already visible, but only to his eyes. The outline of a man took shape.

"Who made the stone man?" I asked.

"Indians," Uncle Nathan said. He held the picture up, as if considering additions. "But I don't know when and I don't know why."

"He could have been there a hundred years," my father said. "Maybe more. There was no way of telling."

"I used to wonder why the Indians chose this hill," Uncle Nathan said. "I still do."

He got up and walked to the window, looking out at the hill and the lake and the ridge. "It may be that it was some sort of holy place to them," he said.

My mother left the cupboard and came across to the table. She picked up Uncle Nathan's drawing. Looking at it, the corners of her mouth twitched upwards.

"You're sure you haven't forgotten anything?" she asked. "Your mother used to say that the stone man was *very* complete."

Uncle Nathan returned her smile. "The pencil's right here, Winnie," he said. "You're welcome to it."

My father spoke quickly. "It was too bad the folks didn't have a camera," he said. "It would have been nice to have a picture of the stone man."

My mother went back to her berries.

"I've always been sorry I was too young to remember him," my father said. "Before he turned into a rock pile, that is."

I hadn't yet got around to wondering about the stone man's disappearance. Now I did. He should still have been on his hillside for me to look at. My father had been a baby when his people came to Willow Bunch, and he couldn't remember the stone man. My uncle had been a young man and could. But the difference in their ages and experience hadn't kept them from sharing a feeling of excitement at the thought of a stone man on our hillside. Why had my grandfather been insensible to this appeal? Hadn't he liked the stone man?

"Liking wouldn't enter into it," my father said. "Your grandfather had a family to feed. He knew where his duty lay."

"There was thirty acres broke when Pa bought this place," Uncle Nathan said. "He thought he needed more. And this hill was the only land he could break without brushing it first."

Somebody else had owned our place before my grandfather, hadn't they? I asked. He hadn't turned the stone man into a rock pile.

"He was a bachelor," my father said.

"The way your grandfather saw it," Uncle Nathan said, "it was a case of wheat or stones. And he chose wheat."

"Which would you have chosen?" I asked Uncle Nathan. "Which did you want?"

"I wanted both," Uncle Nathan said.

"The choice wasn't yours to make." My mother spoke as if she were defending him.

"That's what I thought then," Uncle Nathan said. "I thought when Pa told me to get those rocks picked, that that was what I had to do. I think now I should have spoken up. I know for years I felt guilty whenever I remembered that I had done just what was expected of me."

He looked up, a half-smile on his face. "I know it sounds crazy," he said, "but I felt as if the stone man had more claim on me than my own father did."

"We all of us think some crazy things sometimes," my father said.

From my point of view, Uncle Nathan had only one peculiarity. He had never married. And though I sometimes asked him why, I never found any satisfaction in his answers.

"Maybe it wasn't every girl who took my eye," he told me once. "I'd pity the girl who had to count on me to take care of her," he said another time.

Then my mother told me about the skating party. It had been a dark night in November, and my mother, five years old, had come to our lake with her parents, and spent the night pushing a kitchen chair in front of her across the ice, trying to learn to skate. The party was being held in honour of Uncle Nathan and a girl called Eunice Lathem. They were to be married soon, and their friends planned, after the skating, to go up to the house a present a gift to them. The gift and the fact that the party was in her honour were to be a surprise to Eunice. Nathan, for some reason, had been told about it.

There had been cold that year but no snow, so you could skate all over the lake. My mother remembered them skimming by, the golden lads and girls who made up the world when she was small, and Nathan and Eunice the most romantic of all. Nathan was handsome and Eunice was beautiful and they were very much in love, she said.

She remembered the skaters by moonlight, slim black shapes mysterious against the silver fields. There were a lot of clouds in the sky that night and when the moon went behind one of them, friends, neighbours and parents' friends became alike: all equally unknown, unidentifiable.

My grandfather and Uncle Nathan had built a big wood fire at the near end of the lake. My mother said that it was a grand experience to skate off into the darkness and the perils and dangers of the night, and then turn and come back toward the light, following the fire's reflection on the ice.

Late on, when some people were already making their way up the hill to the house, Eunice Lathem went skating off into the darkness with her sister. They didn't skate up the middle of the lake as most of the skaters had been doing. Instead they went off toward the east bank. There is a place there where a spring rises and the water is deep, but they didn't know that. The ice was thinner there. They broke through.

Near the fire, people heard their cries for help. A group of the men skated out to rescue them. When the men got close the the place where the girls were in the water, the ice began to crack under their feet.

All the men lay down then and formed a chain, each holding the ankles of the man in front of him. Uncle Nathan was at the front. He inched forward, feeling the ice tremble beneath his body, until he came to the point where he could reach either of two pairs of hands clinging to the fractured edge.

It was dark. He couldn't see the girls' faces. All he could do was grasp the nearest pair of wrists and pull. The men behind him pulled on his feet. Together they dragged one girl back to safety. But as they were doing it, the ice broke away beneath them and the second girl went under. The moon came out and they saw it was Eunice Lathem's sister they had saved. They went back to the hole, but Eunice had vanished. There wasn't any way they could even get her body.

"It was an awful thing to have happen on our place," my father said.

"Your Uncle Nathan risked his life," my mother said. Her voice was earnest, for she too believed in identifying heroes and villains.

"There was no way on earth he could save both girls," she said. "The ice was already breaking, and the extra weight of the first one was bound to be too much for it."

Why hadn't he saved Eunice first?

"I told you," my mother said. "He couldn't see their faces."

It troubled me that he hadn't had some way of knowing. I would have expected love to be able to call out to love. If it couldn't do that, what was it good for? And why had the moon been behind a cloud anyway?

"Your grandmother used to say that the Lord moves in a mysterious way," my father said.

"What does that mean?" I asked.

"It means that nobody knows," my mother said.

I'd seen Eunice Lathem's name on a grave in the yard of St. Chad's, where we attended services every second Sunday. If I'd thought of her at all, it was as a person who had always been dead. Now she seemed real to me, almost like a relative. She was a girl who had loved and been loved. I began to make up stories about her. But I no longer skated on the lake alone.

Eunice Lathem's sister, whose name was Delia Sykes, moved away from Willow Bunch right after the accident. She didn't wait until her husband sold out; she went straight to Edmonton and waited for him there. Even when they buried Eunice in the spring, she didn't come back.

Years later, someone from Willow Bunch had seen her in Edmonton. She didn't mention Eunice or the accident or even Willow Bunch.

"It must have been a short conversation," my mother said practically.

Is it surprising that I continued to wonder why Uncle Nathan didn't marry? Some people remember their childhoods as a time when they thought of anybody over the age of twenty-five as being so decrepit as to be beyond all thought of romance or adventure. I remember feeling that way about *women*, but I never thought of men that way, whatever their ages. It seemed to me that Uncle Nathan could still pick out a girl and marry her if he set his mind to it.

"No," he said when I asked him. "Not 'still' and not 'pick out a girl.' A person doesn't have that much say in the matter. You can't love where you choose."

And then, making a joke of it, "See that you remember that when your time comes," he said.

One day my mother showed me a picture of Eunice Lathem and her sister. Two girls and a pony stood looking at the camera. Both girls were pretty. The one who wasn't Eunice was laughing; she looked like a girl who loved to laugh. Eunice was pretty too, but there was a stillness about her, almost a sternness. If she hadn't been Eunice Lathem, I would have said she was sulking.

I felt cheated. Was the laughing one also prettier?

"She may have been," my mother said. "I remember Eunice Lathem as being beautiful. But since Delia Sykes was married, I don't suppose I gave her looks a thought one way or the other."

As I grew older I spent less time wondering about the girl who'd been Eunice Lathem. I'd never wondered about her sister, and perhaps never would have if I hadn't happened to be with Uncle Nathan the day he heard that Delia Sykes had died.

It was the spring I was fifteen. My parents were away for the weekend, attending a silver wedding in Rochfort Bridge. Uncle Nathan and I were alone on the farm and so, if he wanted to talk about Delia Sykes, he hadn't much choice about who to talk to.

It was a morning for bad news. The frost was coming out of the ground, setting the very ditches and wheel-ruts to weeping. Out in the barn, a ewe was mourning her lost lamb. We had put her in a pen by herself and we were saving the dead lamb, so we could use its skin to dress another lamb in case one of the ewes died in lambing or had no milk.

Uncle Nathan and I left the barn and walked out to the road to pick up the mail. The news of Delia's death was in the local paper. "Old-timers will be saddened to learn of the death in Duncan, B.C. of Mrs. Delia Sykes, a former resident of this district," the paper said.

Uncle Nathan shook his head slowly, as if he found the news hard to believe. "So Delia's gone," he said. "She was a grand girl, Delia Sykes. No matter what anybody said, she was a grand girl."

There was a picture of Mrs. Sykes with the death notice. I saw a middle-aged woman who had gone from the hairdresser's to the photographer's. Her cheeks were as firm and round as two peach halves, and she had snappy eyes. She was wearing a white dress. She looked as if she might have belonged to the Eastern Star or the Rebekahs.

Uncle Nathan looked at the picture too. "Delia always was a beauty," he said.

He sat in silence for a while, and then, bit by bit, he began to tell me the story of how he had met Delia Sykes and before her, her husband.

"Only I didn't realize that he was her husband," Uncle Nathan said. "I thought when I met her that she was single; that was the joke of it."

It was late July and late afternoon. Uncle Nathan was teaching school, to make enough money to live on until his farm got going. But he was hoping to get out of it.

"The land was new then and we thought there was no limit to how rich we were all going to be some day. Besides that," he added, "what I wanted to do was farm. School-teaching seemed to me to be no proper job for a man."

There were two things Uncle Nathan wanted. One was to stop teaching. The other was to find a wife.

There were more men than girls around then, he told me, so the man who wanted a good selection had to be prepared to cover a lot of territory.

"Harold Knight and I took in dances and ball games as far away as Hasty Hills," he said.

They'd already seen a fair sampling, but there were still girls they hadn't seen.

"I had a pretty fair idea of what I was looking for," Uncle Nathan said. "I imagine it was the same sort of thing every young fellow thinks he's looking for, but I thought I had standards. I wasn't willing to settle for just anyone."

It was with the idea of looking over another couple of girls that he went to see Harold Knight that late July afternoon. A family with two daughters was rumoured to have moved in somewhere near Morningside School. He'd come to suggest to Harold that they take in the church service at the school the next Sunday.

The Knights, Uncle Nathan said, had hay and seed wheat to sell to people with the money to buy it. When Uncle Nathan walked into their yard that day, he saw that Mr. Knight was talking to a buyer. It was a man he'd never seen before, but he guessed by the cut of the man's rig that he must be well fixed.

"Nathan," Mr. Knight said, "meet Dobson Sykes."

Mr. Sykes was a straight-standing man with greying hair. He put out his hand and Uncle Nathan shook it.

"His driving horses," Uncle Nathan said, "were as showy a team as I'd ever seen—big bays with coats the colour of red willow."

"You'd go a long way before you'd find a better-matched team than that," Mr. Knight said.

"Oh, they match well enough." Dobson Sykes spoke as if that was a matter of little importance to him, as if no effort was made in the acquiring of such a team. "I'd trade them in a minute if something better came along," he said carelessly. "I have a job to keep Spark, here, up to his collar."

"I had a fair amount of respect then for men who'd done well in life," Uncle Nathan told me. "This man was about my father's age, old enough to have made it on his own. When a man like that came my way, I studied him. I thought if I was going to be a farmer instead of a teacher, I'd have to start figuring out how people went about getting things in life.

"I wasn't really surprised when Mr. Knight said that Sykes had a crew of men—men he was paying—putting up a set of buildings for him on a place he'd bought near Bannock Hill. He looked like a man with that kind of money."

"We're not building anything fancy," Dobson Sykes said. "If I'd wanted to stay farming on a big scale, I wouldn't have moved from Manitoba."

After a while Uncle Nathan left the two older men talking and walked out toward the meadow, where Harold was fetching a load of hay for Mr. Sykes.

It was on the trail between buildings and meadow that he met Delia Sykes.

He didn't see her at first because she wasn't sitting up front with Harold. She must have been lying back in the hay, Uncle Nathan said, just watching the clouds drift by overhead. She sat up.

Uncle Nathan saw at once that she was not very old; he had girls almost as old as she was in his classroom. But there was nothing of the schoolgirl about Delia. She was young but womanly. Everything about her curved, from the line of her cheek to the way she carried her arms.

Uncle Nathan saw all this in the instant that she appeared looking down over the edge of the load. He saw too that she had a kind of class he'd never seen around Willow Bunch. She looked like a girl perfectly suited to riding around the country behind a team of perfectly matched bays.

She reached behind her into the hay and came up with a crown of french-braided dandelions. She set it on top of her hair and smiled.

He knew right then, Uncle Nathan said, that his voice wouldn't be among those swelling the hymns at Morningside School next Sunday. And he felt as if he understood for the first time how men must feel when they are called to the ministry. Choosing and decision and standards have nothing to do with it. You're called or you're not called, and when you're called you know it.

The girl smiled and opened her arms as if to take in the clouds in the sky and the bees buzzing in the air and the red-topped grasses stirring in the wind. Then she spoke.

"You've got no worries on a load of hay," she said.

Those were the first words Uncle Nathan heard Delia Sykes say. "You've got no worries on a load of hay."

There was a patch of milkweed blooming near the path where Uncle Nathan was standing. In late July, small pink blossoms appear and the milk, rich and white, is ready to run as soon as you break the stalk. Uncle Nathan picked a branch, climbed the load of hay, and presented it to the girl.

"It's not roses," he said, "but the sap is supposed to cure warts."

She laughed. "My name is Delia Sykes," she said.

"I thought she was Dobson's daughter," Uncle Nathan said, "and it crossed my mind to wonder if he'd have traded her off if she hadn't moved along smart in her harness.

"There didn't seem to be much fear of that. You could see right away she had spirit. If she had too much, it was nothing that marriage to a good man wouldn't cure, I thought."

Uncle Nathan gave a rueful smile. "Of course when we got back to the yard I found out that she wasn't Dobson's daughter but his wife. Later I wondered why she hadn't introduced herself as *Mrs.* Sykes. And she'd called me *Nathan* too, and girls didn't do that then.

"The truth is," Uncle Nathan said, "I had kind of fallen for her."

Did she feel the same way about him?

If she did, Uncle Nathan wasn't willing to say so. "Delia was only nineteen," he said. "I don't think she knew what she wanted."

He was silent for a while. Then he went on with his story. "Once I knew she was married," he said, "I knew right away what I had to do. I remember I gave myself a good talking to. I said, 'If you can fall in love in twenty minutes, you can fall out of love just as fast.' "

"And could you?"

"Some people could, I guess," Uncle Nathan said. "It seemed to take me a bit longer."

The story stopped then because we had to go out to the barn to check the sheep. While we'd been in the house, another ewe had dropped her lamb. We heard it bleat as we came in the barn, and the ewe whose lamb had died heard it too. It was at the far end of the barn, out of sight, but at the sound of it, milk began to run from her udder. She couldn't help herself.

We checked the rest of the sheep and then we went back into the house. I made us a pot of tea.

"I was afraid to go to see Dobson and Delia after they got moved in," Uncle Nathan said. "I think I was afraid somebody would read my mind."

He went, he said, because Delia soon made her house a gathering place for all the young people of the district, and he didn't see how he could be the only one to stay away. Delia didn't make things any easier for him.

"She used to keep saying she'd only been married three months . . . as if that made it any less final. And when she spoke of anything they had—whether it was a buggy or a kitchen safe or the pet dog—she would say 'my buggy' or 'my kitchen safe' or 'my dog.' 'We' and 'us' were words she didn't use at all."

I poured our tea then, trying to imagine the house that Delia Sykes had lived in.

"It was something of a showplace for its time," Uncle Nathan told me. Everything in it was the best of its kind, he said, from the Home Comfort stove in the kitchen to the pump organ in the parlour. What puzzled Uncle Nathan was Delia's attitude to her things. She'd picked them out herself in Winnipeg and ordered them sent, but when they got here, she seemed to feel they weren't important.

"The more things you've got, the more things you've got to take care of," she said. She didn't even unpack most of her trunks.

Dobson was worried. He thought that moving away from her family had unsettled her. "Delia wasn't like this in Manitoba," he said.

"I kept wondering," Uncle Nathan said, "where we would go from here. It never occurred to me that there could be another girl for me. And then Eunice came along."

It was on an October afternernon, Uncle Nathan said, that he met Eunice Lathem.

The sun was low in the southwest when he drove into the Sykes yard, and Dobson, as usual, was out around the buildings showing the younger men his grinding mill, his blacksmith shop, his threshing machine.

Uncle Nathan remembered that the trees were leafless except for the plumes of new growth at the top. He tied up his horse and, as he headed for the house, saw that the afternoon sun was turning the west-facing walls all gold and blue. It looked like a day for endings, not beginnings. But he went into the house, and there stood Eunice Lathem.

Eunice was a year or two older that Delia but she looked just like her. Uncle Nathan noticed that she was quieter.

Supper was already on the table when Uncle Nathan got there. The news of Eunice's arrival had attracted such a company of bachelors that there weren't enough plates or chairs for everybody to eat at once.

"I don't know about anybody else, but I'm starving," Delia announced, taking her place at the head of the table. Eunice, though she was the guest of honour, insisted on waiting until the second sitting.

As the first eaters prepared to deal with their pie, Eunice began to ladle water out of a stonewear crock into a dishpan. Uncle Nathan went to help her. He said something funny and she laughed.

Delia's voice startled them both. "I invited Eunice out here to find a husband," she said with a high-pitched laugh. "I said to myself, 'With all the bachelors we've got around, if she can't find a husband here, there's no hope for her.' "

Delia spoke as if she were making a joke, and there was a nervous round of laughter. Blood rose in Eunice's face.

"If I'd known that was why you were asking me," Eunice said, "I would never have come."

And indeed, Uncle Nathan said, Eunice wasn't the sort of

girl to need anyone's help in finding a husband. She was, if anything, prettier than Delia. Not as showy, perhaps, perhaps not as rounded. But if you went over them point by point comparing noses, chins, teeth and all the rest of it, Eunice might well have come out on top.

Later, when the others had gone, Delia apologized. "I shouldn't have said that," she said. "It sounded awful." She didn't even claim to have been making a joke.

"I want you two to be friends," she said.

In the weeks that followed, Uncle Nathan saw that Delia was pushing her sister his way. He didn't know why, but he didn't find the idea unpleasant.

"I suppose I liked Eunice at first because she looked so much like Delia," he said, "but as I got to know her better it seemed to me that she might be easier to get along with in the long run. I wouldn't be the first man to marry the sister of the girl who first took his fancy, nor the last one either.

"It seemed to me that a man could love one girl as easily as another if he put his mind to it. I reasoned it out. How much did the person matter anyway? That was what I asked myself. It seemed to me that when all was said and done, it would be the life that two people made together that would count, not who the people were.

"I remembered thinking that getting married would be like learning to dance. Some people are born knowing how; they have a natural beat. Other people have to make an effort to learn. But all of them, finally, are moving along to the music one way or the other.

"Anyway," Uncle Nathan said, "I spoke to Eunice, and she agreed, and we decided to be married at Christmas.

"It was September, I think, when we got engaged," Uncle Nathan said. "I remember thinking about telling Dobson and Delia. I could imagine the four of us—Dobson and Delia, Eunice and me—living side by side, spending our Sundays together, raising children who would be cousins and might even look like each other.

"I came over early on the Sunday and we told them. Delia didn't have very much to say then. But in the afternoon when quite a crowd had gathered and Eunice and I were waiting for the rest of them to get there before we made our announcement, a strange thing happened.

"The day before, Dobson had brought home a new saddle pony and Delia had wanted to ride it. Dobson didn't know how well broke it was, or if it could be trusted, and he refused.

I guess that refusal rankled. Delia didn't like to be told she couldn't do a thing or have a thing she had set her heart on.

"Anyway, on Sunday afternoon Eunice was sitting at the pump organ playing for us, and she looked beautiful. We were all sitting around looking at her.

"And then somebody happened to glance out of the window," Uncle Nathan said. "And there was Delia on the pony, and the pair of them putting on a regular rodeo.

"She didn't break her neck, which was a wonder. By the time she finally got off the pony, we were all out in the yard, and somebody had the idea of taking a picture of Delia and Eunice and the pony."

After that, Uncle Nathan said, Delia seemed to want to get the wedding over with as soon as possible. She hemmed sheets and ordered linen and initialled pillow-cases. When November finally came and the neighbours decided on a skating party for Eunice and Uncle Nathan, it was Delia who sewed white rabbit fur around the sleeves and bottom of Eunice's coat, so that it would look like a skating dress.

The night of the party was dark. There was a moon, but the sky was cloudy. They walked down the hill together, all those young people, laughing and talking.

"One minute you could see their faces and the next they would all disappear," Uncle Nathan said. "I touched a match to a bonfire we had laid in the afternoon, and we all sat down to screw on our skates.

"I skated first with Eunice. She wanted to stay near the fire so we could see where we were going. I skated with several other girls, putting off, for some reason, the time when I would skate with Delia. But then she came gliding up to me and held out her hands, and I took them and we headed out together into the darkness.

"As soon as we turned our backs on the fire it was as if something came over us. We wanted to skate out farther and farther. It seemed to me that we could keep on like this all our lives, just skating outward farther and farther, and the lake would keep getting longer and longer so that we would never come to the end of it."

Uncle Nathan sighed. "I didn't know then that in three days Delia would have left Willow Bunch for good, and in six months I would have followed her," he said.

Why had he given up farming?

"Farming's no life for a man alone," he said. "And I couldn't imagine ever wanting to marry again."

He resumed his story. "Once the moon came out and I could see Delia's face, determined in the moonlight.

" 'Do you want to turn back?' I asked her.

" 'I'm game as long as you are,' she said.

"Another time, 'I don't ever want to turn back,' she said.

"I gave in before Delia did," Uncle Nathan said. " 'If we don't turn around pretty soon,' I told her, 'we're going to be skating straight up Pa's stubble fields.'

"We turned around then, and there was the light from the fire and our feet already set on its path. And I found I wanted to be back there with all the people around me. Eunice deserved better, and I knew it."

As they came toward the fire, Eunice skated out to meet them. "I might as well have been someplace else for all the attention she paid me," Uncle Nathan said. Her words were all for Delia.

"If this is what you got me out here for," Eunice said, "you can just forget about it. I'm not going to be your window blind."

"I don't know what you're talking about," Delia said.

She looked unhappy. "She knew as well as I did," Uncle Nathan said, "that whatever we were doing out there, it was more than just skating."

"We were only skating," Delia said. And then her temper rose. "You always were jealous of me," she said.

"Who would you say was jealous now?" Eunice asked.

"We were far enough away from the fire for the girls not to be heard," Uncle Nathan said. "At least I hoped we were.

"What was worrying me was the thought of Eunice having to meet all the people up at the house, and finding out she was the guest of honour, and having to try to rise to the occasion.

"That was why I suggested that the two of them go for a skate. I thought it would give them a chance to cool down. Besides," he added, "I couldn't think of anything else to do."

The girls let themselves be persuaded. They skated off together and Uncle Nathan watched them go. First he could see their two silhouettes, slim and graceful against the silver lake. Then all he could see was the white fur on Eunice's coat. And then they were swallowed up by the darkness.

"It was several minutes before we heard them calling for help," Uncle Nathan said.

Uncle Nathan and I sat silent for some time then: he

remembering, I pondering. "If only you could have seen how beautiful she was," he said at last, and I didn't know whether it was Eunice he was speaking of, or Delia.

"I wonder if I would have felt any better about it if I'd got Eunice instead of Delia," he said. I realized that he'd been trying to make the judgement for thirty years.

"You didn't have any choice," I reminded him. "It was dark. You couldn't see their faces."

"No," Uncle Nathan said. "I couldn't see their faces." The sound of old winters was in his voice, a sound of infinite sadness.

"But I could see their hands on the edge of the ice," he said. "The one pair of arms had white fur around them.

"And I reached for the other pair."

■

Ed Kleiman

Jim Haggarty

Ed Kleiman (1932-   ) was born in Winnipeg's North End—the setting for many of his stories. He presently teaches literature at the University of Manitoba. His fiction has appeared in numerous publications, including *Journal of Canadian Fiction, Canadian Forum, Descant, Antigonish Review,* and *Fiddlehead.* "The Immortals" is the title story of his collection of fourteen stories published in 1980.

THE IMMORTALS

Ed Kleiman

For days in the fall of forty-nine, St. John's High had
buzzed with rumours about whether or not Torchy
Brownstone would be allowed to play in the football game
on Friday. Torchy was our first-string quarterback, a two-
year veteran with the school, and if we were to have any
chance of beating Kelvin—our arch-rivals from River
Heights—then the team could not afford to see him sidelined
with a knee injury. The injury had been sustained in a
practice session last week when a second-string linebacker
had gotten carried away with enthusiasm and tackled
Torchy just as he was coming around the end of a double
reverse. So one of our own players had done what the rest of
the league would have been trying to do all through the fall.

What hurt most was that Torchy should be sidelined when
we were playing Kelvin. The game itself didn't count for
anything. It was an exhibition game, a warm-up before the
regular season began. But what did count was that this was a
contest between the North and South Ends of the city. And
that was no small matter.

The North End consisted mainly of immigrants from
Eastern Europe, labouring classes, small foreign-language
newspapers, watch-repair shops, a Jewish theatrical
company, a Ukrainian dance troupe, small choirs, tap-
dancing schools, orchestral groups, chess clubs and more
radical political thinkers per square block than Soviet
Russia had known before the Revolution. The South
End—or River Heights, as it is more fashionably called—was
basically what that revolution had been against. The mayor,
most of the aldermen, the chairman of the school board and
many of the civic employees—not the street sweepers, of
course—lived in River Heights.

Actually, when you think about it, they had chosen a
curious name for their end of town. If you've ever passed
through Winnipeg, you'll realize that it rests on one of the
flattest stretches of land in the world. In fact, I read in the
school library once that the land falls at the rate of no more
than two feet per mile as it extends northward towards Lake
Winnipeg. So the Heights, you see, can't amount to much

more than six to eight feet, at the most. But people there like to think of themselves as living on a plateau overlooking the rest of the city, as in a sense they do. For the heights they've attained are built on political and economic foundations that give them a vantage point of something more in the order of six or eight hundred feet.

Another way of distinguishing between the two parts of the city is by looking at the street names. In the North End, you'll find such names as Selkirk Avenue, Euclid Street, Aberdeen, Dufferin—names steeped in history, names which suggest the realm of human endeavour, anguish, accomplishment. But if you look at the street names in River Heights, what you'll find, with few exceptions, are such names as Ash Street, Elm, Oak, Willow. Vast expanses of velvet lawns, well-treed boulevards—the area looks like a garden, a retreat from the toil and anguish everywhere visible in the North End. The two cultures meet downtown, where the South End gentry immediately head for the managerial offices, and the North End rabble file past the company clocks with their time cards. After work, countless numbers of expensive cars sweep grandly across the Maryland Bridge back into Eden, while streetcars and buses pass northward beneath the C.P.R. subway into a grim bleak underworld of steel fences, concrete walls, locked doors, and savage dogs that seem capable of looking in three directions at once.

But at the Osborne Stadium in the fall, the traditional roles can be reversed for an evening. There, on Friday nights, the North End may once more experience the heady hours of triumph it knew during the 1919 Strike, when it seemed the World Revolution might begin right here in Winnipeg. So, you see, the fact that Torchy Brownstone had injured his knee in football practice was of major concern to us all.

And then to add insult to injury, the English teacher Mr. Rockwood caught our star tackles, Norm Mittlehaus and Sam Margolis, in Room 41 the day before the game and tried to have them disqualified from playing on Friday. Room 41 is Goldman's drug store—just across the street from the high school—and kids are always sneaking across during the day to have a soda, read a magazine, or have a smoke. And Rockwood is always catching them. Rockwood is about five foot two and weighs about a hundred and eighty, so he's a fairly stocky little guy with huge shoulders and a neck like a bull dog. Needless to say, Rockwood lives in River Heights, and he would have still been teaching at Kelvin if he hadn't swatted one of his pupils one day—the son of a school trustee, as it turned out—and since then he's been our affliction. He often tries to have kids expelled, banned from writing exams, or disqualified from playing football— which drives the football coach, Mr. Powalski, wild. It had always seemed to us that Mr. Rockwood would have been much happier, would have felt more free to express himself, and would have achieved a greater degree of fulfillment if he'd been a guard at Auschwitz.

Anyway, as soon as Mr. Powalski learned that Rockwood had disqualified our star tackles Mittlehaus and Margolis from playing the next night, he rushed up to the principal's office and threatened to resign—again, for what must have been the tenth time that year—if they weren't reinstated.

On the Friday night of the game, the stands were packed. Would Torchy play? And what about Mittlehaus and Margolis? Even I came to the game that night, and I rarely go to football games—or any kind of sports event for that matter. As usual, I was intensely preoccupied with the finer things in life, with art and poetry, and all my evenings then were taken up by an epic poem in hexameters I was working on. But the whole school was caught up in the game that night, and Nate Samuelson, my bench partner in physics lab who had just been elected student president, finally persuaded me that I couldn't stay behind.

So there we all were, glaring across the field at the River Heights stands, where, sitting shamelessly among the staunch supporters of the opposing team, we could make out Rockwood; Peg-Leg Dobson—our physics teacher; Mr. Atkinson—our chemistry teacher and Mr. Clearwater—the principal. Still, Kleinberg, Schultz, Rasmussen and Pollick —all loyal North Enders—had stationed themselves prominently in our end of the stadium.

Rumours abounded. Kelvin was supposed to have all-new football equipment donated by the president of a huge department store. Their new sweaters, it was claimed, were no longer the school colours, cherry and grey, but a regal purple and gold. It was also whispered that the team had been practising secret plays to be unveiled that night. They had a new fullback—a huge two-hundred-pounder, who would make mincemeat of our line. And, most ominous of all, there was talk that the chief referee had bet five dollars on the River Heights team.

But each new rumour of impending doom simply sent our

spirits soaring higher. We shouted taunts across the field, blew up Sheiks and let them float skyward, unveiled posters that displayed a hammer and sickle, beneath which were the words, "Workers, Arise!" bombarded the officials with over-ripe tomatoes and rotten eggs which we'd saved especially for the occasion, and flung rolls of toilet paper into the playing area. Until an exasperated voice in an Oxford accent that had obviously just been acquired that summer asked us all to stand for the National Anthem.

Then the whistle blew, and we kicked off to Kelvin, and, to our horror, that two-hundred-pound fullback really did exist because he caught the ball and ran over three of our tacklers for a touchdown. Less than sixty seconds after the game had started, they had a converted touchdown—worth six points then—and we had three injuries. Suddenly our players in their ripped sweaters and torn pads looked like a pretty shabby lot compared to that Kelvin team, which moved with such military precision in their new uniforms and shiny helmets.

On the next kick-off, our star runner, Cramer, caught the football, and was promptly tackled by their two-hundred-pound fullback, whose name, we learned, was Bruno Hogg. When Cramer finally managed to get up, he was limping. A mighty groan escaped from the North End stands. Jerusalem had just been taken and we were all being marched off to captivity in Babylon. We could see Torchy, down on the sidelines, pleading with the coach to let him in—knee injury and all—but Powalski sent in Marty Klein instead.

When they first caught sight of Marty, the military discipline of the Kelvin team threatened to disintegrate. Marty's all of five foot two and can't weigh much more than one twenty-five, so his appearance caused first titters, then guffaws. Of course they didn't realize that Marty uses his size to advantage. He's the sneakiest player you'll ever see.

Right away, Marty calls a plunge by the fullback. But when they peel the players off our boy, he doesn't have the ball. Then the Kelvin line pounces on the two halfbacks, but they don't have the ball either—and so they throw them away and begin looking around with murder in their eyes for the tailback. By the time they start looking around for Marty, it's too late. He's waving to them with one hand, the ball in the other, from behind their own goal line. Marty had jumped right out of harm's way once the ball had been snapped, and then he strolled off down the sidelines while the Kelvin team

pounced upon one player after another in their frantic
search for the missing football. Somehow we managed to
finish the quarter with a six-all tie.

But in the second quarter, disaster struck. We'd managed to
hold Kelvin in their own end of the field until they had to
kick on third down. Out of their huddle they marched in that
military precision of theirs, and we knew right away
something tricky was up. Three of their backfielders pranced
out to one side behind the kicker, who booted the ball no
more than fifteen yards, and those three ballet stars danced
away with the ball while we were left looking like jerks, with
our coach hastily thumbing through his rule book to see
what it was all about. When Kelvin tried the same stunt a few
plays later, all three of their ballerinas were immediately
flattened. But that was strictly *verboten*, according to the
officials, and we were penalized fifteen yards. Then that two-
hundred-pound fullback of theirs got the ball again, and we
were behind another six points. But at last Powalski found
the section in the rule book dealing with on-side kicks and
brought an end to that particular gimmick.

When we finally got the ball again, Marty Klein called
another plunge by the fullback, but now the whole line piled
on top of poor Marty, and so the fullback—who did have the
ball this time—had already bulldozed his way more than half
the length of the field when his bootlace came undone, and
he tripped over the loose end. Of course Kelvin recovered the
fumbled ball, and we were lucky to finish the half only six
points down.

During the intermission, more rumours swept through the
stands. A doctor had been seen racing down to the stadium
from the North End with a special drug and a set of splints
that would enable Torchy to play in the second half. This
was immediately contradicted by another rumour: the same
doctor had warned that Torchy would limp for the rest of his
life if he played that night.

Someone else hinted that there was a special reason for
those Kelvin players moving about with such stiff, jerky
motions and spastic gestures. All that talk about military
precision and strict training was a bunch of nonsense. Nate
Samuelson had sneaked into the Kelvin dressing room before
the game and sprinkled red pepper into every one of their
jock straps. A little later somebody spotted Nate sitting
beside me, and soon a couple of dozen people were cheering
their new student president. None of us suspected then that

twenty years later, long after he had become a doctor, gotten married and had two children, he would take an overdose of drugs and walk off the MacIntyre Building smack on top of the early morning traffic jam. Nate stood up in the stands that evening, smiled in that sly way of his, and waved his hand to the cheering crowd.

Later still, a few students from the Grade Twelve Industrial Class stormed across the field to pick a fight with some of the River Heights fans, but they got thrown out of the stadium by the police for their efforts. Afterwards, we heard that they had peed in the gas tanks of all the posh cars parked around the stadium—cars which after the game that night were seen to be lurching and stalling through the streets leading back into River Heights.

Then the players came back on the field, and that two-hundred-pound fullback of theirs got the ball, and now we were behind twelve points. It was during the third quarter that they really began to grind our team into the turf. They seemed to be getting stronger by the minute, while our crew looked shabbier than ever. We couldn't understand it. It didn't make sense. Unless perhaps they'd discovered the red pepper. From the way they paraded and strutted across the field, it was clear they'd be prepared for any contingency. We couldn't put anything past them.

When calling plays, they didn't huddle, as we did. Instead their team would line up in two rows, with their backs to us, and their quarterback would stand facing them and bark out the number of the play. They couldn't have cared less if we overheard or not, they were so confident. Then the centre would march out and crouch over the ball, while the rest of the team moved with just as much military precision to their positions. The ball would be snapped and—Quick March!— they had fifteen more yards, while, as likely as not, we had a few more lumps.

Just as we were getting used to the fact that they weren't trying anything fancy now—that this was going to be one of those bruising games where each side tries to pound the other into the earth—their two-hundred-pound fullback started to come round one end, then handed the ball off to the tailback, who scooted round the other end on a double reverse. And we were eighteen points behind.

The mood on our side of the stadium became grim. On the field the game was turning into a rout. Marty Klein, who was playing safety, as well as quarterback, got creamed when he intercepted a Kelvin pass on our one-yard line, and the Ambulance Corps had to carry him off the field. Down on the sidelines, Torchy Brownstone was still pleading with the coach to let him in.

I guess we should have known when Torchy appeared on the bench dressed for the game that the fates had decreed he would play that night. We knew it was crazy, but on to the field he limped with the first-string line: Norm Mittlehaus—a savage tackle who was later to sing with the Metropolitan Opera and eventually become a cantor; Marvin Zimmerman—who'd recently met a bunch of pretty nurses at the General Hospital and was playing with the reckless abandon of someone determined to break a collarbone at least; Sammy Margolis—who never quite came up to expectations, and who, when he was sent to Los Angeles to study dentristry, married the daughter of a clothing manufacturer instead; and Sheldon Kunstler—who later moved to New York and got rich by inventing a machine that bent, folded and stapled computer cards. Across the field they moved, as the voice on the P.A. system announced that Torchy Brownstone was playing against doctor's orders, and we all cheered mindlessly.

St. John's huddled behind their own goal line. A couple of Kelvin linemen—huge Goliaths that seemed to have just wandered in from the battle plains of Judaea—let long thin streams of spit slide from between their teeth to the grass. Their team-mates looked no less contemptuous.

Then the St. John's huddle broke, and Izzy Steinberg, who'd played the Lord High Executioner in *The Mikado* the year before, marched with an exaggerated goose step to his position as centre. About him the rest of the team marched with stiff, jerky steps to their places also. Dressed in their torn sweaters and oversize pants, held up by bits of string and old suspenders, they turned smartly to salute Torchy, who promptly returned the salute, and then as one man they all whirled about to give a "Sieg Heil" to the members of the Kelvin team. As the full impact of the caricature was taken in by the spectators, laughter began to gather within the North End stands until it washed over the Kelvin fans.

The laughter and noise quietened into an expectant hush as Torchy began to call signals. Everyone in the stadium knew that Torchy had the largest sleight-of-hand repertoire of any high school quarterback in the city. Consequently, once the play began, anyone who could conceivably get his hands on the ball—backs, ends—all were immediately flattened by those Kelvin behemoths that came roaring through our line. Which meant that nobody laid a hand on Torchy as he limped down the field, paused briefly to fish the ball out of the hole in his sweater, and then crossed over the River Heights goal line. The quarterback sneak had travelled the whole length of the field.

While the Kelvin players were still complaining to the officials, we could see Torchy calling the St. John's team into a huddle. I don't know what he said, but after the kick-off, our players charged down the field as if they'd been transformed. In the fading sunlight, their torn uniforms looked like golden armour, ablaze with precious stones; their helmets shone with emeralds and sapphires; and they moved with a grace and power that was electrifying. That two-hundred-pound River Heights fullback—who was playing both ways—caught the ball and was promptly hit by Sidney Cohen in the hardest flying tackle any of us had ever seen. After that tackle, Sidney, who had always impressed us as something of a Momma's Boy, was Papa's Boy forever.

The Kelvin fullback had fallen to the earth as if he were the Tower of Babel crumbling beneath the wrath of God. The ball bounced into the air, and Torchy . . . Torchy was where he always is during a fumble. He would have scored touchdowns if he had had to go down the field on crutches. The same, I'm afraid, could not be said for the two-hundred-pound fullback. Bruno Hogg lay unconscious on the field, dreaming strange, alien dreams of knishes and gefilte fish, and blissfully unaware that, for once, he'd met his match and been vanquished utterly. Now we were only six points behind.

During the fourth quarter, the Kelvin line started tackling Torchy on every play. You'd see him out there, limping away from the action of the hand-off, holding up both arms to show everyone he didn't have the ball, and still they'd tackle him. So then Torchy started throwing passes—that way the whole stadium could see he didn't have the ball. But neither the Kelvin tackles nor the officials seemed to care. And that was when Torchy sent word to the bench that it was time for Luther Johnson to come out.

Luther was our secret weapon. Just recently, his family had moved up from a black ghetto in Chicago, where Luther had played end for the city high school champions. He was a lanky six foot five, could lope along for miles faster than most people could sprint, and caught passes thrown anywhere within shouting distance.

Before vanishing in a melee of purple Kelvin seaters, Torchy managed to get away a twenty-yard completion. On the next play, Luther caught a thirty-five-yarder. Suddenly those River Heights players didn't seem to be strutting about so much. From the way they kept pointing, first to one player on our team, then to another, you could see that they were puzzling who to go after. Torchy might just choose to go limping across the goal line for the tying touchdown himself.

Our team wasn't sure, either, what to do next. You could hear them arguing about it in the huddle. Once Norm Mittlehaus's deep baritone voice could be heard demanding that they all call a trick play and throw the ball to him for a change. Finally . . . finally . . . they came out of the conference, but before they could line up, one of the officials blew his whistle to signal they'd lost the down. Too much time in the huddle. So back they went to argue some more.

They were still arguing when they came out for the second down. Torchy looked pretty small out there as he limped into position behind the centre. Even without the limp, though, we would have recognized him by that hard whiplash voice of his, the black hair constantly falling down into his eyes and the fluid way he managed to move once the ball was snapped—hurt leg and all. He was like a particular graceful predatory bird that's injured a wing.

Again the ball was sent arcing through the air, and again Luther was running along in that lope of his—this time across the Kelvin goal line. Everyone on the Kelvin team seemed out to intercept the pass, and all the possible receivers were immediately encircled by River Heights players. The ball, which was soaring a good two feet above everyone's hands, kept rising still, and looked as if it would fall uncaught in the end zone.

Luther didn't need to leap or spring to reach the ball. Suddenly he was just there—his black face a good three feet higher than the distraught white ones looking up at him in disbelief. At that moment, with the players all frozen together in a portrait of triumph and defeat, Luther must have looked—to the Kelvin team—like the Black Angel of Death himself. They hung there for a moment, Luther's eyes ablaze with laughter, his white teeth flashing savagely. Then they all broke apart and tumbled to the ground, and the roaring from the stands broke over them.

As both teams lined up again for the kick-off, Torchy moved toward the sidelines, his limp worse than ever. Though only five minutes remained, now that the score was tied, not a spectator there doubted for a moment that we would go on to win the game. Standing at the bench and looking at his team-mates lining up, Torchy seemed a magician who had just worked a miraculous transformation. The fumbling rabble of players who had dragged out on to the field two hours before now looked like a company of young gods come to try their prowess of the fields of Olympus.

But that was when the Kelvin team began their incredible march down the field. It all started after the kick-off with the referee claiming that we had roughed a receiver. When Mittlehaus objected, he was promptly kicked out of the game for unsportsmanlike behaviour, and the team given an additional penalty of another ten yards. On the next play, Kelvin's pass was incomplete, but we got called for being off-side. A few minutes later and they kicked a single point from our thirty-yard line.

After a moment of doubt and disbelief, a few cheers broke, halting and uncertain, from the River Heights stands. Yet almost immediately a feverish silence gripped the stadium, preventing even the outraged protests of the North End supporters from gathering momentum. Furiously, the St. John's team gathered about the ball. There were only two minutes left in the game, barely enough time to set matters right. Torchy began calling signals, the players snapped into formation, the ball was hiked, and now they were all in motion. Every line in their bodies, the practised way in which they moved, spoke of an assurance and competence toward which they'd been building throughout the game. The fullback slashed into the line. Three yards. Maybe four. Again the players gathered about the ball and signals were barked. Ends criss-crossed over the goal line, players blocked, changed direction, faked. And then the fullback—on a delayed plunge—slashed into the line again. But the Kelvin players held as fast as the walls of Jericho before they finally came tumbling down. Five yards.

For the third down, Kelvin didn't even bother sending back receivers. The play began as another plunge, with the two lines clashing and then becoming still for a moment. Suddenly Torchy began fading back, arm raised to throw— as deadly as a cobra—while Luther burst into the open, shifted to his left, and raced downfield. Torchy waited till the last possible moment as the purple sweaters converged upon him; and then the ball was soaring free out of that jumble of players—as straight and true a pass as any receiver could hope for. Luther loped effortlessly toward where the ball would arc downward into his waiting hands, and we cheered with enough energy to split the stadium apart and bring the walls of that Philistine temple down upon our enemies' heads. And about us, the city shone as if made of molten glass—aflame in the radiance of the setting sun—gates garnished with pearl and gold and all manner of precious stones.

In the dazzled eyes of the frenzied North End fans, Luther, in his dented helmet, torn sweater and baggy pants, was already a figure of glory. But suddenly a look of alarm and disbelief crossed Luther's face as he was brought up short in his tracks, then pitched down, face forward, into the turf— his outstretched arms empty—the ball arcing downward to bound mockingly across the Kelvin goal line, just beyond his fingertips.

His own disbelief was mirrored in the faces of the fans. He had been upended, not by a Kelvin tackle, but by a pair of snapped suspenders which had suddenly catapulted his pants violently downward so that they now hung about his ankles. As the stands erupted in catcalls, laughter, boos and cheers, we glimpsed what looked like a white flag signalling defeat. And then the whistle blew to end the game.

It was right, I suppose, that we should have lost. Anything else would have been a lie. Afterwards, as we pushed and elbowed out way out the gates, we were only too aware of the outraged glances being directed at us by our teachers from across the field. While behind us, in a mighty crescendo of triumph, rose the voices from the River Heights stands:

> Send him victorious,
> Happy and glorious,
> Long to reign over us,
> God Save the King!

Those voices followed us right out of the stadium, and once out of high school, we fled in every possible direction. Marvin Zimmerman raced back to the General Hospital and eventually married one of those pretty nurses; Sam Margolis got his father to mortgage the house and send him to college in Los Angeles; Nate Samuelson, who planned to become a famous heart surgeon, actually entered Medical School; Marty Klein became a delivery man for a local dairy; Luther Johnson got taken on by the C.P.R. as a sleeping-car attendant; and Torchy Brownstone just dropped out of sight. As for Mr. Rockwood, the short, heavy-set English teacher who was the terror of Room 4l, he was at last allowed to return to Kelvin—after his years of penance in the North End—but almost immediately he was forced into early retirement when he swatted a grade-ten student he caught sneaking out to the drugstore on Academy Road. Most of the others—players, teachers, friends—I'm afraid I've lost sight of over the years. But often, when I'm least expecting it, a familiar face that really hasn't changed all that much will stare out at me from the eleven o'clock TV news, or from the society pages of the *Free Press,* or, even occasionally now as the years pass, from the obituary columns. When that happens, I fill in a little write-up of my own beneath a photograph I keep filed away in my memory.

But not only have familiar faces disappeared, familiar landmarks have vanished also, and during the last twenty-five years it has become more and more difficult to keep track of the city I once knew. The Royal Alexandra Hotel, where we held our graduation dance, is gone. Child's Restaurant at Portage and Main, where we'd all meet after a play or movie—no more. Even Osborne Stadium, where we played our football games, has vanished, replaced by a huge, expensive insurance company. Do the shouts of former high school battles ever echo within those heavy stone walls, I wonder, or have they been filed away, along with such names as Norm Mittlehaus, Nate Samuelson, Marvin Zimmerman and the rest, as insurance statistics in grey steel filing cabinets?

With the passage of time, the North End, too, has changed. So final has its defeat become that it has even had thrust upon it a suburb with such street names as Bluebell, Marigold, Primrose and Cherryhill. Over the years, that two-hundred-pound fullback has managed to race clear across the city to score a touchdown right here in our home territory. Now we also have our false Eden.

In an attempt to exact some small measure of revenge, I bought a house in River Heights a few years ago and let the lawn go to seed, allowed the back gate to fall off the hinges, let the torn screens on the veranda go unrepaired, and filled the garage and backyard with old furniture and junk from my grandmother's house. But even I know that this attempt to plant a bit of the North End in the heart of River Heights doesn't begin to restore the balance.

The only time we ever came close to holding our own—and, better still, maybe even winning—was that night years before when a lone figure with a hard whiplash voice and black hair falling into his eyes came limping onto the field for part of a football game. He was one of those figures who, at the time, are filed away in a special place in your memory and are then, unaccountably, forgotten—unless, awakened by some chance occurrence, they spring to life again.

It was just a few days ago, as I was passing a downtown parking lot early in the evening, that I heard a familiar voice barking out directions to some motorists who'd managed to snarl up traffic and block both exits at once. The dark figure of the uniformed attendant moved with a fluid grace that I was sure I had seen somewhere before. There was something familiar about that limp and the way he jerked his head to glance over the lot—like an athlete assessing a new and difficult situation. Back and forth he darted among the honking cars as he signalled some forward, others backward. Until, with a flair that—under the circumstances—was really quite surprising, he had managed to untangle them all.

In the darkness, as he started back toward the booth at the entrance to the parking lot, he seemed to merge with the figure that had limped along the sidelines of the stadium so many years ago and shouted encouragement to a grumbling rabble of players. That night, for almost thirty minutes, under the stadium lights, he had discovered to us all a grace and a strength that flashed electrically from one player to another. And then they were no longer a grumbling rabble of players. They became timeless, ancient, a group of immortals caught up in trials of strength that would never end, Greek athletes who had just come to life out of stone. That night, while we all watched in wonder, the city had flashed about us with sapphires and emeralds, jasper and amethysts. And how we had longed to believe that the city could stay like that forever.

■

Jack Hodgins

Jack Hodgins (1938-   ) was born and raised in a logging and farming community in the Comox Valley on Vancouver Island. This area is the setting for his innovative, imaginative fiction and it is captured well in the film *Jack Hodgins' Island*. He has taught English and creative writing in Nanaimo as well as the University of Ottawa; he edited *The Frontier Experience* (1975) and *The West Coast Experience* (1976). His first collection of short stories was *Spit Delaney's Island* (1976). His novels are *The Invention of the World* (1977), and *The Resurrection of Joseph Bourne* (1979), which won the Governor General's Award for fiction for that year. "The Plague Children" is included in his latest work, *The Barclay Family Theatre* (1981).

THE PLAGUE CHILDREN

Jack Hodgins

Maybe this youth is dangerous and maybe he isn't, nobody knows for sure. What's known is that he's running up the entire length of the Island, end to end. With his track shoes dipped in the Strait of Juan de Fuca he is pumping knees and elbows towards Port Hardy. If he isn't dangerous maybe he's just plain crazy. A sweat-band keeps that long pale hair from getting in his eyes; a beard that looks like rusty wire fans out across his chest; a wrinkled cotton shirt, embroidered like a table-cloth with daisies, flaps and flutters around the waist of his track-suit pants. Whether you see him flicker past behind a screen of trees or catch him stroking head-on up the highway, the effect is much the same. The rhythm of his footsteps never changes, his bone-jarred breaths maintain an even beat, no sweat breaks out across his forehead or soaks that flapping shirt. Maybe this youth is dangerous and maybe he isn't; there are some who even think he may not be human.

Here in Waterville they think they know this youth and what he means: a spy, a scout, an advance guard for a swarm of others. While those legs and elbows pump him north, those eyes are reconnoitering, the brain behind the sweat-band taking notes. In Port Hardy where the highway ends he'll catch his breath and make a phone call south to launch this year's attack. These people have seen it all before. When he passes through this small community of farms they brace themselves for war.

Yet only Frieda Macken acts. Even before the youth is out of sight, she hurries out to the lean-to shed behind her house and roots around in a clutter of rusty machines and broken tools for a sack of lime. In all that settlement of part-time farmers, only Frieda Macken and her husband Eddie get out in their fields to spread the harsh white powder with their hands, squinting into the dust that burns their eyes. The others, seeing that youth thump past with his covetous eyes and his rusty prophetic beard, move inside to wait for what they know is about to happen and still refuse to believe. Not only scout, this youth is harbinger as well. The invading horde is only a day behind.

Read the papers. Find out where they're from. Holland, California, Rome. The Philippines. Some from as near as Vancouver, others from Katmandu. All of them could be here from another planet. A few every year get caught by police and fined. Copenhagen, Tallahassee, Nome, nobody wants to believe the addresses they print in the papers. Nobody believes their names.

For the people who live in Waterville there is something a little incredible in all of this. The place has never wanted to be part of anyone's map. This collection of thirty hobby farms along a four-mile stretch of highway has never wanted to be anything at all but what it is: a General Store and Post Office, a community hall, and houses you pass on your way to somewhere else. They don't even ask you to reduce your speed as you're driving through. Everyone here has been here for fifty years at least, everyone here is middle-aged or older. It's not easy for them to believe that people in Holland, Colombia, Rome, when they hear the name of this settlement, pack their bags and immigrate in order to take part in this annual assault. And yet in Saskatoon, in Florence, and in Oslo, they wrench up whatever roots they have and join the converging exodus around the world towards this place. Word has gone out on some invisible global network that the September rains have come to this part of the world, the magic mushrooms are pushing their way through the ground in record numbers, and a fortune is waiting to be made by those who get here first. Bring your family, bring your friends, bring anyone with a pair of hands and a pair of legs for running away from the law. Fresh air, fresh fruit, and plenty of gardens to raid; a hefty profit and a month of incredible highs.

Dennis Macken sees them first. They lean their bicycles into the ditch outside his field, hide their motorbikes in the bush, and hop off hitch-hiked rides onto the gravel shoulder of the highway. Then they climb over, under, through his strands of barbed-wire fence. They stretch it, twist it, leave bits of their own patched sweaters snagged on it. One fat bearded man in leather shorts grabs a cedar post and levers it back and forth until it breaks off beneath the ground like a rotten tooth. Now he and his long-skirted woman and their four small children can walk unmolested onto Dennis Macken's nearest pasture and start their bent-over search in the damp September grass.

Dennis Macken watches with a hand on the telephone, his tongue exploring a cavity. Unlike his brother and sister-in-law he's done nothing at all to avoid this confrontation. Perhaps he even welcomes it. At any rate he doesn't stop himself from grinning. When it appears that no more of them will be coming this morning he calls the police, then moves out onto the step to watch. A woman with a baby strapped to her back pauses to wave, and smile. There is no one out there who is even half his age.

When the police arrive, he laughs out loud at the sight of that pack breaking up and scattering like panicked cattle— pails emptied, skirts hoisted, long hair flying, children screaming. Through his second fence, or over it, into the bush. By the time the Mounties have crossed the ditch and entered the field there's no one left in sight. The two of them stomp bravely towards the woods and disappear in alder. They come out again pulling a girl who kicks and screams and finally goes limp while they drag her back to their car. At the car she turns and shouts out something, a curse perhaps, at Dennis Macken, at those invisible pickers, at the world. Her words, of course, are in a language he cannot understand.

When the rest have come back to spread out over his field again, Macken moves inside his house and watches from a window. He knows that something is happening here but he doesn't know what it is. He only hopes they will have left for the day by the time he goes out for his evening chores. At sixty-three years old Dennis Macken still believes in the law. These people are trespassing on private property. They're tromping on the field he cleared himself with his home-made tractor. They're breaking down fences he worked hard weeks to build. He imagines himself with a rifle, picking them off from his window; he imagines his pasture a battlefield strewn with bodies; but he still believes in the law. He will phone the police every hour through the rest of this day. And tomorrow. And the day after that. Those young buggers may get their mushrooms in the end, but they'll get plenty of exercise, too.

His neighbour Angel Hopper doesn't believe in waiting for the law, he believes in fighting his battles himself. The sight of the second-day wave of pickers upsets his stomach, gives him migraines, sets his teeth on edge, but he doesn't phone the police. What Dennis Macken has is foolish faith, he says; what Angel Hopper has is a Hereford bull—a thick-necked, thick-shouldered, thick-legged miserable son-of-a-bitch that even Angel Hopper is scared of. A people-hater from birth. He rolls his bulging eyes and swings his head and paws at the ground at even a glimpse of something human, no matter how far away. In a small high-fenced corral behind the barn, he stands up to his knees in muck and swings his tail at flies while he munches hay and dreams of destroying the two-legged race. Sometimes just the sound of Angel Hopper moving around inside the barn is enough to make him circle his pen, work up some speed, and smash his head into the wall.

Hopper isn't half so mean as his bull but he can't help chuckling over what he knows will happen. A treat like this is worth a day off work—no logging company ever went belly-up just because one second-loader stayed home to protect his land. It is also worth the effort of doing it right—which means giving that ragged pack of youths some warning. He waits until all the young men in their crotch-patched overalls and pony-tails and the women in their ankle-length flowered skirts and the children with their pails and paper bags of lunch have crossed the ditch, have cut the strands of his fence and spread out over the field. Then he swaggers down into their midst with his twenty-two in his arms and approaches the only person who looks up, a girl in a purple velvet coat who reminds him of the runaway daughter of Frieda and Eddie Macken. "This is my property you're on," he says, as pleasantly as he knows how, "and I'd like to see you people off of here right away." He pauses and looks at the others, who don't even know he is there. "Please."

The girl frowns into his face as if she sees something at the back of his eyeballs that even he doesn't know is there. "Haven't you heard?" she says. "Nobody owns the earth. You got no business putting up fences and trying to keep us out."

"Thank you," Hopper says and heads for the barn. When the bull has been released to the field Hopper stands on the rusty seat of an abandoned hayfork to watch. Faced with so much humanity all at once, the bull hardly knows where to start. He bawls, drools, trots forward. He lowers his head and flings up dirt with his hoof and trots in a wide curve around the edge of the crowd. At last he charges. He seems to have chosen someone right in the middle. People scatter in all directions, screaming. Angel Hopper hoots and slaps his leg.

No one would ever call him a sadist, but he is having a wonderful time. "Scare the hell out of them all, old Bull!" But Bull is intent on only the one original target, a youth with a rusty beard and a sweat-band who refuses to move. From this distance, Hopper thinks it may be the marathon youth. But marathon youth or whoever he is, this fellow has only to lift his arms and the bull nearly breaks his neck trying to put on the brakes. When he comes to a stiff-legged halt, his head lowered, he appears for a moment to be bowing to the youth. From their positions on top of fence posts and in the lower limbs of trees, the scattered pickers laugh. A few applaud.

The bull backs away from the youth and swings his head as if in apology. Then catching sight of Hopper on the seat of that rusty hayfork, he snorts and tosses his head and starts to run again. This time there's no indecision, the curve in his route is simply because his target is moving, is running towards the house. The bull cuts right through the fence like someone going through spiderweb, drags wire and broken post and several strands of honeysuckle vine behind him across the yard. Unhampered by so many accessories, Hopper is the first to get to the house. He even, for some reason or other, locks the door. While Hopper turns his basement upside down looking for strong enough rope to do something about that bull, the bull discovers a strong desire to travel. Out on the yellow centre line of the highway, he trots northward with his tail switching at flies. Perhaps he has an appointment he wants to keep in someone else's field. Perhaps he has simply developed an ambition to run the length of the Island.

Now all the world is draining into Waterville, it seems. There are people here from Taiwan, Turkey, and Tibet. There are people off the plane from New South Wales, from Ecuador, from Greece. Families of Alabamans. Couples from Japan. Four youths on motorbikes from California, migrant workers on the look-out for a crop more profitable and fun than grapes or beets or oranges. The fields are crowded. The woods are full. No one can escape them now. They hide behind the cattle in the pasture. They camp in the bush and sneak out after dark with miners' lamps beaming from their foreheads. Alan Powers finds a family sleeping in his hayloft. Ossie Greenfield discovers a naked couple making love in the attic of his house. All night long Grandma Barclay listens to the sounds of running footsteps, whispering voices, bodies brushing one another outside her bedroom walls. Strangers sleep in tractor sheds and pick-up cabs and cellars, children's voices cry from under trucks, the air at night is alive with whispers like the rustling sounds of rats.

Dennis Macken wakes at dawn and knows that someone else has slept beside him in his bed. The colour of his dreams has changed and the sheets are strangely warm and limp. Some of his forty-seven hats hanging around the wall are rearranged. He believes it is the marathon youth himself, who intends to push him off his place and use it as a headquarters for his operation. Being a long-time bachelor, Dennis Macken has the neatest house in the district, the most expensive furniture, the newest truck, the cleanest barn, and by far the biggest garden. Naturally, the rusty-bearded runner would choose it for his own. Macken is used to people wanting what he's got.

One of the things that people used to want was Dennis Macken himself. He had his turn as heart-throb for the entire district, years ago. Nearly every woman in Waterville once dreamed of catching him. Star pitcher for the valley baseball team, a heavy drinker, and a player of practical jokes. He also played the field since the field was so willing to be played, then in time chose Frieda Barclay out of all the rest. Amongst other things, he liked her turned-up nose. Frieda, however, like the stronger, thicker nose of Eddie Macken and gave Dennis back his ring. Her choice was to be his sister-in-law instead of wife. His choice was to make no second choice at all from the well-played field but to travel twice around the world and hope to forget her. By the time he stopped his running she was pregnant and he settled into bachelorhood to watch her raise a family. Even after forty years of watching, her nose still drives him crazy. He keeps his place so spick and span not only because it is where she grew up, the Barclay dairy farm he bought from her widowed mother, but also because he knows she despises dirt. He's the only man in the community who can match the floors and windows of her spotless home.

But it isn't Frieda Macken's home that he feels is most at stake. It's his. If he doesn't do something soon to stop that plague of mushroom-pickers from overrunning the settlement they'll soon be crowding him off this earth.

Yet it appears that nothing can stop them now. Everyone knows that police arrests are a joke. These people are happy to forfeit their airline tickets to Norway or Egypt and high-tail it back to the fields. Someone is making a fortune and it isn't the Waterville farmer. His cattle huddle in corners. His garden is picked nearly bare. His wife is afraid to step outside her own house. Coming from town with her station wagon full of groceries, Lenora Desmond finds her house overrun; people in every room. Something they ate has gone bad in their stomachs and they've converted her house to a hospital: people are in her beds, people are throwing up in her toilet, people are wrapped in blankets they've hauled from her closet. The whole house stinks of some foul concoction of weeds a girl is boiling on her stove. "Who is the doctor here?" she says. "Why are you in my house?" But they turn up their sad forgiving eyes and pity her for this bitter uncharity and refuse to move.

Aside from Eddie and Frieda Macken's silent farm, the General Store and Post Office is the only part of the community not alive with strangers. By the fourth day of the siege it is full of residents who've come in for the mail and won't go home. They buy groceries to justify a few more minutes of talk, they stand at the door until Em Madill brings out more chairs from her kitchen. Display shelves are shifted to one end of the room. Counters are cleared. Lenora Desmond moves every loaf of bread to the top of the meat counter so that Angel Hopper can perch to smoke his pipe and Em Madill has somewhere to set up her coffee pot and cups. Women's jaws are set. Men's eyes refuse to see the eyes of other men. They prefer to read the tiny print on the labels of the canned tomatoes.

"It's really very simple," Frieda Macken says. "Nobody picks on our property. Nobody tramples our fences. Nobody scares our cows. You spread lime and the mushrooms don't grow."

"Not that you're gloating," they say.

And she isn't gloating, she understands that no one has followed her lead simply because they can't believe this thing until it's already started to happen. She smiles at a time like this, and almost sings, as if what she's got to offer is astonishing news. "If you gave all of your fields a good dose of it now, would those people still want the mushrooms?"

"Probably yes."

"Those people are crazy, Frieda. They'll find some way of hallucinating on a mixture of mushrooms and lime. They're very young, they're capable of everything."

"The police are trying but they haven't got a hope. That
helicopter of theirs nearly scared my pants off, they thought I
was one of them and chased me right across my own field. I
thought that noisy rig was going to land on my head."

Ernie Butcher tells everyone he fixed up a forty-five-gallon
drum of liquid manure on his tractor and chased these long-
legged freaks all over the field, spraying them. "I even
sprayed their car, but damn if they didn't come back the next
day and I had to do it again." He's getting his field fertilized,
he says, but he isn't doing anything else at all.

Ella Korhonen says she heard that flooding your field with
sea water would solve the problem, too bad this place was too
far inland and all uphill.

Uphill or not, a couple of miles of pipe would be worth it if
it didn't ruin the soil. Ernie Butcher says he's keeping his
own hands off from now on, he saw a bunch of the pickers on
Alan Powers' field yesterday and stopped to holler at them to
get out of there. "They never paid me no attention so I starts
out onto the field myself to give them a piece of my mind and
then old Powers comes roaring out of his house with his
shotgun in his hand and stops on the top of his well-head to
fire. I yelled and waved my arms all over the place but he
blasts off just the same and cripes, you shoulda seen me run! I
heard some of that buckshot whining past my ear.
Somebody's going to get killed if we don't do something
quick."

"It's got so's a person can't even protect what he owns.
Yesterday I heard that Grandma Barclay—Frieda's mother,
eh, and Lenora's—how old is she now? I heard she . . . "

"Eighty-four," Lenora says. "And I know what you're
going to say. Yesterday she came across one of them smoking
in the doorway of our root cellar when she went past to get
me some spuds and without even thinking she hauled off and
hit him with the fork. This morning the guy comes around
with the police and wants to charge her with assault! You can
imagine how far they got with me in the door."

Hell, Alan Powers says, he don't have to worry about that
anymore himself, this big fat fellow moved onto his property
and thinks he owns the place, him and his gang, they chase
everybody else away with sticks and even get into fights.
"That bozo had the bloody cheek to tell me he made sixty
thousand dollars off my place last year and he don't intend to
share it with no one now! I told him, maybe him and that
Back East Mafia is making a fortune off of this farm but

they're tramping down my winter silage as well, which is the same as taking the money right out of my pocket. He laughed in my face. You think I'm going to tangle with him? Forget it."

"It isn't just that we own this land," says Ernie Butcher. "We put a lifetime of sweat into working it. Who do they think they are? If somebody shot just one . . . "

"It wouldn't make any difference," Frieda says. "You'd go to jail and the rest would move into your house."

At the age of sixty, with her white hair and determined jaw, she has the air about her of a woman judge. People will balk at everything she says, but in the end they listen. Her smiling eyes and singsong voice give her an added advantage: she can deliver a judge's orders and pass a judge's sentence as if she's dispensing news that delights and surprises even herself. "We'll go in to town and buy every sack of lime we can find," she says. "Then we'll spend tomorrow spoiling their obscene fun!"

At six o'clock Dennis Macken wakens and feels the heat of a second body in his bed. He knows the heavy breathing isn't his own. He knows the odour of unwashed feet is not his own. Beside him the marathon youth is laid out on his back, asleep. His hands are behind his neck. The hair in his armpits is as bushy as the rusted wire of the beard which rests on his skinny chest. Macken opens his mouth to holler. Then closes it. Who would he holler for? Instead he grunts, and moves to the edge of the bed, ready to leap. He wonders if he left his rifle loaded. He wonders, too, if he's left his senses altogether and taken a step into madness. Who is to say at this time of the morning whether the youth or himself is the intruder? How does he know for sure that this is his house?

Something he knows for sure is that the language he hears is not something he understands. Thick, European, full of sounds in the throat. The youth is awake, grinning. Without taking his hands from behind his neck he stretches his long skinny body, arches it right up off the sheet like a footbridge, then lets it collapse. "Jesus, I overslept," says the youth, in something a little closer to English. And sits up to swing his feet out onto the floor. While Macken still searches for words, the youth crosses the room, and bends to pick up his clothes from the rug.

"Just a minute," Macken says.

The youth drops his flowery shirt down over his

upstretched arms and pushes his head through the neck. He pulls the track pants up his muscled legs. He crouches to lace his shoes. Then, running on the spot, he takes the sweat-band off his head and begins to comb his hair.

"What are you doing here? How the hell'd you get in?"

The youth, still combing, laughs, then takes one of Macken's forty-seven caps down off the wall and tries it on. It's a little small for all that hair but he keeps it anyway.

Macken leans back on his pillow and pulls the covers up to his neck. "Who are you?" he says. He is cold. No, he is frozen. His hands are blue. Ice-water runs through evey vein, out to the ends of his toes, his fingers.

The youth dances like a boxer across the floor to Macken. "That doesn't matter," he says. "But who are you?"

For a moment Macken doesn't know. His name is a foreign sound that people used against him years ago. He can't recall it now. If this stranger should ask him his age, however, that is a different matter. Macken suddenly knows that this is old. "Get out," he says, too weak to put any force in the words. "Get out." He closes his eyes until he is sure there is no one in the room but himself. Even then he doesn't get out of bed.

Not even the sight of Frieda Macken in his bedroom is enough to raise him up. Not even the devastated look on her handsome face, or her plea for help. What are they going to do, she wants to know. She's learned, from people in town who claim to know these things, that lime kills every kind of mushroom you can think of except this psylo . . . psylo . . . whatever it is, this thing. What she and Eddie have done, she supposes, is wasted time and energy spreading lime on fields where none of those things would have had the inclination to grow anyway. And made fools of themselves with their smugness.

Dennis Macken is not surprised to discover that the mushrooms are indestructible. He sees them in his mind's eye multiplying undeterred until they carpet the entire valley, until they are the only crop that grows in this part of the world. All he wants to do is look at his hands. They're old. They're wrinkled and old and covered with splotches like some terrible disease. He's caught it, he thinks, from that youth who slept in his bed, but how can he tell that to Frieda without sounding insane? He can't. He'd rather be silent. He rests his hands on the top of his blankets and hopes she'll notice. She doesn't. His hands look no different to her than her own. It's his eyes she's worried about. His eyes look as if they've seen something they can't accept.

Dennis Macken knows that finding something that will kill the mushroom has nothing to do with anything, that even if every mushroom in the community turns to poison, the plague will not go away. It will increase the energy of its attack, like a horde of starving rats; it will overrun the district, destroying everything in sight. That's why he stays in bed until he's heard Frieda Macken's car pull out of his yard. That's why he listens until he is sure that the pickers are again at work, and gets up to watch from a kitchen window until everything he can see is alive with people. His own fields, Desmonds' fields, Powers' stumpy pasture. Down on their knees with their noses only inches from ground, they part the grass as if they've been told there are diamonds amongst the roots. He knows what they're after, he's seen it himself, a small pointed cap of flesh on a long wiry stem. The first few they find they will eat, to start the day off feeling good, the rest they will hoard in their tins or their plastic bags. He's heard three thousand dollars a pound is what they're worth. Having tasted one once, he can't understand why. All it did was give him a dizzy head.

A dizzy head is what time has given him too, with its incredible speed. Why has it gone so fast? One day you look out a window and dream of all you can do once you've grown into a man; the next, so it seems, you look out the window and find yourself wondering what you've done with it while it flew by. In his case, he wonders what Frieda has done with his life, the one he offered her years ago. Given it back. Having returned it, she seemed to have left everything else up to him. Some travel, a job, this little farm, helping his neighbours a bit—is this what they like to call life?

A pick-up truck slows down and parks in the shallow ditch. Close to a dozen people hop out of the back, and two more out of the cab. On the gravel shoulder they pause for a moment to look over his field, then climb through his fence and drop to their knees to start combing. One of them wears something that looks like pajamas. One is a child with a crutch. They haven't been there for even a minute when the people who got there before them stand up and converge to a knot in the centre of the field. Some carry sticks, a few swing their pails, all of them seem to be shouting. Macken sees, when they break apart and start walking towards the intruders, that the marathon youth takes the lead. Face to face the groups engage in some conversation. An arm is raised. A short piece of lumber is swung. The bodies convulse in a brawl. Even inside he can hear the sounds of their yells. One of the newcomers breaks free and makes for the truck. Others follow his lead. Waving their fists from the back of the pick-up they make their escape, while the rest go back to their work.

Once he is dressed, Dennis Macken crosses the yard and climbs on board his tractor, a monster he's made from a hundred scrapyard wrecks. Big as a tank, it has back wheels that stand higher than he does and a bulldozer blade on the front. Its motor rattles windows. Its tracks cut patterns of three-inch holes in the ground. Its exhaust pipe stretches skyward like a flagpole, and flies his flag—a flowered rag that whips about in the blue exhaust as if it wants to tear free and have a life of its own. A life of his own is what Macken wants too, and up on his tractor he'll claim it.

He starts the engine and manoeuvres out onto the grass. Selecting a cluster of adults down on their knees like pilgrims worshipping their god, he opens her up. Oh holy terror, the screams! Bodies leap up, fall away, scatter. Macken rattles on through. They yell at him, in thirteen different languages. Someone throws a jam tin that clatters against the hood. Someone throws a clod of grass that barely misses his face. He laughs, he laughs, he feels almost young again.

And now he is off to new encounters. This time they haven't the sense to scatter, they run in a pack, and he can't resist the need to give them chase. He stands, he hollers insults, he whoops like a cowboy. He follows them down the length of the field, as close as he dare on their heels. When they turn, he turns. Hair flies. Rags ripple and flap. The girl in a purple velvet coat who looks like Frieda Macken's runaway daughter trips and screams, crawls ahead of the blade, gets up in the nick of time. Macken swings to the left and heads for a new cluster of pickers, he won't be happy until he has them all stirred up, he won't be happy until he's given them all a scare, until he's made their lives so miserable they'll be glad to leave, get off his land, and spread the word that Dennis Macken's not a man to take advantage of. Off to one side he sees a car on the highway backing up for a better look, he sees Angel Hopper getting out of his truck, he sees Frieda Macken running in this direction across the Desmonds' field.

One youth alone stands upright, steady, refuses to move. Macken decides to run over him. But the youth doesn't move, doesn't leap, except onto the top of Macken's blade where he rides with his rusty beard whipped up across his face, his powerful hands on the bar. He is wearing a Macken cap on his hairy head.

Macken stops for no one, not even this wild-eyed youth on his nose. Not even the crowd of neighbours that's collected along his fence. Let them gawk, let them admire his pluck. He sets out on a new crusade. "Get off my field you pack of bastards, git!" But the marathon youth crawls up the engine hood towards Macken's face. "Get out of my way, you creep, I can't see where I'm going!" The eyes are so deep and frightening that Macken can't bear to look at them. The youth pushes his face up close to Macken's face, his breath in Macken's breath, his nose against Macken's nose. He says something that Macken can't understand, some foreign sounds, but he tastes their meaning with his teeth. He won't get out of this alive. Nobody will.

When the youth pulls out the key and rides the tractor to a stop it's already far too late. Behind them a child is lying in the grass and screaming. People are yelling again. People are running to see what Macken has done. Someone hauls him down off his tractor and shoves him towards the commotion. The girl who looks like Frieda Barclay's daughter stops in front of him and spits in his face. Terrified by what he sees, Macken is almost relieved when the marathon youth pushes the others away and hustles him forward towards the child. The crowd from outside his fence is running this way, all of Waterville seems to be here. Macken can hear someone calling his name.

Some faces in this crowd are familiar, some are not. That could be Frieda Macken trying to get to him, but it could be someone else. Macken can't tell his neighbours from these children of the plague. A confusion of bodies. He thinks he sees Angel Hopper pushing someone, he thinks he sees Alan Powers. How carefully does a plague select a territory it will attack? Macken thinks that maybe it doesn't strike blindly at everything in its way, as people believe, he thinks its victims probably select themselves. The magnetic force it can't resist is fear.

The magnetic force he can't resist is that fallen girl. People move back so that he can be pulled towards her. A youth in wire-rimmed glasses is down on his knees in the grass with his eyes squeezed shut and his hands clasped together beneath his chin. A young woman is down in the grass beside him, holding the child's head in her arms. An arm, crushed by one of his wheels, is bleeding, Her mouth is open and her scream is so high and loud that Macken's ears are unable to bear it. He thinks, instead, that he's hearing the sirens that announce the end of the world.

A few of their names are appearing in the papers even now, along with their exotic addresses. Mexico City, Marseilles. Most of the pickers, however, have gone. Like other crops, the magic mushroom has its time and disappears. The marathon youth buys an Oh Henry bar in the General Store and sets off running down the road with his even pace. And where will he go to now? Does he scout for other causes? Will he lead his herd into department stores and onto beaches, will he usher them into picket lines and protest marches and demonstrations? Few have the time to wonder. They pick up liquor bottles and plastic bags and peanut butter jars in the fields. They examine livestock for signs of abuse. They bury smouldering campfires with shovelled sand. Some start giant bonfires of their own to burn up everything those hands have touched. Everyone is fixing fence. Lenora and Albert Desmond scour their house and scrape dried vomit out of corners with a paring knife. Grandma Barclay announces she wants to move into an old folks' home in town. Eddie and Frieda Macken lock up and head for the ferry, in order to spend some time with Frieda's sister Bella in North Vancouver. No one wants to believe what has happened. This collection of thirty hobby farms has never wanted to be anything special at all, except what it's always been. Nearly everyone has lived here for fifty years or longer. Rumour has it that Angel Hopper has decided what he'll do next year when the pickers return, if he hasn't sold out first. He'll sit by the gate and hold out his hand. For a hundred dollars a day— adult or child—he'll let a person pick on his private land and promise not to cause trouble. So what if he's lost a war? Dirty money or not, it's better than breaking bones, it's better than crushing children under your tractor wheels, like somebody else he knows.

Dennis Macken still believes in law, but not the law of the courts. He believes in Macken's law, which will have something to do with magnetic force when he finally figures it out. Watching that youth pump past his fence-line heading south, he knows that some day someone will drag him out of his house and try to convince him with speeches and legal documents and perhaps with a gun that these forty acres don't belong to him any more, or to anyone else that he knows. They'll tell him that everything belongs to this entire race of chidren from another planet who follow that bearded runner in a swarm from place to place throughout the universe harvesting their crop of drugs. Maybe this youth is dangerous and maybe he isn't, nobody knows for sure. What Dennis Macken knows is that there's much he's never thought of in this world, and plenty more to be found. What Dennis Macken knows is that before that plague of mushroom pickers returns he has eleven months to find some way of stopping clocks or step outside of time.

■

Ethel Wilson

Ethel Wilson (1890-1981) was born in South Africa, moved to England, but then made her home in Vancouver from age eight until her death. Although she did not begin to write extensively until after World War II, she nonetheless had a long and distinguished career as a writer of urbane, sometimes satiric, fiction. Among her works are the novels *Hetty Dorval* (1947), *The Innocent Traveller* (1949), *Equations of Love* (1952), *Swamp Angel* (1954) and *Love and Salt Water* (1956). A collection of her stories, *Mrs. Golightly and Other Stories*, was published in 1961.

WE HAVE TO SIT OPPOSITE

Ethel Wilson

Even in the confusion of entering the carriage at Salzburg, Mrs. Montrose and her cousin Mrs. Forrester noticed the man with the blue tooth. He occupied a corner beside the window. His wife sat next to him. Next to her sat their daughter of perhaps seventeen. People poured into the train. A look passed between Mrs. Montrose and Mrs. Forrester. The look said, "These people seem to have filled up the carriage pretty well, but we'd better take these seats while we can as the train is so full. At least we can have seats together." The porter, in his porter's tyrannical way, piled their suitcases onto the empty rack above the heads of the man with the blue tooth, and his wife, and his daughter, and departed. The opposite rack was-full of baskets, bags and miscellaneous parcels. The train started. Here they were. Mrs. Montrose and Mrs. Forrester smiled at each other as they settled down below the rack which was filled with miscellaneous articles. Clinging vines that they were, they felt adventurous and successful. They had travelled alone from Vienna to Salzburg, leaving in Vienna their doctor husbands to continue attending the clinics of Dr. Bauer and Dr. Hirsch. And now, after a week in Salzburg, they were happily on their way to rejoin their husbands, who had flown to Munich.

Both Mrs. Montrose and Mrs. Forrester were tall, slight and fair. They were dressed with dark elegance. They knew that their small hats were smart, suitable and becoming, and they rejoiced in the simplicity and distinction of their new costumes. The selection of these and other costumes, and of these and other hats in Vienna had, they regretted, taken from the study of art, music and history a great deal of valuable time. Mrs. Montrose and Mrs. Forrester were sincerely fond of art, music and history and longed almost passionately to spend their days in the Albertina Gallery and the Kunsthistorische Museum. But the modest shops and shop windows of the craftsmen of Vienna had rather diverted the two young women from the study of art and history, and it was easy to lay the blame for this on the museums and art galleries which, in truth, closed their doors at very odd times. After each day's enchanting pursuits and disappointments,

Mrs. Montrose and Mrs. Forrester hastened in a fatigued state to the cafe where they had arranged to meet their husbands who by this time had finished their daily sessions with Dr. Bauer and Dr. Hirsch.

This was perhaps the best part of the day, to sit together happily in the sunshine, toying with the good Viennese coffee or a glass of wine, gazing and being gazed upon, and giving their senses to the music that flowed under the chestnut trees. (Ah Vienna, they thought, Vienna, Vienna.)

No, perhaps the evenings had been the best time when after their frugal pension dinner they hastened out to hear opera or symphony or wild atavistic gypsy music. All was past now. They had been very happy. They were fortunate. Were they too fortunate?

Mrs. Montrose and Mrs. Forrester were in benevolent good spirits as they looked round the railway carriage and prepared to take their seats and settle down for the journey to Munich to meet their husbands. In their window corner, opposite the man with the blue tooth, was a large hamper. "*Do* you mind?" asked Mrs. Montrose, smiling sweetly at the man, his wife, and his daughter. She prepared to lift the hamper on which the charming view from the carriage window was of course wasted, intending to move it along the seat, and take its place. The man, his wife, and his daughter had never taken their eyes off Mrs. Montrose and Mrs. Forrester since they had entered the carriage.

"*If* you please," said the man loudly and slowly in German English, "*if* you please, that place belongs to my wife or to my daughter. For the moment they sit beside me, but I keep that place for my wife or my daughter. That seat is therefore reserved. It is our seat. You may of course use the two remaining seats."

"I'm sorry," said Mrs. Montrose, feeling snubbed, and she and Mrs. Forrester sat down side by side on the two remaining seats opposite the German family. Beside them the hamper looked out of the window at the charming view. Their gaiety and self-esteem evaporated. The train rocked along.

The three continued to stare at the two young women. Suddenly the mother leaned toward her daughter. She put up her hand to her mouth and whispered behind her hand, her eyes remaining fixed on Mrs. Montrose. The daughter nodded. She also stared at Mrs. Montrose. Mrs. Montrose flushed. The mother sat upright again, still looking at Mrs.

Montrose, who felt very uncomfortable, and very much annoyed at blushing.

The man ceased staring at the two young women. He looked up at the rack above him, which contained their suitcases.

"Those are your suitcases," he asked, or rather announced.

"Yes," said Mrs. Montrose and Mrs. Forrester without smiles.

"They are large," said the man in a didactic manner, "they are too large. They are too large to be put on racks. A little motion, a very little motion, and they might fall. If they fall they will injure myself, my wife, or my daughter. It is better," he continued instructively, "that if they fall, they should fall upon your heads, not upon our heads. That is logical. They are not my suitcases. They are your suitcases. You admit it. Please to move your suitcases to the opposite rack, where, if they fall, they will fall upon your own heads." And he continued to sit there motionless. So did his wife. So did his daughter.

Mrs. Montrose and Mrs. Forrester looked at the suitcases in dismay. "Oh," said Mrs. Forrester, "they are so heavy to move. If you feel like that, please won't you sit on this side of the carriage, and we will move across, under our own suitcases, though I can assure you they will not fall. Or perhaps you would help us?"

"We prefer this side of the carriage," said the man with the blue tooth. "We have sat here because we prefer this side of the carriage. It is logical that you should move your suitcases. It is not logical that my wife, my daughter and I should give up our seats in this carriage, or remove your suitcases."

Mrs. Montrose and Mrs. Forrester looked at each other with rage in their hearts. All their self-satisfaction was gone. They got up and tugged as the train rocked along. They leaned resentfully across the erectly sitting man, and his wife and his daughter. They experienced with exasperation the realization that they had better make the best of it. The train, they knew, was crowded. They had to remain in this carriage with this disagreeable family. With much pulling and straining they hauled down the heavy suitcases. Violently they removed the parcels of the German family and lifted their own suitcases onto the rack above their heads, disposing them clumsily on the rack. Panting a little (they disliked panting), they settled down again side by side with high colour and loosened wisps of hair. They controlled their features so as to appear serene and unaware of the existence of anyone else in the railway carriage, but their hearts were full of black hate.

The family exchanged whispered remarks, and then resumed their scrutiny of the two young women, whose elegance had by this time a sort of tipsy quality. The girl leaned toward her mother. She whispered behind her hand to her mother, who nodded. Both of them stared at Mrs. Forrester. Then they laughed.

"Heavens!" thought the affronted Mrs. Forrester, "this is outrageous! Why can't Alice and I whisper behind our hands to each other about these people and make them feel simply awful! But they wouldn't feel awful. Well, we can't, just because we've been properly brought up, and it would be too childish. And perhaps they don't even know they're rude. They're just being natural." She breathed hard in frustration, and composed herself again.

Suddenly the man with the blue tooth spoke. "Are you English?" he said loudly.

"Yes—well—no," said Mrs. Forrester.

"No—well—yes," said Mrs. Montrose, simultaneously.

A derisive look came over the man's face. "You must know what you are," he said, "either you are English or you are not English. Are you, or are you not?"

"No," said Mrs. Montrose and Mrs. Forrester, speaking primly. Their chins were high, their eyes flashed, and they were ready for discreet battle.

"Then are you Americans?" said the man in the same bullying manner.

"No," said Mrs. Montrose and Mrs. Forrester.

"You can't deceive *me*, you know," said the man with the blue tooth, "I know well the English language. You *say* you are not English. You *say* you are not American. What, then, may I ask, are you? You must be something."

"We are Canadians," said Mrs. Forrester, furious at this catechism.

"*Canadians*," said the man.

"Yes, Canadians," said Mrs. Montrose.

"This," murmured Mrs. Forrester to Mrs. Montrose, "is more than I can bear!"

"What did you say?" said the man, leaning forward quickly, his hands on his knees.

"I spoke to my friend," said Mrs. Forrester coldly, "I spoke about my bear."

"Yes," said Mrs. Montrose, "she spoke about her bear."

"Your bear? Have you a bear? But you cannot have a bear!" said the man with some surprise.

"In Canada I have a bear. I have two bears," said Mrs. Forrester conceitedly.

"That is true," said Mrs. Montrose nodding, "she has two bears. I myself have five bears. My father has seven bears. That is nothing. It is the custom."

"What do you do with your bears?" asked the man.

"We eat them," said Mrs. Forrester.

"Yes," said Mrs. Montrose, "we eat them. It is the custom."

The man turned and spoke briefly to his wife and daughter, whose eyes opened wider than ever.

Mrs. Montrose and Mrs. Forrester felt pleased. This was better.

The man with the blue tooth became really interested. "Are you married?" he asked Mrs. Forrester.

"Yes," she replied. (We'll see what he'll say next, then we'll see what we can do.)

"And you?" he enquired of Mrs. Montrose. Mrs. Montrose seemed uncertain. "Well, yes, in a way, I suppose," she said.

The man with the blue tooth scrutinized Mrs. Montrose for a moment. "*Then,*" he said, as though he had at last found her out, "If you are married, where is your husband?"

Mrs. Montrose took out her pocket handkerchief. She buried her face in her hands, covering her eyes with her handkerchief. She shook. Evidently she sobbed.

"Now you see what you've done!!" said Mrs. Forrester. "You shouldn't ask questions like that. Just look at what you've done."

The three gazed fascinated on Mrs. Montrose. "Is he dead or what is he?" asked the man of Mrs. Forrester, making the words almost quietly with his mouth.

"Sh!!" said Mrs. Forrester very loudly indeed. The three jumped a little. So did Mrs. Montrose.

There was silence while Mrs. Montrose wiped her eyes. She looked over the heads opposite. The wife leaned toward her husband and addressed him timidly behind her hand. He nodded, and spoke to Mrs. Forrester.

"Well," he said, "at least you admit that *you* have a husband. If you have a husband then, where is he?"

"Oh, I don't know," said Mrs. Forrester lightly.

"No, she doesn't know," said Mrs. Montrose.

The three on the opposite seat went into a conference. Mrs.

Montrose and Mrs. Forrester did not dare to look at each other. They were enjoying themselves. Their self-esteem had returned. They had impressed. Unfavourably, it is true. But still they had impressed.

The man with the blue tooth pulled himself together. He reasserted himself. Across his waistcoat hung a watch chain. He took his watch out of his pocket and looked at the time. Then to the surprise of Mrs. Montrose and Mrs. Forrester he took another watch out of his pocket at the other end of the chain. "You see," he said proudly, "I have two watches."

Mrs. Montrose and Mrs. Forrester were surprised, but they had themselves well in hand.

Mrs. Montrose looked at the watches disparagingly. "My husband has six watches," she said.

"Yes, that is true," nodded Mrs. Forrester, "her husband *has* got six watches, but my husband, like you, unfortunately has only two watches."

The man put his watches back. Decidedly the battle was going in favour of the two young women. How horrid of us, he was so pleased with his watches, thought Mrs. Montrose. Isn't it true that horridness just breeds horridness. We're getting horrider every minute. She regarded the man, his wife and his daughter with distaste but with pity.

"You *say*," said the man, who always spoke as though their statements were open to doubt, which of course they were, "that you come from Canada. Do you come from Winnipeg? I know about Winnipeg."

"No," said Mrs. Montrose, and she spoke this time quite truthfully, "I come from Vancouver." Mrs. Forrester remained silent.

"And you, where do you come from?" persisted the man in a hectoring tone, addressing Mrs. Forrester. Mrs. Forrester remained silent, she had almost decided to answer no more questions.

"Oh, do not tell, please do not tell," begged Mrs. Montrose in an anguished way.

"No," said Mrs. Forrester importantly, "I shall not tell. Rest assured. I shall not tell."

"Why will she not tell?" demanded the man. He was tortured by curiosity. So was his wife. So was his daughter.

"Sh!!" said Mrs. Montrose very loudly.

The man seemed ill at ease. By this time nothing existed in the world for him, or for his wife, or for his daughter but these two Canadian women who ate bears.

"How is it," asked the man, "that you no longer buy my trousers?"

"I beg your pardon?" faltered Mrs. Montrose. For a moment she lost ground.

"I said," replied the man, "why is it that you no longer buy my trousers?"

The ladies did not answer. They could not think of a good answer to that one.

"I," said the man, "am a manufacturer of trousers. I make the most beautiful trousers in Germany. Indeed in the world." (You do not so, thought Mrs. Forrester, picturing her husband's good London legs.) "For three years I receive orders from Winnipeg for my trousers. And now, since two years, yes, since 1929, I receive no more orders for my trousers. Why is that?" he asked, like a belligerent.

"Shall we tell him?" asked Mrs. Forrester, looking at Mrs. Montrose. Neither of them knew why he had received no more orders for his trousers, but they did not wish to say so. "Shall we tell him?" asked Mrs. Forrester.

"You tell him," said Mrs. Montrose.

"No, *you* tell him," said Mrs. Forrester.

"I do not like to tell him," said Mrs. Montrose, "I'd rather you told him."

The man with the blue tooth looked from one to the other.

"Very well. I shall tell him," said Mrs. Forrester. "The fact is," she said, looking downward, "that in Canada men no longer wear trousers."

"What are you saying? That is not true, never can that be true!" said the man in some confusion.

"Yes," said Mrs. Montrose, corroborating sombrely. "Yes, indeed it is true. When they go abroad they wear trousers, but in Canada, no. It is a new custom."

"It is the climate," said Mrs. Forrester.

"Yes, that is the reason, it is the climate," agreed Mrs. Montrose.

"But in Canada," argued the man with the blue tooth, "your climate is cold. Everyone knows your climate is cold."

"In the Arctic regions, yes, it is really intensely cold, we all find it so. But not in Winnipeg. Winnipeg is very salubrious." (That's a good one, thought Mrs. Montrose.)

The man turned and spoke rapidly to his wife. She also turned, and looked askance at her daughter. The expressions of the man, his wife, and his daughter were a blend of pleasure and shock. The two liars were delighted.

At last the man could not help asking, "But they *must* wear something! It is not logical."

"Oh, it's logical, all right!" said Mrs. Forrester.

"But what *do* they wear?" persisted the man.

"I never looked to see," said Mrs. Montrose.

"*I* did, I looked," said Mrs. Forrester.

"Well?" asked the man.

"Oh, they just wear kilts," said Mrs. Forrester.

"Kilts? What are kilts? I do not know kilts," said the man.

"I would rather not tell you," said Mrs. Forrester primly.

"Oh," said the man.

Mrs. Montrose took out her vanity case, and inspected herself, powder puff in hand.

"I do not allow my wife and daughter to paint their faces so," said the man with the blue tooth.

"No?" said Mrs. Montrose.

"It is not good that women should paint their faces so. Good women do not do that. It is a pity."

(Oh, Alice, thought Mrs. Forrester in a fury, he shall not dare!) "It is a pity," she hissed, "that in your country there are no good dentists!"

"Be careful, be careful," whispered Mrs. Montrose.

"What do you mean?" demanded the man with the blue tooth.

(She will go too far, I know she will, thought Mrs. Montrose, alarmed, putting out her hand.)

"In our country," said the rash Mrs. Forrester, "anyone needing attention is taken straight to the State Dentist by the Police. This is done for aesthetic reasons. It is logical."

"I am going to sleep," said Mrs. Montrose very loudly, and she shut her eyes tight.

"So am I," said Mrs. Forrester, in a great hurry, and she shut her eyes too. This had been hard work but good fun for Mrs. Montrose and Mrs. Forrester. They felt, though, that they had gone a little bit too far. It might be as well if they slept, or pretended to sleep, until they reached Munich. They felt that outside their closed eyes was something frightening. The voice of the man with the blue tooth was saying, "I wish to tell you, I wish to tell you . . . " but Mrs. Montrose was in a deep sleep, and so was Mrs. Forrester. They sat with their eyes tightly closed, beside the hamper which still occupied the seat with the view by the darkening window. Mrs. Montrose had the inside corner, and so by reason of nestling down in the corner, and by reason of having an even and sensible temperament, she really and truly fell asleep at last.

Not so Mrs. Forrester. Her eyes were tightly closed, but her mind was greatly disturbed. Why had they permitted themselves to be baited? She pondered on the collective mentality that occupied the seat near to them (knees almost touching), and its results which now filled the atmosphere of the carriage so unpleasantly. She had met this mentality before, but had not been closely confined with it, as now. What of a world in which this mentality might ever become dominant? Then one would be confined with it without appeal or relief. The thought was shocking. She felt unreasonably agitated. She felt rather a fool, too, with her eyes shut tightly. But, if she opened them, she would have to look somewhere, presumably at the family, so it seemed safer to keep them closed. The train sped on. After what seemed to her a very long time, she peeped. The wife and daughter were busy. The husband sat back, hands on his knees, chin raised, expectant, eyes closed. His wife respectfully undid his tie, his collar, and his top shirt button. By this time the daughter had opened the hamper, and had taken from it a bottle and a clean napkin. These she handed to her mother. The wife moistened the napkin from the bottle and proceeded to wash her husband, his face, his ears, round the back of his neck, and inside his shirt collar, with great care. "Like a cat," thought Mrs. Forrester, who had forgotten to shut her eyes.

The man with the blue tooth lowered his raised chin and caught her. "You see," he said loudly, "you see, wives should look properly after their husbands, instead of travelling alone and . . ." But Mrs. Forrester was fast asleep again. The whole absurd encounter had begun to hold an element of terror. They had been tempted into folly. She knew—as she screwed up her closed eyes—that they were implicated in fear and folly.

The two young women took care to sleep until the train reached Munich. Then they both woke up.

Many people slept until they reached Munich. Then they all began to wake up.

■

W.O. Mitchell

W.O. (William Ormond) Mitchell (1914-) was born in Weyburn, Saskatchewan, and while growing up spent several years in Florida. He has since lived most of his life in Alberta or Saskatchewan. *Who Has Seen The Wind* (1947) is the classic Canadian novel of a boy growing up on the prairie and has been made into a feature film. His other novels include *The Kite* (1962), *The Vanishing Point* (1975), and *How I Spent My Summer Holidays* (1981). A collection of his works for the stage, *Dramatic W.O. Mitchell* appeared in 1982. "Old MacLachlin Had a Farm" is from *Jake and the Kid* (1961), a collection of short stories based on several hundred episodes first heard on CBC Radio from 1948-58; the book won the 1962 Leacock Medal for Humour.

OLD MACLACHLIN HAD A FARM

W.O. Mitchell

As soon as we get into the yard, I wished we'd come sooner, right away after Mr. Brimacombe said about Old MacLachlin not having his crop in yet. It wouldn't be so good if Old Mac had gone and died without anybody knowing about it. I sure wished Jake and me had come sooner.

Old Mac he wasn't around the yard; there wasn't much of anything living there; no dog came out barking; no chickens were strutting around, just a scaldy-looking rooster pecking at the bare ground. From one of the crazy fence posts a meadowlark said she was spring a couple of times.

I commenced to think how a farm can get old just the way a human being does, just like Old Mac with his grey hair and his mustaches like a couple of grey oat bundles either side of his mouth. All Mac's buildings had got grey, real grey. She's sure awful what the prairie can do to a yard that won't fight back; choke her with weeds; pile her with dust; there isn't any fence can stand up to prairie long.

"Look at there!" That was Jake. He had hold of my shoulder real tight.

"What?" I said.

Jake pointed over to where the seed drill was; it hadn't any wheels on it; they were lying beside it on the ground. But Jake wasn't pointing at the drill; he was pointing at Mac's cow with her udder swelled up, pressing against the sides of her legs. She was pulling some straws out of some old bundles left in a rack from last fall.

"Come on, Kid," Jake said.

I was thinking, please let there not be anything happened to Old Mac, and him with Fergus that's in a prison camp since Dieppe. Jake and me, we're fussy about Mac. He's Scotch; he talks with more burrs than you can pick up in a whole day after gophers. Jake and me should have gone over to see him as soon as Mr. Brimacombe, that's our mail man, came by and said that Sam Botten was angling around to put Mac's crop in for him. Jake claims when Sam dies they'll have to keep an eye on the Golden Gate; he says Sam'll steal her off of the post and make another trip back for the hinges.

There wasn't anybody in Old Mac's kitchen; there wasn't much of anything except an old cook stove in the middle of the floor. Jake he hollered:

"Mac!"

There wasn't any answer. Jake yelled again.

I heard some springs creak in the next room, then:

"Aye?"

We went in.

Even under a log-cabin quilt Old Mac looked big; his both legs lay big down the bed; his hair all mussed up from lying there made his head look bigger than she really was. His eyes they were sort of mad-looking, real fierce under those clumpy-looking eyebrows like grey bunches of wolf willow. There was silver stubble growing bristly out of his face.

On the table beside the cot there was his pipe and a plate half full of old porridge. There was a picture of Fergus, too, with a real broad smile and kilts.

"Ennythin' the matter?" Jake asked.

Old Mac grunted.

"You all right?"

"Aye?"

"Funny time of day fer a fella tuh be takin' him a laydown."

Old Mac just kept right on staring up at us.

"Funny time a day fer . . . "

"I haird ye the furst time. Canna mon no ha'e a rest wi'oot the whole district comin' argy-bargyin' aroon!"

"Nope," Jake said. "Not if he ain't gittin' no crop in this late in thuh spring."

"Is that so? Do ye tell." Old Mac had started to sit up, only he lay back real quick like something grabbed him and she hurt.

Jake grabbed for the corner of the quilt. "Look like you ain't . . . "

"'Tis nothin' at a', an' I'll ask ye tae . . . "

Jake yanked back the quilt. I never saw anybody with a purple leg before; Old Mac's was, all the way from his knee to his ankle.

"Just a sma' bruise," he called it; he said he got it from the drill wheel falling on his leg. When Jake asked him some more questions, we found out the wheels had been taken off, at night. Jake he didn't say anything for a minute after Mac told him that. Then he said:

"Sam Botten bin around to see yuh?"

Mac said he had.

"Before er after them there drill wheels got took off?"

"Before," Mac said. "The day before."

Real slow Jake said, "Now ain't that funny. What'd Sam want?"

"He came fer tae poot in ma crop."

"Whut'd yuh tell him?"

"I'd prefair tae do it ma'sel'."

Jake he didn't say anything right away. I knew what he was thinking. He was thinking about a bay mare fifteen years ago, the one Sam traded him. Sam said Jake'd be tickled to death to see her pull. When Jake got her home, he found out she couldn't pull taffy. Jake told Sam about it, and Sam just laughed. He said she was just the way he claimed; Jake'd be tickled to death to see her pull, and it was just too bad she couldn't.

Nobody ever got the best of Sam. He's one of the kind doesn't go to the trouble of owning any land; he's got two tractors and a couple of combines so he can seed seven or eight sections each year. He does her on shares, and he's always got crops spread clear over Crocus district; whenever anybody's hard up, Sam he's right there to put in a crop. The other fellow always gets the short end of the deal.

Sam he makes money other ways too. He buys scrap iron, and horsehair, and pelts, and beer bottles. He's always offering a person ten or fifteen cents below the going price for skunk or weasel pelts. He's sure fussy about a dollar.

Jake got up off the side of Mac's bed. In a real gentle voice he said, "I figger she's jist about time somebuddy nailed that there Sam Botten's hide to a fence post."

Jake he started in nailing that night. But right about here is where I better tell how the history got tangled up with what came after. Most of the time at Rabbit Hill I don't do so well with history, because I get most of it from Jake, and Miss Henchbaw, that thinks she knows it all, says Jake doesn't know his history right. Whenever I write down Looie Riel was a tall, hungry-looking fellow that wore gold cuff links, chewed Black Judas tobacco, and had a rabbit's foot fob to his watch, she gives me D.

But lately I been getting an H, and that's because of Old Mac's coulee, that some folks call Indian Writing Place because on the rocks at the south end she's all covered over with Indian writing. Most of it is pictures like what the grade ones draw, all mixed up with other stuff, like Imma Shoelack loves Steve Kiziw, and Joe Broomshawe, Broken Shell, 1932; but of course she wasn't, the Indians did that. Ever since we started taking up when the Indians roamed over the Crocus district, I been spending a lot of time around Mac's coulee. Whenever I find an arrow-head, I take her to school and get a good mark. Since I started this spring, I've found a war club, the red stone part of a peace pipe, two dozen arrow-heads, a bone-handled razor, and three dozen beer bottles.

After we moved on to buffaloes, my grades got even better. I found seven skulls half-buried at the foot of the cliff where the coulee cuts down real sharp. And even if there wasn't good grades in her, I guess I'd be fussy about Mac's coulee in spring. Here's how she is:

Still, still as water, with the sun coming kind of streaky through the wolf willow along her edges—what you might call stiff sunlight the way she's full of dust dancing all along her. And when you lie on your belly at the bottom of Mac's coulee, you're in a world; she's your own world, and there's nobody else's there, and you can do what you want with her. You can look close at the heads on the wild oats all real feathery; you can look at the crocuses and they're purple, not out-and-out purple, but not blue either. If you look real close they got real, small hairs like on a person's face close to a mirror. And there's tumbleweeds caught down there; they make you think about umbrellas that got their cloth ripped off of them—like bones, only not stary-white like a buffalo skull. Dead plants are better than anything animal that's dead.

The day Jake and me found Old Mac with his bad leg, I walked home a ways with Jake, until we came to the far end of Mac's back forty, where the coulee is. I left Jake, so I could take a look around for more Indian stuff and buffalo skulls. When I got home for supper, Jake he had told Ma all about Mac. After supper she phoned Mrs. Tincher so she could call a meeting of the Women's Aid and they could rig up a sort of a plan where each one took a day looking after Mac. Right after, Jake phoned Dr. Fotheringham to go take a look at Mac's leg.

The next day Jake spent the afternoon over at Mac's putting the seed drill back together. After school I went over to give him a hand.

The first day two things happened: Sam Botten came over to see Old mac, and Jake told me about the buffalo jumping pound. I better tell about the buffalo jumping pound first;

she's tied up with what happened to Sam later on. You'll see what I mean.

I just got back from school, and I said to Jake:

"Jake, I got H in school today."

"Whut!" Jake straightened up, and he had grease clear across his face. "Has she bin gittin' after you?"

"No, I mean I got a good mark again in history. Brought in a couple more buffalo skulls."

"Oh," Jake said, "that's nice. Whut the heck's skulls got to do with her?"

"We're takin' up about the Indians and the buffalo. Say, Jake, did you ever see a pound?"

"Dang right. Ain't I had tuh go git Queen and Baldy outa . . ."

"Not that kind. Like the Indians had, where they run buffaloes so's they could kill a lot and git meat fer pemmican."

"Oh. Why shore. A course I seen 'em."

"What're they like anyway?"

"Why they're—uh—she bin tellin' you fellas whut they wuz like?"

"All she said was they was a sorta place where they run buffalo, herded 'em, then killed 'em."

"Well, I tell yuh. I seen plenty of 'em, and there wuz one partic'lar kind I—uh—invented myself."

"Did yuh, Jake?"

"Yep." Jake was looking off toward the coulee. "Whut they call a buffalo jumping pound—run 'em over a cliff, like—well—see that there coulee?"

"Yeah."

"Why do yuh figger yuh found so many arras an' skulls round there?"

"Why . . ."

"She's a buffalo jumping pound, the one I'm tellin' you about, the one I figgered out fer Chief Weasel Tail of the South Blackfoot in the early days."

"You mean Mac's coulee!"

"Yep, Mac's coulee. I can remember her like yesterday. Weasel Tail he come to me an' he says, Jake, he says, we gotta have buffaloes. We need her fer meat, an' we need her fer tepees, an' we need her fer moccasins. We need her bad, real bad. There's bin a sorta flint drout around here an' we're all outa arras. The pemmican we was savin' up from last year, the kiyoots got at her. He hitched up his britch clout—he was

a great big slashin' fella, wore nothin' but a britch clout—he
hitched her up, an' he says, my braves ain't touched off but a
couple of buffalo fer two months. What we gonna do, Jake? I
dunno, Weasel Tail, I says; an' he says, Jake, they's a lotta
buffalo hangin' around only we can't git at 'em. You gotta
give us a hand, Jake. She's got me beat, I says to him; an' he
hitches up his britch clout agin the way it was all the time
slippin' down on account of his belly bein' so shrunk up not
havin' enny buffalo to eat. Jake, he says, you gotta figger her
out fer us. Ef we don't git no meat fer our stummicks we
might as well go throw ourselfs over the side a that there
coulee. Well, sir, right there she come to me, she come to me
how tuh git them pore Indians some grub inta their
stummicks. Weasel Tail, I says to him, you go git you all
your braves, build yuh a fence anglin' tuh meet that there
coulee where she's steep, then go round up ever' buffalo fer a
hundred miles around—herd 'em with a hundred drags
behind and two hundred swings to the side, trail 'em right
into that there coulee, an' there's yer grub."

"Gee, Jake!"

"Buffalo!" Jake said. "You never seen so menny in yore
life. Thousands an' thousands of 'em, thicker'n
grasshoppers, large an' small an' medium-sized. Cows with
their calves a-bellerin' after 'em, beardy ol' bulls roarin' so's
you couldn't hardly hear yerself think. An' dust—they riz a
dust that made her just like night fer fifty miles around. They
come on the run, slaverin' at the jaws . . ."

"But if she was . . ."

"Stampedin' like they wuz, the shrink musta bin
somethin' awful on all them buffalo—must dropped a
thousand ton to the mile—made a fella shudder tuh . . ."

"With all that there dust how could you see 'em?"

"See 'em! There wuz a million red lights a-shinin' through
the dust, a million red lanterns where their eyes wuz, two
million bloodshot eyes that lit her up. An' the smell—she
wuz enough tuh give a badger the heartburn—like the inside
of a blacksmith shop a mile square with a million
blacksmiths shoein' a million horses—that wuz how she
smelled. They wuz runnin' on smokin' hoofs—red hot, they
wuz comin' so fast. An' then they hit that there cliff where the
fence angled in. They wuz water there in them days. Soon as
them buffalo commenced to go over, there come a hissin' an'
a roarin' an' a blowin'—cloud a steam came up from them
four million hoofs hittin' that there water—scalded fifteen

braves and fifteen ponies to death. The rest got caught in the blizzard.''

"Blizzard!"

"Yep. Never seen nothin' like it. Steam hit the dust, turned her to mud, an' she started in to mud. She mudded fifteen feet a mud in half an hour—the first mud blizzard I ever see—fifty Weasel Tail's braves got smothered to death a-sittin' on their ponies.''

I looked at Jake a minute. "Jake," I said, "that's real hist'ry. That's—hist'ry!''

"A course," Jake said, "I wouldn't go tellin' that to—to folks that are fussy about hist'ry book hist'ry—the kind that like her sort a watered down. She might be a mite too rich fer Miss Henchbaw.''

But there was where Jake was wrong.

Right about there I thought of something. "Jake," I said, "you claim there was a million of them there buffalo?''

"Yep."

"And they run 'em over the cliff?''

"Yep."

"Where's the bones?''

"Huh?''

"Where's all of them bones? Oughta be more'n a few skulls left outa million buffalo.''

"Yeah. Ye're right there, Kid. Uh—why—the way she wuz—say that there water jug looks kinda dry. Mebbe yuh better—oh—now I—they shore wuz a lotta them bones, a whole mile long that there coulee, hundred feet deep, wide as the coulee. Then we had them real dust storms a coupla years after—covered 'em plumb over. Jist take a look at that there coulee—only 'bout fifty foot deep, ain't she?''

"Yeah.''

"Useta be she wuz two hundred in Weasel Tail's time. Them bones filled her a hundred feet; dust covered her over about fifty. Now she's only fifty—see? What you might call a reg'lar buffalo mine down there, Kid.''

"Jake," I said, "like I said, that there's history.''

I headed for the house to fill the jug for Jake.

She was Mrs. Tincher's day, and she was peeling apples with flour right to her elbows. There was a saucer full of crocuses on the table.

From in Old Mac's room I heard him growling; there came a creak out of the cot spring. Mrs. Tincher she dropped the paring knife and she hit for the doorway. There came another squeal from the springs like when somebody lights on them real hard.

"That's the way, Mr. MacLachlin," Mrs. Tincher said, "you jist hike that there log-cabin quilt up under yer mustache so's you don't catch cold."

The kitchen door opened and I figured she was Jake, till Sam Botten pushed right through the kitchen and into the bedroom. Me right after.

He stood there looking at Old Mac and like always he was sort of chewing; he stood there real tall and skinny, turned kind of sidewise, and I could see the corners of his jawbones going, where the skin was pulled tight across them.

"Heard you wasn't feelin' so good, Mac."

Mrs. Tincher headed for the kitchen.

With his eyes ringed like knot-holes, Old Mac looked up.

I could see he had tight hold of the quilt; he has very old hands, bumpy like tree trunks are bumpy.

Sam said, "Figger we might make us some kinda deal, Mac."

"We canna."

"Land's mighty . . ."

"I'm pootin' her in masel'."

"You've only got . . ."

"Why don't yuh go seed yer brother's?" That was Jake, Mrs. Tincher went to fetch. Sam's brother he doesn't live here any more, not since he moved back to the States and left Sam to sell his land for him. Sam didn't even try; he wrote there weren't any buyers, then harvested a bumper crop off his own brother's land three years in a row.

"Why—hello, Jake," Sam said. He was turned kind of nervous to the doorway. "Dropped in tuh see how Mac wuz doin'."

"Not so well. Doc says he's got some of that high-dro-foby in his leg."

"That so?"

"Yep. Kiyoot."

Sam's jaw quit working; he swallowed; his jaws started in to chewing.

"Kiyoots is bad this year," Jake said. "Aim tuh git me a pelt."

"How?"

"Usin' a little ammunishun outa Old Mac's granary."

"That so?" Sam turned toward the door. "Wouldn't be too shore ef I wuz you."

"On yore way out," Jake said, "don't git too near that there well."

"I ain't likely tuh slip."

"Can't take no chances. She's the only well Old Mac's got."

I guess Looie Riel was beat before he even started to wrassle Jake.

But the next day after school, I found out Sam Botten wasn't beat. I didn't see Jake till just before supper, when I went out to get the wood for Ma. I met Jake. He didn't look so good.

"What's wrong, Jake?"

He pushed past me into the house. I followed.

"Jake!"

He grabbed the basin, dippered some water out of the hot-water tank next the stove, then out to the washstand. I waited til he finished wiping his face.

"What's wrong, Jake?"

"Sam Botten wuzn't foolin'."

"What's he gone and . . ."

"Old Mac's granary—ain't got enough seed in her to fill a hen's crop."

"But . . ."

"Sam he knew there wuzn't none when he wuz over to Mac's yesterday."

"Do you think Sam . . ."

"Shore he did. That there granary's clear down by the bluff. A couple a trips with that there truck a his at night was all he needed. There's tire marks in the dirt right next."

"What can we do? Get the Mounties and . . ."

"Too late fer that," Jake said. "Be thrashin' time afore we kin git her back."

"Wut you gonna do, Jake?"

"I dunno," Jake said, "yet."

All through supper I could see Jake was figuring. And after supper whilst I was doing homework, Jake he sat there on the other side of the table. He didn't seem to be getting anywhere.

Me I was thinking she's awful the way things go; nothing ever goes right all at once. Up till I came home and Jake told me about what happened to Old Mac's seed grain, I'd figured she was a hundred per cent day. Take at school in history when Miss Henchbaw started asking us what we knew about the buffalo, I told all about the jumping pound just like Jake explained to me. Jake he said not to, but I figured if I told her like she came out of a book, Miss Henchbaw would think she was just dandy. She did.

I got another H, and Miss Henchbaw said we'd take a holiday the next day, and go visit Mac 's coulee, and see where the Indians run the buffalo over. Of course I left out about her raining mud and like that.

And then I had to come home and find out about what Sam did; I guess there's got to be some wild oats in every crop.

I heard a cranking sound and I looked up; Jake was on the phone. He phoned for two hours, nearly thirty calls. He didn't say much, just said Old Mac needed grain for seed. On an old letter he marked down the ones that had grain to spare. When he'd made the last call, he turned to me. The way he looked, Sam Botten was beat this time for sure.

"A hunderd fifty-five bushels. Johnny Lammery and Pete Springer, that didn't have none left, is donatin' their teams and wagons to gather her up."

Jake he's smart.

We didn't have school then next day; like she promised Miss Henchbaw took us all to Mac's coulee. That was where we run into Sam Botten again. He looked kind of startled when he saw all us there, and Miss Henchbaw she got to talking with him and she told him why we weren't in school, and she told him all about this being a buffalo jumping pound, and she explained how the dust had covered her over, and think of all the bones of that noble animal the buffalo that were lying there right under our feet, and what a cruel slaughter it had been. She said even if the Indians did need meat, they didn't have to go and run over a million at a time.

Sam he said he never heard about her before, and Miss Henchbaw said didn't he know this was an old Indian camping ground, and wasn't there all the writing on the stone, and hadn't I found seven buffalo skulls this spring. Then Sam he said come to think of her, he'd read where they did discover a bunch of bones in a couple of places that had been covered over, only she was in Alberta. Right there he stopped, and he left his mouth open.

Miss Henchbaw she asked him what was wrong, but he didn't answer her; he was out of there like a licked rooster. There was a funny way for him to act; I decided I better tell Jake when I got home.

Jake he wasn't listening to any talk about pounds that night. Old Mac had baulked at taking the grain folks had gathered up for him; Jake had argued with him, but Mac wasn't giving one inch. "'Tain't no use," Jake said, "she's got me beat."

"But isn't there somethin' . . ."

"Nope. They ain't nothin' nobody kin do. He's bin lyin' there like a old he-bear with all them there wimmen fussin' around him. Says he ain't takin' no charity—ain't havin' his land seeded with neighbours' grain."

"But he can pay 'em back when . . ."

"I never seen nobody so stubborn in all my life—stubborn as a badger—a dang, old, stubborn Scotch badger."

She looked like Jake was beat. All through school I thought about her, and she looked like Jake was beat. Jake was right; Sam Botten was just like a coyote, tricky. Take the way he was all the time chewing, even when he didn't have a chew of tobacco, like he never had enough to eat; and the way he was all the time looking at a person over his shoulder. Right about there I looked up and saw Sam Botten, up in front, right in Rabbit Hill School. Miss Henchbaw she was showing him my buffalo skulls hung up along the top of the blackboard.

I got to remembering how he acted after Miss Henchbaw told him about the buffalo jumping pound; he sure was acting funny. I guessed I'd rather tell Jake for sure when I got home.

And after I told him, she was Jake that was acting funny. He stared at me, and then he bust out laughing so hard I thought he was going to choke; he even cried some, he laughed so hard. And when he finished, he said, "Come on, Kid, you and me's goin' visitin'."

She was still light when we got to Mac's. We found Sam Botten there. He was trying to buy Old Mac's coulee; he just done offering Old Mac fifty dollars for her when we got there.

"Whut yuh want her fer?" Jake said from the doorway.

Sam he turned quick, then he turned back to Old Mac quick. He said:

"There's whut I'm offerin'. Yuh kin take her er leave her."

"Whut yuh want her fer?" Jake said.

"You ain't needed," Sam said. "My bizzness is with Mac."

"Whut good's that there coulee?"

"I said you wuzn't needed."

"I sorta figgered I wuz," Jake said.

"When I want you tuh stick yer nose in, I'll ask."

"He says it's for tae get the gravel," Old Mac said. "I canna figure it oot. There's na gravel in the coulee."

"Kinda white, bony gravel, Sam?" Jake said.

"Kinda felt sorry fer yuh, Mac," Sam said, "laid up like yuh bin. No crop in yet—got no seed— figgered a little money'd go a long ways tuh . . ."

"Yeah," Jake said, "I noticed you shore bin helpin' a lot."

"You keep outa this!" She was just like Sam bared his teeth at Jake for a minute. "Whut yuh say, Mac?"

"Weeel, since I canna . . ."

"Wherever there's a dollar I shore do reely on Sam's judgement," Jake said. "Now, I gotta hundred dollars in the bank, an' she's worth it jist tuh see whut he . . ."

"Two hundred," Sam said quick.

Old Mac he looked up at Sam kind of dazed.

"Three hundred," Jake yelled. Jake he didn't have any three hundred dollars in the bank.

"Four hundred!"

Old Mac he looked real flabbergasted. "I—noo that ye're gettin' sae high—I . . ."

Jake he did a funny thing. He let his left eye drop down at Mac, and he sort of nodded his head so you could hardly see. Then he started in coughing to beat anything, and he headed out to the kitchen like he had to get a dipper of water. He pulled me along with him.

He went right on out the kitchen; he wasn't coughing any more.

"Jake," I said, "why's Old Mac's coulee . . ."

"Kid, when I done her, I never knew helpin' old Weasel Tail wuz gonna pay me back double—seein' them there Indians an' Sam Botten both with their stummick full."

"But what's she all . . ."

"Reg'lar buffalo mine!" It was Sam Botten, and he was waving a piece of paper in his hand. "Same as in Alberta where they run her jist like a mine—buffalo bones at seventeen dollars the ton!" He looked at Jake. "Yuh ain't changed a bit, Jake. Fifteen years ago she wuz that there bay. Now she's Old Mac's coulee. Useta be a jumpin' pound— Indians run over buffalo by the million. We gotta war on now—need explositives, an' they're a-makin' 'em outa bones. Bought me a fifty-thousand-dollar buffalo mine fer four hundred dollars!"

After he'd gone, I turned to Jake. "Jake! What'd . . ."

"Reg'lar buffalo mine," Jake said.

"Old Mac coulda . . ."

"Too bad Sam didn't come tuh the district till '21."

"Old Mac coulda had all them bones . . ."

"Nope."

"Well—if they was all . . ."

"They wuz, Kid, only I fergot tuh tell yuh one thing. This ain't thuh only war we had, yuh know."

"What's that got tuh do with . . ."

"Sam oughta knowed they had tuh have them there explositives last war same as this one."

"Then there . . ."

"Plumb slipped my mind tuh tell him. She wuz mined out in '14—plumb out."

"Then there ain't any . . ."

"Kid, see that there fence post?"

"Yeah?"

"I've nailed me a hide to that there post—kiyoot hide."

Jake spit.

■

Rudy Wiebe

Rudy Wiebe (1934-) was born near Fairholme, Saskatchewan, and now lives in Edmonton where he teaches Canadian literature and creative writing at the University of Alberta. His numerous works, many of which deal with the people and history of western Canada, include the novels *Peace Shall Destroy Many* (1962), *The Mad Trapper* (1980), *My Lovely Enemy* (1983) and *The Temptations of Big Bear* (1973), which won the Governor General's Award for fiction. He wrote the script for his story *Someday Soon*, a television drama seen all over the world, and another story "Tudor King" has been made into a short film. "The Darkness Inside the Mountain" is included in the collection *The Angel of the Tar Sands and Other Stories* (1982).

THE DARKNESS INSIDE THE MOUNTAIN

Rudy Wiebe

Number Three Highway west of Lethbridge, paved, leads through Fort Macleod where at seven-thirty in the morning the black Hutterite men are already swinging off their staked cattle truck in front of the New American Cafe—"To buy ice-cream cones till the back door of the beer parlour opens," Daddy tells me, laughing—and then there's the high prairie of the Piegan Indian Reserve—"Watch for Horse-drawn Vehicles"—and in the emptiness against the foothills a tree has been set up. It couldn't have grown there so thick and all alone, its huge sawn-off branches holding up what at that distance looks like a platform of branches and blankets.

"That's the way they bury them," Daddy says. "Chiefs. High for the crows."

"Crows?" I can see one flapping across the summer shimmer of heat already buckling the hills.

"It's okay, better to fly off than be dragged deeper by worms."

That was one reason Mama didn't want me to go with him all day on his truck run to the Crowsnest Pass. "A girl of ten, Wendell, doesn't need *soaking* in cynicism." "Don't 'Wendell' me." "I didn't give you your name." "You don't have to use it, 'you' is enough." So I am in the red Coca-Cola truck he has driven since spring, bottles leaping in their crates when he can't miss a pothole, the mountains south of Pincher Creek like broken teeth with very bad fillings. The three Cowley elevators drone past, then Lundbreck with half-boarded-up square store fronts—"There's no mine here now, not even a sawmill"—and the pavement ends with a crash and slither of gravel, the bottles going crazy. The railroad bounces doubly under us and against a hill, curves, and suddenly the road silence of a bridge, and thunder. Spray in clouds between cut rock—

"Daddy! Daddy!"

"Yeah, Lundbreck Falls. We'll have a look coming back."

The falls are gone behind an inevitable shoulder of rock and I'll have to wait with a memory of water hanging like brushed grey corduroy, vivid grey, not like irrigation falls, and the quick flash of rapids between trees and rocks, a shimmer spreading behind my eyelids as I squeeze them shut. When I open them there is the smoking cone of the Burmis sawmill but a tiny church also, you'd have to bend to go in, and over a hump the peaked and mortared stone walls of a— no, surely a castle! With all the wooden core of it burned out by a year-long siege, don't tell me!—and I look at Daddy and he doesn't, just grins and gestures ahead to the sudden upthrust of Crowsnest Mountain. Straight down the highway, over the narrow railroad track that cuts the gravel at right angles in front of Bellevue slouched on little hills ahead. We have to stop there while a string of mine cars tugs across the road in front of us.

"You must be good luck," Daddy says. "I never seen them going down the mine before."

Past our broad red nose the little cars are now all seated tight with blackish men facing each other knee to knee, hiproofed lunch buckets in their laps. Each single giant monster eye on the top of each head turns, stares, and one by one they slide into the hole in the hillside, click *click,* click *click,* box after box of them slipping past where the sunlight of the trees and the blue sky stops like a wall. And for one instant that single eye glares from the darkness, and is gone, click *click,* click *click.*

The sun sits on the eastern mountains and I would like to curl up, arrange all this behind my eyelids, there is too much already, how can I possibly remember it all, but Bellevue is there, old stores cut into hillsides and a Chinese cafe and a Ukrainian cafe with bottle cases stacked in cellars, behind gaping fences, crashing as my father heaves them about single-handedly and the blackish faces of the off-work miners leaning across the porch rail of the Bellevue Hotel swivel with us as our long red truck flashes past in the window behind them. We bend around a large grey school and the road splits, straight ahead or down into the valley to a scatter of houses across the river and around a green hill. We drive straight on.

"What about those?"

"There's nobody there," Daddy says, "in Hillcrest, there's nothing there now."

Behind my eyelids I imagine I can see into one of those little houses, look inside its one large room, and there is no ear to hear it as slowly, without a sound, the floor crashes soundlessly into the dark hole of the cellar below and the corners of black begin to move—I jerk my eyes open and a

girl, tiny like me, tilts against the iron fence of the schoolyard
with her hands up as if wired there and I wave, she is the first
girl I have seen and I wave with both hands, desperately, but
she does not even blink, only her head turns like a
mechanism and then we are plunging into the pale
limestone wilderness of the Frank Slide under the ruptured
face of Turtle Mountain. The highway and the railroad so
smooth over and through it, a monumental cemetery for
eighty people buried in two minutes; 1903, Daddy says, and
on the edge of it they found a baby still sleeping in its cradle
untouched. Through piled fields of boulders and past a store
beside Gold Creek and then Turtle Mountain Playgrounds,
and we stop in the noon shadow of that threatening
overhang to eat sandwiches. Last night my mother packed
them, and we wash their dryness down with Coca-Cola ice
cold because my father exchanges two of our extras for cold
bottles from the cooler he services inside.

"See that man," he says, chewing. "He's starting on his
third million. Finished the first two, too."

A slim man—he has arms, legs just like everyone, how
could you see he is rich?—opens the door of a silvery-green
convertible for a thinner woman with hair like a cloud of
gold piled upon her head. O, she is. Rich. The convertible
murmurs, spins away, their heads leaning back together,
they almost touch.

"He was just born," my father says, "that's how he got all
that."

Blairmore is one long street facing lower green mountains,
the CPR station, and the water tower. And a long alley black
with heat and the fried stink of food, the blackness moving,
settling, settling down out of the sky like granular snow in
the blistering day, everywhere. I sort bottles, my hands like
the miners' faces but sticky with pop too, and my father
stacks cases five-high and hauls them in and out, up and
down on the two-wheeled dolly until finally we drive the
length of the street again, bumping through the sunken
sewer ditches that cross in front of every business and past
green mine timbers squared up like tunnels on the cinder
space beside the railroad—a banner, "Welcome to the 52nd
Annual Mine Rescue Games"—and finally, finally, there is
air at the open window and only the grainy blue of
Crowsnest Mountain. By itself like a blessing, and the road
folded left and upward in green arcs toward Coleman. My
father is sweating; his thick hands shake as he rides back and
forth through his ten gears into the hills.

"I can't work a whole day on that horse-p—" He gestures behind him but looks straight ahead. "Not such a killer day."

I had never thought he could. After three grocery and one drug store, four cafes, the Miners' Clubs and the Canadian Legion, he pulls up tight against the bright shade of the alley behind the hotel—"Take a rest, I won't be long"—and is gone. I lock the doors, stretch out and fall into sleep that breaks in sweat, I am gasping on the sweat-hot seat. I pull myself loose, clamber out and up, hand and toe up to the top of the cases on the truck. The bottles burn my fingers. And I cannot open them anyway like my father does by levering two caps together because my hands are too small, and weak.

"I'll open one for you." A whiskered man, grey, his layers of clothing so black with dirt they shine below me in the terrific sun. He reaches up, his horned, gleaming hand takes one bottle from me and his lips draw back on his teeth and he places the top of the bottle there and at one slight grind of his head the hot liquid boils out between his whiskers and over his chin and down his layered front, but he does not notice. Just spits out the cap and looks up at me easily, offering me the hissing bottle.

"It'll make you sick," he says. His voice is as gentle as if he were touching me. "Warm like that."

But I cannot put the bottle to my mouth. Not where his enormous teeth have been. He is something that has risen out of this day, out of the black and overwhelming power of these towns strung between and under mountains and over mines, a heat-blister out of the day, his green eyes glittering through his hair with the snore of the fan blowing beer fumes over me.

"Did you deliver in Hillcrest?" his soft voice asks.

"Hillcr . . . what . . . no, no . . . no."

"You wouldn't. Not today, that's when it happened, June 19, 1914. Forty years, today."

His hands clutch the top cases and I cannot move. He is so close the dirt stands grained and polished in his skin bit by bit.

"A tiny fire jumped up, poof! In those miles of tunnels crossing each other two thousand feet inside Hillcrest Mountain, and then the fire licked along the methane gas bleeding along the tops of the tunnels and found the coal dust, here, there, the pockets where the miners were working and it exploded . . . wauggghhh! . . . and the ventilator shafts blew out and then all the oxygen left in the tunnels burned, bright blue like thunder and lightning breaking, and all the miners . . ." his face, hands, body are changing like a rubber horror mask, bursting from one contortion into another, his body curling up, jerking open spastically . . . "they breathe fire . . . the last oxygen burning, explosion after explosion . . . in the darkness inside the mountain they begin to come apart."

Gradually his face hardens again, his arms, head, shoulders are all there, together.

"Only their brass identification tags gleam in the stinking smoke when the rescue lamps . . . Hillcrest Collieries Limited, June 19, 1914. One hundred eighty-nine men. From Peter Ackers to Michael Zaska."

The coated bottle still sticks in my hand. The truck is twenty cases long: each narrow body is a row of cases, to lay them tight side by side will take nine . . . nine and a half . . .

"That was my shift," his soft voice goes on. "I was called, yes, I was called but my leg ached. So my friend took my shift. There was never a body found with his brass tag on it. His unchangeable number. We found, we assembled one hundred eighty-eight bodies, and then we had one leg left over."

The sun winks between the four chimneys, the immense crossed tipple of Coleman Collieries. A tiny smoke forms there, disappears grey into the brilliant sky.

"Forty years ago, today," the old man says. "Listen, I have to tell you their names. Listen, there was Ackers, Peter. Adlam, Herbert. Albanese, Dominic. Albanese, Nicholas. Anderson . . ."

I have to run, run! But he is below me, between me and the hotel bar door I must reach so I scramble, clanking over the empties and scrape my leg along a case wire but I am down, somehow half-falling and look under the truck—will he move, will he?—and I see one leg there, motionless, beside the tire and then his hair, his head lowers, upside down, it looks like nothing human and at the top of it the terrible mouth is opening on another name and it reaches out for me like a long black tunnel, O sweetest, sweetest Jesus . . .

"I have only one leg," it whispers, "I have only one . . ."

The truck spins past me, his head coming up—"Androski, Geor"—and the door under the beer-scummed fan, and darkness. Like a moist hand clapping shut over me . . . but it is open too, and high everywhere, I reach out my arms and there is nothing. Only this moist, slipping, darkness.

"Daddy . . ."

But there is a light, behind a high narrow table and a shadow moves there, light and glass, misshapen bottles everywhere. And there are other shadows too: quick little double movements of light that come and go, and then I know suddenly that those are the eyes. Turned to me from the vastness of the cavern which I cannot see the end of, that is breathing around me like an animal opening itself endlessly for me into close, moist terror—

"DADDY!"

"Del," a huge voice from the light and as my heart jerks I feel my father's hands on my shoulder, his big hands hold me as only they can. They lift me, completely, and his chest, his neck is there too. His gentle breath.

". . . Prosper. Davidson, John. Demchuk, George," murmers the mound between wall and telephone post. My father places two warm bottles of Coca-Cola beside it. "Demchuk, Nicholas. Dickenson, Matth . . ."

The Crowsnest River burbles between boulders around a small island and then bends, vanishes over Lundbreck Falls in quick, slipping silence. In the water I can see that the western sky between the Crowsnest mountains is covered with giant flames. They do not vanish but grow motionlessly larger, upward from the limits of the world and if it were not for the deep sound of water below, I know I could hear the sky burning there.

"The mines are finished," my father says. "Everything's oil and gas now, coal is nothing."

We move slowly east toward the flat darkness of the prairie. I curl up on the seat, my head in the bend of his thigh. I can hear his muscles shift against my ear as he controls the pedals, the levers, and when we are level at last and up to speed his right hand comes to rest heavy and cupped on my hip. But behind my eyelids I am not asleep; in fact, I may never be able to sleep again.

■

Henry Kreisel

Henry Kreisel (1922-   ) was born in Vienna and escaped to
England during the Nazi occupation. He came to Canada in
1940 and studied at the University of Toronto. He now
lives in Edmonton, where he is University Professor (former
academic vice-president) at the University of Alberta. His two
novels, *The Rich Man* (1948) and *The Betrayal* (1964), have
both been recently re-printed. One of his stories, "The Broken
Globe" has been adapted as both a stage and a television
play. All his short stories have been collected in the book *The
Almost Meeting* (1981).

THE TRAVELLING NUDE

Henry Kreisel

The only thing about the whole affair that worries me a bit is how I am going to explain to my father why I threw up a good job. My father is a very unimaginative man, and I know he has been brooding about me for a long time. Now when he hears about the travelling nude, he's quite likely to become momentarily deranged. But that, I'm afraid, can't be helped.

Ever since the subject was first broached and the debate got passionate, splitting at least one husband and wife right down the middle, I've had a very distinct impression of her. I admit it's quite ludicrous, but you'll admit (though my father isn't likely to) that it has a certain kind of charm.

There she is. Quite good-looking. Not anything spectacular, you understand. The pay is hardly enough to attract anything like that, and the conditions of work are not exactly first class. There's a lot of travelling involved, and the work has to be done mostly in small towns, pop. 1275 or 1423, and she has to stay in rather dingy hotels, even though these hotels have fancy names, like the *Ritz* or the *Imperial*. But she has a pretty good figure, nonetheless. Nicely proportioned. Breasts pretty firm, though perhaps now beginning to droop a little, with the first flush of youth departed. A bit of a fatty fold starting to show round her middle. But the buttocks still firm, and the thighs round and full, and the legs long and shapely. A good nude, take it all in all. Now she goes to all these little places, pop. 1500 and less, a different place each week, and wherever she goes (my father is going to find this hard to understand) she travels in the nude. She wears nothing except a pair of high-heeled shoes. Even in the winter when it's very cold. She's a travelling nude, you see. And she travels out of Edmonton, Alta., pop. 250,000 or so, a fair-sized city.

She takes a taxi from the house she rooms in (that's part of allowable expenses) to either the CPR or CNR or Greyhound Bus station, and there she gets out, proud, head held high, but she's very demure and a bit shy at the same time. So with a nonchalantly grand manner she tips the taxi driver ten cents and walks into the station. He's a bit pop-eyed, and so are most of the other people, but I never worry very much about their reaction. She's accepted, more or less. She's known as the travelling nude and that's all there is to it.

Sometimes, in the winter, I feel I'd like to drape a warm coat around her, but I resist this impulse. She's a hardy soul. She can stand the cold. Anyway, there she goes. Oh, I forgot to tell you. She also carries a handbag. She is, after all, a woman. So she traipses up to the ticket window, and says (her voice is husky, in a feminine, though not exactly seductive way), "One ticket, return, to Great Fish Lake, please." Or it might be Three Bear Hills or Pollux, or Castor, or any number of places, for she is constantly kept busy for eight or nine months of the year. And then she rummages about in her capacious handbag, pays for her ticket, looks somewhat disapprovingly at the astonished clerk who gapes wide-eyed at her slightly drooping breasts (the first flush of youth now gone), not knowing whether to be scandalized or erotically aroused, and then walks over to the newsstand and buys, as is her custom, a copy of the *Ladies' Home Journal* or *Chatelaine* or *Vogue*, for she must know what the well-dressed woman wears this season, or what Dr. Blatz or Dr. Spock thinks this month about the psyche of the preschool child, or what delicious dishes can be concocted this week out of last Sunday's leftover roast. She is a well-informed nude, you see, garnering up bits of useful information as she travels by train or bus.

So she arrives at last in Great Fish Lake, or Three Bear Hills, or Castor, or Pollux, and gets off the bus or the train, and the stationmaster and the local inhabitants look at each other knowingly and say, "Oh, here goes the travelling nude. Guess there's going to be a great deal of activity over at the Community Hall tonight," and they smile and wink broadly at each other, but look very soberly as she walks past them, and doff their hats and say, "Good afternoon, ma'am. Not too cold for you, I hope," and she smiles back graciously, showing as she does so a gap (unfortunate blemish!) in the upper row of her teeth.

And the desk-clerk at the *Great Fish Lake Imperial* or the *Three Bear Hills Ritz*, wooden buildings, once painted white, with name emblazoned in black block letters, looks down the main street and sees her coming, and says to a man drowsing in a sagging, brown, cracked leather chair, "There's the travelling nude. That means the old Community Hall is going to be all lit up tonight," and winks at the man in the sagging chair, who rouses himself with a startled snore and looks at her as she walks towards the hotel, balancing delicately on her high-heeled shoes, her handbag now slung across her shoulder.

The desk-clerk has her key ready. "Same room as last time, ma'am. 14A." The number 13 is delicately skipped at the *Great Fish Lake Imperial* or at the *Three Bear Hills Ritz*.

She smiles her gap-toothed smile, thanks him, and taking her key, walks up the stairs, and the two men look thoughtfully at her firm buttocks swaying lightly from side to side as she mounts to the first floor and lets herself into her room.

Once in, she sighs deeply and lies down on her bed. A long evening's work now stretches before her, and she does not anticipate it with particular pleasure. The work is tiring, and she feels tired already, even before it's begun, for she's no longer quite as energetic as she once was.

Evening comes. A few street lights in the main street go on, and the grey-haired, mustachioed caretaker gets everything ready, and then, singly or in groups, they begin to emerge from the small houses in the unlit streets or from farmhouses further away, making their way on foot or in cars that bump along rutty roads, and so at last converge upon the Community Hall, and, carrying satchels and sundry other equipment, greet each other and go into the Hall and sit down busily on chairs arranged in a wide semi-circle, and now, talking to each other, they wait. There are pinched-looking women, resigned to spinsterhood, and middle-aged matrons, their child-rearing task now done; there are a few youngish couples, and two or three single men.

"Are we all here?" says a cheerful female voice. "Good. Now we must really work tonight. She'll be here in a minute. Take advantage of your opportunity. Remember, she won't be here for another six months or so."

Out of the satchels come sheets of drawing paper and charcoal pencils, and they all sit there, poised, expectant, ready for action.

The door opens and with stately steps, head held high, her bearing almost regal, the travelling nude enters, makes her way smiling, as if bestowing royal grace, to a chair in the middle of the semi-circle and sits down. Her work has now begun.

"Now, class," says the cheerful female, who teaches in the local elementary school during the day, "tonight we'll try and draw the sitting nude. Tomorrow we'll draw the nude standing, and the day after the reclining nude. I hope you'll all be here again then, for as Mr. Mahler told us, we cannot become painters without learning to draw the human figure exactly, can we now?" And smiles all round the semi-circle, and then nods pleasantly at the sitting travelling nude.

The travelling nude arranges herself on her chair, trying to make herself as comfortable as possible. She now seems oblivious of the faces staring at her. Each new face now sees her from its own angle. There is a pause while each drinks in the vision of "Figure. Female. Sitting. Nude." At last they begin to sketch away, now satisfied, now frustrated; erase, start again; look over their shoulders to see what their neighbours are doing, while all the while the cheerful female circulates among them, admonishing, guiding, calling on the team to give their all. "Be sure and remember that Mr. Mahler comes next month," she cries, "and that we want to show him that we've really been making progress."

So for three evenings they sketch the travelling nude until their creative energies are quite exhausted, their paper all used up, their pencils blunt.

Early in the morning, on the fourth day after her arrival, the travelling nude departs. She is glad the work for this week is over. Looks forward to lounging about for a few days in Edmonton. She is quite tired, for the accommodation is dingy, the food stale and steamy, and the work is strenuous, exhausting even. And yet she knows that in the following week she will set out again and spend three days in some little town to help along the growth of culture in the land.

II

Perhaps it would be better if I made up some commonplace story and never said anything at all about the travelling nude to my father. For if I told him the truth, I would only succeed in calling forth his Job-like posture. On such occasions he sighs deeply, lifts his head towards the ceiling of the room, as if God sat there in a corner, rolls his eyes, and spreads his arms out wide, resigned to his martyrdom. "Everybody has some cross to bear," he told me once. "You are my cross." I'm sure he thinks I am mad.

It occurs to me that you might think so, too. Let me assure you that I am as sane as you. I am an artist. My name is Herman O. Mahler. I am aware that "Mahler" is the German word for painter. So perhaps long ago one of my ancestors was a painter, and the thought that this familial talent, after lying dormant for many generations, burst forth again and manifested itself in me, makes me quite excited, creating a bond between me and that remote ancestor whose name proclaimed his art. My father sneered at the notion. So far as he knew or cared to admit the Mahlers were all respectable businessmen, ever since the first Canadian Mahler, my grandfather, established a general store in Orillia, a small Ontario town. I myself was born in Toronto twenty-seven years ago.

When I announced my intention of becoming a painter, my father stormed up and down our living room, crying incessantly, "Why did I slave all these years? For what? For what? What was the point? What?"

I, for my part, kept on saying, "I don't see any logical connection here," but he merely repeated, "Why did I slave all these years? For what? For what?"

My mother didn't take any of this seriously. She thought my ambition would burn itself out. I was only seventeen at the time. But when the flames burned ever lustier, my mother, who is a realistic woman, persuaded my father to let me go to the Ontario College of Art.

He looked the place over and was quite impressed by its size and general air of stolidity. As he put it to my mother, "The building is beautiful. Big solid pillars. Good stone. Nice trees all around. And the inside, too. Respectable. Quiet. Clean. Not like those attics you hear about. Well, maybe there's something to this art business after all."

I studied at the Ontario College of Art for three years, learned to draw "Figure. Female. Reclining. Nude." "Figure. Female. Sitting. Nude." Learned to work in oil, tempera, and various other media, took several courses in the history of art, and emerged at last a duly certified Mahler.

By the time I was twenty-four or twenty-five I had already passed through several well-recognizable periods. My first period was the blue period, and it is astonishing what nuances of blue I could produce. My style then was generally realistic, although my father, on seeing one of my paintings, exclaimed, "Blue horses! Why that's impossible! Who ever saw a blue horse?"

I moved on to my pink period and painted in pink more or less the same subjects which I had hitherto painted in blue. "Pink horses!" my father exclaimed. "Why, that's impossible! Who ever saw a pink horse?"

I moved rapidly on to my Cubist period, in which I

produced at least one remarkable painting, a largish oil, entitled, "Nude Descending Staircase," which practically caused my father to suffer an apoplexy and to mutter darkly about fraud and the corruption of the young. It was the title that annoyed him, for he could recognize no nude in the picture itself. My mother contented herself with a clicking of her tongue and a modest statement that these things were beyond her.

After my Cubist period came my Abstract period, and at last I felt that I had found my style. Here imagination was not restricted. I felt free, with all nature at my feet. I was a conqueror. Neither space nor time could now contain me. My father was now quite certain that I was mad.

In five years of painting I sold paintings totalling two hundred dollars, and even my poor mathematical brain managed to compute that this amounted to only forty dollars per annum. What was most irksome, however, was the fact that since I continued to live at home and was therefore in a manner of speaking a kept man, my father, who was after all doing the keeping, felt himself entitled to keep up a consistent, sniping, carping sort of criticism about the noble art of painting in general and my own activity in particular. He wondered why this curse had been wished on his only son, for whom he had envisaged a bright and rosy future in the retailing business. The idea that I was carrying on the tradition established by a remote Mahler he dismissed with contempt.

At last he began to insist that I earn my own living. What was I to do? I refused to prostitute my original, God-given talent, for I felt that if I did so I would in some obscure way be betraying the honour and integrity of that remote Mahler who had passed on his mantle to me and was now watching to see what I would do with it. Imagine my joy, therefore, when I read in an art magazine that the Extension Department of the University of Alberta was looking for an Extension lecturer in art, whose business it would be to travel the length and breadth of the province and give a series of short courses (none longer than a week) in various small towns. What marvellous vistas opened up before me! I would be a true servant of the noble art of painting. What hidden talents I would discover, what rough diamonds I would unearth, polish, and present to the world! And I would go on painting myself. Thus I could pursue the noble art to which I had dedicated myself and keep on eating at the same time without relying on the charity of my father or prostituting the inner me.

I applied for the job and was duly appointed.

III

I resigned from this position largely because of the travelling nude.

I must be frank. The rough diamonds I hoped to find turned out to be chunks of coal. And not even coal of the first grade, either. But they were most pleasant pieces of coal, kind and most appreciative. I became known in the little towns and in the pokey hotels, and held forth in sundry Community Halls on the elements of the noble art of painting as taught in the Ontario College of Art. Thus is the light spread into the furthermost corners of the land.

Most of my students were unfortunately wholly intent on reproducing mountains and lakes and flowers with a passion that depressed me. "More imagination!" I cried. "Use all the imagination you have!" Whereupon dear Mrs. McGregor, when next I arrived in her neck of the woods, showed proudly a canvas on which she had painted a desert sheik, in long white robes and red fez, sitting in a posture meant to be majestic on an improbable-looking Arabian horse, and staring at what was unquestionably a frozen lake in front of him, and the snow-capped Rocky Mountains ringing him all round. The critical mind stood awed and aghast. All I could mutter was, "You could improve the folds in the sheik's robe."

I did not despair. My earnest hope was to guide my charges away from nature and lead them, via the human figure, to the glory and perfect freedom of Abstraction. I began first by having one or another of my students pose, and I showed them how a face could be broken down into its geometrical components. It was rather more difficult to demonstrate how the clothed body could so be broken down, and it was in Three Bear Hills that I made the fatal remark.

"What we need for a real study of the human figure," I said, "is someone to model for us in the nude."

Well, the ice descended on the Three Bear Hills Community Hall. Shocked looks crissed and crossed, and dear Mrs. McGregor looked at me with infinite pain, as if to say, "You wouldn't surely mean me?"

I found myself shaking my head and mumbling, "No. No. That is not what I meant at all," when suddenly there was the unmistakeable gravel voice of Thomas Cullen breaking the icy silence with a loud, "Hear! hear!"

I turned to look at him, and there he was, as sprightly a sixty-year-old as ever you saw, small and wiry, with a little bald-pated head, looking straight at Nancy Hall, a fair to middling thirty-year-old blossoming bud, and "Hear! Hear!" he cried again. "That's what we need all right."

"Shame!" cried dear Mrs. McGregor. "Shame!"

"For academic purposes merely," said Thomas Cullen saucily.

"Shame!" cried Mrs. McGregor again. "Shame!"

I managed to smooth things over, but the fertile seed continued to sprout in Thomas Cullen's bald-pated head and the following June bore glorious fruit in Medicine Hat.

Once a year there is a meeting of the Community Art Classes in one of the larger centres, and whoever has the time gathers there for a shindig lasting a day. There are discussions in small groups about how things could be improved and then all the students exhibit their pictures, and in the evening there's a banquet and there's a guest speaker, and afterwards the group chairmen present a series of resolutions and everybody votes on them, and then, in a softly-glowing mood of togetherness and comradeship the group dissolves, thinking that the art of painting has been truly and nobly served.

As leader and travelling mentor I was expected to arrange this annual event, and things went pretty smoothly. That ancient Mahler might have thought the guild of medieval painters had been miraculously revived, until of course, he'd seen the paintings. After the discussions and the exhibition we all gathered in the banqueting room of a restaurant, and sat on hard, narrow chairs around long tables eating tough chicken and soggy boiled potatoes and dried-out coleslaw. After the dessert, I rapped a teaspoon against a glass and introduced our guest speaker, a nice enough fellow who'd come out from Edmonton at my request, and now began to warble about the aesthetics of modern art, and threw names about, like Leger, and Braque, and Mondrian, and Picasso, and everybody nodded knowingly, feeling cultured and really dead centre, if you know what I mean. At last he finished warbling and sat down amid polite applause.

The next item on the agenda was "Resolutions". It's funny, but I can never think of the word "resolutions" without at once seeing a wastepaper basket. I guess that is what Freud meant by free association. A procession of wastepaper baskets now began to march through my head as our little band of devotees resolved in various ways to make the cultural desert bloom.

It was getting pretty hot and my chair seemed to be getting smaller, and just as I thought we were all done, there was the loud clearing of a throat, and Thomas Cullen cried out, "I have another resolution, Mr. Chairman."

Another wastepaper basket strutted slowly through my head. "But," I said, "you didn't chair one of the groups, did you, Mr. Cullen?"

"No," said Thomas Cullen, "I did not. This is a private resolution." He cleared his throat again and took a sip of water. Then he got up, straightened his tie, reached deep into the inner recesses of his breast-pocket and brought out a piece of paper.

"Inasmuch and because no painter can call himself a painter unless he knows the anatomy of the human figure," Thomas Cullen read solemnly, "and inasmuch as it is impossible to study and know the human figure unless that figure is nude be it therefore resolved that the authorities in question secure a travelling nude who would go from community to community . . ."

Thomas Cullen had more to say, but I didn't hear it. For, like Venus rising from the waves, the travelling nude rose in my mind, fully fashioned, although with the first flush of youth now gone.

The next voice I heard distinctly was that of Mr. Edward Nash, who sat next to his wife, and who now said loudly and clearly, "I second the motion."

His wife turned on him with a startled look that froze on her face and gave me some idea of what Sodom and Gomorrah must have been like. "You wouldn't," she hissed. "You wouldn't."

"I second Mr. Cullen's motion," said Edward Nash stoutly. "A travelling nude—that's what we need to perfect ourselves as painters."

"You men!" said Mrs. Nash indignantly. "You're all alike. Painters, indeed! Travelling nudes! Mountains and horses are good enough to practice on."

"I'm sure the gentlemen are acting from highest motives," I said, trying to soften things up.

"Lowest motives," cried Mrs. McGregor, "if you ask me."

"Now, now," I said sternly. "Let's have an orderly debate."

"I don't see what there is to debate," said Mrs. Nash. "Lechery. That's all."

In the far corner portly Mr. Barrhead rose. He was about fifty, and he specialized in painting lakes. He was, I believe, a lawyer. "There's some merit in the resolution before us," he began. "However, the whole thing is premature. Our fellow citizens would undoubtedly misconstrue this—this business, and the Community Art Classes would likely get a bad name. In fact, this thing would likely kill the whole development."

"I disagree emphatically, Mr. Chairman," protested Thomas Cullen. "If we get a travelling nude it would be the biggest shot in the arm that painting ever got in this province."

It was at this moment that I saw the travelling nude demurely walk to the hotel in her high-heeled shoes, and I was so engrossed in my vision that I missed most of what followed, though Mrs. Nash threw herself into the battle with renewed vigour and her voice dominated all.

"Question!" someone shouted. "Question!"

"Before we vote," cried Thomas Cullen, obviously trying desperately to save his resolution, "let's ask Mr. Mahler what he thinks."

The noise subsided. All turned to me.

"I think it's an excellent idea," I said firmly. "If there's anything you people need more than anything else it's a travelling nude."

"You can't mean that," cried Mrs. Nash after a moment of stunned silence.

"I do," I said firmly, for my mind was filled with the vision I had seen.

"I knew it," cried Mrs. McGregor. "I knew it all the time." I have often wondered since what exactly it was that Mrs. McGregor knew.

The vote was taken. Fifty-two against, and one for. Mr. Edward Nash half-raised his hand to vote "aye", but after a quick look at his furious spouse, he dropped it again, and abstained.

IV

It was about two weeks after this memorable scene that my boss in Edmonton summoned me to his office. He's a very nice fellow, though more interested in oil wells than in oil paint, and our relations had always been pleasant enough.

"Ah, Mahler," he greeted me. "It's good to see you. Sit down." He was sucking on a pipe, and began to rummage about for something on his desk. "Everything all right?" he asked casually.

"Fine," I said. "Everything's fine. One more trip to Three Bear Hills and other points South, and that's it for this year. Thank God."

He gave me a quick look. "Why 'Thank God'?" he asked. "Aren't you happy in your work?"

"Oh, sure," I said. "But I'm . . ."

"Quite so," he interrupted. "Quite so." It was quite obvious that he wasn't really much interested. He was filling his pipe and lighting it, and in between puffs he said, "I called you in, Mahler, because of this," and he held up a letter that he had unearthed from a pile on his desk. "It's nothing," he said nonchalantly. "I'm sure you can explain."

I was getting a bit annoyed, I must admit. If it was nothing, then what was there to explain?

"It's a complaint," he said. "Signed by about fifteen of your students. I think it's a joke or something. But it appears that you are strongly in favour of a travelling nude."

I looked him straight in the eye. "That's right," I said. "It's got to the point where you can't have any kind of development of the community art classes unless you get a travelling nude. And the sooner the better." I leaned forward and tapped my knuckles on his desk for emphasis.

"You're not serious," he said.

"I was never more serious in my life," I said. "And what's more, we need the kind of nude that'll really travel in the nude."

"You're not serious," he said again, incredulously. His pipe went out and he sucked on it desperately.

"Furthermore," I continued, quite reckless now, "unless we get a travelling nude, I can't possibly continue to instruct here. I'm sick and tired of mountains and lakes. Our students have to be initiated into the secrets of female, figure, sitting, nude."

"Mahler!" he said, and there was alarm in his voice, "you must be mad."

"Drink deep or taste not the Pierian spring," I said.

"Mahler!" he cried. "What the . . ."

"The original resolution called for the authorities to secure a travelling nude," I informed him calmly. " 'Authorities' in this case means you. So if I were you, I'd start advertising."

"Mahler," he said. His hands were trembling, and he put his pipe down on his desk. "Please go and see a doctor."

"I will not be insulted," I said haughtily. "I have my artistic pride. It runs in the family. You will have my letter of resignation in the morning."

I left him speechless, poor fellow. I think deep down I must have wanted to give up this job. Don't you?

Oh, I forgot to tell you. The name of the travelling nude was Valerie. She had no surname. Or if she did, I never knew it.

■

Aritha van Herk

Aritha van Herk (1954-   ) was born in Alberta, and grew up on a farm near the town of Edberg. She has published stories in numerous magazines, and with Rudy Wiebe co-edited the anthology *More Stories From Western Canada* (1980). Her first novel, *Judith*, about a young woman who runs a pig farm, was published in 1978 after winning the Seal First Novel Award; it has now been published in seven languages. Her second novel, *The Tent Peg*, appeared in 1981. She has taught at the universities of Calgary and British Columbia and now writes and lives in Vancouver.

NEVER SISTERS

Aritha van Herk

You would never believe that we are sisters. If you see us together, you might think we are friends or cousins, but never sisters. Unless you are perceptive enough to notice that we have the same hurried walk, the same unsympathetic way of speaking. But she is far more beautiful than I am, emanating a suggestion of whispy frailness that completely contradicts my stocky build. And in contrast to her dark hair and eyes, I am fair and freckled, without the clear olive tone of her skin. Or the decisiveness of her actions. Whatever I may seem like, I am not jealous. Although I will admit, as a child I worried that she would be forever beyond my grasp. Older, slimmer, always an edge of knowledge, her hands flying easily where mine fumbled. That is the advantage an older sister will perpetually have: she experiences long before you possibly can.

She is older than I am by eight years. An odd situation. I have a menage of brothers (four of them), but only this one sister. My brothers used to be important, but that has changed and now it is my sister who preoccupies me. I suppose we ought to be close. But somehow, in the patterns of years, we have admitted distance. Eight years is an enormous gap when you are young. And perhaps it was for the best. Throughout my childhood she was my second mother, a surrogate. Now that I am old enough to be called adult, there are those years between us so that we do not compete, there is no severing dragon of jealousy. Instead, time interfered. We are not close; I must say that. We never were.

I was ten when she left home. I stand at the window and watch the car drive away; Hannike sits very straight on the front seat beside my father. The picture has the clarity of illusion: she wears a creamy blouse and a wine-coloured jumper and in her ears are the pearl earrings my mother has given her that morning. In that instant I see only a flash of her fine dark hair drawn back off her forehead and then the car is gone.

In a certain sense, she ceased to exist, no longer the cool inviolable sister who moved among my brothers so effortlessly. And so unlike me. I fought and kicked and yelled, learned all of the boys' bad habits and none of the good. My mother often wished aloud that I had been born a boy so that she could treat me like one. Sometimes she even dared to ask me why I was not more like Hannike. I pretended not to care, but I felt hurt, secondhand.

Hannike and I shared the same bedroom. When the car turned out of the driveway, it was that I thought of, her sleeping beside me for as long as I could remember. For the first time, I would sleep alone. The idea paralysed me—not that I would sleep alone, but that *she* would sleep alone far away in a strange bed while I had the comfort of our familiar room. And lying still and awake that night I cried for her more than for myself.

In bed. I suppose that was when we were the closest. After all, we spent little time together during the day. I was locked into my child's world of play while she had gone a step further into the labyrinth of chores and responsibility. It was her room. She was the oldest and she shared it with me, but it was still her room. There was never any question about that. I was tolerated. Still, there was an intimacy about it that I appreciate only now.

I was a pretender. I lie awake in bed until she comes upstairs and closes the bedroom door behind her. I lie perfectly still with my eyes shut until she thinks she is sure that I am asleep. I can peek through my eyelashes at her without her ever guessing that I am awake. She hesitates and stands at the window for a moment, looking out into the darkness. Then she turns back to the room, stilled and reluctant, almost compliant. I thought that she was cautious and quiet for me, but now I believe her stillness was something else.

She was the first naked woman I ever saw. My own nakedness was shameful and wretched—I had the straight body of a boy. Watching her step out of her skirt and shuck off her blouse to stand fragile and a little stooped in white panties and bra emphasized my inadequacy, how hopelessly far behind I was. I could have watched her for hours, the turns of her body as smooth and pale as those of a ceramic figure. And it was not her sexuality, the white cotton bra easily unhooked and flung onto the dresser, the panties kicked from around her ankles, that made me hold my breath, but the fragility of her bones, the angularity of her back and hips, her long slender legs moving in a blurred sibilance of lambent skin. I wanted to touch that skin, feel the texture of it, but I never did, knowing my grimy child's hand would be a kind of violation.

Propped against the pillows, with the book resting on her knees, she would read. I shifted closer and closer until, through my eyelashes, I could almost see the page. I didn't want to read her book, I only wanted to be close to her, to watch her read. But she sensed my awareness always, caught me immediately.

"Get over on your own side!"

I am instantly quiet as a shell, feigning perfect slumber.

"You can't fool me, Marikje. Turn over and get to sleep."

That was the year I could never fall asleep. I lay awake for hours, listening to the sounds the old house made around me. And always she was there, Hannike my sister, the sprawl of her dark hair, the fluidity of her body in sleep, even the smell of her faint and dark like thin-skinned oranges at Christmas.

If she was angry, she would shove me over, her hands pushing at my rigid and resistant body. I never said a word, as if I thought silence would confirm my innocence, that I wasn't really awake at all. She was never cruel. Rather, she used a form of practicality on me that was sometimes humiliating, sometimes comforting.

"Go to sleep. You'll be too tired to go to school tomorrow."

That was true. In the mornings I could not move; I had to be prodded and shoved and pulled at until I was walking down the driveway to the end of the road to wait for the school bus.

She was different at school, one of the older kids who moved smoothly between the separate circles of home and learning. For us they were still two isolated worlds, so radically different we could hardly think of them together, let alone merge them. The long and jolting bus ride divided them completely.

For her, there was no separation. Outwardly at least, she made the transitions easily. I am still envious that she could have become an adult before I was even aware that I was a child, or so it seemed to me. It was strange that she was old enough to be a babysitter and a stand-in mother, but young enough to have to listen to my parents. Her eight years superiority became my incessant preoccupation. When I'm as old as Hannike . . . Of course, I will never catch up.

She will tell you that we were very different, but neither of us is remembering the way I used to imitate her, emulate her, wish to be her. To all outward appearances, I have given that up now and so the memory remains unjogged. But her shape was always there. My childhood has no memories that do not include her.

Did I say that she was an adult before I was even a child? She had to be. We were all younger than she; we were all her responsibility. I know she wishes she had been the youngest, had been absolved of our weight. But there it was; older children do what they have to do and then leave home.

When she was left with us she was the boss, we had to listen to her. Of course we were unwilling, disobedient, eager to imagine new forms of misbehaviour. Jan broke his ankle jumping out of the hayloft. Dad found the horse in the next county after we let her out. And always Hannike was stoic and responsible. I think she sometimes even took the blame.

The old bureau in the attic was full of pictures and books and boxes of letters. They were the leftovers of my parents' past; a lock of my grandmother's hair, a christening gown wrapped in tissue. We were allowed to play drum corps in the attic but were supposed to stay out of the bureau. I didn't open the drawer and find the picture of my father in a uniform, holding a gun, but we were suddenly fighting over it and then we tore it. I remember her lighting among the five of us like a hailstorm, yanking at us in a silent fury. Her small fists useless against us, she flashed away and in a moment was back wielding my mother's wooden butter paddle. How could she possibly catch us? We were Indians, monkeys, devils going in five directions at once. And she chased us all, furiously and frantically while we laughed and ran and whooped at her. It was only when she stomped back to the house with such anger written in every line of her body, the paddle dangling from her hand, that we stopped, sobered.

She locked us out of the house that afternoon. Locked all the doors and wouldn't open them for anything. Left us to our own devices as if she didn't care if we were dead, or would all kill ourselves. We slunk around the porch, hoping she would relent, hoping for anger rather than icy withdrawal. We knew only that she was crying, crying and crying with that helpless inevitability that we sometimes glimpsed in her. And we were terrifyingly ashamed.

And then there is the other picture. I stand at the end of the driveway with Hannike and my brothers waiting for the bus. The trees are heavy with frost, the bus is late, and we have been waiting for fifteen minutes. I am in grade two. I carry a lunchkit but no books. Inside my red mittens my hands are cold, so cold I am unable to hang onto the handle and I drop the lunchpail with a clatter. I curl my hands into fists but they only seem to be getting colder.

Hannike is looking down the road for the bus, squinting into the brilliant ice-sun as if she would challenge it. Her boots scrunch the snow and she is standing beside me. "Are you cold, Marikje?"

I nod, huddled inside my coat like a turtle.

"Stamp!" she says.

I stamp my feet hard on the ground so that needles of fire race through my legs.

"It's my hands."

"Put them in your pockets."

I shove them into the pockets of my coat but still they feel stiff and bloodless.

"Are they still cold?"

I nod, miserable. "Isn't the bus coming?"

"It's probably stuck." She takes my mittened hands in hers, rubs them absently. Suddenly she turns her back to me. "Here. Take off your mitts and put your hands under my coat."

I drop my stiff mittens at my feet and shove my hands under her coat, into the warmth trapped there.

"Is that better?" she says over her shoulder.

"Yes." My hands are still curled into fists.

"Put them under my sweater."

I fumble with the layers of clothing, the suddenly acute sensation of rough wool on the backs of my hands in opposition to the smoother crispness of her blouse on my palms and fingertips. And suddenly I am afraid, afraid of touching her. I pull my hands away from her blouse, her body underneath it.

"Marikje, you're letting all the cold air under my sweater!" She is suddenly ruthless, authoritative, "Look, put your hands under my shirt and on my back and stand still."

For an instant I am petrified, then slowly, slowly I obey her, moving deeper under the cocoon of her clothes, my fingers stumbling onto the incredible softness of her warm skin. Entranced, I open my hands and touch her, lay my spread palms on her. It is as if I am touching some magical source of heat that thaws my fingers immediately, but more, leaves them with a tingling ache of sensation. Her skin is like warm water, perfectly still and smooth, unshrinking. Under my fingers I can even feel the shape of her ribs. I marvel at that now, the intimacy of it, the liberty she allowed me, my cold hands warming themselves on the flush of her skin. That was my sister.

When I am twelve, she comes home on weekends. Now she is totally beyond me, a woman from another place who does not belong here anymore. She even laughs with me. She is free of having to protect me, free of having to punish me. I am fascinated by her. She is free of my parents too; free as I know I will never be, too young and malleable to tear myself away. The turn of her head and the fine line of bone along her chin have left us behind completely, another transition accomplished. While she has grown more graceful, I have become clumsy and awkward. I break dishes and stumble; my hair is lank and colourless.

She still sleeps in the big bed with me and now she talks to me before we go to sleep. About the residence and about going to university and about taking courses and becoming a teacher. I want to do exactly what she is doing; I want to retrace every step she makes. Her life seems as perfect to me as mine is not. She falls asleep before I do and I lie staring at the sloping ceiling above me and wishing I could be her, free of having to wait, waiting for everything. Beside me her body is restless and suddenly she turns over.

"No," she mumbles. "No."

I am instantly motionless. "What? Hannike?"

"Mmmmn."

She is still asleep; her voice comes out of the depths of her dreams. I am suddenly frightened, something somewhere has leaped beyond me.

She flings out her arm. "No, I don't want to."

I sit up and stare down at her. Now I am even afraid to touch her, to waken her.

She mumbles something else and then is quiet.

I sit frozen upright, not wanting to hear, yet I cannot stop myself from listening and I cannot bring myself to wake her.

She stirs. "I won't," she says clearly. "I hate them all. I won't take care of them anymore."

"Hannike, Hannike." I shake her shoulder hard. "Wake up. Don't you feel well?"

She opens her eyes for a moment, then sighs and turns her back to me.

"Go to sleep, Marikje," she says. "Go to sleep. You have to go to school in the morning."

I lay awake beside her then, trying to fit the pieces together. Her endless stooped endurance, the oldest of the six of us, the liberties she allowed us, the gleam of her creamy skin in the light. And I knew that she had made a transition that I would never even get to, let alone make, a spoiled child with an older sister.

When Hannike was married, two years later, I was fourteen. I was her youngest bridesmaid; I wore a yellow dress and carried pink flowers. But what I remember most is her standing in her bathrobe before she put on her dress, standing lost and defenseless as if she would cry, as if there were no hope or escape. I was dispassionate. I didn't want to be like her anymore. I would never marry and have children. I had decided.

And I remember that my father cried, that he stood beside my mother and the tears slipped down his brown face. He never cried when I got married, eight years later. I know because I watched him. I wanted to see if he would. That was the difference between Hannike and I.

A year later she was heavy and awkward with her first child, as if she had never denied anything, only affirmed it. She had slipped away from me. At fifteen I did not understand pregnancy and I did not like small children. Her body seemed to be a gross intrusion on her small, light frame and I was afraid for her. She did not want my fear. She was happy, she said, and the corners of her mouth tilted upwards.

Now everyone says that her daughter looks like me when I was a child. I do not see the resemblance. She seems to me to look more like Hannike. But then, I do not see her often. Only often enough to remind her of my strangeness and that I am a disinterested aunt. Hannike and I live in the same city but we are far away from each other. She has four children now. I have none.

When we are home together, my father sometimes asks me when will I have a child and I smile and say, "Not yet, Dad." And Hannike looks at me very quickly out of the corner of her eye, but she says nothing.

■

Anne Cameron

Glen Erikson

Anne Cameron (Cam Hubert) (1938-) lives in Nanaimo,
British Columbia, and is the author of several feature
screenplays including the highly popular *Ticket to Heaven* as
well as numerous poems and short stories. Her novel
Dreamspeaker (1978) won the Gibson Literary Award, and is
an acclaimed film for television as is *Drying Up the Streets*.
Her fiction is influenced by the oral story-telling traditions of the
native people of Vancouver Island, especially matrilineal
societies.. Her novel *The Journey* was published in 1982, and
"The Lost Gold Mine" appears in the collection of stories told to
her by Vancouver Island natives, *Daughters of Copper
Woman* (1981).

THE LOST GOLDMINE

Anne Cameron

It had been gray and heavy all day, the fog hiding the sharp slopes of old Catface, closing in on us until you could hardly see the outlines of the house next door, and then, just before supper time, the wind started to blow with a vengeance, all the fog blew away, and the rain came down on us, driving almost sideways, hitting the windows with a sound like handsful of sand, seeping in under the doors and around the window frames while the screaming wind tried to take the cedar shakes off the roof and move them back into the forest where they'd been for two hundred years before they got cut.

Radio reception wasn't fit to listen to, just static and humming noises, and one by one people drifted over to visit us, bringing some tea bags or a few ounces of coffee grounds, or maybe some cookies or fresh-baked bread, and we sat around for a while playing cards and talking, and some of the people worked on their knitting or their carving, or whatever it was they did in their quiet times.

Granny was working on a cedar basket, her bucket of water on the floor by her feet, the cedar strands soaking, staying pliable. Her old hands are wrinkled, the knuckles swollen and knotted now, but she still makes the best baskets on the coast, so fine and tight and even, the designs showing clear and sharp.

When she started to tell her story she didn't look at any of us, she kept her eyes on her work, and let the words fall softly into the quiet. We didn't have to listen, she wasn't trying to Teach us anything, she was just offering a story for anybody who wanted to listen. Sometimes strangers get uneasy talking to my Granny because she doesn't always look directly at them when she talks. When Granny looks at you, she fixes you with her deep black eyes until you feel like she's looking right into the inside of your head, but it isn't always polite to do that, it doesn't leave a person much privacy, and there are times we find it impolite to force even our gaze on someone. Also, Granny doesn't always look at you when you talk to her, so sometimes people who aren't from here think she hasn't heard them, but there isn't much goes on my Granny misses. It's just that she uses her ears to listen, not her eyes, so she doesn't have to look at you, she looks off at something else, or watches her hands, or maybe sits nodding at the floor, listening and giving you all the room you need to find words and express yourself.

We sat where we felt most comfortable, letting the wind scream at the roof and tug at the door. Once in a while someone would get up quietly and add another piece of alder to the fire in the big black stove with the worn nickel designs. When it's warm we have a gas ring for heating water or cooking, and there are full bottles of gas that come in on the freight boat regularly, so we don't have to worry about running out of gas. But when it's cold or damp, Iike it is all winter and part of the autumn, we light a fire in the wood-burning stove, and there's always lots of alder for fuel. The crackling of the fire in the stove made a peaceful sound that sometimes filled in the pauses between words as Granny wove her basket, and her story, which probably won't ever get into the history books in the schools and only survived for us to hear because other people, before my Granny was born, memorized it and told it to their students who memorized it and told it to younger people.

"Just about the same time the people up-coast were introduced to the Keestadores, the people down-coast met up with'em too.

"Now there's some people say us Nootka are hard-nosed and belligerent, but them as aren't Nootka are always jealous of us as are, and their opinion doesn't count for much anyway. We're the singers, the Kwagewlth are the carvers, the Salish are the politicians. And the Cowichan are the philosophers. Real gentle people, most of the time, always able to look at two or three or all sides of a question and always willin' to study with and share ideas and stories with other people. They've got the reputation for the most poetic language on the coast, but I don't know because I don't speak any of it or understand it spoken to me.

"Maybe it was because the Cowichan were so gentle, or maybe it's just that gold does that to people. We had a lot of gold here, but we never mentioned it, not to keep it a secret, but because we didn't think it was good for anythin'. It won't hold a cuttin' edge, and there was more of it than there was of natural copper, so we figured the copper was the precious metal, and used it for jewelry and ornaments. Maybe the Cowichan thought the Keestadores, who seemed to know a lot about metal, might know what to do with the stuff, so they showed it to them and asked what it was good for, which makes me wonder about havin' a mind that always looks for new ideas. In no time at all the Cowichan were faced with a choice of slavin' in a gold mine or bein' dead from a Spanish sword.

"They cut and blasted a big hole in the mountain and started whippin' and beatin' people to get'em to haul out rocks and gold. Men, women, and all but the little bitty kids or the very old were workin' and the ones not workin' were penned up in the middle of the village and held hostage. Anyone did anythin' wrong, they got beat and the hostages got abused. A person might take a beatin' for herself, but when you know your sister or some little kid is gonna get beat if you don't behave, you think twice about tryin' anythin'.

"A couple of people tried to get away and let other tribes know what was goin' on, but what happened was so awful, and the small and the old suffered so much, they all decided it wasn't worth it, so the Keestadores had it pretty much their own way.

"There was a girl had been livin' with the Tse-Shaht, learnin' how their women caught babies and teachin' the Salish weavin' she'd learned from someone else, and she was on her way home when she noticed this big mess on the hill. She didn't feel good about it, and the Cowichan, they always respect their feelin's, so she got the pullers takin' her home in the dugout to pull into a small crik and stay outta sight for a while, and she snuk close and just let her eyes find out the story. She seen the Keestadores whippin' at people and takin' them up the path to the mess, and she seen how wore out the ones comin' back were, and she went back and got the pullers to turn around and take her back up-coast, fast.

"The Tse-Shaht, like the rest of us, had just found out about the two little girls when she got back, and everyone believed what she had to say. When the Chesterman thing was done and the sacred sisters honoured, the whole fleet headed south.

"On the way down, other bands and tribes joined. There were fast two-and four-puller sealin' dugouts goin' on ahead to tell the people that the fleet wasn't just on a raidin' party or tryin' to invade anyone's fishin' territory. As soon as they said why it was headin' down, people joined in, either because they liked the Cowichan or because they figured maybe they'd be next. And, too, I guess it's true some people just like a good fight.

"Half way down the sealers came racin' back to say there was a Keestadore boat headin' up and the fleet hid itself and had a long talk about whether to try to take'em now or later. At first everyone was so steamed up they were all for now, but then they figured there was sure to be some noise, and people would get hurt or killed and they needed all the Fighters they could get because gettin' the Cowichan out from under was the important thing, so they just lay quiet and let the big galleon go by, and they planned plans and dreamed dreams for later.

"They hid the dugouts again a mornin's walk from the village, and they snuk in real close and just watched. They saw the Cowichan taken up the mountain path, and they saw the others brought down, wore out and some with marks from the whips, and they planned, and figured, and prayed, and waited.

"That night they hid themselves on either side'a the path goin' up to the mess and when the Cowichan was brought up in the mornin', all the Fighters were ready. A Keestadore officer up front, and Keestadore guards along the file, and another officer bringin' up the rear. There'd be five or six or maybe ten Cowichan, and then a Keestadore with a whip slappin' at them, and then some more Cowichan, and another Spaniard, and like that all the way down the line.

"When the whole bunch had gone past the woman at the foot of the hill, why she stepped out real quiet. She knew there was no sense tryin' for the head because'a the helmet, and the back and chest was covered with armour, so she just grabbed the officer by his bearded chin, lifted his head and slit his throat before he could even gurgle, let alone yell.

"Of course the Cowichan weren't goin' to raise the alarm. They just kept walkin' up the mountain, actin' just like they always did, makin' sure she was hid from sight while she put on the Keestadore armour and took his place. If the officer at the front had turned around all he'd'a seen would have been the metal hat glintin' in the early mornin' sun, just like always.

"The next Spaniard in front of her, he got the same treatment when another Fighter stepped out of the bush, real quiet, and did the same thing to him. One by one, workin' from back to front, they slit the Spanish throats and put on the armour. When the officer looked around, everythin' looked just the same to him as it was supposed to, right up until his own chin was grabbed and the last thing he saw was his own blood spurtin'.

"The Cowichan knew where he kept his key, and how to use it to unlock the chains around them, and they did that, but didn't take'em right off, they wanted to arrive lookin' as close to normal as they could. They all hid knives and such that the Confederacy Fighters gave them, and when they got to the mess at the top of the path, they shuffled and kept their heads bent, and looked at the ground, same as always, and the Spanish guards moved forward to change wore out workers for fresh ones and it was all over in no time flat. All the Spaniards were dead, and their bodies all thrown in the hole in the hill.

"The rest of the Cowichan were unchained, and the Keestadore swords'n'armour were divided up, and everyone trooped almost all the way back down to the village again. They stopped and re-formed a pretend column of Cowichan. They had chains around them, but they weren't locked shut, and everyone had a knife, and a lot of reason to use it.

"One of the Cowichan chiefs snuk carefully down to his own house and went inside and got his family war club. He'd got it from his mother's oldest brother who'd gotten it from *his* mother's oldest brother, and it was somethin' every Fighter envied. It was as long as a tall man's arm, and so heavy only the strongest men could lift it, and it looked mean. It had been part of the root of an old arbutus tree, and there was a big rock in the end of it where the root had grown around it in the ground, a hundred years before it was undercut by a creek and toppled over with the roots pulled up out of the earth by the weight of the tree. The rock was as big as two fists clenched together, and all around it, set into the wood, were whales' teeth and some pieces of walrus tusk, so it crushed and stabbed and cut all at the same time. When he swung it, the wind swished between the rock and the wood, between the teeth and the tusks, and it screamed like an eagle does sometime.

"The Confederacy Fighters and the freed Cowichan were right in the middle of the village when the Cowichan Chief came outta his house with his club held up, and he swung it, and it screamed for him and then he let out the most godawful yell, and the fight was on and it was here-we-go time.

"Some of the Keestadores tried to get their boat underway but it takes a long time to get the sails up and they didn't have all the pullers they needed for the long oars that stuck out the sides and down to the water. They tried to make a fight of it with the big guns, but the dugouts were already too close. Some of the Fighters had stayed back with the dugouts and were waitin' just out of sight around the point, and when the yellin' and fightin' started, the navy came in at full speed, every puller sweatin' and keepin' the rhythm just exactly. They got in so close to the big wooden ships that the Spanish couldn't point the guns down enough, they fired right over the heads of the pullers and into the sea. The firelances did it to the sails, and then they just hitched cedarbark ropes to the big boat and steered her on the rocks and let the sea do most of the work for them.

"The sailors and Keestadores on the wooden ship had to swim for it, but they didn't have a chance. The dugouts closed in on them one at a time, and the steerman or steerswoman just leaned over and bashed in the heads of the swimmers or sent a whalin' harpoon through'em.

"They took the Keestadore dead up to the mine and tossed'em inside, and then let the priests go in and pray over the dead. And while the blackrobes were prayin', the Confederacy used Keestadore powder to bring the hill down over the hole, buryin' the whole lot of'em in with the gold they'd wanted so much.

"But then they saw how raw the earth looked there, and they knew it would be easy to tell there was Somethin' there, and it wouldn't take much figurin' to know what, so they got the idea to hide the evidence and suck in that other Keestadore boat at the same time, and they lit fire to the bush.

"Some of the holy people were upset about that because cedar and hemlock are sacred and arbutus is blessed and balsam is holy, and destruction is a sin, but when people have smelled a lot of blood their brains go funny, and they lit the bush.

"Between the blast that sealed the mine and the smoke from the bush fire, the other Spanish boat came back in a rush. From where they were it must'a looked like the Keestadores was chasin' the Cowichan for water and stuff to fight the fire. They could see the other boat bust on the rocks, and of course they wanted to help, and with their attention turned to two wrong directions, they didn't see the navy dugouts until they were up close, and the big guns were no use again.

"It wasn't easy to get the last big boat because the sails were already up, but they threw bladders of oil through the holes where the oars stuck out and sent fire arrows and lances in and started some small fires. Some of the dugouts were sunk this time, and the big wooden ships just rode right over 'em, splittin' the cedar and crushin' and drownin' men and women.. There was so many dugouts, and so many Fighters, and the fires were spreadin' and the sails were startin' to burn and the ship didn't have much room to manoeuvre in the bay and the smoke from the fire was makin' it hard to tell what was goin' on. Finally it was the same as before, the boat burnin' and people tryin' to swim to safety and not findin' any safe place, swimmin' in water red with blood, hearin' the chant of the paddlers comin' closer, and then not seein' anythin' at all, and all of'em died.

"Before anyone got to celebrate, the wind shifted and the Cowichan and the Confederacy had to get away or burn like the bush they'd set afire. They headed north in dugouts, and it was like the bush wanted vengeance. The fire crowned and chased after'em, sometimes missin' entire stands of timber, like around Nitinat, fed by the wind, leapin' from the top'a one tree to the top'a another, faster than a swift runner can move, and the heat so hot some of the small lakes boiled like pots on the stove and people who'd tried to find safety in them died of hot water and no air to breathe.

"Before it was over, a third of the island had been burned, a lot of people were dead or homeless, and innocent animals who'd had nothin' to do with any of it were gone forever."

She put her basket-work aside and got up from the sofa and walked to the bathroom. We made a pot of tea, and waited for her to come out and tell us some more. But when she came out of the bathroom finally, she didn't look at us or speak to us, she just went to her bedroom, went inside and closed the door. So we finished our tea, washed the cups and left them to dry on the countertop, then everyone else went home and I went to bed to listen to the wind howlin' and the rain splashin' and to think about what it must have been like long before my Granny's granny was born.

∎

Margaret Laurence

Doug Boult

Margaret Laurence (1926-) was born and grew up in Neepawa, Manitoba; she lived in England, Somaliland, Ghana and Vancouver before she settled in Lakefield, Ontario. A major concern of her fiction is the exploration of people in and from her invented Manitoba town: Manawaka. Her novels include *This Side Jordan* (1960), *The Stone Angel* (1964), *The Fire Dwellers* (1969) and two which won the Governor General's Award for fiction, *A Jest of God* (1966) and *The Diviners* (1974). *A Jest of God* was made into a feature movie, *Rachel Rachel.* Her writing has received many other awards and honors, and she was made a Companion of the Order of Canada in 1971. "A Bird in the House" is the title story of her 1970 collection of short stories; it has been made into a television feature by the CBC. An excellent documentary film on her life and writing is *First Lady of Manawaka.*

A BIRD IN THE HOUSE

Margaret Laurence

THE PARADE would be almost over by now, and I had not gone. My mother had said in a resigned voice, "All right, Vanessa, if that's the way you feel," making me suffer twice as many jabs of guilt as I would have done if she had lost her temper. She and Grandmother MacLeod had gone off, my mother pulling the low box-sleigh with Roddie all dolled up in his new red snowsuit, just the sort of little kid anyone would want people to see. I sat on the lowest branch of the birch tree in our yard, not minding the snowy wind, even welcoming its punishment. I went over my reasons for not going, trying to believe they were good and sufficient, but in my heart I felt I was betraying my father. This was the first time I had stayed away from the Remembrance Day parade. I wondered if he would notice that I was not there, standing on the sidewalk at the corner of River and Main while the parade passed, and then following to the Court House grounds where the service was held.

I could see the whole thing in my mind. It was the same every year. The Manawaka Civic Band always led the way. They had never been able to afford full uniforms, but they had peaked navy-blue caps and sky blue chest ribbons. They were joined on Remembrance Day by the Salvation Army band, whose uniforms seemed too ordinary for a parade, for they were the same ones the bandsmen wore every Saturday night when they played "Nearer My God To Thee" at the foot of River Street. The two bands never managed to practise quite enough together, so they did not keep in time too well. The Salvation Army band invariably played faster, and afterwards my father would say irritably, "They play those marches just like they do hymns, blast them, as though they wouldn't get to heaven if they didn't hustle up." And my mother, who had great respect for the Salvation Army because of the good work they did, would respond chidingly, "Now, now, Ewen—" I vowed I would never say "Now, now" to my husband or children, not that I ever intended having the latter, for I had been put off by my brother Roderick, who was now two years old with wavy hair, and everyone said what a beautiful child. I was twelve, and no one in their right mind would have said what a beautiful child, for I was big-boned like my Grandfather Connor and had straight lanky black hair like a Blackfoot or Cree.

After the bands would come the veterans. Even thinking of them at this distance, in the white and withdrawn quiet of the birch tree, gave me a sense of painful embarrassment. I might not have minded so much if my father had not been among them. How could he go? How could he not see how they all looked? It must have been a long time since they were soldiers, for they had forgotten how to march in step. They were old—that was the thing. My father was bad enough, being almost forty, but he wasn't a patch on Howard Tully from the drugstore, who was completely grey-haired and also fat, or Stewart MacMurchie, who was bald at the back of his head. They looked to me like imposters, plump or spindly caricatures of past warriors. I almost hated them for walking in that limping column down Main. At the Court House, everyone would sing "Lord God of Hosts, be with us yet, lest we forget, lest we forget." Will Masterson would pick up his old Army bugle and blow the Last Post. Then it would be over and everyone could start gabbling once more and go home.

I jumped down from the birch bough and ran to the house, yelling, making as much noise as I could.

> I'm a poor lonesome cowboy
> An' a long way from home—

I stepped inside the front hall and kicked off my snow boots. I slammed the door behind me, making the dark ruby and emerald glass shake in the small leaded panes. I slid purposely on the hall rug, causing it to bunch and crinkle on the slippery polished oak of the floor. I seized the newel post, round as a head, and spun myself to and fro on the bottom stair.

> I ain't got no father
> To buy the clothes I wear
> I'm a poor lonesome—

At this moment my shoulders were firmly seized and shaken by a pair of hands, white and delicate and old, but strong as talons.

"Just what do you think you're doing, young lady?" Grandmother MacLeod enquired, in a voice like frost on a windowpane, infinitely cold and clearly etched.

I went limp and in a moment she took her hands away. If you struggled, she would always hold on longer.

"Gee, I never knew you were home yet."

"I would have thought that on a day like this you might have shown a little respect and consideration," Grandmother MacLeod said, "even if you couldn't make the effort to get cleaned up enough to go to the parade."

I realised with surprise that she imagined this to be my reason for not going. I did not try to correct her impression. My real reason would have been even less acceptable.

"I'm sorry," I said quickly.

In some families, *please* is described as the magic word. In our house, however, it was *sorry*.

"This isn't an easy day for any of us," she said.

Her younger son, my Uncle Roderick, had been killed in the Great War. When my father marched, and when the hymn was sung, and when that unbearably lonely tune was sounded by the one bugle and everyone forced themselves to keep absolutely still, it would be that boy of whom she was thinking. I felt the enormity of my own offense.

"Grandmother—I'm sorry."

"So you said."

I could not tell her I had not really said it before at all. I went into the den and found my father there. He was sitting in the leather-cushioned armchair beside the fireplace. He was not doing anything, just sitting and smoking. I stood beside him, wanting to touch the light-brown hairs on his forearm, but thinking he might laugh at me or pull his arm away if I did.

"I'm sorry," I said, meaning it.

"What for, honey?"

"For not going."

"Oh—that. What was the matter?"

I did not want him to know, and yet I had to tell him, make him see.

"They look silly," I blurted. "Marching like that."

For a minute I thought he was going to be angry. It would have been a relief to me if he had been. Instead, he drew his eyes away from mine and fixed them above the mantelpiece where the sword hung, the handsome and evil-looking crescent in its carved bronze sheath that some ancestor had once brought from the Northern Frontier of India.

"Is that the way it looks to you?" he said.

I felt in his voice some hurt, something that was my fault. I wanted to make everything all right between us, to convince him that I understood, even if I did not. I prayed that Grandmother MacLeod would stay put in her room, and that

my mother would take a long time in the kitchen, giving
Roddie his lunch. I wanted my father to myself, so I could
prove to him that I cared more about him than any of the
others did. I wanted to speak in some way that would be
more poignant and comprehending than anything of which
my mother could possibly be capable. But I did not know
how.

"You were right there when Uncle Roderick got killed,
weren't you?" I began uncertainly.

"Yes."

"How old was he, Dad?"

"Eighteen," my father said.

Unexpectedly, that day came into intense being for me. He
had had to watch his own brother die, not in the antiseptic
calm of some hospital, but out in the open, on the stretches
of mud I had seen in his snapshots. He would not have
known what to do. He would just have had to stand there
and look at it, whatever that might mean. I looked at my
father with a kind of horrified awe, and then I began to cry. I
had forgotten about impressing him with my perception.
Now I needed him to console me for this unwanted glimpse
of the pain he had once known.

"Hey, cut it out, honey," he said, embarrassed. "It was
bad, but it wasn't all as bad as that part. There were a few
other things."

"Like what?" I said, not believing him.

"Oh—I don't know," he replied evasively. "Most of us
were pretty young, you know, I and the boys I joined up
with. None of us had ever been away from Manawaka before.
Those of us who came back mostly came back here, or else
went no further away from town than Winnipeg. So when
we were overseas—that was the only time most of us were
ever a long way from home."

"Did you want to be?" I asked, shocked.

"Oh well—" my father said uncomfortably. "It was kind
of interesting to see a few other places for a change, that's
all."

Grandmother MacLeod was standing in the doorway.

"Beth's called you twice for lunch, Ewen. Are you deaf,
you and Vanessa?"

"Sorry," my father and I said simultaneously.

Then we went upstairs to wash our hands.

That winter my mother returned to her old job as nurse in my father's medical practice. She was able to do this only because of Noreen.

"Grandmother MacLeod says we're getting a maid." I said to my father, accusingly, one morning. "We're not, are we?"

"Believe you me, on what I'm going to be paying her," my father growled, "she couldn't be called anything as classy as a maid. Hired girl would be more like it."

"Now, now, Ewen," my mother put in, "it's not as if we were cheating her or anything. You know she wants to live in town, and I can certainly see why, stuck out there on the farm, and her father hardly ever letting her come in. What kind of life is that for a girl?"

"I don't like the idea of your going back to work, Beth," my father said. "I know you're fine now, but you're not exactly the robust type."

"You can't afford to hire a nurse any longer. It's all very well to say the Depression won't last forever—probably it won't, but what else can we do for now?"

"I'm damned if I know," my father admitted. "Beth—"

"Yes?"

They both seemed to have forgotten about me. It was breakfast, which we always ate in the kitchen, and I sat rigidly on my chair, pretending to ignore and thus snub their withdrawal from me. I glared at the window, but it was so thickly plumed and scrolled with frost that I could not see out. I glanced back to my parents. My father had not replied, and my mother was looking at him in that anxious and half-frowning way she had recently developed.

"What is it, Ewen?" Her voice had the same nervous sharpness it bore sometimes when she would say to me, "For mercy's sake, Vanessa, what is it *now?*" as though whatever was the matter, it was bound to be the last straw.

My father spun his sterling silver serviette ring, engraved with his initials, slowly around on the table.

"I never thought things would turn out like this, did you?"

"Please—" my mother said in a low strained voice, "please, Ewen, let's not start all this again. I can't take it."

"All right," my father said. "Only—"

"The MacLeods used to have money and now they don't," my mother cried. "Well, they're not alone. Do you think that's all that matters to me, Ewen? What I can't bear is to see you forever reproaching yourself. As if it were your fault."

"I don't think it's the comedown," my father said. "If I were somewhere else, I don't suppose it would matter to me, either, except where you're concerned. But I suppose you'd work too hard wherever you were—it's bred into you. If you haven't got anything to slave away at, you'll sure as hell invent something."

"What do you think I should do, let the house go to wrack and ruin? That would go over well with your mother, wouldn't it?"

"That's just it," my father said. "It's the damned house all the time. I haven't only taken on my father's house, I've taken on everything that goes with it, apparently. Sometimes I really wonder—"

"Well, it's a good thing I've inherited some practicality even if you haven't," my mother said. "I'll say that for the Connors—they aren't given to brooding, thank the Lord. Do you want your egg poached or scrambled?"

"Scrambled," my father said. "All I hope is that this Noreen doesn't get married straightaway, that's all."

"She won't," my mother said. "Who's she going to meet who could afford to marry?"

"I marvel at you, Beth," my father said. "You look as though a puff of wind would blow you away. But underneath, by God, you're all hardwood."

"Don't talk stupidly," my mother said. "All I hope is that she won't object to taking your mother's breakfast up on a tray."

"That's right," my father said angrily. "Rub it in."

"Oh Ewen, I'm sorry!" my mother cried, her face suddenly stricken. "I don't know why I say these things. I didn't mean to."

"I know," my father said. "Here, cut it out, honey. Just for God's sake please don't cry."

"I'm sorry," mother repeated, blowing her nose.

"We're both sorry," my father said. "Not that that changes anything."

After my father had gone, I got down from my chair and went to my mother.

"I don't want you to go back to the office. I don't want a hired girl here. I'll hate her."

My mother sighed, making me feel that I was placing an intolerable burden on her, and yet making me resent having to feel this weight. She looked tired, as she often did these days. Her tiredness bored me, made me want to attack her for it.

"Catch me getting along with a dumb old hired girl," I threatened.

"Do what you like," my mother said abruptly. "What can I do about it?"

And then, of course, I felt bereft, not knowing which way to turn.

My father need not have worried about Noreen getting married. She was, as it turned out, interested not in boys but in God. My mother was relieved about the boys but alarmed about God.   "It isn't natural," she said, "for a girl of seventeen. Do you think she's all right mentally, Ewen?"

When my parents, along with Grandmother MacLeod, went to the United Church every Sunday, I was made to go to Sunday school in the church basement, where there were small red chairs which humiliatingly resembled kindergarten furniture, and pictures of Jesus wearing a white sheet and surrounded by a whole lot of well-dressed kids whose mothers obviously had not suffered them to come unto Him until every face and ear was properly scrubbed. Our religious observances also included grace at meals, when my father would mumble "For what we are about to receive the Lord make us truly thankful Amen," running the words together as though they were one long word. My mother approved of these rituals, which seemed decent and moderate to her. Noreen's religion, however, was a different matter. Noreen belonged to the Tabernacle of the Risen and Reborn, and she had got up to testify no less than seven times in the past two years, she told us. My mother, who could not imagine anyone's voluntarily making a public spectacle of themselves, was profoundly shocked by this revelation.

"Don't worry," my father soothed her. "She's all right. She's just had kind of a dull life, that's all."

My mother shrugged and went on worrying and trying to help Noreen without hurting her feelings, by tactful remarks about the advisability of modulating one's voice when singing hymns, and the fact that there was plenty of hot water so Noreen really didn't need to hesitate about taking a bath. She even bought a razor and a packet of blades and whispered to Noreen that any girl who wore transparent blouses so much would probably like to shave under her arms. None of these suggestions had the slightest effect on Noreen. She did not cease belting out hymns at the top of her voice, she bathed once a fortnight, and the sorrel-coloured hair continued to bloom like a thicket of Indian paintbrush in her armpits.

Grandmother MacLeod refused to speak to Noreen. This caused Noreen a certain amount of bewilderment until she finally hit on an answer.

"Your poor grandma," she said. "She is deaf as a post. These things are sent to try us here on earth, Vanessa. But if she makes it into Heaven, I'll bet you anything she will hear clear as a bell."

Noreen and I talked about Heaven quite a lot, and also Hell. Noreen had an intimate and detailed knowledge of both places. She not only knew what they looked like—she even knew how big they were. Heaven was seventy-seven thousand miles square and it had four gates, each one made out of a different kind of precious jewel. The Pearl Gate, the Topaz Gate, the Amethyst Gate, the Ruby Gate—Noreen would reel them off, all the gates of Heaven. I told Noreen they sounded like poetry, but she was puzzled by my reaction and said I shouldn't talk that way. If you said poetry, it sounded like it was just made up and not really so, Noreen said.

Hell was larger than Heaven, and when I asked why, thinking of it as something of a comedown for God, Noreen said naturally it had to be bigger because there were a darn sight more people there than in Heaven. Hell was one hundred and ninety million miles deep and was in perpetual darkness, like a cave or under the sea. Even the flames (this was the awful thing) *did not give off any light.*

I did not actually believe in Noreen's doctrines, but the images which they conjured up began to inhabit my imagination. Noreen's fund of exotic knowledge was not limited to religion, although in a way it all seemed related. She could do many things which had a spooky tinge to them. Once when she was making a cake, she found we had run out of eggs. She went outside and gathered a bowl of fresh snow and used it instead. The cake rose like a charm, and I stared at Noreen as though she were a sorceress. In fact, I began to think of her as a sorceress, someone not quite of this earth. There was nothing unearthly about her broad shoulders and hips and her forest of dark red hair, but even these features took on a slightly sinister significance to me. I no longer saw her through the eyes or the expressed opinions of my mother and father, as a girl who had quit school at grade eight and whose life on the farm had been endlessly drab. I knew the truth—Noreen's life had not been drab at all, for she dwelt in

a world of violent splendours, a world filled with angels
whose wings of delicate light bore real feathers, and saints
shining like the dawn, and prophets who spoke in ancient
tongues, and the ecstatic souls of the saved, as well as deni-
zens of the lower regions—mean-eyed imps and crooked
cloven-hoofed monsters and beasts with the bodies of swine
and the human heads of murderers, and lovely depraved
jezebels torn by dogs through all eternity. The middle layer
of Creation, our earth, was equally full of grotesque pres-
ences, for Noreen believed strongly in the visitation of ghosts
and the communication with spirits. She could prove this
with her Ouija board. We would both place our fingers
lightly on the indicator, and it would skim across the board
and spell out answers to our questions. I did not believe
whole-heartedly in the Ouija board, either, but I was cautious about the kind of question I asked , in case the answer
would turn out unfavourable and I would be unable to forget
it.

One day Noreen told me she could also make a table talk.
We used the small table in my bedroom, and sure enough, it
lifted very slightly under our fingertips and tapped once for
Yes, twice for *No*. Noreen asked if her Aunt Ruthie would
get better from the kidney operation, and the table replied
No. I withdrew my hands.

"I don't want to do it any more."

"Gee, what's the matter, Vanessa?" Noreen's plain placid
face creased in a frown. "We only just begun."

"I have to do my homework."

My heart lurched as I said this. I was certain Noreen would
know I was lying, and that she would know not by any ordinary perception, either. But her attention had been caught by
something else, and I was thankful, at least until I saw what
it was.

My bedroom window was not opened in the coldest weather.
The storm window, which was fitted outside as an extra wall
against the winter, had three small circular holes in its frame
so that some fresh air could seep into the house. The sparrow
must have been floundering in the new snow on the roof, for
it had crawled in through one of these holes and was now
caught between the two layers of glass. I could not bear the
panic of the trapped bird, and before I realised what I was
doing, I had thrown open the bedroom window. I was not
releasing the sparrow into any better a situation, I soon saw,
for instead of remaining quiet and allowing us to catch it in

order to free it, it began flying blindly around the room, hitting the lampshade, brushing against the walls, its wings seeming to spin faster and faster.

I was pertrified. I thought I would pass out if those palpitating wings touched me. There was something in the bird's senseless movements that revolted me. I also thought it was going to damage itself, break one of those thin wing-bones, perhaps, and then it would be lying on the floor, dying, like the pimpled and horribly featherless baby birds we saw sometimes on the sidewalks in the spring when they had fallen out of their nests. I was not any longer worried about the sparrow. I wanted only to avoid the sight of it lying broken on the floor. Viciously, I thought that if Noreen said, *God sees the little sparrow fall*, I would kick her in the shins. She did not, however, say this.

"A bird in the house means a death in the house," Noreen remarked.

Shaken, I pulled my glance away from the whirling wings and looked at Noreen.

"What?"

"That's what I've heard said, anyhow."

The sparrow had exhausted itself. It lay on the floor, spent and trembling. I could not bring myself to touch it. Noreen bent and picked it up. She cradled it with great gentleness between her cupped hands. Then we took it downstairs, and when I had opened the back door, Noreen set the bird free.

"Poor little scrap," she said, and I felt struck to the heart, knowing she had been concerned all along about the sparrow, while I, perfidiously, in the chaos of the moment, had been concerned only about myself.

"Wanna do some with the Ouija board, Vanessa?" Noreen asked.

I shivered a little, perhaps only because of the blast of cold air which had come into the kitchen when the door was opened.

"No thanks, Noreen. Like I said, I got my homework to do. But thanks all the same."

"That's okay," Noreen said in her guileless voice. "Any time."

But whenever she mentioned the Ouija board or the talking table, after that, I always found some excuse not to consult these oracles.

"Do you want to come to church with me this evening, Vanessa?" my father asked.

"How come you're going to the evening service?" I enquired.

"Well, we didn't go this morning. We went snow-shoeing instead, remember? I think your grandmother was a little bit put out about it. She went alone this morning. I guess it wouldn't hurt you and me, to go now."

We walked through the dark, along the white streets, the snow squeaking dryly under our feet. The streetlights were placed at long intervals along the sidewalks, and around each pole the circle of flimsy light created glistening points of blue and crystal on the crusted snow. I would have liked to take my father's hand, as I used to do, but I was too old for that now. I walked beside him, taking long steps so he would not have to walk more slowly on my account.

The sermon bored me, and I began leafing through the Hymnary for entertainment. I must have drowsed, for the next thing I knew, my father was prodding me and we were on our feet for the closing hymn.

> Near the Cross, near the Cross,
> Be my glory ever,
> Till my ransomed soul shall find
> Rest beyond the river.

I knew the tune well, so I sang loudly for the first verse. But the music to that hymn is sombre, and all at once the words themselves seemed too dreadful to be sung. I stopped singing, my throat knotted. I thought I was going to cry, but I did not know why, except that the song recalled to me my Grandmother Connor, who had been dead only a year now. I wondered why her soul needed to be ransomed. If God did not think she was good enough just as she was, then I did not have much use for His opinion. "Rest beyond the river"—was that what had happened to her? She had believed in Heaven, but I did not think that rest beyond the river was quite what she had in mind. To think of her in Noreen's flashy Heaven, though—that was even worse. Someplace where nobody ever got annoyed or had to be smoothed down and placated, someplace where there were never any family scenes—that would have suited my Grandmother Connor. Maybe she wouldn't have minded a certain amount of rest beyond the river, at that.

When we had the silent prayer, I looked at my father. He sat with his head bowed and his eyes closed. He was frowning deeply, and I could see the pulse in his temple. I wondered then what he believed. I did not have any real idea what it might be. When he raised his head, he did not look uplifted or anything like that. He merely looked tired. Then Reverend McKee pronounced the benediction, and we could go home.

"What do you think about all that stuff, Dad?" I asked hesitantly, as we walked.

"What stuff, honey?"

"Oh, Heaven and Hell, and like that."

My father laughed. "Have you been listening to Noreen too much? Well, I don't know. I don't think they're actual places. Maybe they stand for something that happens all the time here, or else doesn't happen. It's kind of hard to explain. I guess I'm not so good at explanations."

Nothing seemed to have been made any clearer to me. I reached out and took his hand, not caring that he might think this a babyish gesture.

"I hate that hymn!"

"Good Lord," my father said in astonishment. "Why, Vanessa?"

But I did not know and so could not tell him.

Many people in Manawaka had flu that winter, so my father and Dr. Cates were kept extremely busy. I had flu myself, and spent a week in bed, vomiting only the first day and after that enjoying poor health, as my mother put it, with Noreen bringing me ginger ale and orange juice, and each evening my father putting a wooden tongue-depressor into my mouth and peering down my throat, then smiling and saying he thought I might live after all.

Then my father got sick himself, and had to stay at home and go to bed. This was such an unusual occurrence that it amused me.

"Doctors shouldn't get sick," I told him.

"You're right," he said. "That was pretty bad management."

"Run along now, dear," my mother said.

That night I woke and heard voices in the upstairs hall. When I went out, I found my mother and Grandmother MacLeod, both in their dressing-gowns. With them was Dr. Cates. I did not go immediately to my mother, as I would have done only a year before. I stood in the doorway of my room, squinting against the sudden light.

"Mother—what is it?"

She turned, and momentarily I saw the look on her face before she erased it and put on a contrived calm.

"It's all right," she said. "Dr. Cates has just come to have a look at Daddy. You go on back to sleep."

The wind was high that night, and I lay and listened to it rattling the storm windows and making the dry and winter-stiffened vines of the Virginia creeper scratch like small persistent claws against the red brick. In the morning, my mother told me that my father had developed pneumonia.

Dr. Cates did not think it would be safe to move my father to the hospital. My mother began sleeping in the spare bedroom, and after she had been there for a few nights, I asked if I could sleep in there too. I thought she would be bound to ask me why, and I did not know what I would say, but she did not ask. She nodded, and in some way her easy agreement upset me.

That night Dr. Cates came again, bringing with him one of the nurses from the hospital. My mother stayed upstairs with them. I sat with Grandmother MacLeod in the living room. That was the last place in the world I wanted to be, but I thought she would be offended if I went off. She sat as straight and rigid as a totem pole, and embroidered away at the needlepoint cushion cover she was doing. I perched on the edge of the chesterfield and kept my eyes fixed on *The White Company* by Conan Doyle, and from time to time I turned a page. I had already read it three times before, but luckily Grandmother MacLeod did not know that. At nine o'clock she looked at her gold brooch watch, which she always wore pinned to her dress, and told me to go to bed, so I did that.

I wakened in darkness. At first, it seemed to me that I was in my own bed, and everything was as usual, with my parents in their room, and Roddie curled up in the crib in his room, and Grandmother MacLeod sleeping with her mouth open in her enormous spool bed, surrounded by half a dozen framed photos of Uncle Roderick and only one of my father, and Noreen snoring fitfully in the room next to mine, with the dark flames of her hair spreading out across the pillow, and the pink and silver motto cards from the Tabernacle stuck with adhesive tape onto the wall beside her bed—*Lean on Him, Emmanuel Is My Refuge, Rock of Ages Cleft for Me.*

Then in the total night around me, I heard a sound. It was my mother, and she was crying, not loudly at all, but from somewhere very deep inside her. I sat up in bed. Everything seemed to have stopped, not only time but my own heart and blood as well. Then my mother noticed that I was awake.

I did not ask her, and she did not tell me anything. There was no need. She held me in her arms, or I held her, I am not certain which. And after a while the first mourning stopped, too, as everything does sooner or later, for when the limits of endurance have been reached, then people must sleep.

In the days following my father's death, I stayed close beside my mother, and this was only partly for my own consoling. I also had the feeling that she needed my protection. I did not know from what, nor what I could possibly do, but something held me there. Reverend McKee called, and I sat with my grandmother and my mother in the living room. My mother told me I did not need to stay unless I wanted to, but I refused to go. What I thought chiefly was that he would speak of the healing power of prayer, and all that, and it would be bound to make my mother cry again. And in fact, it happened in just that way, but when it actually came, I could not protect her from this assault. I could only sit there and pray my own prayer, which was that he would go away quickly.

My mother tried not to cry unless she was alone or with me. I also tried, but neither of us was entirely successful. Grandmother MacLeod, on the other hand, was never seen crying, not even the day of my father's funeral. But that day, when we had returned to the house and she had taken off her black velvet overshoes and her heavy sealskin coat with its black fur that was the softest thing I had ever touched, she stood in the hallway and for the first time she looked unsteady. When I reached out instinctively towards her, she sighed.

"That's right," she said. "You might just take my arm while I go upstairs, Vanessa."

That was the most my Grandmother MacLeod ever gave in, to anyone's sight. I left her in her bedroom, sitting on the straight chair beside her bed and looking at the picture of my father that had been taken when he graduated from medical college. Maybe she was sorry now that she had only the one photograph of him, but whatever she felt, she did not say.

I went down into the kitchen. I had scarcely spoken to Noreen since my father's death. This had not been done on purpose. I simply had not seen her. I had not really seen anyone except my mother. Looking at Noreen now, I suddenly recalled the sparrow. I felt physically sick, remembering the fearful darting and plunging of those wings, and the fact that it was I who had opened the window and let it in. Then an inexplicable fury took hold of me, some terrifying need to hurt, burn, destroy. Absolutely without warning, either to her or to myself, I hit Noreen as hard as I could. When she swung around, appalled, I hit out at her once more, my arms and legs flailing. Her hands snatched at my wrists, and she held me, but still I continued to struggle, fighting blindly, my eyes tightly closed, as though she were a prison all around me and I was battling to get out. Finally, too shocked at myself to go on, I went limp in her grasp and she let me drop to the floor.

"Vanessa! I never done one single solitary thing to you, and here you go hitting and scratching me like that! What in the world has got into you?"

I began to say I was sorry, which was certainly true, but I did not say it. I could not say anything.

"You're not yourself, what with your dad and everything," she excused me. "I been praying every night that your dad is with God, Vanessa. I know he wasn't actually saved in the regular way, but still and all—"

"Shut up," I said.

Something in my voice made her stop talking. I rose from the floor and stood in the kitchen doorway.

"He didn't need to be saved," I went on coldly, distinctly. "And he is not in Heaven, because there is no Heaven. And it doesn't matter, see? *It doesn't matter!*"

Noreen's face looked peculiarly vulnerable now, her high wide cheekbones and puzzled childish eyes, and the thick russet tangle of her hair. I had not hurt her much before, when I hit her. But I had hurt her now, hurt her in some inexcusable way. Yet I sensed, too, that already she was gaining some satisfaction out of feeling sorrowful about my disbelief.

I went upstairs to my room. Momentarily I felt a sense of calm, almost of acceptance. "Rest beyond the river." I knew now what that meant. It meant Nothing. It meant only silence, forever.

Then I lay down on my bed and spent the last of my tears, or what seemed then to be the last. Because, despite what I had said to Noreen, it did matter. It mattered, but there was no help for it.

Everything changed after my father's death. The MacLeod house could not be kept up any longer. My mother sold it to a local merchant who subsequently covered the deep red of the brick over with yellow stucco. Something about the house had always made me uneasy—that tower room where Grandmother MacLeod's potted plants drooped in a lethargic and lime-green confusion, those long stairways and hidden places, the attic which I had always imagined to be dwelt in by the Spirits of the family dead, that gigantic portrait of the Duke of Wellington at the top of the stairs. It was never an endearing house. And yet when it was no longer ours, and when the Virginia creeper had been torn down and the dark walls turned to a light marigold, I went out of my way to avoid walking past, for it seemed to me that the house had lost the stern dignity that was its very heart.

Noreen went back to the farm. My mother and brother and myself moved into Grandfather Connor's house. Grandmother MacLeod went to live with Aunt Morag in Winnipeg. It was harder for her than for anyone, because so much of her life was bound up with the MacLeod house. She was fond of Aunt Morag, but that hardly counted. Her men were gone, her husband and her sons, and a family whose men are gone is no family at all. The day she left, my mother and I did not know what to say. Grandmother MacLeod looked even smaller than usual in her fur coat and her black velvet toque. She became extremely agitated about trivialities, and fussed about the possibility of the taxi not arriving on time. She had forbidden us to accompany her to the station. About my father, or the house, or anything important, she did not say a word. Then, when the taxi had finally arrived, she turned to my mother.

"Roddie will have Ewen's seal ring, of course, with the MacLeod crest on it," she said. "But there is another seal as well, don't forget, the larger one with the crest and motto. It's meant to be worn on a watch chain. I keep it in my jewelbox. It was Roderick's. Roddie's to have that, too, when I die. Don't let Morag talk you out of it."

During the Second World War, when I was seventeen and in love with an airman who did not love me, and desperately anxious to get away from Manawaka and from my grandfather's house, I happened one day to be going through the old mahogany desk that had belonged to my father. It had a number of small drawers inside, and I accidentally pulled one of these all the way out. Behind it there was another drawer, one I had not known about. Curiously, I opened it. Inside there was a letter written on almost transparent paper in a cramped angular handwriting. It began—*Cher Monsieur Ewen*—That was all I could make out, for the writing was nearly impossible to read and my French was not good. It was dated 1919. With it, there was a picture of a girl, looking absurdly old-fashioned to my eyes, like the faces on long-discarded calendars or chocolate boxes. But beneath the dated quality of the photograph, she seemed neither expensive nor cheap. She looked like what she probably had been—an ordinary middle-class girl, but in another country. She wore her hair in long ringlets, and her mouth was shaped into a sweetly sad posed smile like Mary Pickford's. That was all. There was nothing else in the drawer.

I looked for a long time at the girl, and hoped she had meant some momentary and unexpected freedom. I remembered what he had said to me, after I hadn't gone to the Remembrance Day parade.

"What are you doing, Vanessa?" my mother called from the kitchen.

"Nothing," I replied.

I took the letter and picture outside and burned them. That was all I could do for him. Now that we might have talked together, it was many years too late. Perhaps it would not have been possible anyway. I did not know.

As I watched the smile of the girl turn into scorched paper, I grieved for my father as though he had just died now.

■

Sam Selvon

Kevin Roberts

Sam Selvon (1923-) was born in Trinidad of Indian parents and began his career as a writer with the *Trinidad Guardian*. He moved to London in 1950 and for thirty years lived there as a writer, producing scripts for radio, television and film, short stories, and numerous novels. Among them latter are *The Lonely Londoners* (1956), *The Plains of Caroni* (1970), and *Moses Ascending* (1975). His first novel, *A Brighter Sun* (1952), has been acclaimed as a Caribbean classic; his early stories are collected in *Ways of Sunlight* (1957, reissued 1978). He came to Canada in 1979 and is now a Canadian citizen living in Calgary. *Moses Migrating*, a new novel, will be published in 1983; he has been appointed writer-in-residence at the University of Alberta for 1983-84.

RALPHIE AT THE RACES

Sam Selvon

Ralphie lost his image standing in front of the narrow mirror on the bathroom door of his apartment. No matter how much he twisted his head and hunched his shoulders to try and get a glimpse of the skin at the back of his neck, as he leaned sideways the upper part of his body just vanished off the mirror as if it had never existed. Eventually, persevering in the contortions, he was rewarded with his head at an awkward angle, but he froze in the position and gingerly brushed his fingertips on the area.

There was no doubt about it. He, a landed immigrant from tropical Trinidad only eleven degrees off the Equator, was sunburnt. The thin outer pigment of black was peeled away to reveal pink and even white patches.

What made matters worse as he stood there examining the rest of his body was the discovery of bumps on his arms from mosquito bites. In spite of himself Ralphie had to laugh. Sunburnt, *and* mosquito-bitten. Here he was in Calgary, in the "frozen north," just beginning to get accustomed to the weather, and if he wrote a letter home to tell them it was so hot that he was sunburnt for the first time in his life, and itching with mosquito bites, they would never believe him.

It was Friday morning, and in a way the hot summer was responsible for an unusual chain of circumstances which had started for Ralphie at the beginning of the week. On Monday, listening to the weather forecast predict an indefinite run of fine weather, he got to thinking that he was falling into a rut. He felt he should make some effort to get up and about, as there was so much he hadn't done or seen since he settled down in Calgary. He didn't want to be like so many other immigrants who get into a routine the day they find a job and a place to live and lose their original interest in the new environment and exploring the things about them. A good example was his best friend Angus, a fellow Trinidadian, who had been living in Calgary for seven years and was now a Canadian citizen, and hadn't even been up to the top of the Calgary Tower.

When Ralphie explained his feelings, Angus merely shrugged.

"I see the tower every day, man," he said, "what I want to go up there for, to catch birds?"

"You don't feel funny that you living here so long and up to now you haven't been?" Ralphie asked him.

"Why I should feel funny? I bet a lot of other people who born here haven't been either. Besides boy, the weather too hot these days to do anything."

"Too hot?" Ralphie scoffed. "A Trinidadian like you complaining that it's too hot?"

"Weather like this, the best place to be is the racetrack," Angus said. "Let the horses and the jockeys provide the action while you sit back, and at the same time you could come away with a few bucks in your pocket."

"You could also lose the shirt off your back," Ralphie reminded him, knowing that Angus spent all his spare time at the races.

"Not a bad idea in this kind of weather," Angus laughed.

"That's the trouble with you guys," Ralphie said, "you make a joke of everything. But I bet by the time the summer is over, I will know more about Calgary than you do."

"Good luck," Angus said, still laughing, "maybe you will be able to take me on a conducted tour of the city to see the sights and places of historic interest!"

"Laugh all you want," Ralphie retorted, "but I intend to take advantage of this good weather we're having."

But he almost had to give up the idea when he was driving to work on the Wednesday and his car broke down. Ironically enough, the damage was caused by his engine getting overheated with the temperature soaring into the upper twenties. And it was more trouble than he thought when he found it couldn't start. He had to be towed away, and the people at the garage told him it would take a couple of days and cost a hundred and fifty bucks.

It had not taken Ralphie long to realize that in this country without transport one might as well be stranded on a desert island. The only walking anyone did was to and from a parking lot, or shopping in the malls. But where would he find that sort of money with payday not until the following week? And what about his plans to get about and see the local sights? He had been thinking of driving to the mountains over the weekend—he'd heard about the cool mountain lakes, and felt sure that he would have no trouble tempting Angus to go along with him to get away from the hot and humid city for a while.

As he thought of Angus it occurred to him that friends were there to help a guy get out of a jam, and he phoned him and explained the situation. Angus said he didn't have the money right away, but he was sure he would have it by Friday and would lend it to him, no sweat.

Ralphie was so relieved that he did not mind having to leave the car. One of his workmates gave him a drop home that evening, but when he got up on Thursday he had to get to work by bus. It was only when he was using his own two feet to get to the bus stop that he realized how hot it really was. He was perspiring and out of breath. I must be out of shape, he thought, I ought to be doing some exercise.

That was why, during the lunch hour, instead of sitting in the cafeteria around the corner as he usually did, he bought a sandwich and took a stroll in the neighbourhood. It turned out to be more of an exploration, for he saw shops and business places that he never knew existed, and suddenly, at the end of a street, he came across a greenbelt area. It excited him—this was exactly the sort of thing he was telling Angus about, calling yourself a Calgarian, but ignorant of what the city was like just a couple of blocks or so from the place where you worked!

In spite of the heat Ralphie lingered in the area. There were other people about, some of them stretched out on the grass in the open baking in the sun . . . why should *he* grumble?

When he got home that evening he headed straight for the fridge, dying for an ice-cold beer, only to discover he had run short. If he had the car he could easily drive down to the liquor store. The thought was irritating—and so was his body, sore and itchy from his unaccustomed walk in the sun. Anyway, tomorrow was Friday, he'd get the money from Angus to pay for the car, thank God for that.

He reminded himself of this in the morning when he discovered the results of his lunchtime walk, and gave thanks again that the car was equipped with air conditioning. He was almost consoled when the phone rang and he answered.

It was Angus.

"You're early," Ralphie said.

"Yeah, I wanted to catch you before you went to work."

Something in Angus' tone alarmed Ralphie and he asked abruptly: "You got the money?"

"That's what I called about. I went to the races last night . . ." *and here it comes, Ralphie thought* . . . "and I lost. A streak of bad luck, boy . . ."

"Go on," Ralphie said, as Angus' voice trailed away.

"What d'you mean 'go on?' That's it, all I got left is about fifty bucks."

"You call yourself a friend?" Ralphie said bitterly, scratching his arm. "I got sunburn and mosquito bite walking about in the heat, and now you let me down. I was planning to go to the Rockies tomorrow, too."

"Look Ralphie, I'm sure I'll have it for you tonight, I can't be so bad-luck-ed twice in a row."

"You mean you're going back?"

"Sure. I can't miss the Wild Rose Stakes meeting, the stands will be packed. Why don't you give it a whirl?"

"I never been to a racetrack in my life, and I don't intend to start now."

"You could dump that old Chevvy and buy a new car."

"Yeah, I could lose the little money I got, too."

"At least think about it. With an expert like me you can't go wrong. If you change your mind give me a call and I'll pick you up after work."

All morning, as he went about his job in a downtown repository, Ralphie thought of Angus with mixed feelings. He was disappointed in his friend, but he could not help a grudging admiration for his carefree style and having the nerve to gamble on horses. Perhaps he himself was being too cautious, and should take a chance for once—how else could he pay for the car short of a miracle? If he tightened his belt, he could afford to risk about twenty-five dollars. Would that be enough? He hadn't the faintest clue. Maybe he'd have to dress for it—Canadians seemed to have special clothing for every damn thing, curling, golfing, baseball, fishing, ice-skating ... why not horse-racing? As his resistance weakened, he began to think of it as just another way to get out of the routine and do something different, which was just what he was planning all along.

Late in the afternoon he phoned Angus. "Look, about this evening . . ."

Angus didn't wait for him to finish. "That's great, boy, maybe you'll have beginner's luck."

"I haven't even been near to a horse all my life, Angus. I don't even know where the racetrack is."

"Stampede Park—I said I'd pick you up."

"Have I got to wear a jockey cap or something?"

Angus laughed so loudly Ralphie had to shift the phone off his ear. "Come on Ralphie, you're not as dumb as all that.

Look, just get a paper and study the form, if you like. I'll pick you up after work, okay?"

Before Ralphie could raise any more objections or questions Angus hung up on him.

When they got to Stampede Park that evening, Ralphie had made up his mind about two things. The first was he wasn't going to make himself appear a complete fool to Angus even if he had to bluff and bluster. The second was that he was going to be careful and hold on tight to his money. No bets in the first race, or the second, or even the third and fourth. He would case the joint, as it were, and feel his way into this new experience before he invested any part of his twenty-five bucks—well, twenty-three, he corrected himself, deducting the two-dollar entrance fee which he felt Angus should have paid, and thinking uneasily that he was down two bucks already and he hadn't even seen a horse or heard one neigh.

Angus was anxious to get doing. He wore a cap which he assured Ralphie had nothing to do with the attire of race-goers ("it always bring me good luck if I wear it") and a pair of binoculars dangled on his chest from a leather strap around his neck ("I will lend it to you now and then if you want to get a close-up of the race; I bought it with my first winnings.")

As they went through the turnstiles and walked towards the pavilion, Angus said, "We mustn't miss the daily double."

"Yeah," Ralphie muttered, feeling ill-at-ease and gazing around at the crowds of people moving about in complete familiarity with their surroundings. He also suspected that Angus was trying to impress him, putting on airs as if he was the Chief Steward of the meeting or something: as they were passing some stairs he gestured and said, "When I'm in the money I go up there to the clubhouse, but seeing as this is your first visit I'll stick around with you—or rather, you stick around with me."

"I'll be okay, don't worry about me," Ralphie said.

They went out to the open stands and Angus led Ralphie to his usual place in the back row of the yellow section. Once seated he immediately became engrossed in studying the form, checking the list of horses and jockeys, what time they made at previous meetings, and what tips he could get from the newspapers: he even looked up at the sky as if seeking a sign from the few puffy clouds that drifted above the park.

All of which had Ralphie baffled, he could not make head or tail of it as Angus frowned and concentrated like he was trying to work out Einstein's theory of relativity. Ralphie looked across the central stage or platform at the tote board flashing figures and letters on and off giving information which was totally useless to him, how could anyone make sense of it?

Suddenly a woman came out on the platform, dressed up like English people when they are going to chase the foxes with the hounds. She had a bugle under her arm and she marched up like a soldier to a microphone and she played a little tune, army reveille or something it sounded like to Ralphie.

"Where's the rest of the band?" Ralphie asked, hopeful for some music to divert his thoughts.

"Ten minutes to go," Angus muttered, "you putting anything on the daily double?"

"I will hold my horses for a while," Ralphie said, unconsciously making the pun.

The riders began to come out on the track to warm up and get in position for the start.

"Number five look good," Ralphie volunteered, for no other reason than the feeling that he had to say something.

"You think so?" Angus frowned like a man tortured by indecisions, and consulted the program. "Two point eleven . . . two point ten . . . that's the worse time in the lot."

"All the same, if I was you I would put my money on number five," Ralphie persisted.

"I am taking number three, and number six for the second race," Angus said. "Take it from me, that's the best bet."

"Six is an unlucky number," Ralphie was beginning to enjoy his deception. "I would chose seven if I was you."

Angus chuckled. "Boy, I could understand why you keep away from the racetrack, and leave it to the experts like me!" And he went off to place his bet.

Needless to say, number five came in first, and in the second race, number seven finished a whole length in front of the others.

"And they're paying three hundred bucks for the double," Angus said mournfully.

"What!" Ralphie sat up. He couldn't believe it, although Angus pointed it out on the tote board, and said that if he had only had a little guts to bet a mere two dollars, he would have had three hundred in his pocket now.

"Three hundred and twenty-three, including my capital," Ralphie choked.

Angus was too much the regular gambler to let it upset him, but Ralphie did a hop and a dance in dismay.

"I lost my chance, I lost my chance!" He wailed.

"It got other races," Angus said. "And besides, look at all the other losers."

"I don't see any! Everybody win excepting me!"

"Cool it. Can't you see all those bits of paper scattered around," Angus waved a hand about the stands, already the ground was strewn with discarded tickets. "Forget what's gone, man, that's spilt milk, water under the bridge. See what you could do in the next race."

"That's easy for a hardened gambler like you to say," Ralphie could not recover from the blow. He got up and wandered about the stands with his hands in his pockets, kicking disgustedly at any tickets he saw on the ground. Lady Luck had smiled at him and he had spurned her advances. He went out on the grounds and leaned against the rails, and as the horses came around the last bend he imagined they were running the first two races again and this time he had bet every cent he had.

He was so bitter and disappointed he was tempted to get out of Stampede Park and go home, but he came across the Rodeo Bar as he strayed about. Perhaps a double scotch chased with a beer might console him.

As he sipped the drink he did feel better, and he thought, what the hell, I might as well have another, at least I'm enjoying this instead of trusting my money on jockeys and horses that I know nothing about—and I'm not the only one, if you ask me the bar doing more business than the races!

"I had the daily double," he said conversationally to a stranger standing next to him.

"Yeah?" the man replied, "you caught them, eh?"

"Yeah." Ralphie drained his glass. "But I didn't bet."

"Tough luck." He gave Ralphie a curious glance and turned back to his own friends.

Ralphie wasn't sure how long he'd been away, but when he got back Angus asked him if he'd won anything.

"I wasn't betting," he replied. "Just moseying around ."

"Well, a quinella is coming up now."

"Quin-ella? Where?"

"Pick two horses, it doesn't matter which comes in first or second."

"Oh yeah, quinella . . . how've you been doing, you make a big kill yet?"

"Not too good, Ralphie. You better start betting if you want that car for the weekend. You didn't pick up any tips on your wanderings?"

Ralphie took a random peep at the program. "Sure, I heard two Chinese guys arguing about *Ruby Morning* and *Victor Brave Boy* for that quinella thing."

"Yeah?" Angus was too experienced a punter to take any tip lightly, no matter from what source. Many times he'd stood behind some Chinese guy in the payout line and seen him strain to pick up the load of notes he'd won. But when he looked up the card selections he read "continues to disappoint" for one, and "needs mini-miracle" for the other. He shook his head and went back to his own convictions and calculations.

The girl in the fox-hunting garb came out and blew her bugle and the horses came out for a preliminary canter. Ralphie was too miserable to care. He had ten dollars left and was just impatient to get home and forget the whole thing.

"Jesus!" Angus exclaimed as the race ended, tossing away his tickets like so many other. "Victor Brave Boy and Ruby Morning! Man, this is *twice* you make a correct forecast and you didn't bet!"

"Because I am a moron, the most stupid man in Calgary!" This time Ralphie was on the verge of tears.

"The most stupid here today, that's for sure. I don't know how you do it, boy, but whatever it is, it works. And you better stop depending on me to take the car out, I just lost again."

"Let's go home." Ralphie was dejected. "I never coming back to a racetrack again. This must be a sign that I should never gamble."

"The last race is coming up," Angus said. "Cowards die many times before their deaths is one saying, but they have another, which is 'third time lucky.' In fact, I will go against my better judgement and back your tip. Look at this list of eight horses and pick the winner."

But Ralphie had nothing to say. He hung his head in utter despair, and his eyes couldn't even focus properly on the clusters of unlucky tickets lying at his feet and around him. If he had had the courage to buy one, *just one*, his worries would have been over.

Suddenly he stood up and without a word to Angus he

strode off determinedly to the nearest betting window. For a moment he paused, wondering what to say. Then he pulled the ten dollars out and put the money down and shut his eyes and said, "All that on the last race."

The girl looked at him. "What bet?"

"Oh. Ah. To win."

"What horse . . . what number?"

"Er . . . number ten."

She smiled a little. "There's no number ten running in this race."

"Oh. What's the next number, nine?" he asked.

"You want ten dollars on number nine to win?"

"Yeah, yeah. That's it."

He rejoined Angus silently and sat down.

Angus left him alone, except for a quick glance of sympathy. Like a true punter, he appreciated what agonies a man suffered when he did not take advantage of an inspired forecast and watched the horse come in a winner. Ralphie had a lot to learn, though, he should not give up, he should take his blows like a man and come out fighting in the next rounds.

Through the race Ralphie kept his head down and forced himself to think of anything but horses. Already he was regretting his rashness, he would be leaving the racetrack without a cent in his pocket, couldn't even afford to buy some lotion from the drugstore for his sunburn, though it didn't bother him much unless he touched the tender skin . . . as for driving to the mountains over the weekend, well, it was just too bad, he would have to wait until next payday . . .

He tried not to listen to the commentator's excited voice as the race progressed, but Angus's yelling was too close to shut out.

"Number eight! Come on eight! That's it baby, come on! It's eight! Eight in the lead!"

And that's the end of that, he told himself, let it be a lesson to you, better to spend your money on women and drink . . .

Then he heard Angus swearing. "Oh hell . . . it's a photo-finish, there's an inquiry . . ."

Photo-finish? Inquiry? Was that the name of a horse or something? Perhaps they would have to run the race again, and this time . . . this time . . .

After what seemed ages he heard Angus swearing again. "Blast it! Eight come in second . . . nine is the winner!"

Ralphie looked up and gaped at Angus. "Nine? Win?"

"Yeah. You bet on nine?"

He couldn't speak. He was trembling with excitement and could barely lift his hand to show Angus the ticket.

"Jesus, nine was a rank outsider, Ralphie! You must have hit it rich, boy!"

As they moved to go inside Angus was so elated for his bewildered friend that he clapped him heartily on the shoulders and was about to voice congratulations again when Ralphie let out a mighty yell of pain.

"Oh Christ, Angus, my sunburn!" He hunched and staggered a little and the ticket slipped from his nervous fingers, but he grabbed wildly on the ground for it, elbowing in the jostling crowd.

"Sorry, Ralphie . . . I forgot all about that in the excitement . . . I'll just check the full results on the telly, you better join the payline before it get too big."

Ralphie was among the first winners, so excited that he was breathing in short gasps and trying to control his body from shaking.

When he put his ticket down the cashier looked at it closely then frowned at him.

"You've made a mistake."

"Yeah." He was grinning all over his face and the words did not register until she spoke again.

"This is for the ninth race, and it isn't a winning number. Move aside and check it, please."

Looking for Ralphie, Angus found him down on all fours near the spot where he had dropped the ticket, scrambling about hopelessly in the litter of betting tokens and muttering to himself like a madman.

■

Brenda Riches

Theresa Heuchert

Brenda Riches (1942-) was born in Jubbulpore, India, and moved to England at the age of four. She came to Saskatoon in 1974 and began writing seriously after she came into contact with Saskatchewan writers. She now lives in Regina and writes both short fiction and poetry. Her work has appeared in *Grain, The Capilano Review, event, Dandelion, Fiddlehead,* and *Freelance,* as well as the anthologies *The Story So Far* (5) and *The Best of Grain.* "Gall" is included in her first book, a collection of poems and stories called *Dry Media,* published by Turnstone Press (1980). She is fiction editor of *Grain* magazine.

GALL

Brenda Riches

September 13

Her name is Sara. The new girl, the intruder. Red-haired
Sara with the fluttering eyes. Who does she think she is,
prancing in and choosing the desk in front of Matthew? Who
is she, that she gets A's first time?

If they gave marks for what I'm good at I'd get A's. But
what would you know about that, precious Mrs. Kirk? You're
married to your damn classroom, your withered old specimens.

Those who can't, teach. And today we did the nuptial
flight of bees. It figures. Matthew's all eyes for the sleek head
in front of him. They'd have garish children, those two.
Swarming creatures with striped red and yellow hair.

She can have him. I don't care.

October 13

Today Mrs. Kirk brought a dead stem of goldenrod and
told us the lump on it was a gall. It's an abnormal growth
induced by a parasite, she told us, and we had to study it and
write down our observations.

I wish I could grow on Matthew.

Gall: 1) Before dissection. (I wrote)

This swelling has forced veins to pull and widen, and
magnified the colour so that you can see clearly the
shades of silken sand that harbour the grub, the tracery
that shelters it. The veins have pulled the skin inwards
and I am aware of stress because the parts between have
a bloated shape like a peeled tangerine. The swelling is
dry and rigid, and when I tap it against my thumb the
stem vibrates.

2) After dissection.

The insect is puffy in its tight cavity. The razor has
exposed it and I prod it with the ribby stem of the dead
plant. I prod. It's like gelatine. The inner faces of the
segments are polished chalk under my fingers.

Mrs. Kirk read it through quickly and told me I was supposed to be recording not romanticising, that I shouldn't use

first person in scientific observation and that you can't mag-
nify colour. Sara smiled into her book. She got the best mark
of course. She's so *precise.* Matthew commented that gall is
also that bitter stuff we carry inside us somewhere. Mrs. Kirk
said he should make his comments more accurate and told
him to go and look up the word in a recognized dictionary.
Sara's invited Matthew to Thanksgiving dinner. She hasn't
wasted any time, wasping her way in.

November 13

Mrs. Kirk, dear Mrs. Kirk. Cast your eye on this observation. Will you give it an A?

GALL

At the butterfly brief time of the year when lakes have frozen and before snow covers the ice, I skated. The lake was
fringed with cattails, reeds and tall gatherings of pampas. I
arrived at noon in the clear expectation that the sun would
cover the ice and I would skate on gold glass. It would be an
afternoon lifted out of time, precious and unreal.
Not so. Skating in the direction of my shadow I was on ice
that was grey and black and pitted with trapped bubbles. Little clusters of shredded snow rested like feathers on the surface, and dead leaves were caught on the tops of some of
these, so that when I pulled one off it left its imprint behind
as a glass fossil.
As I skated towards the bend of the lake, it pleased me to
see Sara's face beneath the ice. I stopped for a better look. It
was under a part that was cracked, and the jagged edges cut
through her face from just above her left eye, and continued
diagonally, severing her nose from which spurted a dark red
weed, then took a vertical course splitting her soft mouth.
Tributary cracks webbed outwards to break her hair close to
the scalp, below her ears and level with her throat. The geo-
graphy of disfigurement was entrancing. I glided about
twenty feet away, turned, and skimmed back over her.

December 13

It hasn't stopped snowing for three days. Even when I
close my eyes all I can see is white. It's as if the ground and
my brain, both of them together, were being wrapped for
burial.

I can't sleep. If I keep Sara under the lake she will feed on its rank and winter feast. She will turn into something with wings.

January 13

Sara is oppressive like a sky that stretches over me, a smothering grey that reaches all the way down to my horizon. Matthew has offered to teach her how to ski. He leaned forward when Mrs. Kirk wasn't looking (when does she ever really look?), touched the back of Sara's neck lightly with one finger, and she turned to face him. He whispered very quietly, but I heard what he said, and I saw her eyes light up. I wanted to throw icy water at them. That would be really something. Sara of the spitting eyes.

February 13

Sara skis *incredibly* well. She must do. Matthew has said so five times so far. Another A for Sara.

Mrs. Kirk is droning on about the way bees dance. On and on like a buzz saw. My eyes are closed.

Sara skis. Yes, I can see her. Sending her body along tracks Matthew has made for her. Sara the quiet shadow, trailing behind him with a noise like taffeta. Now she falls in the snow. She sits up, laughing. He pulls her to her feet and brushes the snow off her clothes. Now they've come to a dusk of pine trees. Sara and Matthew moth-winging to a dark place where they will kiss.

March 13

Today the sun shining through the window pane woke up a bluebottle. Its glossy buzzing lulled me. Its wings were thin. So thin. How could they send that full body winging through the air? Mrs. Kirk complained about the noise so Sara squished it dead with her thumb. I wish Matthew had been in the room to see her smile as she did it.

April 13

Matthew looks different. He's wearing a loose yellow shirt. Even Mrs. Kirk commented. Button your shirt, Matthew, she told him. Sara is flighty in a new dress. Her mouth is gaudy with lip gloss.

I've written a poem.

Butterfly

Painted lady
I'm watching you
flapping there
over my yellow flower.
How would you like
to be pinned
under glass?
How would you like
to be spread
permanently.

May 13

Earlier this evening I walked down Matthew's back lane.
Your fence has gaps in it, Matthew. You should do something about that. Get your backside off the grass and mend
your rotten fence.

What keeps you on the grass, Matthew? Sara the scarlet
flounce? Tumble-skirted Sara who wants you to smooth her
out with your sunwarmed hands?

June 13

At four o'clock I watched them walk out of school. They
were holding hands. Their fingers were so twisted together
that they looked like one grotesque knot.

Sara and Matthew. Knotted together.

"It's an abnormal growth, induced by a parasite."

■

Alice Munro

Alice Munro (1931-) was born in Wingham, Ontario, lived for twenty years in British Columbia and now makes her home in Clinton, Ontario. Her first collection of short stories, *Dance of the Happy Shades* (1968) won the Governor General's Award for fiction. She is the author of the novel *Lives of Girls and Women* (1971), and further collections of short stories, *Something I've Been Meaning To Tell You* (1974), *Who Do You Think You Are?* (1978) and *The Moons of Jupiter* (1982). Several of her stories, including "The Peace of Utrecht" and "A Trip to the Coast", have been made into films.

FORGIVENESS IN FAMILIES

Alice Munro

I've often thought, suppose I had to go to a psychiatrist, and he would want to know about my family background, naturally, so I would have to start telling him about my brother, and he wouldn't even wait till I was finished, would he, the psychiatrist, he'd commit me.

I said that to Mother; she laughed. "You're hard on that boy, Val."

"Boy," I said. *"Man."*

She laughed, she admitted it. "But remember," she said, "the Lord loves a lunatic."

"How do you know," I said, "seeing you're an atheist?"

Some things he couldn't help. Being born, for instance. He was born the week I started school, and how's that for timing? I was scared, it wasn't like now when the kids have been going to play-school and kindergarten for years. I was going to school for the first time and all the other kids had their mothers with them and where was mine? In the hospital having a baby. The embarrassment to me. There was a lot of shame about those things then.

It wasn't his fault getting born and it wasn't his fault throwing up at my wedding. Think of it. The floor, the table, he even managed to hit the cake. He was not drunk, as some people thought, he really did have some violent kind of flu, which Haro and I came down with, in fact, on our honeymoon. I never heard of anybody else with any kind of flu throwing up over a table with a lace cloth and silver candlesticks and wedding cake on it, but you could say it was bad luck; maybe everybody else when the need came on them was closer to a toilet. And everybody else might try a little harder to hold back, they just might, because nobody else is quite so special, quite so center-of-the-universe, as my baby brother. Just call him a child of nature. That was what he called himself, later on.

I will skip over what he did between getting born and throwing up at my wedding except to say that he had asthma and got to stay home from school weeks on end, listening to soap operas. Sometimes there was truce between us, and I would get him to tell me what happened every day on "Big

Sisters" and "Road of Life" and the one with Gee-Gee and Papa David. He was very good at remembering all the characters and getting all the complications straight, I'll say that, and he did read a lot in *Gateways to Bookland*, that lovely set Mother bought for us and that he later sneaked out of the house and sold, for ten dollars, to a secondhand book dealer. Mother said he could have been brilliant at school if he wanted to be. That's a deep one, your brother, she used to say, he's got some surprises in store for us. She was right, he had.

He started staying home permanently in Grade Ten after a little problem of being caught in a cheating-ring that was getting math tests from some teacher's desk. One of the janitors was letting him back in the classroom after school because he said he was working on a special project. So he was, in his own way. Mother said he did it to make himself popular, because he had asthma and couldn't take part in sports.

Now. Jobs. The question comes up, what is such a person as my brother—and I ought to give him a name at least, his name is Cam, for Cameron, Mother thought that would be a suitable name for a university president or honest tycoon (which was the sort of thing she planned for him to be)— what is he going to do, how is he going to make a living? Until recently the country did not pay you to sit on your uppers and announce that you had adopted a creative life-style. He got a job first as a movie usher. Mother got it for him, she knew the manager, it was the old International Theatre over on Blake Street. He had to quit, though, because he got this darkness-phobia. All the people sitting in the dark he said gave him a crawly feeling, very peculiar. It only interfered with him working as an usher, it didn't interfere with him going to the movies on his own. He got very fond of movies. In fact, he spent whole days sitting in movie houses, sitting through every show twice then going to another theatre and sitting through what was there. He had to do something with his time, because Mother and all of us believed he was working then in the office of the Greyhound Bus Depot. He went off to work at the right time every morning and came home at the right time every night, and he told all about the cranky old man in charge of the office and the woman with curvature of the spine who had been there since 1919 and how mad she got at the young girls chewing gum, oh, a lively story, it would have worked up to

something as good as the soap operas if Mother hadn't
phoned up to complain about the way they were
withholding his pay cheque—due to a technical error in the
spelling of his name, he said—and found out he'd quit in the
middle of his second day.

Well. Sitting in movies was better than sitting in beer
parlours, Mother said. At least he wasn't on the street getting
in with criminal gangs. She asked him what his favourite
movie was and he said *Seven Brides for Seven Brothers.* See,
she said, he is interested in an outdoor life, he is not suited to
office work. So she sent him to work for some cousins of hers
who have a farm in the Fraser Valley. I should explain that
my father, Cam's and mine, was dead by this time, he died
away back when Cam was having asthma and listening to
soap operas. It didn't make much difference, his dying
because he worked as a conductor on the P.G.E. when it
started at Squamish, and he lived part of the time in Lillooet.
Nothing changed, Mother went on working at Eaton's as she
always had, going across on the ferry and then on the bus; I
got supper, she came trudging up the hill in the winter dark.

Cam took off from the farm, he complained that the
cousins were religious and always after his soul. Mother
could see his problem, she had after all brought him up to be
a freethinker. He hitchhiked east. From time to time a letter
came. A request for funds. He had been offered a job in
northern Quebec if he could get the money together to get up
there. Mother sent it. He sent word the job had folded, but he
didn't send back the money. He and two friends were going
to start a turkey farm. They sent us plans, estimates. They
were supposed to be working on contract for the Purina
Company, nothing could go wrong. The turkeys were
drowned in a flood, after Mother had sent him money and we
had too against our better judgment. Everywhere that boy
hits turns into a disaster area, Mother said. If you read it in a
book you wouldn't believe it, she said. It's so terrible it's
funny.

She knew. I used to go over to see her on Wednesday
afternoon—her day off—pushing the stroller with Karen in
it, and later Tommy in it and Karen walking beside, up
Lonsdale and down King's Road, and what would we always
end up talking about? That boy and I, we are getting a
divorce, she said. I am definitely going to write him off. What
good will he ever be until he stops relying on me, she asked. I
kept my mouth shut, more or less. She knew my opinion. But

she ended up every time saying, "He was a nice fellow to have around the house, though. Good company. That boy could always make me laugh."

Or, "He had a lot to contend with, his asthma and no dad. He never did intentionally hurt a soul."

"One good thing he did," she said, "you could really call it a good turn. That girl."

Referring to the girl who came and told us she had been engaged to him, in Hamilton, Ontario, until he told her he could never get married because he had just found out there was hereditary fatal kidney disease in his family. He wrote her a letter. And she came looking for him to tell him it didn't matter. Not at all a bad-looking girl. She worked for the Bell Telephone. Mother said it was a lie told out of kindness, to spare her feelings when he didn't want to marry her. I said it was a kindness, anyway, because she would have been supporting him for the rest of her life.

Though it might have eased things up a bit on the rest of us.

But that was then and now is now and as we all know times have changed. Cam is finding it easier. He lives at home, off and on, has for a year and a half. His hair is thin in front, not surprising in a man thirty-four years of age, but shoulder-length behind, straggly, graying. He wears a sort of rough brown robe that looks as if it might be made out of a sack (is that what sackcloth is supposed to be, I said to Haro, I wouldn't mind supplying the ashes), and hanging down on his chest he has all sorts of chains, medallions, crosses, elk's teeth or whatnot. Rope sandals on his feet. Some friend of his makes them. He collects welfare. Nobody asks him to work. Who could be so cruel? If he has to write down his occupation he writes priest.

It's true. There is a whole school of them, calling themselves priests, and they have a house over in Kitsilano, Cam stays there too sometimes. They're in competition with the Hare Krishna bunch, only these ones don't chant, they just walk around smiling. He has developed this voice I can't stand, a very thin, sweet voice, all on one level. It makes me want to stand in front of him and say, "There's an earthquake in Chile, two hundred thousand people just died, they've burned up another village in Vietnam, famine as usual in India." Just to see if he'd keep saying, "Ve-ery ni-ice, ve-ery ni-ice," that sweet way. He won't eat meat, of course, he eats whole-grain cereals and leafy vegetables. He came into the kitchen where I was slicing beets—beets being forbidden, a root vegetable—and, "I hope you understand that you're committing murder," he said.

"No," I said, "but I'll give you sixty seconds to get out of here or I may be."

So as I say he's home part of the time now and he was there on the Monday night when Mother got sick. She was vomiting. A couple of days before this he had started her on a vegetarian diet—she was always promising him she'd try it—and he told her she was vomiting up all the old poisons stored up in her body from eating meat and sugar and so on. He said it was a good sign, and when she had it all vomited out she'd feel better. She kept vomiting, and she didn't feel better, but he had to go out. Monday nights is when they have the weekly meeting at the priests' house, where they chant and burn incense or celebrate the black mass, for all I know. He stayed out most of the night, and when he got home he found Mother unconscious on the bathroom floor. He got on the phone and phoned *me*.

"I think you better come over here and see if you can help Mom, Val."

"What's the matter with her?"

"She's not feeling very well."

"What's the matter with her? Put her on the phone."

"I can't."

"Why can't you?"

I swear he tittered. "Well I'm afraid she's passed out."

I called the ambulance and sent them for her, that was how she got to the hospital, five o'clock in the morning. I called her family doctor, he got over there, and he got Dr. Ellis Bell, one of the best-known heart men in the city, because that was what they had decided it was, her heart. I got dressed and woke Haro and told him and then I drove myself over to the Lions Gate Hospital. They wouldn't let me in till ten o'clock. They had her in Intensive Care. I sat outside Intensive Care in their slick little awful waiting room. They had red slippery chairs, cheap covering, and a stand full of pebbles with green plastic leaves growing up. I sat there hour after hour and read *The Reader's Digest*. The jokes. Thinking this is how it is, this is it, really, she's dying. Now, this moment, behind those doors, dying. Nothing stops or holds off for it the way you somehow and against all your sense believe it will. I thought about Mother's life, the part of it I knew. Going to work every day, first on the ferry then on the bus. Shopping at the old Red-and-White then at the new Safeway—new, fifteen years old! Going down to the Library one night a week, taking me with her, and we would come home on the bus with our load of books and a bag of grapes we bought at the Chinese place, for a treat. Wednesday afternoon too when my kids were small and I went over there to drink coffee and she rolled us cigarettes on that contraption she had. And I thought, all these things don't seem that much like life, when you're doing them, they're just what you do, how you fill up your days, and you think all the time something is going to crack open, and you'll find yourself, *then* you'll find yourself, in life. It's not even that you particularly want this to happen, this cracking open, you're comfortable enough the way things are, but you do expect it. Then you're dying, Mother is dying, and it's just the same plastic chairs and plastic plants and ordinary day outside with people getting groceries and what you've had is all there is, and going to the Library, just a thing like that, coming back up the hill on the bus with books and a bag of grapes seems now worth wanting, O God doesn't it, you'd break your heart wanting back there.

When they let me in to see here she was bluish-gray in the face and her eyes were not all-the-way closed, but they had rolled up, the slit that was open showed the whites. She always looked terrible with her teeth out, anyway, wouldn't let us see her. Cam teased her vanity. They were out now. So all the time, I thought, all the time even when she was young it was in her that she was going to look like this.

They didn't hold out hope. Haro came and took a look at her and put his arm around my shoulders and said, "Val, you'll have to be prepared." He meant well but I couldn't talk to him. It wasn't his mother and he couldn't remember anything. That wasn't his fault but I didn't want to talk to him, I didn't want to listen to him telling me I better be prepared. We went and ate something in the hospital cafeteria.

"You better phone Cam," Haro said.

"Why?"

"He'll want to know."

"Why do you think he'll want to know? He left her alone last night and he didn't know enough to get an ambulance when he came in and found her this morning."

"Just the same. He has a right. Maybe you ought to tell him to get over here."

"He is probably busy this moment preparing to give her a hippie funeral."

But Haro persuaded me as he always can and I went and phoned. No answer. I felt better because I had phoned, and justified in what I had said because of Cam not being in. I went back and waited, by myself.

About seven o'clock that night Cam turned up. He was not alone. He had brought along a tribe of co-priests, I suppose they were, from that house. They all wore the same kind of outfit he did, the brown sacking nightgown and the chains and crosses and holy hardware, they all had long hair, they were all a good many years younger than Cam, except for one old man, really old, with a curly gray beard and bare feet—in March, bare feet—and no teeth. I swear this old man didn't have a clue what was going on. I think they picked him up down by the Salvation Army and put that outfit on him because they needed an old man for a kind of mascot, or extra holiness, or something.

Cam said, "This is my sister Valerie. This is Brother Michael. This is Brother John, this Brother Louis." Etc., etc.

"They haven't said anything to give me hope, Cam. She is dying."

"We hope not," said Cam with his secret smile. "We spent the day working for her."

"Do you mean praying?" I said.

"Work is a better word to describe it than praying, if you don't understand what it is."

Well of course, I never understand.

"Real praying is work, believe me," says Cam and they all smile at me, his way. They can't keep still, like children who have to go to the bathroom they're weaving and jiggling and doing little steps.

"Now where's her room?" says Cam in a practical tone of voice.

I thought of Mother dying and through that slit between her lids—who knows, maybe she can see from time to time— seeing this crowd of dervishes celebrating around her bed. Mother who lost her religion when she was thirteen and went to the Unitarian Church and quit when they had the split about crossing God out of the hymns (she was for it), Mother having to spend her last conscious minutes wondering what had happened, if she was transported back in history to where loonies cavorted around in their crazy ceremonies, trying to sort her last reasonable thoughts out in the middle of their business.

Thank God the nurse said no. The intern was brought and he said no. Cam didn't insist, he smiled and nodded at them as if they are granting permission and then he brought the troupe back into the waiting room and there, right before my eyes, they started. They put the old man in the centre, sitting down with his head bowed and his eyes shut—they had to tap him and remind him how to do that—and they squatted in a rough sort of circle round him, facing in and out, in and out, alternately. Then, eyes closed, they started swaying back and forth moaning some words very softly, only not the same words, it sounded as if each one of them had got different words, and not in English of course but Swahili or Sanskrit or something. It got louder, gradually it got louder, a pounding singsong, and as it did they rose to their feet, all except the old man who stayed where he was and looked as if he might have gone to sleep, sitting, and they began a shuffling kind of dance where they stood, clapping, not very well in time. They did this for a long while, and the noise they were making, though it was not terribly loud, attracted the nurses from their station and nurses' aids and orderlies and a few people like me who were waiting, and nobody seemed to know what to do, because it was so unbelievable, so crazy in that ordinary little waiting room. Everybody just stared as if they were asleep and dreaming and expecting to wake up. Then a nurse came out of Intensive Care and said, "We can't have this disturbance. What do you think you're doing here?"

She took hold of one of the young ones and shook him by the shoulder, else she couldn't have got anybody to stop and pay attention.

"We're working to help a woman who's very sick," he told her.

"I don't know what you call working, but you're not helping anybody. Now I'm asking you to clear out of here. Excuse me. I'm not asking. I'm telling."

"You're very mistaken if you think the tones of our voices are hurting or disturbing any sick person. This whole ceremony is pitched at a level which will reach and comfort the unconscious mind and draw the demonic influences out of the body. It's a ceremony that goes back five thousand years."

"Good Lord," said the nurse, looking stupefied as well she might. "Who are these people?"

I had to go and enlighten her, telling her that it was my

brother and what you might call his friends, and I was not in on their ceremony. I asked about Mother, was there any change.

"No change," she said. "What do we have to do to get them out of here?"

"Turn the hose on them," one of the orderlies said, and all this time, the dance, or ceremony, never stopped, and the one who had stopped and done the explaining went back to dancing too, and I said to the nurse, "I'll phone in to see how she is, I'm going home for a little while." I walked out of the hospital and found to my surprise that it was dark. The whole day in there, dark to dark. In the parking lot I started to cry. Cam has turned this into a circus for his own benefit, I said to myself, and said it out loud when I got home.

Haro made me a drink.

"It'll probably get into the papers," I said. "Cam's chance for fame."

Haro phoned the hospital to see if there was any news and they said there wasn't. "Did they have—was there any difficulty with some young people in the waiting room this evening? Did they leave quietly?" Haro is ten years older than I am, a cautious man, too patient with everybody. I used to think he was sometimes giving Cam money I didn't know about.

"They left quietly," he said. "Don't worry about the papers. Get some sleep."

I didn't mean to but I fell asleep on the couch, after the drink and the long day. I woke up with the phone ringing and day lightening the room. I stumbled into the kitchen dragging the blanket Haro had put over me and saw by the clock on the wall it was a quarter to six. She's gone, I thought.

It was her own doctor.

He said he had encouraging news. He said she was much better this morning.

I dragged over a chair and collapsed in it, both arms and my head too down on the kitchen counter. I came back on the phone to hear him saying she was still in a critical phase and the next forty-eight hours would tell the story, but without raising my hopes too high he wanted me to know she was responding to treatment. He said that was especially surprising in view of the fact that she had been late getting to hospital and the things they did to her at first did not seem to have much effect, though of course the fact that she survived the first few hours at all was a good sign. Nobody had made much of this good sign to me yesterday, I thought.

I sat there for an hour at least after I had hung up the phone. I made a cup of instant coffee and my hands were shaking so I could hardly get the water into the cup, then couldn't get the cup to my mouth. I let it go cold. Haro came out in his pyjamas at last. He gave me one look and said, "Easy, Val. Has she gone?"

"She's some better. She's responding to treatment."

"The look of you I thought the other."

"I'm so amazed."

"I wouldn't 've given five cents for her chances yesterday noon."

"I know. I can't believe it."

"It's the tension." Haro said. "I know. You build yourself up ready for something bad to happen and then when it doesn't, it's a queer feeling, you can't feel good right away, it's almost like a disappointment."

Disappointment. That was the word that stayed with me. I was so glad, really, grateful, but underneath I was thinking, so Cam didn't kill her after all, with his carelessness and craziness and going out and neglecting her he didn't kill her, and I was, yes, I was, sorry in some part of me to find out that was true. And I knew Haro knew this but wouldn't speak of it to me, ever. That was the real shock to me, why I kept shaking. Not whether Mother lived or died. It was what was so plain about myself.

Mother got well, she pulled through beautifully. After she rallied she never sank back. She was in the hospital three weeks and then she came home, and rested another three weeks, and after that went back to work, cutting down a bit and working ten to four instead of full days, what they call the housewives' shift. She told everybody about Cam and his friends coming to the hospital. She began to say things like, "Well, that boy of mine may not be much of a success at anything else but you have to admit he has a knack of saving lives." Or, "Maybe Cam should go into the miracle business, he certainly pulled it off with me." By this time Cam was saying, he is saying now, that he's not sure about that religion, he's getting tired of the other priests and all that not eating meat or root vegetables. It's a stage, he says now, he's glad he went through it, self-discovery. One day I went over there and found he was trying on an old suit and tie. He says he might take advantage of some of the adult education courses, he is thinking of becoming an accountant.

I was thinking myself about changing into a different sort of person from the one I am. I do think about that. I read a book called *The Art of Loving*. A lot of things seemed clear while I was reading it but afterwards I went back to being more or less the same. What has Cam ever done that actually hurt me, anyway, as Haro once said. And how am I better than he is after the way I felt the night Mother lived instead of died? I made a promise to myself I would try. I went over there one day taking them a bakery cake—which Cam eats now as happily as anybody else—and I heard their voices out in the yard—now it's summer, they love to sit in the sun. Mother saying to some visitor, "Oh yes I was, I was all set to take off into the wild blue yonder, and Cam here, this *idiot*, came and danced outside my door with a bunch of his hippie friends—"

"My God, woman," roared Cam, but you could tell he didn't care now, "members of an ancient holy discipline."

I had a strange feeling, like I was walking on coals and trying a spell so I wouldn't get burnt.

Forgiveness in families is a mystery to me, how it comes or how it lasts.

∎

Audrey Thomas

David Robinson

Audrey Thomas (1935-   ) was born in Binghamton, New York, came to Canada in 1959 and, after two years in Ghana, now lives in Vancouver and Galiano Island. Her stories have appeared in many magazines, as well as Canadian and American anthologies. Her first story collection was *Ten Green Bottles* (1967) which also contains "Xanadu"; two other collections are *Ladies and Escorts* (1977) and *Real Mothers* (1981). She has also written six novels including *Songs My Mother Taught Me* (1973), *Blown Figures* (1974) and *Latakis* (1979).

XANADU

Audrey Thomas

In the beginning it was hardly paradise. That first night, "the night of the dreadful overture," as she was to call it later, when they had arrived at last at the house, bones aching from the long drive up from the harbour (over a road so pock-marked with holes it looked, as her husband said, "as though an army had blown it up as they retreated,") heads reeling from that first sensuous shock which Africa invariably delivers to the European consciousness, only to discover that the house was in utter darkness and the steward who had been engaged for them by the university was dead drunk on the front verandah (had quite literally stumbled upon this last discovery and experienced a thrill of horror, thinking for a moment, that the man was dead, not drunk); when they had solved the mysteries of hanging mosquito nets and sent the children off to bed with the remains of the picnic inside them ("we couldn't find so much as a can opener"); when she had inhaled the general atmosphere of damp and decay (which even two Bufferin tablets and a large whisky failed to dispel), had succumbed to self-pity and despair and anger, as she did the ony sensible thing a woman can do in such circumstances—put her head in her hands and wept. "The whole thing seemed a vast conspiracy," she said to her friends later, "and I felt, somehow, that a large and highly organized 'unwelcoming committee' had been at work." Then she would add, with a small laugh at her own idiosyncrasies, "I attach great importance to beginnings, to signs and portents you might say. My Irish ancestry I suppose." What made it worse was the fact that her husband insisted upon treating the whole thing as a joke, an adventure. "Jason seemed to find it all so interesting, so novel. He kept sticking his head out the door and sniffing—like a great dog who wanted to be let out, or a child on his first night of vacation. I honestly think that if I had been the violent sort—" (a pause while she impishly regarded her listeners and smiled the delightful smile which had made her such a favourite with both men and women) "—if I had been the violent sort I would have killed him on the spot. There is nothing more irritating," she would continue in a half-humorous, half-philosophic tone, "than the sight of another person enjoying a situation which you yourself find absolutely intolerable. *He* couldn't wait for daylight because he wanted to explore. *I* couldn't wait for daylight because I wanted to find the way to the nearest travel office."

Yes, it made for an amusing tale, in retrospect, but it could hardly be called an auspicious beginning. The next morning, in spite of the terrible and tiring events of the day before, she awoke early; and being unable to return to sleep or to endure the sight of her husband's peaceful face on the pillow beside her, she dressed quickly and went down to the kitchen. She was surveying with distaste a platoon of small ants who were breakfasting off the dirty dishes of the night before when she heard a light tap, tap ("almost like a discreet cough") on the kitchen door. Thinking it might be someone from the university, someone who would apologize for their not having been met; for their having to arrive in the dark, the pouring rain, alone and helpless; for the drunken steward, the missing can opener, the musty sheets, for the whole initial fiasco, she flung open the door "as full of righteous indignation as a balloon about to pop." There on the stoop stood a large black man, the blackest man she had ever seen. He was clad only in a pair of khaki shorts and a tattered string vest. She was still in that state, not at all unusual for a European, when all Africans look alike; so, although she had seen the steward of the night before, had seen him clearly in the light of her husband's torch, she did not realize at first that the two men bore very little resemblance to one another and she immediately assumed that they were the same. Naturally she was furious, and she spoke to him very sharply. ("I nearly sent him away!")

"I thought my husband made it very clear to you last night that your services would no longer be required. And if you think you're getting any wages for yesterday's performance you're very much mistaken." He watched her, impassive yet without hostility, and waited politely until she had finished. "There was I, screaming at the poor man like some fishwife, and he never moved a muscle; never even, as I recall, batted an eye." (Of course she was elaborating a little here. In actual fact she had never raised her voice, was furiously calm, spoke slowly and methodically as though, with each word, she were giving him a sharp but precise blow from an unseen hammer. But it made a better story the other way, and she enjoyed the implication that she, who seemed the mildest of women, had been, at the outset, the typical European bitch. "I was positively archetypal," she would cry, and wrinkle her delightful nose with laughter and pretended self-distaste.) Yet when she had finished her little speech, the man did not go away as she expected and she spoke to him again. "Well? What is it you want? You can hardly expect us to give you a reference, can you?"

"No, Madame. Please, Madame, I know nothin' about yesterday. I have only just arrived. Do you want a steward, Madame?" It was then that she looked at him closely, *really* looked at him, and realized her terrible mistake, her awful blunder.

"I'm terribly sorry," she said, and smiled her brilliant smile—the smile that had endeared her to countless cab-drivers, milkmen and meter-readers (not to mention her wide circle of friends) back home. "I thought you were someone else. Our steward, I mean the steward engaged for us, was drunk when we arrived. We sent him away, and I thought you were he. I've been very rude to you. Forgive me." She found herself offering an apology where no apology had in fact, been demanded. Perhaps precisely because none had been asked for, not even hinted at in the man's impassive but polite silence; or perhaps because the awareness of centuries of what one might call, euphemistically, European bad manners made her feel that an apology was due and overdue. He accepted the apology in the same way in which he had accepted the accusations—with a polite silence. Yet this very silence seemed to comfort her, seemed to indicate that he understood and approved first, the anger, and second, the apology. But all he did, verbally, was to repeat, "Please, Madame, do you need a steward?"

"Can you cook?" she asked. He could.

"Can you read and write?" He could do this as well. ("Although why I asked that question, then, when all I needed, all I was desperate for, was someone who could clean and scrub and make the wretched stove light, who could bring domestic order out of the chaos into which we had been plunged, I'll never know." She did not remember that she had overhead a woman on the boat say that it was a tremendous advantage if "they" could read and write.)

"Well, then," she said, "you're hired."

"Just like that?" her listeners would ask in wonder and admiration. "Just like that," she would reply with a laugh. "Call it instinct, call it what you will; I somehow felt that he was what we wanted, what we needed, and that it would be ridiculous to ask for letters of reference, or his job book, with all those ants crawling around and the children about to wake up and want their breakfast. It was as though I had rubbed a lamp and the genie had appeared. "One doesn't," she added with a laugh, "ask a genie for his testimonials."

And indeed, it did seem like magic. In minutes the dishes were done, the kitchen swept ("the broom seemed to appear from nowhere") and a large pan of bacon and eggs was frying merrily on the stove. Full of excitement she ran up the stairs which she had descended with such foreboding just half an hour before. She found her husband in the children's room, searching through suitcases for clean underwear and socks, for dry sandals (the eldest had managed to step in a puddle the night before), and a missing Teddy bear. The room was in chaos, and for a moment she experienced a renewal of despair as she glanced at the disorder and the all-too-obvious grime of the room itself. But then she remembered her errand, her news. "Listen, Jason, we've got a steward." "We had a steward, you mean," he replied from the corner, where he was trying to persuade the eldest that one brown sandal and one red would look very gay.

"No," she shook her head slowly, triumphantly, "we've got one—a new one. I just hired him."

"Good," he said. And that was all. No questions were asked—nothing. It seemed to him the most natural thing in the world that a steward should appear out of nowhere, and that his wife should hire him on the spot. She was a little put out, a little irritated, that her announcement did not, somehow, seem worthy of blaring trumpets and waving flags. Something (it couldn't have been spite) made her ask, "What if he isn't any good?"

"He'll be good," said her husband. And he was. By the time they all trooped down to breakfast, the sitting-room had been swept, the ashtays emptied, and the table laid with an almost military precision. A pot of coffee stood ready (a hot pad placed carefully under it, she noted with approval), a bowl of fruit was waiting at each place, and she settled herself at the head of the table with a shy, triumphant smile—like a soldier modestly returning home, his erect back and grave smile bearing mute witness to battles won and obstacles endured. Everything was delicious: crisp bacon, solid but not solidified eggs, a veritable regiment of toast lined up for their inspection. And all the time the steward was moving to and fro, his sandals slapping efficiently on the terrazzo floor. Plates were whisked away and clean plates substituted; a second rack of toast appeared, more steaming coffee: all this done so quickly, so quietly that the large black man might have been another Ariel with hosts of spirits at his command. The children were delighted, intrigued.

"Did *he* get the breakfast, Mommy? What's his name?" It came as a shock to her, almost as a sensation of good manners breached, that she had, in fact, forgotten to ask him his name. So when he appeared again she turned her shy, brilliant smile on him once more, extended her smile to him, offered it, the way a friend will convey apology with the soft pressure of a hand.

"I'm terribly sorry. I forgot to ask your name."

"Joseph, Madame." And then, a bit confused as to how to end the brief interview (for she had never dealt with servants before), she simply played her smile over his face once once more and reached for the marmalade.

By noon, when they had all returned from an exploratory trip around the compound, had met the registrar and gracefully accepted his equally graceful apologies for thinking that their ship was due in on the tenth, not the ninth; had explained to him about the drunken steward and the lack of electricity; had been assured that the man, if he could be found, would be dealt with, and had been informed, again with a graceful apology, that the electricity was always off on Thursday evenings; when they had collected their mail and bought a few things at the little shop, they discovered that the chaos of the bedrooms had disappeared. Suitcases had been unpacked and set out on the upstairs verandah to air, the children's clothes had been carefully sorted and put away, beds had been stripped of their musty sheets and mattresses laid outside to absorb the sun. They discovered Joseph in the bathroom, kneeling over the tub and methodically kneading dirt out of the mosquito nets. Even the missing Teddy bear had been found. And later, after a (by now) predictably delicious lunch, as she lay on her immaculate bed in a state of happy exhaustion and listened to the laughter of the children, who were taking turns on an ancient swing which her husband had discovered at the bottom of the garden, she decided that things had, after all, turned out for the best. She felt, somehow, that she almost owed that miserable creature of the night before a vote of thanks. For if they hadn't had to send him away, then she, in turn, would have sent Joseph away that morning. A bad beginning, she reflected philosophically, just before she dozed off, does not necessarily imply a bad ending.

Thus the days slipped by, each one like some perfect, exotic jewel set carefully and expertly into her golden chalice of contentment. What of mosquitoes? Joseph examined the nets each day, and sprayed the lounge each evening after dinner while they sipped a cup of coffee on the verandah. What of the rains? At the first tentative rumble Joseph ran swiftly through the house, shutting the louvres, bringing in the washing, checking that the candlesticks were ready if the electricity should go off and remain off after dark. What of the orange lady, the bean man, the itinerant traders—the steady stream of merchandise which arrived each day? Joseph took care of it all—made certain that only the biggest oranges at the smallest price, the choicest beans, the largest bunch of bananas, the most serious traders, ever passed her threshold. For the first time in more years than she cared to remember she felt "caught up" with the sheer mass of business necessary to maintaining a comfortable, well-run home. For the first time she could wake up in the morning without a moral hangover, sense of things left undone or done too hastily, of buttons still missing or unmatched socks. Instead at six o'clock came the gentle, cough-like knock announcing the arrival of morning tea. Then they dressed, and while her husband shaved and collected the books he would need that morning, she dressed the children for school. By 6:30 breakfast was on the table; by seven her husband had left; by 7:30 the eldest child had been picked up by the little school bus which travelled the compound. She read and played games with the little one until it was 8:15 and his turn to be picked up for nursery school. How strange it seemed, at first, to take her coffee out on the verandah and contemplate the day before her, the day that would unroll like a red carpet under her feet, to choose what she wanted to do, to ignore unmade beds and dirty dishes, washing and ironing, what to serve for lunch. She felt almost as though she were a convalescent who was now recovering slowly but happily, aware perhaps for the first time of the small beauties of the world, the large beauty of being alive at all. Joseph took care of everything— everyone; moved swiftly and noiselessly in and out of their days, a dark brown shuttle weaving a gay-coloured carpet for her delight.

Yet with all this idleness, this new and unaccustomed leis-

ure, she wasn't bored—not for a minute. She embarked, first
of all, on a plan of self-improvement, sent away for books
which she had always meant to read, decided to brush up on
her French, to begin German. "After all," she said to Jason
one evening as they sat on the verandah observing the
strange, almost embarrassed pink of the tropical sunset, "I
may never have this chance again."

"Which chance is that?"

"The chance to spread my intellectual wings a bit, to
grow—as a person, I mean."

"Begin," he said with a teasing smile, "by keeping still
and watching that sky."

But his teasing never bothered her, and she was perceptive
enough to realize that even the most sympathetic of husbands
could not possibly understand what it was like to be suddenly released from all the never-ending pressures of housework, the domestic cares that had always, since the birth of
their first child, hovered over her like a swarm of angry bees.
"It was not that I really minded, of course at the time. I'm
old-fashioned enough to believe that a woman's place *is* in
the home, not in the office. It's just that one gets so run
down, spiritually as well, without even noticing it—without
having *time* to notice it I should say." Now, for the first time
in many years, she could read a magazine through from cover
to cover if she felt like it, at one sitting; she could have
friends in for dinner without being conscious, as the evening
wore on, of the great stack of unwashed dishes which would
have to be dealt with when the final goodbyes had been said.
Now, while the guests sipped their coffee on the verandah
she could hear, as one hears a delightful, far-off tune, the
sound of Joseph washing up in the kitchen. And every evening before the children were bathed and put to bed (always
clean pyjamas, always a fresh and spotless towel), she sat
down with them and read a story: one that they chose, however long, and not one that she had chosen because it was
short and quickly gotten through. This hour with the children became very precious to her, and she would even linger
over it, as one lingers over a delicious meal, asking the children questions about the characters, reading favourite bits
again. The children responded gaily, affectionately,
giggling with delight as she changed her voice and became
the wicked old witch, the dwarfs, the three bears. She felt like
a flower that had been tightly curled and suddenly, in the
embrace of the sun, begins to expand.

Then too, there were the coffee mornings when she met the other faculty wives and discussed the advantages and disadvantages of life in the tropics; how difficult it was to get butter and tea, how easy to get fresh fruit. And, of course, they discussed the stewards. It took several weeks before she realized just how lucky they had been. Tales of broken crockery, sullenness, petty thievery; gradually it dawned on her that Joseph was something of a miracle, a paragon. Each week some new disaster was reported. One steward had been caught wearing his master's vests, another had burned a large hole in an heirloom tablecloth. Yet another had disappeared for five days and returned with no explanation at all (and was duly sacked). One woman, who had arrived only three months before, was on her eleventh boy, and *he* didn't seem at all satisfactory. She would come away from these coffee mornings feeling like a healthy woman who has just been regaled with stories of ghastly operations; she found it all hard to believe. But there was, of course, the initial experience, that first night, and almost as though she felt it necessary to defend herself, to justify her good fortune, she would recall her own lurid introduction and speculate with her friends on what would have happened if—? For she could, in truth, find no fault with Joseph at all. "As a matter of fact," she confided shyly to her new friends, "he is far better at managing a household than I am." Then she would smile her delightful smile and throw up her hands in a pretty gesture of mock despair. It was as though they had all been panning for gold and she, the lucky one, had by chance discovered the richest hoard, the deepest vein, was carrying Joseph's virtues around in her pocket like a sack of golden pebbles. Every Tuesday, early, before the sun had begun to beat down in earnest, she and Joseph would set off in the station wagon for town. Wandering from shop to shop, a gay straw basket on her arm, she did the weekly marketing. (And always Joseph behind her like a cool black shadow.) She enjoyed these Tuesday mornings, enjoyed the colourful pageantry of the busy town, the gay clothes of the men and women—"black Romans in bright togas. How pale and insipid they make the Europeans look." She enjoyed bargaining with the boys who came rushing up with grapefruit, limes, oranges; enjoyed haggling with the "Mammys" over vegetables. Sometimes they would go to the large open-air market where it was her turn to wait quietly while Joseph quickly bargained for yams and sweet potatoes, bananas and pineapples. (He had explained to her, very politely, that the prices were raised for a white woman, and he could therefore obtain more value for her money if he bargained for her; said all this in a manner which indicated full recognition of this deplorable practice and yet somehow managed to convey the idea that such bargaining would be a pleasure for him because it would serve her and "the Master.") Although she could not understand what he said to the various traders, she accepted his prices as absolute and would never dream of interfering in these sometimes long and rather tedious harangues. And if she needed something at the end of the week, she did not hesitate to send him off alone, knowing that her money would be well spent and that he would not add on a sixpence here or a shilling there, as was the practice of many of her friends' boys. "There is something almost regal about him," she commented once to her husband. "It is as though everything that he does for me, for us, is done because he genuinely likes us, because he accepts us as people and not as employers. He serves without being servile—if you know what I mean."

They became familiar figures in the town, the small, fair woman in the straw hat and the huge black man. Even when she refused a purchase she would flash her smile and the sting was taken out of the refusal. And when the chattering, the crowding around became too much, she had only to turn to Joseph with a smiling, half-despairing look; a few sharp words in the vernacular and the vegetable boys, the fruit boys, the little crowd of beggars and loungers, would scatter like so many dark birds. It was wonderful to feel so protected, so well-looked-after. And of course, as though to keep her ever mindful of just exactly how wonderful it all was, there were always the Sundays—Joseph's day off. On Sunday morning there was no welcoming cup of tea, no immaculately laid breakfast table, no strong brown arms to deal with the tidying and washing up. On Sundays the magic world, her enchanted island as it were, disappeared. Joseph, like a huge black Prospero, retired to his cell, and she was left to work her own miracles. Strangely enough, in spite of the fact that she was rested and content, things always went wrong for her on Sundays. As though she were a bride of a few months, she found herself burning toast, over-cooking eggs, dropping a precious jar of marmalade on the floor. Jason and the children were really quite brutal about it, teased her unmercifully. "Who's Joseph's stand-in?" her husband would say to the eldest child. "I think she might do for a small-boy, don't you, but she'll never make a cook-steward." At first she entered into the game, dropping serviettes on purpose, laying the table backwards, making faces and muttering, "Yes, Master, yes, Master," under her breath or "Sorry, Master." But after a while it began to hurt a bit, this patronizing attitude of theirs, and one Sunday, when the youngest had wept bitter tears because Joseph wasn't there to chop up the eggs in a special way, she left the table in anger and wept a few bitter tears of her own. After all, in the terrible heat, with a cantankerous stove, they could hardly expect her to be perfect. However, they all filed shyly up to apologize and she soon forgave them with her brilliant, if this time somewhat watery, smile. Nevertheless, although she may have forgotten and forgiven, something remained at the back of her consciousness, something unnamed, unobserved, as infinitesimal as a grain of sand in an oyster, as quiet as the hum of a solitary mosquito. Monday came, Joseph returned to work and everything seemed, on the surface, to be back to normal. If a bit of the old magic was gone, she would have been the last person to admit it, perhaps the last person to understand why. And except for the incident of the snake, things might have gone on, indefinitely, very much as before.

However, one morning, as she made her way across the courtyard with a small basket of wet clothes (for she refused to allow Joseph to wash out her underthings, felt, somehow, that this was too much to ask any man to do), a large python sluggishly uncurled itself from the clothes pole not three feet away from her. For the space of a heartbeat she stood rooted to the spot, hypnotized with terror. Then she ran, screaming into the house. She was still locked in the farthest bedroom when her husband and the children came home for lunch. When she had been assured that the snake had been killed, she ventured forth and allowed herself to be led to the table. The children were very excited, for apparently Jospeh had killed the snake and it was stretched out on a pole behind his quarters. Already a group of admiring neighbours had been to see it and marvelled over its length and ugliness. It appeared that the eldest child knew all about snakes. "A python won't bite you, Mother. It crushes you to death. Or anyway, it crushes animals and things." He gazed at her with a condescending smile. But the terror of the morning was still so great in her mind that she scarcely heard the child, and his words bounced off her consciousness without wounding. She ate and drank mechanically and then, at her husband's insistence, went back upstairs to lie down. She had not yet spoken to Joseph, had not yet thanked him for killing the snake. To tell the truth, she was somewhat embarrassed about the whole thing. It was not that anyone would blame her for running away, for screaming, or even for hysterically locking herself in the bedroom. She knew that most people, men as well as women, have a violent reaction to snakes whatever their size. No, she was all right there, and her hasty retreat could hardly be called a social blunder. (As a matter of fact, the one woman on the compound who did show an interest in reptiles was thought by many of the others to be a bit "queer" and certainly slightly unfeminine.) Her embarrassment had to do with Joseph. Lying on the immaculate bed, shutters drawn against the glare, she faced up to the unpleasant fact that she did not want to thank her steward, that in fact she wished the snake had managed to get away. Now she was somehow in his debt, owed something to this dark man who could cope with anything. ("Something?" whispered a voice in her ear. "Everything.") She felt, for the first time, that she belonged to Joseph and not Joseph to her. And yet, the more she thought about it, the more she realized that the incident of the snake was just one example of the way in which Joseph had gradually made himself indispensable. Suddenly she heard the voices of her husband and the children, directly below the window. They must be coming back from viewing the snake, and the littlest child was obviously a bit frightened. "Will Joseph kill all the snakes, Daddy?" she heard him ask in an anxious voice. "Of course. That's what he keeps the big stick for." "But what will we do on Sundays?" said the child, and began to cry. "I'll tell you what," said his father, trying to jolly the child and unaware, of course, that he was being overheard. "On Sundays, if we see any snakes we'll take some of Mummy's toast and hit them right between the eyes. I should think they wouldn't come round here a second time." The child began to giggle, and all three moved around the corner and out of earshot. This was the crowning blow. Not only had Joseph made himself a necessity in their household, but he was making her a family joke. Each time that he increased in importance, she diminished. It was unbearable. She felt stifled, afraid. All the little helps which Joseph had performed for her, all the larger duties which he had removed from her weary shoulders—each act now seemed like a golden thread binding her tighter and tighter to a conception of herself as a totally incompetent, albeit delightful, woman. She felt as though she had been tricked out of her rights, deceived. She lit a cigarette and lay smoking, while she examined the problem, explored the wound the way a child will explore with his tongue the raw hole where a tooth should be. By tea time she had come to a decision.

The next morning, after her husband had left, after the children had been kissed and put on the bus, she gave Joseph a pound note and asked him to go into the market for some fruits and vegetables. She stood at the window for a long time, watching his erect figure grow smaller and smaller until he turned the bend of the road and disappeared. Almost regretfully she opened the silver chest and selected three coffee spoons, holding the heavy silver in her hands for a moment, hating to part with it for even a few hours. Then, with the spoons in her pocket, she made her way slowly, determinedly, across the courtyard toward the servants' quarters at the back of the house.

∎

Jane Rule

Jane Rule (1931-   ) was born in New Jersey, and has made her home in Canada since 1956; she presently lives on Galiano Island, B.C. She writes essays of criticism and social commentary, but she is known primarily as a fiction writer who has published five novels, including *Desert of Heart* (1964), *The Young in One Another's Arms* (1977) and *Contract with the World* (1980). "A Television Drama" appears in her collection of short stories *Theme for Diverse Instruments* (1975). Her most recent collection of stories and essays is *Outlander* (1981).

A TELEVISION DRAMA

Jane Rule

At one-thirty in the afternoon, Carolee Mitchell was running the vacuum cleaner, or she would have heard the first sirens and looked out. After the first, there weren't any others. The calling voices, even the number of dogs barking, could have been students on their way back to school, high-spirited in the bright, cold earliness of the year. Thinking back on the sounds, Carolee remembered a number of car doors being slammed, that swallow of air and report which made her smooth her hair automatically even if she wasn't expecting anyone. But what caught her eye finally was what always caught her eye: the flight of a bird from a treetop in the ravine out over the fringe of trees at the bottom of her steeply sloping front lawn, nearly private in the summer, exposed now to the startling activity of the street.

Three police cars were parked in front of the house, a motorcycle like a slanted stress in the middle of the intersection, half a dozen more police cars scattered up and down the two blocks. There were men in uniform up on her neighbour's terrace with rifles and field glasses. Police with dogs were crossing the empty field at the bottom of the ravine. More cars were arriving, police and reporters with cameras and sound equipment. Mingling among the uniforms and equipment were the neighbors: Mrs. Rolston from the house across the street who had obviously not taken time to put on a coat and was rubbing her arms absent-mindedly as she stood and talked, Jane Carey from next door with a scarf tied round her head and what looked like one of her son's jackets thrown over her shoulders, old Mr. Monkson, a few small children. Cars and people kept arriving. Suddenly there was a voice magnified to reach even Carolee, surprised and unbelieving behind her picture window.

"Clear the street. All householders return to or stay in your houses. Clear the street."

Mrs. Rolston considered the idea for a moment but did not go in. The others paid no attention at all. Carolee wondered if she should go out just to find out what on earth was going on. Perhaps she should telephone someone, but everyone she might phone was already in the street. Was it a gas main?

Not with all those dogs. A murder? It seemed unlikely that anyone would kill anyone else on this street, where every child had his own bedroom and most men either studies or basement workshops to retreat into. In any case, it was the middle of the afternoon. Mrs. Cole had come out on her balcony with field glasses focused on the place where the dogs and police had entered the ravine. Field glasses. Where were Pete's field glasses? Carolee thought she knew, but she did not move to get them. She would not know what she was looking for in the undergrowth or the gardens.

"Clear the street. All householders return to or stay in your houses."

Police radios were now competing with each other. "Suspect last apprehended in the alley between . . ." "House to house search . . ." "Ambulance . . ."

If one of those policemen standing about on the street would come to search the house, Carolee could at least find out what was going on. Was that a t.v. crew? Dogs were barking in the ravine. Did police dogs bark? Nobody on the street seemed to be doing anything, except for the motorcycle policeman who was turning away some cars. Maybe Carolee should go empty the dishwasher and then come back. It was pointless to stand here by the window. Nothing was happening, or, if something was happening, Carolee couldn't see the point of it. She went to the window in Pete's study to see if she could discover activity on the side street. There were more policemen, and far up the block an ambulance was pulling away without a siren, its red light slowly circling. Carolee watched it until it turned the corner at the top of the hill. Then she turned back toward the sound of barking dogs and radios, but paused as she turned.

There, sitting against the curve of the laurel hedge by the lily pond, was a man, quite a young man, his head down, his left hand against his right shoulder. He was sick or hurt or dead. Or not really there at all, something Carolee's imagination had put there to explain the activity in the street, part of a collage, like an unlikely photograph in the middle of a painting. But he raised his head slightly then, and Carolee saw the blood on his jacket and trousers.

"I must call the police," she said aloud, but how could she call the police when they were already there, three of them standing not seventy feet away, just below the trees on the parking strip? She must call someone, but all the neighbours were still out of doors. And what if the police did discover him? He might be shot instead of helped. Carolee wanted to help him, whoever he was. It was such an odd way he was sitting, his legs stretched out in front of him so that he couldn't possibly have moved quickly. He might not be able to move at all. But she couldn't get to him, not without being seen. Suddenly he got to his feet, his left hand still against his right shoulder and also holding the lower part of his ducked face. He walked to the end of the curve of hedge as if it was very difficult for him to move, and then he began a stumbling run across the front lawn, through the trees, and out onto the parking strip. There he turned, hesitated, and fell on his back. Carolee had heard no shot. Now her view was blocked by a gathering of police and reporters, drawn to that new center like leaves to a central drain.

"Suspect apprehended on . . ."

What had he done? What had that hurt and stumbling boy done? Carolee was standing with her hand on the transistor radio before it occurred to her to turn it on.

"We interrupt this program with a news bulletin. A suspect has been apprehended on . . ."

He had robbed a bank, run a car into a tree, shot a policeman, been shot at.

"And now, here is our reporter on the scene."

Carolee could see the reporter quite clearly, standing in the street in front of the house, but she could hear only the radio voice, explaining what had happened.

"And now the ambulance is arriving . . ." as indeed it was. "The suspect, suffering from at least three wounds, who seems near death, is being lifted onto a stretcher . . ." This she couldn't see. It seemed to take a very long time before police cleared a path for the ambulance, again silent, its red light circling, to move slowly down the block and out of sight.

A newspaper reporter was walking up the front path, but Carolee didn't answer the door. She stood quietly away from the window and waited until he was gone. Then she went to the kitchen and began to empty the dishwasher. It was two o'clock. She turned on the radio again to listen to the regular news report. The details were the same. At three o'clock the hospital had reported that the policeman was in the operating room having a bullet removed from his right lung. At four o'clock the suspect was reported in only fair condition from wounds in the shoulder, jaw, leg and hand.

At five o'clock Pete came home, the evening paper in his

hand. "Well, you've had quite a day," he said. "Are you all right?"

"Yes," Carolee said, her hands against his cold jacket, her cheek against his cold face. "Yes, I'm all right. What did the paper say?"

"It's all diagrams," he said, holding out the front page to her.

There was a map of the whole neighbourhood, a sketched aerial map, a view of the roof of their house Carolee had never had. She followed the dots and arrows to the hood of a car crumpled under a flower of foliage, on again across the ravine, up their side hill, and there was the laurel hedge and the jelly bean lily pond, but the dots didn't stop there, arced round rather and immediately down through the trees to a fallen doll, all alone, not a policeman or reporter in sight, lying there exposed to nothing but a God's eye view.

"You must have seen him," Pete said.

"Yes," Carolee agreed, still looking down on the roof tops of all her neighbours' houses.

"Did it frighten you?" Pete asked.

"Not exactly. It was hard to believe, and everything seemed to happen so very slowly."

"Did you get a good look at him?"

"I guess not really," Carolee said. Had he sat there by the laurel hedge at all, his long, stiff legs stretched out in front of him? The map didn't show it.

"Something has got to be done about all this violence," Pete said.

His tone and the look on his face made Carolee realize that Pete had been frightened, much more frightened than she was. Those dotted lines across his front lawn, that figure alone in the landscape—Carolee felt herself shaken by a new fear, looking at what Pete had seen.

"I'll get us a drink," Pete said.

Once they sat down, Carolee tried to tell her husband what it had been like, all those women just standing out in the street. She told him about the guns and field glasses and dogs and cameras. She did not tell him about the man, hurt, by the laurel hedge.

Pete turned on the television, and they watched three minutes of fast-moving images, first the policeman lifted into an ambulance, then officers and dogs running through the field, finally glimpses of the suspect on the ground and then shifted onto a stretcher; and, while they watched, a voice told them of the robbery, the chase, the capture. Finally several people were quickly interviewed, saying such things as, "I saw him go over the fence" or "He fell practically at my feet." That was Mrs. Rolston, still rubbing her cold arms in the winter day.

"I'm glad you had the good sense to stay inside," Pete said. He was holding her hand, beginning to relax into indignation and relief.

Carolee wasn't there, nor was the man there. If she had spoken to that reporter, if she had said then, "I saw him. He was sitting by the laurel hedge," would the dots in the paper have changed? Would the cameras have climbed into their nearly exposed winter garden? Would she believe now what she couldn't quite believe even then, that she stood at that window and saw a man dying in her garden?

Now a labour union boss was talking, explaining the unfair practices of the compensation board. Nearly at once, young marines were running, firing, falling. Planes were dropping bombs. Carolee wasn't there, but it seemed real to her, terribly real, so that for a moment she forgot Pete's hand in hers, her safe house on a safe street, and was afraid.

■

Sinclair Ross

Sinclair Ross (1908-) was born on a homestead near Prince Albert, Saskatchewan and worked for the Royal Bank from 1924 to his retirement in 1968. Since then he has lived in Greece and Spain before returning to live in Montreal. His first novel, *As For Me and My House* (1941) is probably the finest novel yet written about Canadian prairie life, and his short stories echo that achievement. "One's A Heifer" is taken from the collection *The Lamp at Noon* (1968); his other novels are *The Well* (1957), *Whir of Gold* (1970) and *Sawbones Memorial* (1974). Several of his stories, including "The Lamp at Noon" and "Cornet at Night," have been produced as films.

ONE'S A HEIFER

Sinclair Ross

My uncle was laid up that winter with sciatica, so when the blizzard stopped and still two of the yearlings hadn't come home with the other cattle, Aunt Ellen said I'd better saddle Tim and start out looking for them.

"Then maybe I'll not be back tonight," I told her firmly. "Likely they've drifted as far as the sandhills. There's no use coming home without them."

I was thirteen, and had never been away like that all night before, but, busy with the breakfast, Aunt Ellen said yes, that sounded sensible enough, and while I ate, hunted up a dollar in silver for my meals.

"Most people wouldn't take it from a lad, but they're strangers up towards the hills. Bring it out independent-like, but don't insist too much. They're more likely to grudge you a feed of oats for Tim."

After breakfast I had to undress again, and put on two suits of underwear and two pairs of thick, home-knitted stockings. It was a clear, bitter morning. After the storm the drifts lay clean and unbroken to the horizon. Distant farmbuildings stood out distinct against the prairie as if the thin sharp atmosphere were a magnifying glass. As I started off Aunt Ellen peered cautiously out of the door a moment through a cloud of steam, and waved a red and white checkered dish-towel. I didn't wave back, but conscious of her uneasiness rode erect, as jaunty as the sheepskin and two suits of underwear would permit.

We took the road straight south about three miles. The calves, I reasoned, would have by this time found their way home if the blizzard hadn't carried them at least that far. Then we started catercornering across fields, riding over to straw-stacks where we could see cattle sheltering, calling at farmhouses to ask had they seen any strays. "Yearlings," I said each time politely. "Red with white spots and faces. The same almost except that one's a heifer and the other isn't."

Nobody had seen them. There was a crust on the snow not quite hard enough to carry Tim, and despite the cold his flanks and shoulders soon were steaming. He walked with his head down, and sometimes, taking my sympathy for granted, drew up a minute for breath.

My spirits, too, began to flag. The deadly cold and the flat white silent miles of prairie asserted themselves like a disapproving presence. The cattle fields stared, and the sky stared. People shivered in their doorways, and said they'd seen no strays.

At about one o'clock we stopped at a farmhouse for dinner. It was a single oat sheaf half thistles for Tim, and fried eggs and bread and tea for me. Crops had been poor that year, they apologized, and though they shook their heads when I brought out my money I saw the woman's eyes light greedily a second, as if her instincts of hospitality were struggling hard against some urgent need. We too, I said, had had poor crops lately. That was why it was so important that I find the calves.

We rested an hour, then went on again. "Yearlings," I kept on describing them. "Red with white spots and faces. The same except that one's a heifer and the other isn't."

Still no one had seen them, still it was cold, still Tim protested what a fool I was.

The country began to roll a little. A few miles ahead I could see the first low line of sandhills. "They'll be there for sure," I said aloud, more to encourage myself than Tim. "Keeping straight to the road it won't take a quarter as long to get home again."

But home now seemed a long way off. A thin white sheet of cloud spread across the sky, and though there had been no warmth in the sun the fields looked colder and bleaker without the glitter on the snow. Straw-stacks were fewer here, as if the land were poor, and every house we stopped at seemed more dilapidated than the one before.

A nagging wind rose as the afternoon wore on. Dogs yelped and bayed at us, and sometimes from the hills, like the signal of our approach, there was a thin, wavering howl of a coyote. I began to dread the miles home again almost as much as those still ahead. There were so many cattle straggling across the fields, so many yearlings just like ours. I saw them for sure a dozen times, and as often choked my disappointment down and clicked Tim on again.

II

And at last I really saw them. It was nearly dusk, and along with fifteen or twenty other cattle they were making their way towards some buildings that lay huddled at the foot of the sandhills. They passed in single file less than fifty yards away, buy when I pricked Tim forward to turn them back he floundered in a snowed-in water-cut. By the time we were out they were a little distance ahead, and on account of the drifts it was impossible to put on a spurt of speed and pass them. All we could do was take our place at the end of the file, and proceed at their pace towards the buildings.

It was about half a mile. As we drew near I debated with Tim whether we should ask to spend the night or start off right away for home. We were hungry and tired, but it was a poor, shiftless-looking place. The yard was littered with old wagons and machinery; the house was scarcely distinguishable from the stables. Darkness was beginning to close in, but there was no light in the windows.

Then as we crossed the yard we heard a shout, "Stay where you are," and a man came running towards us from the stable. He was tall and ungainly, and, instead of the short sheepskin that most farmers wear, had on a long black overcoat nearly to his feet. He seized Tim's bridle when he reached us, and glared for a minute as if he were going to pull me out of the saddle. "I told you to stay out," he said in a harsh, excited voice. "You heard me, didn't you? What do you want coming round here anyway?"

I steeled myself and said, "Our two calves."

The muscles of his face were drawn together threateningly, but close to him like this and looking straight into his eyes I felt that for all their fierce look there was something about them wavering and uneasy. "The two red ones with the white faces," I continued. "They've just gone into the shed over there with yours. If you'll give me a hand getting them out again I'll start for home now right away."

He peered at me a minute, let go the bridle, then clutched it again. "They're all mine," he countered. "I was over by the gate. I watched them coming in."

His voice was harsh and thick. The strange wavering look in his eyes steadied itself for a minute to a dare. I forced myself to meet it and insisted, "I saw them back a piece in the field. They're ours all right. Let me go over a minute and I'll show you."

With a crafty tilt of his head he leered, "You didn't see any calves. And now, if you know what's good for you, you'll be on your way."

"You're trying to steal them," I flared rashly. "I'll go

home and get my uncle and the police after you—then you'll see whether they're our calves or not."

My threat seemed to impress him a little. With a shifty glance in the direction of the stable he said, "All right, come along and look them over. Then maybe you'll be satisfied." But all the way across the yard he kept his hand on Tim's bridle, and at the shed made me wait a few minutes while he went inside.

The cattle shed was a lean-to on the horse stable. It was plain enough: he was hiding the calves before letting me inside to look around. While waiting for him, however, I had time to realize that he was a lot bigger and stronger than I was, and that it might be prudent just to keep my eyes open, and not give him too much insolence.

He reappeared carrying a smoky lantern. "All right," he said pleasantly enough, "Come in and look around. Will your horse stand, or do you want to tie him?"

We put Tim in an empty stall in the horse stable, then went through a narrow doorway with a bar across it to the cattle shed. Just as I expected, our calves weren't there. There were two red ones with white markings that he tried to make me believe were the ones I had seen, but, positive I hadn't been mistaken, I shook my head and glanced at the doorway we had just come through. It was narrow, but not too narrow. He read my expression and said, "You think they're in there. Come on, then, and look around."

The horse stable consisted of two rows of open stalls with a passage down the centre like an aisle. At the far end were two box-stalls, one with a sick colt in it, the other closed. They were both boarded up to the ceiling, so that you could see inside them only through the doors. Again he read my expression, and with a nod towards the closed one said, "It's just a kind of harness room now. Up till a year ago I kept a stallion."

But he spoke furtively, and seemed anxious to get me away from that end of the stable. His smoky lantern threw great swaying shadows over us; and the deep clefts and triangles of shadow on his face sent a little chill through me, and made me think what a dark and evil face it was.

I was afraid, but not too afraid. "If it's just a harness room," I said recklessly, "why not let me see inside? Then I'll be satisfied and believe you."

He wheeled at my question, and sidled over swiftly to the stall. He stood in front of the door, crouched down a little, the lantern in front of him like a shield. There was a sudden stillness through the stable as we faced each other. Behind the light from his lantern the darkness hovered vast and sinister. It seemed to hold its breath, to watch and listen. I felt a clutch of fear now at my throat, but I didn't move. My eyes were fixed on him so intently that he seemed to lose substance, to loom up close a moment, then recede. At last he disappeared completely, and there was only the lantern like a hard hypnotic eye.

It held me. It held me rooted, against my will. I wanted to run from the stable, but I wanted even more to see inside the stall. And yet I was afraid to see inside the stall. So afraid that it was a relief when at last he gave a shamefaced laugh and said, "There's a hole in the floor—that's why I keep the door closed. If you didn't know, you might step into it—twist your foot. That's what happened to one of my horses a while ago."

I nodded as if I believed him, and went back tractably to Tim. But regaining control of myself as I tried the saddle girths, beginning to feel that my fear had been unwarranted, I looked up and said, "It's ten miles home, and we've been riding hard all day. If we could stay a while—have something to eat, and then get started—"

The wavering light came into his eyes again. He held the lantern up to see me better, such a long, intent scrutiny that it seemed he must discover my designs. But he gave a nod finally, as if reassured, brought oats and hay for Tim, and suggested, companionably, "After supper we can have a game of checkers."

Then, as if I were a grownup, he put out his hand and said "My name is Arthur Vickers."

III

Inside the house, rid of his hat and coat, he looked less forbidding. He had a white nervous face, thin lips, a large straight nose, and deep uneasy eyes. When the lamp was lit I fancied I could still see the wavering expression in them, and decided it was what you called a guilty look.

"You won't think much of it," he said apologetically, following my glance around the room. "I ought to be getting things cleaned up again. Come over to the stove. Supper won't take long."

It was a large, low-ceilinged room that for the first moment or two struck me more like a shed or granary than a house. The table in the centre was littered with tools and harness. On a rusty cook-stove were two big steaming pots of bran. Next to the stove stood a grindstone, then a white iron bed covered with coats and horse blankets. At the end opposite the bed, weasel and coyote skins were drying. There were guns and traps on the wall, a horse collar, a pair of rubber boots. The floor was bare and grimy. Ashes were littered around the stove. In a corner squatted a live owl with a broken wing.

He walked back and forth a few times looking helplessly at the disorder, then cleared off the table and lifted the pots of bran to the stove. "I've been mending harness," he explained. "You get careless, living alone like this. It takes a woman anyway."

My presence, apparently, was making him take stock of the room. He picked up a broom and swept for a minute, made an ineffective attempt to straighten the blankets on the bed, brought another lamp out of a cupboard and lit it. There was an ungainly haste to all his movements. He started unbuckling my sheepskin for me, then turned away suddenly to take off his own coat. "Now we'll have supper," he said with an effort at self-possession. "Coffee and beans is all I can give you—maybe a little molasses."

I replied diplomatically that that sounded pretty good. It didn't seem right, accepting hospitality this way from a man who was trying to steal your calves, but theft, I reflected, surely justified deceit. I held my hands out to the warmth, and asked if I could help.

There was a kettle of plain navy beans already cooked. He dipped out enough for our supper into a frying pan, and on top laid rashers of fat salt pork. While I watched that they didn't burn he rinsed off a few dishes. Then he set out sugar and canned milk, butter, molasses, and dark heavy biscuits that he had baked himself the day before. He kept glancing at me so apologetically all the while that I leaned over and sniffed the beans, and said at home I ate a lot of them.

"It takes a woman," he repeated as we sat down to the table. "I don't often have anyone here to eat with me. If I'd known, I'd have cleaned things up a little."

I was too intent on my plateful of beans to answer. All through the meal he sat watching me, but made no further attempts at conversation. Hungry as I was, I noticed that the wavering, uneasy look was still in his eyes. A guilty look, I told myself again, and wondered what I was going to do to get the calves away. I finished my coffee and he continued:

"It's worse even than this in the summer. No time for meals—and the heat and flies. Last summer I had a girl cooking for a few weeks, but it didn't last. Just a cow she was—just a big stupid cow—and she wanted to stay on. There's a family of them back in the hills. I had to send her home."

I wondered should I suggest starting now, or ask to spend the night. Maybe when he's asleep, I thought, I can slip out of the house and get away with the calves. He went on, "You don't know how bad it is sometimes. Weeks on end and no one to talk to. You're not yourself—you're not sure what you're going to say or do."

I remembered hearing my uncle talk about a man who had gone crazy living alone. And this fellow Vickers had queer eyes all right. And there was the live owl over in the corner, and the grindstone standing right beside the bed. "Maybe I'd better go now," I decided aloud. "Tim'll be rested, and it's ten miles home."

But he said no, it was colder now, with the wind getting stronger, and seemed so kindly and concerned that I half forgot my fears. "Likely he's just starting to go crazy," I told myself, "And it's only by staying that I'll have a chance to get the calves away."

When the table was cleared and the dishes washed he said he would go out and bed down the stable for the night. I picked up my sheepskin to go with him, but he told me sharply to stay inside. Just for a minute he looked crafty and forbidding as when I first rode up on Tim, and to allay his suspicions I nodded compliantly and put my sheepskin down again. It was better like that anyway, I decided. In a few minutes I could follow him, and perhaps, taking advantage of the shadows and his smoky lantern, make my way to the box-stall unobserved.

But when I reached the stable he had closed the door after him and hooked it from the inside. I walked round a while, tried to slip in by way of the cattle shed, and then had to go back to the house. I went with a vague feeling of relief again. There was still time, I told myself, and it would be safer anyway when he was sleeping.

So that it would be easier to keep from falling asleep myself I planned to suggest coffee again just before we went to bed. I knew that the guest didn't ordinarily suggest such things, but it was no time to remember manners when there was someone trying to steal your calves.

IV

When he came in from the stable we played checkers. I was no match for him, but to encourage me he repeatedly let me win. "It's a long time now since I've had a chance to play," he kept on saying, trying to convince me that his short-sighted moves weren't intentional. "Sometimes I used to ask her to play, but I had to tell her every move to make. If she didn't win she'd upset the board and go off and sulk."

"My aunt is a little like that too," I said. "She cheats some-times when we're playing cribbage—and, when I catch her, says her eyes aren't good."

"Women talk too much ever to make good checker players. It takes concentration. This one, though, couldn't even talk like anybody else."

After my long day in the cold I was starting to yawn already. He noticed it, and spoke in a rapid, earnest voice, as if afraid I might lose interest soon and want to go to bed. It was important for me too to stay awake, so I crowned a king and said, "Why don't you get someone, then, to stay with you?"

"Too many of them want to do that." His face darkened a little, almost as if warning me. "Too many of the kind you'll never get rid of again. She did, last summer when she was here. I had to put her out."

There was silence for a minute, his eyes flashing, and wanting to placate him I suggested, "She liked you, maybe."

He laughed a moment, harshly. "She liked me all right. Just two weeks ago she came back—walked over with an old suitcase and said she was going to stay. It was cold at home, and she had to work too hard, and she didn't mind even if I couldn't pay her wages."

I was getting sleepier. To keep awake I sat on the edge of the chair where it was uncomfortable and said, "Hadn't you asked her to come?"

His eyes narrowed. "I'd had trouble enough getting rid of her the first time. There were six of them at home, and she said her father thought it time that someone married her."

"Then she must be a funny one," I said. "Everyone knows that the man's supposed to ask the girl."

My remark seemed to please him. "I told you didn't I?" he

said, straightening a little, jumping two of my men. "She was so stupid that at checkers she'd forget whether she was black or red."

We stopped playing now. I glanced at the owl in the corner and the ashes littered on the floor, and thought that keeping her would maybe have been a good idea after all. He read it in my face and said, "I used to think that too sometimes. I used to look at her and think nobody knew now anyway and that she'd maybe do. You need a woman on a farm all right. And night after night she'd be sitting there where you are—right there where you are, looking at me, not even trying to play—"

The fire was low, and we could hear the wind. "But then I'd go up in the hills, away from her for a while, and start thinking back the way things used to be, and it wasn't right even for the sake of your meals ready and your house kept clean. When she came back I tried to tell her that, but all the family are the same, and I realized it wasn't any use. There's nothing you can do when you're up against that sort of thing. The mother talks just like a child of ten. When she sees you coming she runs and hides. There are six of them, and it's come out in every one."

It was getting cold, but I couldn't bring myself to go over to the stove. There was the same stillness now as when he was standing at the box-stall door. And I felt the same illogical fear, the same powerlessness to move. It was the way his voice had lowered, the glassy, cold look in his eyes. The rest of his face disappeared; all I could see were his eyes. And they held me as the lantern had held me, held me intent, rigid, even as they filled me with a vague and overpowering dread. My voice gone a whisper on me I asked, "And when you wouldn't marry her—what happened then?"

He remained motionless a moment, as if answering silently; then with an unexpected laugh like a breaking dish said, "Why, nothing happened. I just told her she couldn't stay. I went to town for a few days—and when I came back she was gone."

"Has she been back to bother you since?" I asked.

He made a little silo of checkers. "No—she took her suitcase with her."

To remind him that the fire was going down I went over to the stove and stood warming myself. He raked the coals with the lifter and put in poplar, two split pieces for a base and a thick round log on top. I yawned again. He said maybe I'd like to go to bed now, and I shivered and asked him could I have a drink of coffee first. While it boiled he stood stirring the two big pots of bran. The trouble with coffee, I realized, was that it would keep him from getting sleepy too.

I undressed finally and got into bed, but he blew out only one of the lamps, and sat on playing checkers with himself. I dozed a while, then sat up with a start, afraid it was morning already and that I'd lost my chance to get the calves away. He came over and looked at me a minute, then gently pushed my shoulders back on the pillow, "Why don't you come to bed too?" I asked, and he said, "Later I will—I don't feel sleepy yet."

It was like that all night. I kept dozing on and off, wakening in a fright each time to find him still there sitting at his checker board. He would raise his head sharply when I stirred, then tiptoe over to the bed and stand close to me listening till satisfied again I was asleep. The owl kept wakening too. It was down in the corner still where the lamplight scarcely reached, and I could see its eyes go on and off like yellow bulbs. The wind whistled drearily around the house. The blankets smelled like an old granary. He suspected what I was planning to do, evidently, and was staying awake to make sure I didn't get outside.

Each time I dozed I dreamed I was on Tim again. The calves were in sight, but far ahead of us, and with the drifts so deep we couldn't overtake them. Then instead of Tim it was the grindstone I was straddling, and that was the reason, not the drifts, that we weren't making better progress.

I wondered what would happen to the calves if I didn't get away with them. My uncle had sciatica, and it would be at least a day before I could be home and back again with some of the neighbours. By then Vickers might have butchered the calves, or driven them up to a hiding place in the hills where we'd never find them. There was the possibility, too, that Aunt Ellen and the neighbours wouldn't believe me. I dozed and woke—dozed and woke—always he was sitting at the checker board. I could hear the dry tinny tickling of an alarm clock, but from where I was lying couldn't see it. He seemed to be listening to it too. The wind would sometimes creak the house, and then he would give a start and sit rigid a moment with his eyes fixed on the window. It was always the window, as if there was nothing he was afraid of that could reach him by the door.

Most of the time he played checkers with himself, moving his lips, muttering words I couldn't hear, but once I woke to find him staring fixedly across the table as if he had a partner sitting there. His hands were clenched in front of him, there was a sharp, metallic glitter in his eyes. I lay transfixed, unbreathing. His eyes as I watched seemed to dilate, to brighten, to harden like a bird's. For a long time he sat contracted, motionless, as if gathering himself to strike, then furtively he slid his hand an inch or two along the table towards some checkers that were piled beside the board. It was as if he were reaching for a weapon, as if his invisible partner were an enemy. He clutched the checkers, slipped slowly from his chair and straightened. His movements were sure, stealthy, silent like a cat's. His face had taken on a desperate, contorted look. As he raised his hand the tension was unbearable.

It was a long time—a long time watching him the way you watch a finger tightening slowly on the trigger of a gun—and then suddenly wrenching himself to action he hurled the checkers with such vicious fury that they struck the wall in front of him and clattered back across the room.

And then everything was quiet again. I started a little, mumbled to myself as if half-awakened, lay quite still. But he seemed to have forgotten me, and after standing limp and dazed a minute got down on his knees and started looking for the checkers. When he had them all, he put more wood in the stove, then returned quietly to the table and sat down. We were alone again; everything was exactly as before. I relaxed gradually, telling myself that he'd just been seeing things.

The next time I woke he was sitting with his head sunk forward on the table. It looked as if he had fallen asleep at last, and huddling alert among the bed-clothes I decided to watch a minute to make sure, then dress and try to slip out to the stable.

While I watched, I planned exactly every movement I was going to make. Rehearsing it in my mind as carefully as if I were actually doing it, I climbed out of bed, put on my clothes, tiptoed stealthily to the door and slipped outside. By this time, though, I was getting drowsy, and relaxing among the blankets I decided that for safety's sake I should rehearse it still again. I rehearsed it four times altogether, and the fourth time dreamed that I hurried on successfully to the stable.

I fumbled with the door a while, then went inside and felt my way through the darkness to the box-stall. There was a bright light suddenly and the owl was sitting over the door with his yellow eyes like a pair of lanterns. The calves, he told me, were in the other stall with the sick colt. I looked and they were there all right, but Tim came up and said it might be better not to start for home till morning. He reminded me that I hadn't paid for his feed or my own supper yet, and that if I slipped off this way it would mean that I was stealing too. I agreed, realizing now that it wasn't the calves I was looking for after all, and that I still had to see inside the stall that was guarded by the owl. "Wait here," Tim said, "I'll tell you if he flies away," and without further questioning I lay down in the straw and went to sleep again . . . When I woke coffee and beans were on the stove already and though the lamp was still lit I could tell by the window that it was nearly morning.

V

We were silent during breakfast. Two or three times I caught him watching me, and it seemed his eyes were shiftier than before. After his sleepless night he looked tired and haggard. He left the table while I was still eating and fed raw rabbit to the owl, then came back and drank another cup of coffee. He had been friendly and communicative the night before, but now, just as when he first came running out of the stable in his long black coat, his expression was sullen and resentful. I began to feel that he was in a hurry to be rid of me.

I took my time, however, racking my brains to outwit him still and get the calves away. It looked pretty hopeless now, his eyes on me so suspiciously, my imagination at low ebb. Even if I did get inside the box-stall to see the calves—was he going to stand back then and let me start off home with them? Might it not more likely frighten him, make him do something desperate, so that I couldn't reach my uncle or the police? There was the owl over in the corner, the grindstone by the bed. And with such a queer fellow you could never tell. You could never tell, and you had to think about your own skin too. So I said politely, "Thank you, Mr. Vickers, for letting me stay all night," and remembering what Tim had told me took out my dollar's worth of silver.

He gave a short dry laugh and wouldn't take it. "Maybe you'll come back," he said, "and next time stay longer. We'll go shooting up in the hills if you like—and I'll make a trip

to town for things so that we can have better meals. You need
company sometimes for a change. There's been no one here
now quite a while."

His face softened again as he spoke. There was an expression in his eyes as if he wished that I could stay on now. It
puzzled me. I wanted to be indignant, and it was impossible.
He held my sheepskin for me while I put it on, and tied the
scarf around the collar with a solicitude and determination
equal to Aunt Ellen's. And then he gave his short dry laugh
again, and hoped I'd find my calves all right.

So I went from stall to stall, stroking the horses and making comparisons with the ones we had at home. The door, I
noticed, he had left wide open, ready for me to lead out Tim.
He was walking up and down the aisle, telling me which
horses were quiet, which to be careful of. I came to a nervous
chestnut mare, and realized she was my only chance.

She crushed her hips against the side of the stall as I
slipped up to her manger, almost pinning me, then gave her
head a toss and pulled back hard on the halter shank. The
shank, I noticed, was tied with an easy slip-knot that the
right twist and a sharp tug would undo in half a second.
And the door was wide open, ready for me to lead out Tim—
and standing as she was with her body across the stall diagonally, I was for the moment screened from sight.

It happened quickly. There wasn't time to think of conse-
quences. I just pulled the knot, in the same instant struck the
mare across the nose. With a snort she threw herself backwards, almost trampling Vickers, then flung up her head to
keep from tripping on the shank and plunged outside.

It worked as I hoped it would. "Quick," Vickers yelled to
me, "the gate's open—try and head her off" but instead I just
waited till he himself was gone, then fairly flew to the box-
stall.

The door was fastened with two tight-fitting slide-bolts,
one so high that I could scarcely reach in standing on my
toes. It wouldn't yield. There was a piece of broken whiffle-
tree beside the other box-stall door. I snatched it up and
started hammering on the pin. Still it wouldn't yield. The
head of the pin was small and round, and the whiffle-tree
kept glancing off. I was too terrified to pause a moment and
take careful aim.

Terrified of the stall though, not of Vickers. Terrified of
the stall, yet compelled by a frantic need to get inside. For the
moment I had forgotten Vickers, forgotten even the danger of

his catching me. I worked blindly, helplessly, as if I were confined and smothering. For a moment I yielded to panic, dropped the piece of whiffle-tree and started kicking at the door. Then, collected again, I forced back the lower bolt, and picking up the whiffle-tree tried to pry the door out a little at the bottom. But I had wasted too much time. Just as I dropped to my knees to peer through the opening Vickers seized me. I struggled to my feet and fought a moment, but it was such a hard, strangling clutch at my throat that I felt myself go limp and blind. In desperation then I kicked him, and with a blow like a reflex he sent me staggering to the floor.

But it wasn't the blow that frightened me. It was the fierce, wild light in his eyes.

Stunned as I was, I looked up and saw him watching me, and, sick with terror, made a bolt for Tim. I untied him with hands that moved incredibly, galvanized for escape. I knew now for sure that Vickers was crazy. He followed me outside, and, just as I mounted, seized Tim again by the bridle. For a second or two it made me crazy too. Gathering up the free ends of the reins I lashed him hard across the face. He let go of the bridle, and, frightened and excited too now, Tim made a dash across the yard and out of the gate. Deep as the snow was, I kept him galloping for half a mile, pommelling him with my fists, kicking my heels against his sides. Then of his own accord he drew up short for breath, and I looked around to see whether Vickers was following. He wasn't—there was only the snow and the hills, his buildings a lonely little smudge against the whiteness—and the relief was like a stick pulled out that's been holding up tomato vines or peas. I slumped across the saddle weakly, and till Tim started on again lay there whimpering like a baby.

VI

We were home by noon. We didn't have to cross fields or stop at houses now, and there had been teams on the road packing down the snow so that Tim could trot part of the way and even canter. I put him in the stable without taking time to tie or unbridle him, and ran to the house to tell Aunt Ellen. But I was still frightened, cold and a little hysterical, and it was a while before she could understand how everything had happened. She was silent a minute, indulgent, then helping me off with my sheepskin said kindly, "You'd better forget about it now, and come over and get warm. The calves came home themselves yesterday. Just about an hour after you set out."

I looked up at her. "But the stall, then—just because I wanted to look inside he knocked me down—and if it wasn't the calves in there—"

She didn't answer. She was busy building up the fire and looking at the stew.

■

Sandra Birdsell

Gerry Kopelow

Sandra Birdsell (1942-) grew up in Morris, Manitoba, and lived in various other Manitoba towns before settling in Winnipeg. She began writing fiction in 1976 and in the same year published her first short story. Since then her work has appeared in many literary publications and has been heard on CBC. She completed her first novel in 1979. "Truda" appears in her first collection of short stories, *Night Travellers* (1982).

TRUDA

Sandra Birdsell

"It's time to do something about all your drawings," Mika
said to Truda. She knelt on the floor searching the bottom of
the bedroom closet for plastic rain coats and hats. "Cloudy,
possible showers this morning, some sunny patches in the
southern regions, above normal temperatures," the announcer
said. The radio in Mika's bedroom was turned up loud. Mika
backed from the closet with a roll of Truda's drawings in her
hand.

"Look at this mess, will you? You can't keep these drawings forever. The wax in the crayons will attract mice."

Mice had moved into the house during the flood, taking
over the top floor, eating all of Mika's plants down to the
earth in the pots and burrowing inside to get at the roots.
Mice had chewed holes in their curtains, pulled strips of
wallpaper loose from around the baseboards, gnawed at the
plaster beneath, leaving behind hollows lined with delicate
grooves like veins in a leaf. The mice had also left behind a
furry smell, a grey mouldy odour that Mika scrubbed free
with Lysol. Mika had worked diligently, had reclaimed the
house from the flood waters, and the mice had been banished, nothing of them remained except for the imagined
fine whiskers twitching in the corners, the soft scurrying in
the dust beneath the bed at night.

"I don't think mice like wax," Truda said.

"Mice or no mice, you can't keep all these drawings. It's
getting out of hand. That's all you do, day and night, and
it's not good for your eyes."

Truda was the only Lafreniere to wear glasses. Her mother
couldn't understand it. Lack of carrots, her father said. Not
only do carrots give you good eyesight, they also give you
hair on your chest. Look at me, Maurice said, living proof.
Swallow a fruit pit and a tree will grow inside, bee stings are
really smooches for sweet children. Truda doubted it. She
knew the reason for her poor eyesight. At one time, she'd
cried too much.

Mika unrolled the drawings and spread them across the
floor. "Where did you ever get all the paper?" she asked. She

was practical, wondered more about the gathering of paper rather than why or what was in the drawings.

Truda couldn't decide whether or not to answer. She ran her tongue across her top teeth to keep the words inside. It was still easier for her to remain silent than it was to speak. When she sat at the washstand on her stool facing the window drawing pictures, she could go the whole day without speaking to anyone.

"From the bakeshop. The girl gave it to me."

"You crossed the highway alone?"

Caught. Truda felt sweat on her palms. Words were traps. "Betty came with me."

"That's neither here nor there. You can't keep every single drawing. Pick out the best ones and throw the rest out."

"I can't."

"There's no such word as can't."

Then why did you just use it yourself, Truda wondered.

"I didn't say to get rid of all of them. Just some, okay? Where would I be if everyone collected junk? Snowed under." Mika began shuffling through the drawings as though looking for some redeemable quality that might justify keeping them. She looked for genius and saw crude shapes of houses, barns, farm machinery, gardens, chickens. She picked out a drawing, pointed to the figure of a young girl. "Is this you?" she asked. "Have you drawn yourself into the pictures? Is that why you want to keep them?"

Of course it's not me. How could she be so ridiculous? The girl had black curly hair, she didn't wear glasses. "No, that's not me."

The pictures were drawings of the farm where she'd stayed during the flood. The girl was the one who'd been in the photograph on the piano with her eyes closed, a circle of flowers in her hair. Truda gathered the drawings together quickly. But Mika's attention had already begun to wander. "Where did I put those rain coats?" she asked herself. She got up from the floor and stepped over Truda. "Well, do what you want. But if you spent as much energy running and playing as you do on these drawings, then you wouldn't be so fat."

Truda didn't mind. She knew her mother's comment was punishment for not being agreeable, but she was able to keep the drawings. She listened as Mika went downstairs. She heard Lureen talking in the kitchen below. That was the way she liked the house to be. She preferred to be alone and still have people moving about, talking to each other. If she stayed in her room drawing and suddenly it grew silent beneath her, she went looking until she found them. She rolled up the drawings. She would need to find a safe place for them somewhere against any tampering that could later be blamed on a mouse, in the same way silence could be blamed on a cat.

"Oh good, you're here, finally," Mika said as Truda entered the kitchen. "Have some cereal."

Truda ate the cold breakfast cereal without tasting the blue-tinged powdered milk or the dry papery flavour of the puffed wheat kernels. She closed out the voices of her brothers and sisters and planned her next drawing. Everything about the farm had been backwards. When you came in the door there were latches on the wall in the porch. Latches that held brooms and mops firmly snapped into place. In one corner had been the cream separator with a checkered cloth draped over the bowl and in the other corner, a blue metal pie plate on the floor and cats feeding around it, wild frightened cats that zig-zagged out of her path when she entered the porch.

"I've got a job for you to do today," Mika said to Truda.

"I was going to ask if Truda could come with me after school when I go for the eggs," Betty said.

"Afraid to go alone?" Lureen's voice was strident. "What a suck."

"Well, sorry, but Truda can't go with you. I need her to pull weeds in the garden."

"How come?" Lureen asked. "Why do I have to stay in after school and wash sealers in the basement while Truda gets to do the garden? It's not fair. I always do the garden."

Their voices jabbed against Truda like a fork stabbing peas on a plate. There had been a window above the cats' feeding dish. And dried-up flies cradled in a spider's web. When you entered the farm house, instead of the kitchen there was a large dining room filled with dark furniture. Then to the left, sliding doors, a cramped parlour, a piano with a photograph of a young girl in a coffin. Stop: before that, the yard. She needed to remember the yard. She needed to reconstruct all parts of the farm because although she'd lived there almost six months, it was as though it had been a dream. She looked up at the refrigerator where she kept the bucket of crayons, out of reach of the little ones who would colour the walls or eat the crayons, Mika said. They were gone.

"My crayons," Truda said. Had Mika discovered the way to stop the drawings?

"Look here," Mika said to Lureen. "If you'd done a better job weeding the garden last time, you'd be doing it now. Besides, it won't hurt Truda to get some fresh air."

"My crayons are missing."

"If Truda can come with me to get the eggs, I'll help her do the garden," Betty said.

"Well, I'm not sitting in this dumb house all day washing jars. What about my fresh air, eh? I could die down there. Why is it only Truda who needs fresh air?"

"You'll do as I tell you."

A spoon clattered to the floor. "And where are you off to?" Mika asked Truda. Truda was halfway across the kitchen.

"To look for my crayons. They're gone. Someone took them."

"Who would take them, a mouse?" Mika asked. "You don't need your crayons this very minute. Come and sit down. Don't slow things down; I've got so much to do." She turned to Betty. "Alright, I don't care. Truda can go with you just as long as everything gets done."

My crayons, my crayons, Truda thought. She's taken them. Mika reached for the Bible resting on top of the radio. She set the Bible down on the table with a thump and opened it to the place where a bay leaf had been stuck between the pages as a marker.

Thou shalt not steal, Truda thought. The delicate scent of the bay leaf was released as Mika began to read.

After school Truda and Betty walked along the highway to the small yellow cottage where Betty would pick up three dozen eggs. "I know it was her," Truda said. "I know she took my crayons." They had walked two blocks and then the houses dwindled and gave way to open fields. Their running shoes and legs were covered in a yellow dust from the fresh gravel on the shoulder of the road. Truda walked with her head down. She'd once seen a boy at school catch the sun in a glass and beneath the glass, paper smouldered and burned. The same thing would happen to her eyes if she looked at the sun. She disliked the clicking sounds that the grass-hoppers made in the ditch along the highway. At the farm, she'd had an insect jump down the front of her dress. They'd laughed, teased her, took her dress off in the middle of the field. It wasn't pleasant laughter, but nevertheless it had been laughter which was scarce on the farm where everyone had their job to do and did it as though tomorrow wouldn't come if they didn't. In the small cramped parlour, the photograph of the little girl, and also on top of the piano, the mantle clock, striking the hour as she entered the house. Each time it bonged, the sound froze her mind. The sound of it was an old yellowing wooden sound and a lemon polish, warm milk and silverware cleaner sound. Beyond the kitchen, stairs to the attic had black rubber treads with grooves in them that made her think, black licorice; but they weren't that, they tasted bitter when she put her tongue on them.

I'm coming up one step—dropping buns
I'm coming up two steps—dropping buns
I'm coming up three steps—dropping buns
I'm coming up fourteen steps— dropping buns
And there I met a horse who was—dropping buns.

The attic: along one wall, a chest with an embroidered cloth on top of it. A fold-down cot with a crochet spread beside a mangle iron.

"She doesn't want me to draw and so she took away my crayons," Truda said.

Betty squeezed Truda's hand. "She only put them away for the summer. Wait and see."

"I want to go home." And look for them.

"Well you can't. And there's a lot to see outside of your room if you'd only look." Betty nudged Truda's chin upwards.

"Look, what do you see?"

She saw nothing. Fields, the sky. At the farm, a strange humming sound had risen up out of the fields and the people on the fields were like specks of dust moving across the horizon into the midst of the humming. And then she saw something else, like water, running overtop the highway. It sparkled and jumped beneath the sun. It was glassy blue and spilled off the highway into the fields. "A lake," she said. "I see a lake."

Betty laughed. "That's what I thought too when I first saw it. But it isn't a lake, I've been out there and you know, it gets further away, you can never reach it."

"I see waves," Truda said. She was excited. They thought she was still blind. They forgot, she could see now, even the leaves on the trees. And she could see the lake. It wasn't the yellowish brown of the river either, creeping up step by step until they'd had to climb into a boat and paddle away from town. The lake was like Betty's eyes, it was glassy blue.

"What you see are heat waves rising off the highway. I

don't know how it happens. It just does." They crossed the highway and approached the cottage where Betty would get the eggs.

"But it looks real, like a lake."

Betty led Truda down into the shallow ditch beside the highway. A car shot past and Truda watched as the car met the lake on the highway, cut through and vanished. "Come," Betty said. "We'll sit for a while and rest our legs." She set the cartons down and flopped back into the grass. Truda lay down beside her. She heard the humming sound coming up from the fields. She heard the cry of the Franklin gulls and shaded her eyes to find them.

She had sat on the cot in the attic room at the farm and listened to the birds circling above the fields. The farm woman was awkward, thought Truda couldn't dress herself and complained as she forced Truda's arms into the armholes of a cotton blouse she'd ironed on the mangle. The cotton squeaked as the buttons were pushed through holes which were too small. The blouse was the colour of goldenrod. It belonged to the dead girl on the piano. Draw: birds, grey with some blue shining in the grey wings. Their beaks made funny *kapoka* sounds on the gravel. They muttered and complained and once she thought she'd heard her name mentioned. She stood still, heart pumping blood wildly, fearful that they would smell her and fly away. The people were all on the fields. They were the specks in the dust coming to the house when they had breakdowns or for the prepared food. It made it easier to keep her vow not to speak when there was no one to talk to, except for the birds. She scooped chicken feed from the sack and scattered it around the yard. She moved among the birds slowly, speaking the sad soft cooing call of the male, and they rose up quickly, their wings fanning the air. She followed them, wheeling over the blue spruce, the willows at the far end of the pond, across the fields spread out below, golden patches on a huge quilt of green and blue, to Agassiz. To her home and her family.

Truda raised her arm and followed a single bird's flight with a finger, guided it down towards the lake but at the last moment, it veered away. She thought she could hear waves and the sound of it reminded her of the flood. She felt as though she carried her own Franklin gull sound inside her chest, overwhelming her with its terrible lonely cry. It was how she'd felt when she'd been at the farm, awake in the attic, waiting and waiting for the flood to be finished.

"Guess what, Truda? You have a new baby brother. I've named him Peter. Isn't that wonderful?" Static on the telephone wire, it was the sparrows bouncing on the wire outside the window, making Mika's words break into fragments . . . guess . . . baby . . . wonder . . .

I said. I said. I said. I said. The sparrows one after another fluttered from the wire. It shivered, a silver arc, then it straightened and dissolved into the sky. Silence.

I said, don't leave me here. When are you coming to get me?

"Have you got nothing to say? Cat's got your tongue?"

"Don't worry, it's a little thing," the farm woman said. "Once you come she'll find her tongue again. We didn't want to worry you. It's a little thing and you have your hands full with the new baby."

After that, the rain began falling, making everything blurred around the edges and so she missed seeing her mother's face at the car window. She had stood crying in the house, looking out across the yard at the road through a rain-spattered window and it was the flood. That's what made everything so wet. That and her crying. The rain came and the road past the house dissolved and oozed black dirt into deep waterfilled gulleys on each side. A man pushed the car down the road away from the farm. They couldn't stop and come for her because of the new baby, the slippery road, the rain, the flood, her crying. Even though it was her seventh birthday, and they'd promised to come, they didn't stop. And so she didn't get to see her mother's white moonshaped face at the car window. Look, look, she's waving, someone said. But Truda doubted it. See, there's your mother, girl. Stop crying for once. Don't you know, water attracts water? But she couldn't stop crying and so her two weeks' stay turned into three months and then another three months. Crying made everything worse. She'd ruined her eyes.

Ooowee, oowee, the gull inside her chest cried. *Ooowee.*

"Did you know that this land was once all under water?" Betty asked. "Once upon a time it was a large lake."

Happy Birthday to you, crying made everything worse. But she'd discovered that crayons and paper made it better. Drawing was a bird moving against a clean sky the way you wanted it to.

"Hey, are you sleeping?"

"Next time, take me with you," Truda said. "I don't want to go to the farm. I'll run away if they make me stay there.

Next time—"

Betty laughed and slid her arm beneath Truda's neck, pulling her head onto her shoulder. "What's this next time business? We probably won't have another flood. And even if we do, we have the dikes now. So forget about the flood once and for all and listen. Thousands of years ago, this was all lake. Lake Agassiz." Betty sat up and pointed across the fields. "A hundred miles away is the nearest shoreline. In the Pembina Hill. Miss Janzen showed us on a map at school."

"Will it ever come back?" Like the flood, a trickle first across the basement floor and later, a rushing waterfall and sealers bobbing about in the muddy water.

Betty gathered the egg cartons up and got to her feet. "No, it won't come back. Not in a million years. We've got nothing to worry about." She pulled Truda's ear. They crossed planks that led across the ditch to the yellow cottage. They stopped outside the gate.

"Like it out here?" Betty asked.

"Yes." The sun didn't hurt her eyes the way she thought it would.

"Good. Wait until the flax is blooming. It looks just like a lake too."

"There is a lake out there. I can hear waves."

"It's all in your head, believe me," Betty said. "Now wait right here. I won't be long."

Truda waited. She leaned into the fence and looked at the lake. It jumped forward and channels of water tipped down the highway towards her. It was all in her head but she could smell fish and see shells and sand. The gulls flew low, crossing and crisscrossing each other's flight paths. She could see their black feet tucked up against white-grey bottoms. She looked down and saw milky water receding before her feet, leaving wet crescent marks on the ends of her navy sneakers. Beige sand, dappled with curious flat grey pebbles, rounded perfectly smooth, was left in the water's wake. She stooped, picked several pebbles and dropped them into her pocket before the white frothy water rushed back up, cold, overtop her shoes and then up around her ankles. She lifted her eyes to the lake. The gulls cried with joy and bounced their solid bodies against the lake. It was like nothing she had ever drawn. She didn't need crayons when she had all this in her head. Mika could never take away her head. Her own gull rose. She felt the cold water around her calves, at her knees and then it swirled about her thighs. She took a deep breath and dove under. She didn't need to draw the farm. The farm was gone and her imagination was a tree growing inside and green leaves unfolding one by one.

■

Jake MacDonald

Jake MacDonald (1949-) was born in Winnipeg and continues to live there as a full-time writer. During the summer he guides in northern Ontario or lives in a houseboat; he has written numerous radio plays and short stories, and his first novel, *Indian River* (1981), tells a story of how pollutants (chemical and human) gradually corrupt and destroy a northern community. At present he teaches creative writing to students in rural Manitoba schools. "Becoming" first appeared in *The NeWest Review* (February, 1982).

BECOMING

Jake MacDonald

The blizzard hit at mid-afternoon.

Later in the day, with darkness descending on the city, Nimitz realized he wasn't going to get away clean. It was just before supper time and he had turned off all the lights in his apartment; he heard footsteps coming in the outside hall. They were heavy footsteps, creaking, stealthy, and he was into the broom closet, peering through the crack, when they kicked the apartment door in.

One of them was a heavyset, bleary-eyed man. The other was a woman, mid-twenties, attractive, carrying a microphone in her left hand and a tape recorder in her right. Her lips were moving as she held the mike. The big man stepped past the splintered door jamb and beckoned for the young woman to follow. He gestured for absolute quiet. They moved down the hall towards the bedroom and out of Nimitz's line of sight.

His heart pounded in his ears. He was torn between anger, pure rage that they would barge into his apartment like this, and an intense embarrassment that at any moment he would be discovered. Then suddenly they were coming.

They walked right up Nimitz's cluttered hall and stood in front of the broom closet. The fat man planted his hands on his hips, and shook his head in disgust as he looked around. "I don't know what to tell you, ma'am. The crazy guy, he could be anywhere."

The big man was Nimitz's landlord. He always paid his rent on time but nonetheless the landlord seemed to hate him. It was not unheard of for the landlord to go around kicking doors in. He was a self-made man, a rumoured millionaire, and often declared that he hadn't worked his ass off all his life so that people could tell him what he could or couldn't do. Accordingly he often browsed through Nimitz's mail, and often could be heard at strange hours of the night, squeaking down the outer hallway with his guard dog.

The young woman, carrying the tape recorder in the crook of her arm, moved down the hall and studied the big colour posters that he'd taped to the walls. Nimitz watched. She paused in front of the beautiful Kodachrome blowup of the fan coral, his favourite too.

"He certainly does like the sea, doesn't he."

The landlord tossed a hand. "Aw, summabitch. He's a nutcase, eh? All I know is, he says he's going to the ocean to be a fish, who's paying the rent, eh?"

The landlord fingered a rip in the wallpaper where Nimitz had tacked a large photo of a hammerhead shark. The hall window ticked, betraying a windblown gust of sleet. Nimitz's luggage was still piled in the hall, where he'd hurriedly abandoned it after hearing their approach. The young woman, who in her black leather coat, tightly pinned hair and red lips looked vaguely feline and untrustworthy to Nimitz, eyed the luggage and glanced casually at the broom closet door, slightly ajar. "Well I'd certainly like to talk to him, anyway." she sighed. "I, uh . . . don't want to disturb this young man's privacy but I think he has a most interesting idea . . . a very clever advertising gimmick. Don't you think so? I mean, with these awful prairie winters . . . what a promotion scheme!"

Nimitz was gritting his teeth, jammed into the closet, standing on one leg. Curses, he thought to himself, I never should have rented that billboard. Now I've even got reporters after me.

With the last dregs of his bank account he'd commissioned a billboard at the corner of Stradbrook and Main, showing him in his fish outfit, bidding Winnipeg adieu with a lifted fin. SO LONG WINNIPEG—the caption read—I'M OFF TO THE OCEAN TO BECOME A FISH! And he'd signed his name. This public statement, which he'd intended strictly as a sincere farewell, had backfired horribly. The billboard company, after charging him $400 erected the message a day ahead of schedule and caught Nimitz unprepared. He'd hoped to be well underway, jetting his way south to the Caribbean by the time the billboard went public, but the phone had started ringing by early afternoon and hadn't stopped. He'd been besieged by relatives, family, employer, neighbours—each demanding, no doubt, an explanation. But each time he'd taken to the broom closet. So far it had worked.

His landlord ground coins in his pocket, impatient. The lady reporter kept exploring the apartment, lifting, poking, spinning the fat papier-mache fish that hung on threads from the ceiling. Her head shook slowly, a tight smile played on her mouth.

"I gotta get back to my hockey game," said the landlord.
"It's Gretzky," he explained.

"Well thank you very much for showing me his apartment," the young woman said. "I hope he's not out wandering around in this blizzard tonight . . ." She glanced at the broom closet. "The weather is so bad that they've cancelled all the flights at the airport. Perhaps I'll leave my card, in case he decides to contact me." She smoothed the leather coat over her hips and walked to the broom closet. Her eyes were unfocused, abstract, her lips parted as she wedged the card in the door jamb, her face perhaps six inches away. This woman, Nimitz thought to himself, has taken advantage of men before.

Nimitz caught a cab to a hotel near the airport.

The storm was at its height. The streets were empty. It was suppertime, but dark as wild eerie midnight. Nimitz sat in the back of the cab, clutching a huge stack of paraphernalia on his lap—mylar fins, ribbed with old car aerials, a scaly skin fashioned from a body stocking and large sequins, spiny dorsals, sheet metal gills. The cab wallowed and skidded though the snow-clogged streets. Occasionally snowplows would lunge across the street in front of them, their disaster lights spinning crazily.

"You're going to a masquerade party on a night like this?" the cab driver remarked.

"No . . ." said Nimitz quietly, the lights of the city playing over his face one last time. "I'm going to the ocean. To become a fish."

The cabbie nodded. "Sorry I asked."

At the hotel door the cabbie sulked, refusing to help Nimitz unload his gear. Nimitz paid him with a five dollar tip, his bare hands freezing in the bitter January wind, and then carted his equipment to the brightly-lit aquarium of the hotel entrance.

He stood in front of the desk, his fins piled beside him, and rubbed his hands together for warmth. Bits of snow melted in his tousled hair.

"Mr. uh . . . don't I know you?" the desk clerk asked.

"I doubt it," retorted Nimitz. "I'm on my way to the ocean. I'd like to rent a room for a few hours, until the airplanes start moving again."

"Of course, sir."

"And I'm expecting a call from the airlines regarding my

reservation. Other than that I want privacy, alright? No visitors—I want to get some rest."

"Yes sir, of course," the desk clerk tossed a finger, a bellhop materialized at Nimitz's side.

"You take the suitcase. I'll take the fish outfit," said Nimitz.

The bellhop led him down the hall.

He wasn't in his room more than ten minutes, testing the shower, testing the colour television, ripping the sanitary band off the toilet seat, when a key sounded in the door and the lady reporter came into the room. "I'd like to introduce myself," she said.

Nimitz relented.

The girl said her name was Kate Matthews, free lance journalist, down on her luck. "At a hundred bucks a story do you think I'm getting rich?" she said. She was already sitting on the edge of the bed, but there was a resigned look on her face as if she expected to be expelled from the room as quickly as she had come in. Her leather coat was unbuttoned, and she didn't have a light for her cigarette. Nimitz didn't smoke.

"I'll talk to you for five minutes. These rules please . . . no tape recorder, and no story until I leave town."

"Okay," she said. "No sweat." She was still looking for a match for her cigarette. She found one, lit her cigarette, and slipped out of her leather coat. She was wearing black slacks, fawn sweater and a crimson silk scarf knotted around her throat. Nimitz appraised her bosom. This is one thing I'll miss, he thought to himself. A female trout or salmon is gorgeous, admittedly, but the human female isn't that bad either.

Settled, with her knees crossed, her Benson & Hedges aloft, her hair loosed and shaken down, she glanced at Nimitz and smiled. "Now . . . what's this about becoming a fish. Is this another one those Fly-to-the Sun promotions?"

Nimitz explained that he was serious. He showed her his fins, his weight belt, his underwater topographical maps of various ocean regions—all tucked away in waterproof pouches —his scaly outfit, designed so that other fishes would accept him, and most important of all, his solid-state rebreather. He laid all the gear out on the bed, explaining the function of each, and told her that he'd test the outfit one more time, to make sure he hadn't forgotten anything.

Kate Matthews watched with a look of disbelief as he

stripped down to his jockey shorts and climbed into the fish outfit. In a matter of minutes he was fully dressed—in silver scales, rattling gills, and a great quivering array of gaudy fins. From around his neck, in the manner of a French cavalier, hung a lacy ruffle of quills. He waddled carefully to the mirror, studying his image with narrowed eye. "I put a lot of thought into this. You know, your average person would think I was crazy. They'd say 'Nimitz, you're crazy. Why not become a dolphin if you're going to all that trouble?' But that's just their own prejudice coming through. Dolphins share a lot of similarities with human beings, so naturally we think that dolphins are wonderful. And nobody mentions that the Japanese slaughter them by the thousands, so there's a real risk involved. And not only that . . . dolphins breathe air and I don't want to have to go up to the surface all the time, I've had enough of that."

He stood sideways, glancing at himself in the mirror, and awkwardly rearranged one of his ventral fins. "I finally settled on the rooster fish. I'm one of the most grotesque creatures in the ocean, in a sort of flamboyant way, and also . . ." he added with a modest smile "I'm deadly poisonous."

Kate Matthews stared at him for a long moment. "This is a joke." she said flatly.

Nimitz shook his head. His gills rustled. "But you don't have to stay here, if you don't believe me. I mean you asked, and I'm telling you."

"Well you can't just become a fish!"

He sat on the edge of the bed, crossed his fins patiently in his lap. "Well yes, actually . . . I can."

She stared at him, as if making some quick appraisal of his sanity, and he stared back. There was the faint sound of winter buffeting the outside walls. "You see," he began, "it's a well-accepted fact, these days, that the physical world is really just an idea. It's not real, but just a sort of stage setting that we've all decided to work on. Any physicist will tell you that. Any physicist will tell you that once you divide an atom a certain number of times there's nothing left. Nothing! At some level, then, there's no such thing as matter!"

She nodded sourly. "Heavy."

"So if being here, in this room, in this city, in this world, is just an idea, then I'm changing my mind, that's all. I'm just changing my mind."

"If you're just changing your mind, why do you need all this equipment?"

"Well . . . I don't have the mental power of say, a yogi or somebody like that so I have to cheat a bit. I don't expect to turn right into a fish just by snapping my fingers. I'm more reasonable than that. I figure I'll have to be down there, concentrating real hard for a couple of weeks before I get any results."

She nodded, then shook her head. "You can't do this. You can't take these philosophies and apply them to real life, they're not meant for that. Where will you live when you're down there? How will you swim with all that crap on? What will you eat? How will you . . . breathe?"

Nimitz smiled benignly and displayed his solid-state rebreather, which was a black steel and rubber device resembling a harmonica. "With this . . . I can breathe underwater just like a fish. It's good for up to two years . . . Cousteau designed it years ago but suppressed it because it would kill off his SCUBA royalties. Not many people know about it. I had to buy the plans off this Florida smuggler I know, and it cost me plenty."

She examined it dubiously. "This little thing?"

"Sure. It works just great. You just pop it in your mouth and breathe through it. It separates the H_2 from the O. Hydrogen bubbles shoot out those little vents on the side and oxygen flows in through the mouthpiece. It'll have to do until I get my gills operating."

She peered at his gills, several layers of clinking sheet metal with meticulously handpainted scales. "But . . . where will you live? You can't just swim around like a fish with that monkey suit on."

He unbuttoned his gills at the throat and smiled. "Of course not. I'll tend to settle down off reefs in about forty feet of water. I prey on crustaceans so you'll tend to find me where there's a steady run of shrimp or squid or lobster. Give me some clear, clean water, a sand bottom, and maybe a bit of riprap or coral nearby and I imagine I'll do very well."

"Really," she said. She was regarding him with unwavering fascination. "And you seriously think you can get away with this? You don't work for some goofy ad agency?"

He stared back at her, his eyes equally intent. "No I do not."

"And you think that . . . mouth organ thing will let you cruise around underwater indefinitely?"

"Oh yeah. I just got to keep it filled with baking soda."

"You've got to keep it filled with . . . baking soda?"

"Yeah . . . the baking soda makes the bubbles. Along with the H_2. Here, let me show you. I should test it anyway."

Nimitz stood up, clumsy because of the way the fish skin bound his legs together, and wiggled into the bathroom. He heard her coming behind him, but couldn't see with the ruff of fins around his neck. He bent over stiffly and turned on the bathroom tap, and spoke loudly over the water's roar. "My name is Nimitz, by the way," he said.

"I know. . . . Your name is on the billboard, remember?"

"Yes. But I'd like to forget. I hadn't intended to become a notorious figure so early, but my plans fouled up."

She was turning over the breathing device in her hand, looking up at him expectantly. He was taller than her but not by much.

"Allow me." Nimitz said. He shut the tap off and took the rebreather from her hand, paused for a moment and gazed down into the half-tubful of swinging water. Bright lights from the ceiling, reflected in the bath, moved like thought on Nimitz's face. He clamped the rebreather in his mouth, looked at her, waved goodbye, and then plunged his head into the water.

Seconds passed, and more seconds, and then she thought she detected a queer tremor in his shoulders. She seized him by the gills and dorsal fins and wrestled him bodily from the bathtub. He fell backwards onto the floor, she, falling in a tangle beneath him, and as he gasped and coughed violently she scrambled to one knee, forced him to lie flat on the wet floor, and prepared to administer mouth-to-mouth recusitation. Nimitz floundered and the more he coughed and struggled the harder she pinned.

"Easy, easy . . ." she soothed. "You're not going to drown."

"I know I'm not going to drown!" he protested, his voice nasal from the thumb and forefinger clamped on his nose. "I was going to be fine! There was no problem! Didn't you see the H_2?"

"No I didn't see the H_2," she retorted, mimicking the quack in his voice. "If it was working so well why is your face purple?"

"Eh!?"

"Why is your face purple?"

He sat up, straightened his fins. "Excitement I guess . . . I don't know! You try it. If you don't think it's exciting to be breathing air under water, man's oldest dream . . ."

She made a cynical snort.

"Looks like I spilled a little water on you." Nimitz said.

She nodded, looking down at the water splotches in her slacks, the thin sweater drenched and clinging to her bust. "I guess I got excited," she said. She gave him a crooked smile.

At that moment the telephone rang. Nimitz wriggled and flopped on the floor struggling to get up.

"Here, let me help," she said.

"Get the phone."

Nimitz lay on the floor and listened as she answered the phone. Water, his element, soaked in through the fish skin and established a chilly presence in his undershorts. "It's the airline," she called out. "There's some flights starting to operate again. You've got a reservation on Flight 203 to Cozumel, but that's postponed until sometime tomorrow morning. And you've got a reservation on Flight 109 to Miami, but the flight is held over in Toronto . . . And you've got—"

"All I want is to get to the sea!" he blurted. "Anywhere on the sea! Doesn't she have anything tonight, going to the sea?"

There was a long interval, and Nimitz listened intently to the voice in the other room. Kate's voice was calm and pleasant. Nimitz was beginning to think that she was a little unbalanced.

"There's a Skybus to Vancouver at midnight. It's leaving on time, and there's still two seats left."

Nimitz struggled to his feet. "Yes! I'll take it."

Kate Matthews cooed into the telephone. "Wonderful. We'll take both of them," she said.

In front of the airport there were taxi cabs clustered like predators, their lights flashing in ominous synchronization. The cab containing Nimitz and Kate Matthews slid to an icy halt in the loading zone. Nimitz paid the cabbie and exited clumsily. Still in his fish costume, having committed himself to never again remove that freely-chosen badge of identity, he slipped on the packed snow and bent one fin against the taxi door. Kate Matthews exited from the cab behind him, carrying a luggage bag and taking his arm as they slipped and skidded across the road. "It's only a caudal fin," said Nimitz "I'll hardly ever need it. Anyway . . . maybe it'll heal."

"I'll get some tape somewhere," Kate Matthews said.

Overhead, above the streetlights, the cloud cover had torn off and the sky was clearing. There were several stars, tiny chinks of light, visible in the huge dark emptiness but the wind still blew, swirling chips of ice into their faces, and they both exclaimed aloud as they rushed towards the door. Kate Matthews, her own clothes thoroughly soaked from the debacle in the hotel bathroom, had changed into an outfit assembled from Nimitz's suitcase. As she expected, his clothes were somewhat too large and consistently fish-oriented, with "Save the Whales" and "I'm a Bass Buster" tee shirts predominant, along with sweaters plastered with fishing club crests, "Tackle Tester" and "Go Barbless" baseball hats etc., but she managed to put together an outfit she thought reasonably anonymous. Wearing wool breeches, an old British army khaki shirt, canvas vest, straw creel hung over her shoulder as a purse, and a crush hat, festooned with numerous tiny trout flies, she thought she might pass for somebody marginally normal, perhaps even chic. However, as they entered the cavernous light of the airport terminal, aswarm with strangers, she drew near to Nimitz's fin. "I feel a bit conspicuous," she whispered, as they walked to the CP ticket desk.

"How do you think I feel?" he replied.

Nimitz paid for their tickets. "I won't need money where I'm going," he sighed. There was a two dollar bill in his hand. "This is it. The last money I have as a human. Should we blow it foolishly?"

"Let's save it." she said. "You never know."

They secured their tickets, checked their luggage and walked to the boarding gate. Nimitz went through the metal detector first. A female security officer, smiling as if she were overjoyed to see them, ran a hand detector up and down their bodies. Nimitz, at first concerned that his fish costume would cause consternation at the security gate, saw that amongst the other passengers lined up for the Vancouver flight—aging hippies, loggers, painted ladies, seven-foot-tall Rastifarians, radical nuns, skeletal drug addicts—he was barely noticed. They walked down the hall and down the long umbilical tunnel into the DC8. They sat, waited, there was a whine, the engines staggered thunderingly alive and they began to roll, squeaky as a carriage, across the concrete ramp towards the runway. Nimitz pressed his forehead against the window and mentally photographed all that he would never see again—

lights of the city, crawling headlights, cold pavement swept by even colder snow. A moment later the landscape swung through an abrupt ninety-degree arc and the jet braked to a stop. There was a long moment, a total silence inside the gloom of the aircraft.

Nimitz looked at Kate Matthews. She was pretending to look straight ahead, but he had the sense that she was studying him. She seemed sneaky, but in a constant and predictable and quite playful way. The trout fisherman's hat was perched on her abundant hair in a roguish tilt and she was twiddling her thumbs. As if reading his mind she whispered to him from the corner of her mouth, "I saw your picture on the billboard and that's why I'm here. I'm not really after a story. I'm after you. I know what kind of man I like and the face on the billboard sparked my interest. And then I found out that you're probably crazy and that was two strikes. And then I found out that you're going away and never coming back, so that was three strikes and I'm out."

She proffered her hand, palm up, as if they were making a deal.

Nimitz took her hand, profoundly moved. He hesitated, as if searching for the proper words. "If you were a rooster fish," he finally whispered, "I would like to spawn with you."

"Oh thank you, Nimitz," she replied, squeezing his hand.

The jet began its takeoff roll. With the thunder of engines they were pressed deep into their seats. Nimitz was imagining what it would be like to spawn with Kate Matthews. "Do you know how to swim?" he asked, as the plane lifted off.

It was like the hell-bound plane, Nimitz thought to himself. A full moon slanted in through the heavy plastic port-holes and the plane bucked and swooped its way westward. At one point the pilot announced that were flying into a one hundred and twenty mile an hour headwind, thus the buffeting, but though he changed altitudes the bouncing continued. Their departure time from Winnipeg was midnight and their estimated time of arrival in Vancouver was midnight, and as they rocketed westward, locked in time, the strange-looking passengers who hulked up and down the gloomy aisles, or brayed drunkenly throughout the airplane, seemed like flies caught in amber, living exhibits in some future museum. Nimitz, with a leaden despair for his own species, studied the plastic moldings, vinyl seat backs and mysteriously patterned rivets around him and tried to divine the process by which human civilization had come to this noxious climax. Personally, he suspected that evolution made its first mistake when the first amphibians crawled up out of the sensible sea.

Finally the plane began to descend. Kate Matthews, who had been sleeping with her head upon his shoulder, stirred drowsily and he patted her knee. He felt like they were married. "We're going down."

She leaned across him, her elbows heavy in his lap, and peered out the porthole. A moment later she said, "Look, there's the lights of the city."

They landed at Vancouver International and picked up their bags. Even inside the terminal, teeming with crowds, they could smell the damp west coast air. They went outside and it was lightly raining. The everpresent cabs idled at the curb and a tangle of roads, black and shiny as oil under the streetlamps, all led towards the lights of the city. "What now?" Kate Matthews asked.

"This way," Nimitz said. "I used to know a guy . . ."

They walked down the road for half a mile. When they were out of sight of the main door of the airport Nimitz went down into the ditch and spread the barbed wire fence. "Hop through," he said. He was shivering. Already the rain had leaked through the hand-sewn scales of his fish skin.

"What gives?" she said, as they began to slog across the muddy field.

"This is actually an island, Sea Island. When they built the airport there were some people living on this island, but they kicked them all off. I know a guy who's sort of a hobo who lives in one of the old houses up here. He's a good guy, we used to work together. Anyway, maybe he'll put us up for the night. He's thinking of becoming a fish too."

Soon a dark row of houses, with not a light on, loomed ahead. The wind seemed to be picking up and Nimitz moved boldly through the yards, hurrying against the quickening rain. "It's this one," he whispered loudly. "But it doesn't look like he's home."

Around the back door, which was piled with fresh-cut firewood, there were many signs of occupancy—dog dish, rubber boots, swede saw. Kate Matthews spied a note on the door, "Look."

"DEAR STRANGER," the note read "COME ON IN AND HELP YOURSELF. BUT PLEASE REPLACE WHAT YOU USE. SPLIT WOOD IF YOU GOT NO

MONEY. PERSONAL FRIENDS PLEASE IGNORE THIS
SIGN. I'M SHANGHAIED TO BELLA COOLA. CY."

They went in the door and Nimitz groped through the
kitchen, locating a lantern and a wooden match. The room
flared alight—kitchen at one end, fireplace halfway through
the room and old double bed at the far end. "I want a coffee," Kate Matthews said.

"Me too . . . I'm cold."

"Take off that fish outfit. You must be soaked."

"I'll take it off and light a fire. I don't mind going human
tonight, since it's my last night as a hairless primate, or, if
you prefer, a homo sapiens."

Nimitz lit the fire and took off his fish skin. His shorts
were also wet and he removed them, hanging everything by
the heat of the fire. His torso, hardened by years of travelling
and outdoor labour, was sculpted in shadow by the firelight.
He was not ashamed to be naked in front of a woman he
barely knew. It was his preference for basics that convinced
him to become a fish in the first place. He got into the bed
and pulled the blankets to his chin, shivering.

"Hurry up," he said. "I'm warming it up."

"Warming what up?"

She came to the bedside with two steaming mugs of coffee.
Nimitz watched her undress. He decided that she was undoubtedly the most straightforward, witty and nubile woman he'd
ever had the pleasure to watch disrobe. She climbed under
the heavy quilts, shivered wildly from the cold and wrapped
herself around him. "Oh my," she said. "Oh my . . ."

Afterward, in the total dark, with the fire down to only
crawling embers, she stirred her sleepy warmth against him
and kissed the side of his neck. "Nimitz . . . are you still
awake?"

"Of course," he said.

"Well . . . what's that strange noise outside? That . . .
thumping, swishing noise. It can't be that windy, can it?"

Nimitz smiled, she could tell by the movement of his
cheek. "What, didn't you realize? No . . . I guess in the dark
you couldn't see and I forgot to tell you. That sound is the
surf hitting as the tide comes in. We're only about fifty yards
from the sea."

Dawn broke stormy and dismal. For hours, as wind and
rain slapped the windows, Nimitz and Kate Matthews dozed
under the covers. Occasionally they would waken, nuzzle like

cats, and ease their limbs into some new model of entwine-
ment. Outside, the sea growled patiently.

Finally, after sleeping all of the morning and much of the
afternoon, Kate Matthews opened her eyes to sunlight in the
window. She rolled over to tell Nimitz but he was already
awake, staring up at the ceiling. "When are you going?" she
asked.

He looked at her. "Soon, I guess. I was going to go early
in the morning but I hate to go swimming when it's
overcast."

They rose from the bed and dressed. Kate Matthews wriggled into Nimitz's old fisherman's sweater and moved about
the kitchen making coffee, her hair a luxuriant mane. Nimitz, strapping on his gills, gazed at her fixedly. His eyes were
soft but the muscles of his jaw twitched with determination.
Finally he moved up behind her and placed a fin on her
shoulder. "Kate," he said.

She sobbed and threw her arms around him. "I don't *want*
you to become a fish!"
Her tears ran onto his scaly chest.

"Kate, Kate . . ." he whispered. "It's not what you want, or
what I want, or what anybody wants that's important. It's
bigger than that. It's survival of a species. At one time we
crawled out of the sea, and now it's time for us to go back,
don't you see?"

She nodded.

They drank their coffee and went outside.

It was a brilliant day, the sky blue as a flag. The sea was a
darker purple, redolent with salty breezes, and across a line of
dunes, drift logs, and cane grass the surf was dumping lazily
on the beach. Nimitz walked boldly through the sand, his
ostentatious rooster quills shivering colourfully in the wind,
and seagulls swerved drastically overhead, screaming.

There was a rowboat on the beach and together they
pushed it into the water. "Do you know how to row?" he
asked.

"Shut up," she replied.

She rowed and he sat in the rear of the boat, going over his
maps. "I'm going to swim out to the end of the Strait of Juan
de Fuca," he told her. "And then hang a left and head south
down the edge of the continental shelf. If I keep travelling I
should make the Coronado Islands in four or five weeks.
There's lots happening down there, the waters are teeming
with life . . . I'll take it easy there for a while, rest up, prey on

the plentiful crustaceans, then it's make westering . . . head out. I got seven thousand miles of Pacific Ocean to explore, not to mention what lies beyond, like the Great Barrier Reef, Sunda Straits, South China Sea . . ."

She stopped rowing. They were fifty yards from shore, bobbing gently. Her chin was propped on her hand and she wasn't looking at him. And then she looked up at him and she was focused, bright. "Good luck Nimitz," she said.

He shrugged. "As long as I don't get speargunned by some tourist or netted by some Russian trawler I should be alright."

He pulled the fringed collar and fish hood up over his head. The glassy eyes, large as saucers, stared at her unseeing. "Next time you're at a fancy cocktail party," he said, the large fat lips flapping, "Take a good look at the seafood hors d'oeuvres. It might be me."

She pried open the huge lips and took one last look at the human face inside. She kissed him, he kissed her. "Good-bye," he said.

"If you change your mind you'll find me back in Winter-peg, working for a living."

"Evolution can't reverse itself," he said.

He stood up, put the rebreather in his mouth and leapt into the sea. Water exploded around him, flashes of coloured light. Jeeze it's cold! He was going to shout, but realized with his weight belt he was already sinking. He breathed deeply, once, twice, and a rapture began to flood into his brain. Below him he saw the deep sandy bottom coming up to meet him, and scattered on it were dappled spots of sunlight that looked exactly like dancing gold.

■

Leon Rooke

Kim

Leon Rooke (1934-) was born in Roanoke Rapids, North Carolina and settled in Victoria, B.C. in 1969 where he still lives. He began his writing career as a playwright; *Sword/Play* was produced both in Vancouver (1973) and New York (1975) but he is known primarily for his fiction. He has published two novels, including *Fat Woman* (1980), and numerous collections of stories: *Last One Home Sleeps in the Yellow Bed* (1968), *The Love Parlour* (1977), *Cry Evil* (1980) and *The Birth Control King of the Upper Volta* (1983). "Deer Trails in Tzityonyana" is from the collection *Death Suite* (1981).

DEER TRAILS IN TZITYONYANA

Leon Rooke

The limousine, black with a maroon top and not new, was parked out of the sun a few hundred yards up the street from the school. The motor was purring. The driver up front wore a maroon cap and was smoking a cigarette. The man in the back opened the door as Itzy drew near. She was the last person out of the school yard and was in a hurry to get home. Her nose as usual was in a book, this one called *Deer Trails in Old Tzityonyana*.

"Get in," the man said.

Itzy looked up, astonished that anyone should speak to her and especially like that. She looked up and down the street, squinting against the sun, and retreating a few steps backwards. Then she closed her book and cautiously approached the open door. She looked inside, wrinkling her nose. The interior smelled of the driver's cigarettes, but the seats were wide and cushiony and the radio was softly playing. She stepped in. There was so much room between the front and back seats and the roof was so high that she could practically stand without bending. Everything up the street looked different through the windshield, tangled and misty and all the trees a shining green because earlier it had been raining.

"Sit down," the man beside her said, and reaching over, he closed the door.

"Yes sir," Itzy said.

He wore dark glasses and sat with one knee crossed over the other, his hands folded one above the other in his lap. He stared straight ahead, as did Itzy, although not before she noticed the thick gold ring on his finger and wondered to herself what such a ring would cost. She thought it silly for a man to wear jewelry, even a ring. No one spoke.

In a few minutes they were out of her neighbourhood and heading away from town. The man up front drove at a slow steady speed and did not once look around at the two in the back; he lit up another cigarette and turned the radio up slightly. The volume was still faint, however, and Itzy could hardly hear it. The car motor had a nice soft whirr and she liked that better.

When they were about five miles out, with the Aurilian Springs cemetery stretching along both sides of the road, the man reached over and lifted the book out of Itzy's hands. He studied the cover, which showed a green forest and in a clearing deep in the forest, at a small pool, three deer feeding themselves. He settled the book back in the girl's lap without opening it.

"Junk," he said.

Itzy murmured "Yes sir," although one could tell by the slanted look she gave him that she did not agree.

At Estherville, the first town down the road, the limousine crept slowly through Main Street, turned and climbed a high hill to another part of town, and eventually came to a stop under a wide red awning held up by four brightly-painted men carved out of wood and blowing on trumpets. The brass of the trumpets shone in the sun and past the last of these Itzy could glimpse the sea.

"Stay here," the man told her.

She remained as she was, sometimes looking up to stare at the driver's maroon cap and sometimes squinting up her eyes and glancing outside as if to determine for herself what had made this or that odd sound, but for the most part she kept her nose in the pages of *Deer Trails in Old Tzityonyana*.

The man returned. "Take this," he said.

Itzy accepted the ice cream cone. It was up high, in three scoops of different flavours, and she licked immediately at the chocolate on the bottom.

"Good?" the man asked.

Itzy absently nodded. She was already back into her reading of *Deer Trails in Old Tzityonyana*.

The driver guided the limousine carefully back down the long incline and slowly back through Estherville's quiet Main Street; on the highway he got the machine up again to its steady, silent speed and kept it there, smoking, and now and then nodding his head to some beat of music from the radio which Itzy could hear only faintly.

At the Aurilian Springs cemetery a long, slow procession of automobiles was turning tediously off the highway, and here the man in the rear with Itzy pulled the shades down over the windows and sat back against the cushion, drumming his fingers on his knees, until they could again continue.

A few minutes later they were once more in Itzy's neighbourhood.

"Not too near, Horace," the man told his driver.

Horace pulled over to the curb, stopping under a drooping willow that covered much of the road. The sun was still strong and with the windows closed it was very hot inside the limousine.

Itzy made no move yet to get out. She was looking at the driver.

"Do you want any money?" the man asked.

"What for?" She did not look at him.

She saw the driver reach out and turn the radio dial. She heard a broken word or a stab of music from one station after another, but the driver kept on turning the knob. She wondered what he was looking for.

"Is there anything you would like?" asked the man beside her.

Itzy scratched herself. After a while she said: "I would like his cap." She pointed at Horace.

The man contemplated this request. It did not seem to amuse or surprise him, nor did he appear to think it odd.

"Give her your cap," he said.

The driver took off his cap and passed it over the seat without looking back. Itzy took it, and the man reached across her to open her door. Itzy backed out, still staring at Horace. The driver's head was quite bald. It seemed to her that he was too young to have no hair. He looked silly, and she wondered whether this ever made him unhappy.

The man in the rear pulled her door shut.

The limousine at once lumbered heavily away, but before it had gone even a few yards Itzy had turned her back to it and was racing across green grass, steering for the hole in a neighbour's hedge, taking short-cuts home.

"You're late!" called her mother from the kitchen.

Itzy didn't answer. She was out of breath, and her face felt warm. She plopped down into a big recliner chair, pushed her weight back, and let the platform come out and lift her feet up. Although the room was already in darkness, she closed her eyes.

"Where were you?"

Her mother was beside her, looking down, wiping her hands on a towel.

"Nowhere," Itzy said.

When her mother continued to stand there wiping her hands and staring down on her, Itzy shrugged and again said, "Nowhere."

"You've been running," her mother said.

"Have I?"

"You're not in any trouble, are you?"

"I think not," Itzy said.

Her mother looked confused. Itzy wished she would go on about her business. She was about to say *leave me alone*, but she stopped herself in time, knowing that would be a mistake.

"What have you been doing all day?" she asked.

Her mother didn't answer at once. Then she backed away and in a quiet, edgy voice said: "The usual. What do you think?" She went to the sofa and sat down with her knees together, spreading the towel over them like a serviette. "I've been working on my puzzle," she said.

"Was that fun?"

Her mother glared at her. But then her expression softened and she said: "It's a Wildwood scene. Very pretty on the box cover. But I can't find the right pieces."

"You never can."

Her mother did not take offense at this, although she might have.

"Will you help me?"

"Over the weekend," Itzy said, "if I have time."

Her mother sighed, sinking back against the sofa cushions. Itzy shifted over on her side, bringing her knees up under her chin so that the book rested only a few inches from her face.

"You'll get eye-strain again," her mother said. "You'll have headaches." She stared across at Itzy, studying her intently, in the meantime raking her hand aimlessly through the puzzle pieces spread out on the coffee table in front of her.

Itzy, her small mouth puckered in concentration, was tracing one finger under the lines of type to keep them from running together. Her body threw a dark shadow over the pages and her eyes were squinted up so narrowly, and her body was so still, that one might easily have assumed she was asleep, except for her racing finger.

"You'll go blind," her mother said. She did not get up to turn on the lights, however, or to open the curtains. Nor did it occur to her to command Itzy to do one of these things.

"Where did you get that silly cap?" her mother asked.

She had to repeat this.

"A friend gave it to me," Itzy eventually replied. "I like it."

For the next several minutes Itzy's mother worked over her puzzle.

"There is supposed to be a chimney," her mother declared.
"There is supposed to be the rest of a chimney somewhere,
but I can't find it. I don't believe it is here."
"I'm trying to read," Itzy told her. "Stop talking to me."
Feeling her mother's eyes continually on her, Itzy finally
looked up, shrugging. "It's there somewhere," she said.
"Why do you buy one with so many pieces? I keep telling
you."

Itzy's mother looked from her daughter to the spread-out
puzzle and suddenly her hands flew out and she scrambled up
the assembled pieces, hissing angrily.

Itzy ignored this. She had her own problems. Her hands
were sticky, she had stained the book pages with ice cream,
and her stomach was rumbling.

Her mother walked over to where the window curtains
were drawn. She smoothed out several folds in the rich, deep
cloth. "Five thousand pieces," she murmured. "It's absurd."
She turned to Itzy who was scowling up at her. "I'm going to
get new drapes," she said. "I'm going to get some brightness
into this house."

Itzy flung down her book, audibly groaning. Her mother
returned to the sofa and once more sat down. She sat with her
hands together in her lap, regarding Itzy closely. "I gather
you don't care. I take it that you have no opinion."

Itzy shoved herself back into the chair; she stretched out
almost in a prone position and closed her eyes.

"I'm not hungry this evening," she heard her mother say
in a new voice. "Do you mind if we skip dinner?"

Itzy's eyes opened and she stared anxiously up at the dark
ceiling; it seemed to her that the house had the same low
hum, and the same gentle vibrations, that earlier had marked
her time in the limousine.

"I may never eat again," her mother said.

Itzy let out a small clap of laughter.

"That's right, laugh!" her mother said. "You don't have to
worry about what men think when they look at you."

Itzy's eyes rolled. She covered her face with the book,
although she could not hide her body's shaking.

Several minutes passed in silence. Then Itzy heard her
mother sweeping the puzzle back into its box. When she
opened her eyes her mother was standing above her. "How is
the book?" she asked softly.

Itzy's reply held the same quality. "It's junk, I guess."

"But I thought you liked it!"

"You thought wrong."

The strength went out of her mother's shoulders; she stood a moment, shivering. "Wash up," she then said. "We will be eating soon." She passed on into the kitchen.

Later in the evening they had their baths, first Itzy, then her mother, then they went to bed.

From across the hall, somewhere about midnight, her mother's voice called to her: "Go to sleep!"

Itzy muttered under her breath; after a few seconds she yawned, and rolled over to turn off the light. For a time her mind wandered, then she thought of nothing.

The next day Itzy did not go to school. She had a stomach ache, she said, and her mother was content to let her remain home. In the morning they worked together on her mother's puzzle and in the afternoon they walked to a nearby grocery, and in the evening they made more headway on the Wildwoods scene.

A quiet weekend followed, both of them going about drowsily through the heat of the day, and sinking down gratefully into sleep once darkness fell. On Sunday the two fell asleep together, reading from the same book in her mother's narrow bed.

Thus it was Monday before Itzy again came out of the school yard to find the black and maroon limousine waiting under the tree up ahead.

"Where is your cap?" the man asked her once they were underway.

Itzy was momentarily confused; she had forgotten all about receiving the cap and once she remembered, she could not think where she had left it. She shrugged her shoulders. The man stared off in a distracted way into the blue afternoon.

Today the driver was wearing a new cap, identical to the first, although it did not fit him nearly so well. It perched high on his head and looked silly, Itzy thought, and with this one she could see that he had no hair. His ears stuck out and the skin had tiny blue veins running all over.

A light rain came up and perhaps because of this, half-way to Estherville, only a little way beyond the cemetery, the car turned around and they drove back. Near the side of the road a green awning had been put up, with freshly-dug dirt stacked up around a gaping hole, although the cemetery itself was deserted.

It seemed to Itzy that the driver was going much more hurriedly that was his usual habit.

"Where is your book?" the man beside her asked.

"Mother says I have to rest my eyes," Itzy told him.

The man nodded. He peered at her briefly but made no further comment and his own eyes were shielded behind his dark glasses.

They did not take her back to her neighbourhood but instead twice drove up and down the business district of her own small town, a distance only of several bleak and impoverished blocks with a court house at one end; then they turned off onto a high curving road that swept up above the shoulders of the town and on past an unseen but marked waterfall which Itzy could hear thundering away behind a tangled rise of tree and mountains; they swept on up the narrow, twisting road so thick with vines and hugging trees that for some minutes all view of the sky was obscured. Then the road crested and Itzy caught one brief sight of the sea before the road elbowed back upon itself and they passed swiftly on through a tall and sculpted black iron gate over which was slung a mossy panel of brass or bronze containing a swirl of italic script. Carefully groomed hedgerows to either side came up to meet them and over the top of hedge, holding its place against the vacant blue sky, Itzy could see the orange roof tiles of a massive house, the clay wet and streaming, though still glistening in the sun. The limousine glided to a stop outside a two-story Tudor garage set back in deep shade.

"Get out," the man told her.

She did so, waiting by the door until the man had come around in front of her.

"Come along," he said.

She followed him, with her head down and watching the lift of his black heels as he paced briskly up the winding flat-stone walk past a rose garden and timidly-gurgling pools to the front door.

"Come in."

He stood aside to let her pass. She entered the dark hallway, there pausing, waiting. She could just see, just the bare outlines of heavy tables and urns and paintings up on walls and her own shoes on the cool quarry floor. Then the door closed and even that fell away. He felt for her hand, found it, and quickly led her along. Her feet dragged behind and he yanked on her arm, saying, "Don't be silly." Then he stopped and she bumped lightly against him. She was crying.

"Stop that!" he said.

He shoved open a door and pulled her in front of him.

"Through there," he said.

In the distance, through another door, Itzy could see a faint thread of light, and from someplace, the drone of music, dismal and melancholy.

The man stayed close to her.

A grey silent darkness embraced the room she came into, and Itzy wondered where the light could have gone.

"Look around if you want to," the man said. He was over by a long wall, half-hidden by the drapes, and by the weary indifference of his tone this time Itzy knew he was not thinking of her. The drapes hiding him were emerald green like the sea when shaded and they were as high and wide as a theatre curtain. Over the opposite wall two enormous rugs were displayed and they seemed to have innumerable paths of what Itzy took to be gold spun into them. Great gawking statues arrested in flamboyant motion, some of them taller than Itzy, were up on pedestals, their surfaces smooth and cold and hard as rock to her touch. A creature of some sort, black as fury, was crouched down on all fours, guarding the hearth. It was too large to be a dog, and too still to be living; all the same, Itzy did not allow herself to go near it.

"Come here," the man instructed her.

She walked into a ribbon of sunlight blinding to her eyes, and flung both hands up over her face. Then she looked again, squinting up her eyes. The house was perfectly poised over a splendid long valley. In the valley floor she could see isolated roof tops and the church steeples of her small town; an inch or so above that, sandwiched in between a layer of green, was what would be Estherville. In the far, far distance the valley was chopped off by the sea and the shoulders of numerous other mountains curved gracefully down. Where water met sky a round black speck showed, its size increasing and decreasing, like a shrunken head severed from its body ever to float there.

Then the weighted curtain fell back into place and the room was pitch-black once more.

"Sit down," the man told her.

She stumbled against something, hurting her leg, although she did not cry out and the man was behind her to catch whatever it was. She fumbled her way into one of the black stuffed chairs and brought her legs up beneath her, looking around for but not finding him.

"Perhaps you should call your mother," she heard him say. He was right up next to her.

She waited until her breathing had leveled out. Then: "Why should I do that?"

"So she won't worry."

"What will I say?" Her voice was querulous and altogether bad-tempered, as if she believed he had placed an impossible burden on her. He didn't reply at once, and she was aware again of the music, far off, the notes thin and squeaky.

"I don't know," he said.

Itzy sighed, stretching herself out. The chair was very, very comfortable, filled with down perhaps, and she wondered what it would be like to fall asleep here. She heard the soft tinkle of ice in a glass from some place in the room and realized he was mixing himself something to drink. She wondered how he was able to do this in the dark.

"I want an ice cream," she said.

The music surged in once more, with more volume this time and more pleasant, and Itzy closed her eyes. When next she opened them his shadowy figure was over against the fireplace mantle, bent, one foot resting on the back of the creature beneath him on the hearth.

"We don't have any ice cream," he said. He asked her what else she might like.

She was about to say she did not know what else she wanted, that she wanted nothing, when all at once with a violent frenzy the music rushed in, discordant and tuneless, as if a door had abruptly opened to let it through; hands over her ears, she sat shivering, her eyes scrunched up and her teeth clamped tightly together; she remained this way only momentarily, however, for when her hands came down the door had closed and the music had ceased altogether. There was no sound whatsoever. She stared out over the room, amazed, sucking in her breath, alarmed by the tricks her own mind seemed to be playing. The gold paths in the carpets on the wall were rippling and the statues up on their pedestals had somehow gone whiter and more menacing. Then she gave a loud shriek, cowering back in her chair; her skin crawled. The black creature on the hearth had suddenly reared up and was now walking slowly towards her.

"Down, Horace," the man said.

The creature immediately turned and retreated and once

again shrunk down on the hearth.

Itzy had heard no one come in. Yet she gasped, aware that someone had. She saw a black head silently regarding her from the shadows of the opposite chair. She could hear the person breathing, and knew that it was a woman. The dark shape did not move. Then a lit cigarette swept up through the blackness, burned bright orange for a time, at last to sweep back down out of sight.

This time Itzy was not frightened when the hearth creature rose up and came silently across the room, slowly spun, and dropped down in a heap by the person's chair.

The man passed in front of Itzy, leaving the room. She wanted to grab his hand and go out with him, but this, she knew, was unacceptable. She found her voice.

"I am Itzy," she said. "Are you Claire?"

The woman did not speak, although her breath deepened, and for some minutes both remained as they were. Itzy wondered what it must be like to be that woman and to live in a house this big, without relief from the darkness which crouched everywhere and which seemed to her to have endured over this place for a billion years.

From time to time the cigarette arched up and the tip burned larger, then it swung down again. Whenever this happened the creature at the woman's feet would lift its head, then when the cigarette descended its head would again sink back to the floor.

Itzy was startled when finally the woman spoke.

"You did not bring your book," she said. The voice was soft and surprisingly melodious and for reasons not clear to Itzy it reminded her of her mother's voice in those years before their troubles had come. Yet she did not know what to think of the woman's remark.

"No," she said, "I finished it." She stared down into her black lap, aware only now of the hot pain along her thighs and wondering why this should be, not realizing that she had been scraping her nails into her skin since the moment she first entered this room.

The room stank of the woman's smoke and there floated in it too the scent of heavy perfume.

"Are you pretty?" the woman asked.

Again, Itzy did not know how to respond.

"I don't know," she eventually said.

They said nothing more, yet still they sat on. It seemed to Itzy that hours went by before the man returned. He appeared, a dark form come to stand silently behind the woman's chair. Then the woman stood up, the shadows swirled around her, the creature at her feet rose up and padded back to its place by the hearth, and Itzy too found herself standing.

"Horace will take you home," the man said.

The woman's face came close to Itzy's own, though she did not touch her, and Itzy closed her eyes to keep from seeing her.

"You should not hate us," the woman said.

Then Itzy saw the black side of the woman moving away through the darkness, one arm extended as though to rearrange that darkness or perhaps to forestall any assistance the man or anyone else might think to give her. The darkness swallowed her up.

During the brief run down the mountain back to Itzy's town she sat alone in the back seat, weeping. Limousine headlights swept like fine white arrows over the tops of trees, into trench and crevice, through formless thickets. A rabbit, frozen at the road's edge, was scooped up by the night, the woods sang in their silence, and when they passed near the waterfall she imagined she could feel the mist of its spray and see it hanging in the sky like the white plume of a gigantic living bird. She cried for nothing, cried for sheer wonder of it all. This was as Old Tzityonyana might have been, undomesticated wilderness, with no trails made and herself alone to make them. Her mother would be upstairs in bed, waiting—perhaps asleep, perhaps dreaming. Itzy would sink down beside her, press kisses on her closed eyes, say, *"Sleep mother, Itzy's grown up now, she will look after you."*

■

Edna Alford

Reg Silvester

Edna Alford (1947-) was born in Saskatchewan and now spends her winters in Tulliby Lake, Alberta and her summers at her home in Livelong, Saskatchewan. She was a founding editor of *Dandelion* magazine and has published both peotry and prose in such literary magazines as *Journal of Canadian Fiction, Prism International* and *Fiddlehead.* "Under the I" appears in *A Sleep Full of Dreams* (1981), her highly acclaimed first collection of short stories for which she won the Lampert Memorial Award for the Best First Book published in Canada that year.

UNDER THE I

Edna Alford

Harold Sampson stamped his work boots on the coco mat two or three times, then scraped them backward like a dog after defecation, flinging snow against the doorsill behind him. This was his ritualistic winter entrance, a prairie habit he hadn't been able to leave behind when they sold the farm and moved to Calgary fourteen years ago.

There was a long white banner tacked on the bulletin board to his right. "BINGO," Harold read in large red letters, "THURSDAY, JANUARY 7, 8 P.M., SOUTHMOUNT LEGION HALL."

He hunched his shoulders and shook spasmodically. His large hands were clenched in fists, red from the cold, with white knuckles and fingernails. He stuck long arms straight out in front of him, like stovepipes extended to conduct the heat back into his body. He coughed loudly, too many times, for he smoked heavily these days. He drew the phlegm up to the front of his mouth between his teeth and spat on the floor to this right.

He had thick lips which were always somewhat wet with spittle on the inner edges; a common face, flat and wide and grey-bristled on the lower cheeks and chin. He had a round inoffensive nose and he was the sort of person who is always slightly brown, winter and summer. His grey eyes weren't small but looked that way because of the suggestion of a squint caused by the fine lines that grew like webs from the corners.

The spitting ceremony complete, Harold stuck his hands into his parka pockets and cocked his head, which was covered with one of those plaid wool caps with fleece ear flaps. He looked around the entrance of the hall for Mavis. She had run in from the cold while he parked the truck. Mavis wasn't there; probably in the ladies, he thought.

He waited, surveying the entrance hall. Wouldn't be too many out for the bingo tonight what with the blizzard blowing up so fast. He hadn't been taken with the idea of going out tonight but Mavis had insisted, saying that the bingo was pretty well all the fun she got out of life. So they had come.

He absently read the announcements on the bulletin board:

Garage Sale. Sat. Jan. 9. 1322 42 Ave. S.W. Trike, crib, skates, doilies, and other household oddments. 10 a.m. - 4 p.m.

Funeral for Mrs. Bertha McNaughton, Sat. Jan. 9, 2:30 p.m. Legion Hall. Baking and sandwiches to be brought to Alice Thackeray 10 a.m. kitchen.

Ladies Auxiliary Meeting Tues. Jan. 12. Legion Hall. Election of officers.

Again he looked to the top of the stairway for Mavis and this time she was there, beckoning him to come up. She wore her brown cloth coat with imitation leather trim on the collar, the cuffs, and in a narrow panel down the front. The plastic leather had cracked in the cold and was scarred with tiny fissures. The coat was shapeless. Her winter boots, imitation sealskin, looked strange, like paws on the ends of her short thick legs. She had pincurled her hair that morning and it stuck out mouse-brown, fluffy and festive. And she had put on lipstick. The fluffy hair and lipstick didn't soften her features as they might have but rather accentuated her sharp nose, tiny pig-like eyes, and thin mouth set low in a pointed chin. She never wore her hat after she had curled her hair, not even in this weather.

She looked sort of happy, Harold thought as he climbed the stairs slowly, for he had had a hard day at the plant, one of those long dark winter days where nothing had gone wrong exactly, but nothing had gone right either. The story of their lives. Nothing really terrible, but no breaks in the monotony. That was why Mavis liked the bingos, he figured, not so much for the chance to make a little extra money although, God knows, they could use it, but for the excitement.

Harold hated the bingos. Mostly women who were strangers to him yacking, smoking, drinking coffee and shrieking "BINGO" so loud you'd think they'd just jumped over the moon instead of winning $13.50 in quarters. But Mavis didn't drive so he had to come, especially tonight with the weather so bad; she couldn't depend on the buses.

When he got to the top of the stairs they went into the hall without speaking, Harold with his hands still stuck in his parka pockets. From an attendant, Mavis accepted a narrow white sheet of paper on which was listed the order of the bingos and what they were—"snowballs," "sandwiches," "postage stamps," "blackouts"—the list looked endless to Harold.

He had been wrong about the turnout. The Legion Hall

was packed with people sorting their cards, getting coffee in white styrofoam cups from tall aluminum urns with black plastic spouts, establishing their separate territories like animals at the long plywood tables. They were mostly women, Harold was right about that, mostly middle-aged and older, with scarves, caps, and heavy stockings, hovering around their chairs which were wood and metal and could be stacked against the far wall after the bingo.

Mavis picked their seats and Harold followed her like a large friendly dog. She took off her coat, draped it over the back of her chair and said to Harold, "Take off your cap; you'll cook in here. How many cards you want?"

"Oh six, I guess. Might's well," Harold said. He swiped his cap off his head and dropped it on the floor beside him. His stubble-grey hair was flattened in a ring by the sweat band inside the cap.

Mavis went over to the table in the corner where the cards were stacked. There were a lot of people jostling around the table, snatching stacks of cards out from under each other, flipping through them rapidly, discarding the "bad ones" and grabbing more. They were searching diligently for the "right ones," the "good cards." Harold could never figure out how they could tell the good cards from the bad. Maybe that was his trouble, he thought. But he knew Mavis always took a great deal of care choosing the cards and although he did not himself know the ins and outs of the process, he had always trusted her judgment in these matters.

While she was gone, Harold looked around the hall. At first glance it looked large and open and well-lit but this first impression was deceptive. The walls were two-tone, painted pea-green on the upper half and dirty sand on the lower half. These colours were divided by a narrow dark brown line which ran around the room, a sinister line like an elastic band you could expect to tighten imperceptibly or snap at any moment without warning.

Harold noticed there were almost as many fluorescent rods on the ceiling here as at Woolco, but fluorescent lighting never seemed to give enough light—he had noticed that wherever he went. No matter how many rods they put in, only the top half of the room seemed to be lit. And it was the same here. The bottom half, where the people were, was dingy somehow and he found himself squinting more than usual. The painters at the plant said fluorescent bulbs even changed the actual colour of a thing—you couldn't tell what the real colour was, they said, till you got it outside in the natural light.

He looked toward the stage where the caller would soon be seated. To the right of the bingo machine hung a picture of the Queen. To the left, a picture of Prince Philip. And in the centre, above the stage, an enormous Red Ensign had been tacked to the wall. Like most Legions, thought Harold. Most of them had the same kind of decoration. Some hung scrolls with names of the local war dead on them in that strange writing so an ordinary person couldn't read them.

By and by Mavis brought back fifteen cards, six for him and nine for her. She was pretty good at keeping track of them all so she always got nine instead of six, and tonight she had bought a Bonanza card, six cards full of numbers on one sheet to be played after the regular cards. She picked up a clean ashtray from one of the other tables and placed it between them. Harold reached into his shirt pocket and pulled out his package of Exports; he flicked one out by tapping the package expertly and lit the cigarette. Mavis smoked Matinee.

"They're just about ready to start, Harol'," said Mavis. She had never pronounced the "d" at the end of his name. "Why don't you run over and get us a coffee."

Harold got up and stood in line at one of the urns and got two cups of coffee, both with cream and sugar, both with little pink plastic stirsticks in them. As he was carrying them back to the table, the caller began reading the Legion announcements. They were the same ones Harold had already read, and he only half-heard the voice. He was concentrating on not spilling the coffees. "The funeral for Mrs. B. McNaughton," the voice said, "will be held in the Legion Hall Saturday, January 9 at 2:30 p.m. All you ladies are to bring your baking and sandwiches to the kitchen by 10 a.m. and give them to Mrs. Thackeray—," and so on.

By the time Harold returned to his seat, the caller had begun and Mavis glared at him for being late so that he jerked a little setting the coffees and slopped some onto two of Mavis' Cards. Mavis stiffened and hissed at him to "Hurry up, Harol'." As he sat down, he sucked in his breath and sort of whistle-sighed it all out. For some reason this habit was of comfort to him when he was in Mavis' "bad books," although he knew full well that it irritated her even further.

The little white balls, housed in a small wire cage situated to the right of the caller, bounced frenetically. Each was marked with a number and the caller had only to place his hand over an orifice at the top of the cage and a numbered ball would pop into the palm of his hand. The number on that ball was what he called into the microphone, out to the crowd. And the Legion had just installed a new device for the bingos, a large electronic scoreboard which had been placed high above the caller's head and on which all the numbers called lit up.

This impresed Harold. He was always happy when they introduced a new machine at the plant. Kind of made some excitement in his day, he thought. Even so, the scoreboard rather frightened him, seeing his bad luck in lights. The thought never occurred to Harold that he might win. He never had. It was the same at the plant. He never thought about being promoted. Always someone else had been chosen. He was used to it.

"Under the O clickety-click sixty-six, O sixty-six," the caller said. His voice was strong and clear, slightly nasal, but confident, like the rest of the world, it seemed to Harold, like he was the caller for the whole world.

The balls spewed relentlessly and the caller called them arbitrarily and without passion. Number after number until finally a woman's voice cried out "Bingo!" The voice seemed detached from any person, like what Harold had heard about in the church, "speaking in tongues," he thought they called it, or was it "with tongues?" It didn't matter, he thought; it was all the same anyway. He looked down at his own cards while the caller checked the first bingo. There were a few spaces blacked out by the plastic slots with tabs on the cards, but no orderly row, no cause for excitement.

Harold butted his cigarette in the ashtray and absently flicked all the tabs back so the numbers showed again. Mavis did the same, only she was very businesslike about it, efficient, in fact. For her the process was like a job, to be accomplished with skill. For some reason it didn't represent loss to her, or the reiteration of loss as it did to Harold.

The next set of bingos was what they called a "postage stamp combination." "You better keep your mind on the cards this time if you know what's good for you, Harol'," Mavis said. Harold didn't look up at her, but stared at the patchwork of numbers on his bottom left card.

While everyone prepared for this game, a woman spoke to Harold from across the table. Harold hadn't noticed her before. She must have come in when he was off fetching the coffees. She was an old woman, about seventy-five or eighty he guessed, and she was all gussied up but in a poor way. That is she wore a lot of lipstick and an old but brightly coloured silk scarf pinned at the throat with a rhinestone brooch. The brooch had some of the strategic stones missing so you couldn't really tell what the pattern was supposed to represent. A bit like a bird, thought Harold. Yes, it was probably a bird. She had snow-white hair, curly, that stuck out from under an absurd pink felt hat which nestled in a cloud of chartreuse net and pink feathers. Maybe that was why he thought of the bird.

She had remarkable eyes, hollow grey eyes that had no sparkle, no light in them. But that's the kind of thing age does to some, he thought, makes them spooky. What the woman said to him, however, was not remarkable. "I never miss a bingo," she said.

"Oh, s'at so," said Harold.

"Never in twenty-five years have I missed one week of the bingos. Before we came to the city, I used to play in Sundre, at the hall there. Better days, those were. I knew everybody in the hall. Here, I come alone and I go alone. And there was none of this fancy stuff then. Plain bingo. You have to be a mathematician these days jest to play."

"Oh," said Harold. He was not honestly interested but he had a way about him he couldn't seem to change. He listened to everybody no matter how boring, how tedious, how insignificant the conversation seemed to him. He was always tangled up with one lonely person or another, listening, not knowing how to stop listening to their stories. Mavis really hated this. She was always the one who had to drag him away.

Mavis, in fact, now put her finger to her lips and made a shushing sound. The caller had started again. "Under the B, the wee one, B one," he said, "B one." The voice became hypnotic after a while and table after table of human robots obeyed his every command, sliding the slots shut over their numbers. "More and more, under the N forty-four, N number forty-four."

Finally, after all the postage stamps had been filled and someone yelled "Bingo!", there was a break in the action. The lady across the table began to talk to Harold. He tried to appear busy sliding the slots back but it was useless and eventually he looked up at her and listened.

"I like the old way," she said, "when we used the corn

kernels or the pennies to cover the numbers. Can't get used to these silly slidin' cards, you know. Oh well," and this next part interested Harold, "I never win anyway," she said, "so what's the difference?" She smiled.

And Harold smiled showing his crooked teeth, ochre with nicotine. "Same with me," he said, "been comin' for years and I never won a cent."

"The cards are good, Harol'," interrupted Mavis. "I picked them as best I could. Maybe if you paid more attention."

"I don't see you winning nothin' tonight Mavis," he said, and as soon as he said it he knew he had gone too far. Mavis appeared to stop breathing for an instant as if he'd slapped her face. Then she grew cold and sat silent, her small eyes as glazed as a dead woman's. She stayed that way, waiting for the caller. Harold thought he shouldn't have done it, spoiled her night out is what she would say and maybe it was so, but nothing short of winning could turn it back—he knew that. She wouldn't be talking again till they got in the truck to go home, and then he would hear about it.

The old woman understood. He could see that by the way she looked at him and then at Mavis. He was getting to like her, warming up to her as they put it.

"So you never won in all them years," he said, half smiling, hoping she would accept this as an apology for his harsh behaviour.

"Not once," she replied. "But this my night. I'm going to win the big one tonight."

Harold laughed. "That's what they all say," he snorted, but he was sorry he had said that too. Her face was deadly serious.

"I'm not joking, young man," she said and Harold liked that. It had been a very long time since anyone had called him "young man." The old woman shifted her weight forward so that she was leaning toward him and she whispered conspiratorially. "Tonight, I know. I know I'm going to hit the jackpot tonight."

"If you say so," said Harold. He crossed his legs defensively, picked up his Exports and tapped one out. Before he lit it, he gulped down some of his sweet lukewarm coffee. He felt uneasy. Not that he wanted to disappoint the old girl. But he began to think she was a bit off, a little touched. Meeting someone like that always scared him.

The caller began again. A short one, he said, a "snow-ball," he called it. "Under the O, the old age pension number sixty-five. Ladies and gentlemen, O sixty-five."

"That one's for you," Harold said to the old woman.

"You bet'cher life," she laughed back at him as she carefully pushed a slot shut on one of the cards. She only played two cards. "Gettin' old," she told him, "though I never played more than two. Never could manage to keep track of more."

"You're not the only one," Harold said, feeling more and more of an affinity to this strange old woman.

No more than a dozen or so numbers had been called when someone yelled "Bingo" and the snowball was over. The caller marched verbally through the letters "L" and "X" and the "sandwiches," calmly articulating number after number, event after event, according to the program. Finally he took a break, said he'd be back in ten minutes and that then they would go for the "total blackout" and the winner would take the jackpot which tonight was $377.50.

The old woman smiled to herself, then looked up at Harold. "Don't worry about me," she said, "I mean the not winning. It's never been any different for me. I had two boys and one of them died, the good one. They say it's always so. You put me in mind of him somehow. The other, I don't know where he got to. He was a drunk and no good for nothin', even on the farm.

"We never had a thing. My man was no farmer neither. If it wasn't for my cream and egg money, we'd a starved. If there was hail around, it always hit us and if there were hoppers, we had the worst of 'em. Not one bit different when we left the farm. Hand to mouth all them years. I'm glad I'm done with it."

Here he was again, listening. Good old Harold. But it was somehow different this time. All of it sounded so familiar. Everything rang a bell, as they say, until Harold was fairly ringing all over inside. He felt an uncomfortable lump like a cold stone in his chest when she talked about the farm. Life had been the same for him and Mavis. All but for the kids. They had none to miss. He didn't know quite what to say. He felt he was expected to say something but all he could think of was, "No, life ain't easy for none of us."

"I know," she replied, almost mischievously, "that's why I'm so glad I'm done with it."

Harold shifted uneasily in his chair, jerked it backward,

clanking Mavis' chair as he did so. "So ya feel lucky tonight do ya?" He tried to change the subject. He was secretly afraid that she might drop dead right in front of him. They said old folk could do that sort of thing, kind of will themselves to die. That wasn't the kind of excitement he was looking for. The thought spooked him.

"I don't *feel* lucky, young man. I have it on the best and highest authority that I will win the jackpot tonight." She rolled her sallow eyes upward and sat silent for a moment as if she could see through the clouds, through even the stars.

She was serious, Harold could tell, dead serious. Lord, how did he ever manage to get himself tangled up with these people. Awkwardly, he clamped his fingers round his styrofoam cup and said, "Well, I guess I'll get another cup before he starts up again." He looked over at Mavis who did not respond at all but sat, it seemed to Harold, like a lady chipped from ice. Humiliated, he turned to the old woman. "You want one?" he asked sheepishly.

"Why thank you so much for thinking of me but I don't drink it no more," she replied politely. Harold felt like a gentleman. Must bother her stomach, he thought. The old ones can't take too much of that sort of thing. He had a thought that maybe she might have a drink of warm milk after she got home tonight, but somehow that didn't fit either.

Harold arrived back at his table just as the caller returned to the stage. He pretended to hurry to make himself ready for the jackpot bingo—a total blackout. Every single slot on the card had to be shut. He hoped the old woman would think he had no time to talk. She didn't speak.

The bingo began. Under the B, number ten; under the O, sixty-five; under the I, eighteen; G, fifty-five, number fifty-five. The caller droned on and on while each person at each chair flicked and flicked and flicked the numbers dark, blacking them out like days on a calendar. Harold noticed that the old woman played only one card this time and had pushed her other card to the side. He also noticed that she seemed to flick a number shut every time one was called. After twenty-three numbers, the caller remarked jokingly to the crowd, "Folks, if it really is your lucky night, you could do it with the next number. For $377.50, the grand jackpot, under the I—"

Harold didn't learn until later what number actually was called, for the old woman threw her hand into the air and shrieked, "Bingo! Bingo! Bingo!" before he had a chance to hear it. The number made no difference to him. His cards were only pocked here and there with a few shut slots.

"The lady says she has a bingo," said the caller evenly. "We'll just have one of the girls check that out, ladies and gentlemen. Do not clear your cards." He sounded sceptical and so was Harold, but Harold hoped—more than that, he wished so strongly he very nearly prayed that she had won the jackpot, that everything was in order.

A middle aged woman marched toward them in a business-like manner, briskly. She whisked the card from the old woman's hand and began reading the numbers back to the caller. B-10, O-65, and so on, all of them correct. Even Mavis began to regard the old woman with interest, almost with respect.

Harold was convinced the old woman had been right about her luck. So she had finally won, he thought, and then with some personal excitement and delight, he completed his thought—that a loser could win; just because you never won didn't mean you never could. And in his throat and chest the lump which had been lodged for the better part of the evening, ever since the talk about the farm, mysteriously dissolved and he began to feel hope, not much hope, true enough, but unmistakably hope for himself and for his life and for his very existence.

The woman who was checking the card came to the final number. She flicked the shutter open. Where there should have been a number, there was only a blank white space. The old woman sat quietly, smiling, her hands confidently folded in her lap. She didn't appear in the least nervous. The room hushed. Then the checker spoke. "There's a number missing on this card," she called out. "Could you give us the last number called."

The man at the front spoke dispassionately. "There's no such a thing as a blank in this game. Under the I, sixteen, ma'am was the last number called. No bingo. All right ladies and gentlemen," he continued without pause, "for $377.50, under the N, thirty-five, N number thirty-five."

Harold looked up at the electronic scoreboard. I-16 all right. The machine couldn't be wrong. Must have been a mistake at the printing plant, he thought. That sort of thing happened every so often. But why hadn't the old lady seen it. She said she'd played bingo all her life. She should have known there was no such a thing as a blank. But then the old ones couldn't always see so well, he thought—or the young ones either for that matter. He had trouble keeping track himself.

"No!" the old woman cried out. "It was under the I-Zero that was called. I know it, sure as I'm sitting here. I was suposed to win. I did win." She was near to tears and so was Harold for that matter. Moreover he was angry. What kind of luck is that, he thought; a blank space for God's sake. They should have let her have it, just this once.

The caller looked up and out toward the old woman. "Ma'am," he said, "even if there was such a thing as a zero in the game it would be under the B, not the I." There was a roar of laughter from the crowd.

Meanwhile, the woman who had checked the card was trying to explain, rationally, but the old lady wouldn't listen. "No! No!" she said and she thumped her frail fist on the plywood table. "It ain't fair!" Harold watched helplessly as the old woman wept, sniffling into the unravelling embroidered roses of her yellowed hankie. Harold was embarrassed for her. He had thought she was stronger. He reconsidered his thought about the strength of will the old ones were supposed to have. Now he guessed it wasn't so.

People nearby were glaring at the old woman now. Some, including Mavis, were making shushing noises which sounded like angry oblique whispers people made when a baby was crying in a crowded theatre. They couldn't hear the caller, they said—"The old bat probably can't see her hand in front of her face, shouldn't be here anyway," someone said.

Harold was sure she heard that remark. She immediately straightened herself, wiped her nose one last time, picked up her bag and rose proudly, effortlessly, he thought, for a woman her age.

She turned to leave; then as if to spite the hostile players around her and at the same time to discomfort Harold, she glanced back at him and said clearly in a thin but loud voice, "All right then, so be it. But I'll be back next week. I won't rest till I win." With that, she shuffle-glided between the tables and out the doorway.

"Good riddance," Mavis snapped.

Harold regarded his wife incredulously, as if he had never seen her before. He felt badly for the old lady. He was no longer interested in his cards, not even for appearances' sake. The more he thought about it, the more unfair the whole thing seemed to him, and that feeling grew to include not only the bingo but finally the whole world. She did have spunk after all, he thought, said she'd be back and he bet she would too. She was a woman who'd been through a lot. A little setback like this wouldn't stop her.

Finally, someone yelled "Bingo!" and the blackout was over. Harold thought the guy who won that one took dirty money. Harold himself wouldn't have taken a cent of that money home.

Mavis efficiently cleared and stacked her nine cards beside her and was spreading out the Bonanza cards when Harold turned to her and said, "I guess I'll go start the truck, get her warmed up."

Mavis looked up and nodded. "Better put on your cap then," she said. He reached under the table and fetched his cap. He put it on and pulled the fleece flaps down over his ears. Then he left.

On his way out he remembered the paralyzing cold and wondered how the old lady made out in this kind of weather. Because almost everyone played the Bonanza cards, the stairway was deserted but for a few of the menfolk who were on their way down to the bar in the Legion basement. Halfway down the stairs, Harold looked out through the plate glass doors, at the bottom of the landing. He stopped for a moment, then muttered to himself, but out loud, "Jesus, it *is* her." He could see the body of the old woman crumpled on the ground just a few yards from the door. He could see her pink hat laying beside her.

He ran down the stairs and heaving his shoulder against the doors, spread them easily. He lumbered through the drifting snow.

The wind had already begun to sting red blotches on his face and hands by the time he got there. When he knelt down on one khaki knee beside the body, his leg sank deep into the snow. He found the old woman motionless, undisciplined spittle running slowly out of her slack blue mouth, her hollow eyes rolled up toward the snowflakes driven like tiny arrows in the Legion light. She was dead.

He lifted the plastic handbag out of one half-open hand, gloved in pink angora. He opened the bag. Identification, he thought. He took out a billfold, snapped it open and held a card up to the light. It was an old age pension card. An address was what he was looking for, someone to call—there it was in finely typed letters—Mrs. Bertha Louise McNaughton, Pine Mountain Lodge, 1632 - 13 Avenue N.W. There was a phone number, 358-6924.

On the way to the hall, Harold's mind flicked back to the bingo, to his fear that she might drop dead. He had been right about that, he thought. Goddammit if she didn't do just that. But he had been wrong about the loss of the jackpot not bothering her. He should have known, maybe should have gone after her, talked to her. A stroke, likely, or a heart attack maybe, he thought. Too worked up. The old ones can't take it. Harold suddenly felt guilty, sick and guilty.

He stamped his workboots mechanically two or three times on the coco mat at the door. When he got to the pay phone near the entrance, he took out his Exports, tapped one out and lit it, coughing badly. He spit on the floor and took a drag from the cigarette. His hand shook. He took a dime out of his pocket, dropped it into the slot of the phone, and hearing the buzz at the end of the line, he dialed the number for the lodge.

"Good evening, Pine Mountain Lodge, Matron Benstone speaking."

"Ya," stammered Harold, "ah, this is Harold Sampson here. I'm at the Legion Hall up on Southmount, at the bingo, like, and I found an old woman in the parking lot here. I think she's dead—must've had a heart attack or somethin'. Her I.D. says she lives there at the lodge. Name's Mrs. Bertha McNaughton, it says. Should I call an ambulance, er—ah what should I do. Maybe you should send somebody down."

There was a long silence at the other end of the line. Then the voice said, quietly, "Ah—thank you very much for calling us, Mr. Sampson, but Mrs. McNaughton couldn't be there. You see she did pass away—of a heart attack—there, last week after the bingo. As a matter of fact her funeral is on Saturday afternoon at the Legion Hall. Are you sure it's Mrs. McNaughton?" There followed another even longer silence than the first.

Then Harold said, "Ya, ya, I'm pretty sure, I think. Can you hold on a minute. I'll just go check. Hold on, will ya." Harold dropped the receiver and heard the voice from the dangling apparatus reassure him, "Yes Mr. Sampson, certainly I'll hold." He was already to the plate glass doors.

He cupped his hands over his eyes and squinted toward the parking lot, staring hard at that spot in the parking lot where the body was supposed to be. It was no longer there. Harold pushed open the door and ran to the spot. Still there was no body, no hat, no bag. There wasn't even the indentation from his knee. Frightened, Harold glanced at the sky, expecting something—he didn't know what. There was nothing, only the flick flick of tiny snow arrows in the Legion Light.

He ran back into the hall. People were pouring noisily down the stairway and out the doors. He stamped his feet on the mat, scraping them backward, flinging snow against the doorsill. He loped through the crowd to the phone, grabbed the dangling receiver and almost shouted into it. "Must have been a mistake. I guess so. Sorry to bother you."

"That's perfectly all right, Mr. Sampson. You're sure everything is all right?"

"Ya, it's ok. It's ok."

"Goodbye then, Mr. Sampson."

"Goodbye." Harold replaced the receiver.

His eyes fell on the bulletin board which was directly to his right beside the pay phone. There it was. The second announcement. That was why the name had sounded so familiar to him. He felt slightly relieved. Yet, as he stood listlessly waiting for Mavis, he began to realize that nothing really was explained at all. Except maybe that he had been right in the first place about the will of the old ones, more right than he wanted to be.

He longed desperately to tell someone about it, to tell someone that something very special had happened to him. But who? Mavis? She would think he had finally lost all his marbles. Of all people, she would understand the least. The fellas at the plant? No, they would laugh, say, "Old Harold always was a joker. You sure can tell some tall ones, Harold. You should write 'em down some day. Make a million."

Besides, and this was what bothered Harold the most, maybe he was losing his grip on things. Harold was afraid of those who were, as they said, touched. And he knew that no matter how bad things were now, no matter how boring and stale and tedious his life had been, things could get worse. He had learned that along the way. So he set his mind to never telling anyone about it.

He reached into his parka pocket where he had stuffed the old age pension card. He would tear it up, he thought, throw it away. But no matter how deeply he shoved his hand into the pocket, no matter how he fumbled, all he could come up with was a half-empty match packet, a shirt button and a small wad of lint.

Now he was even more frightened, had never been so afraid in his life. The worst of it was it showed on his face. When Mavis came up to him, the first thing she said was, "My God, Harol', you look like you seen a ghost. What's the matter?"

"Nothin'," said Harold. "let's go. You ready?" He lit another Export.

"Ya, I'm ready." Mavis was smiling. "I won the Bonanza! $78.75! Did you hear that Harol'? You shoulda been there." Her face was flushed, red-mottled. She wore a crooked, self-satisfied smile and she was excitedly twisting and folding and carressing the paper money with her thick, short-fingered hands. "And no one else bingoed, Harol'. I didn't have to share a cent. Well, when that guy called out my last number, I yelled 'Bingo!' then and there. First thing tomorrow morning I'm going down to the Betty Shop and see if I can't find myself a new coat, one of them imitation moutons or—"

"That's fine, Mavis, just fine," Harold interrupted weakly.

"I hope you're not coming down with the flu, Harol'. That's all we need." Her tone of voice had changed already.

"Could be," said Harold, "I don't feel too good all right." All the warmth seemed to have left his body. He shivered uncontrollably now. His yellow teeth clattered and clicked without his consent. His lips were dry.

They didn't speak again until they were in the truck, half-way home. At the last set of lights on Southmount, he finally said it, quietly, "I'm tellin' you right now Mavis, so's you'll know for good an' for all—wild horses couldn't drag me to another goddamn bingo game."

Harold riveted his eyes to the windshield, to the spray and hiss of flakes against the glass. Mavis snapped her head toward him, flung her face close to his, spitting words. "You never could stand me ha;in' a good time, could you Harol'? Could you Harol'?"

∎

Helen J. Rosta

Nikki Christophers

Helen J. Rosta was born and raised in Alberta; she now lives in Edmonton. She has worked as a social worker, and as a fiction editor for *Branching Out*. Her stories have been published in various magazines such as *Flare, The Journal of Canadian Fiction*, and *Fiddlehead*, and anthologized in *Getting Here, Wild Rose Country*, and *More Stories From Western Canada*. Her first collection of short stories, *In The Blood*, includes "Midsummer Feast". "Hunting Season", another story in that collection, has been made into a film.

MIDSUMMER FEAST

Helen J. Rosta

"I have to go now," Nancy Ann said, looking up into the glare of the brassy sun that had already crossed the midpoint of the sky and was lying a little to the west, over the highest tower. In the harsh light the city was colourless, the towers bleached to the shade of ashes, the windows like burnt-out eyes. "I have to go," Nancy Ann repeated and wriggled her toes in the powdery brown hill of soil that she had just hoed around a potato plant.

Carol Jane rapped Nancy's ankle with a hoe handle. "Stop that! Don't you want to eat this winter?"

Nancy sat down in the dirt and began to pull a scab off her knee. It came away whole, leaving a tiny depression underneath, white at the edges and crimson in the middle where it had stuck. She ate the scab.

"Get going," Carol said.

Nancy examined her knee, squeezed it, put her lips to the wound and sucked but there was no blood.

Carol Jane glanced at the sky. "It's getting late. You'd better go home and help your mother."

Alice Marion stopped working. Shoulders hunched, she leaned on her hoe handle, squinted at Nancy. "Go home," she commanded.

"Leave me alone."

One by one the others braced themselves on their hoe handles and fixed their eyes on Nancy. "What's the matter with Nancy Ann Nancy Ann Nancy Ann?"

"Shut up," Nancy snapped and turning her back on them, dragged her feet through the potato hill and out of the garden.

"You're making more work for us," Alice Marion yelled after her.

"I don't care."

"You eat as much as anyone."

Nancy shuffled down the sidewalk, kicking at the crumbling cement. She turned west, heading home, but halfway there she paused, picked up a sharp stone and, squatting, sketched a narrow, long-nosed face on the sidewalk. She drew in a big mouth, filled it with a mass of pointed teeth, and scratched the name "Alice Marion" under the picture. A thin whiff of cement dust rose like smoke to her nostrils.

She got to her feet, put the stone in her mouth, rolling it over her tongue with little slurps. Finally, she blew it out, aiming at the window in front of her. The stone hit with a small ping.

Far down and across the street the Bank sat, a square, massive building encircled by a heavy chain fence. Nancy looked carefully around. There was no one in sight. She ran down the street, her calloused soles making slapping noises on the pavement. Outside the fence she stopped, glanced over her shoulder, slid under, and scurried into the shadows of the north wall. The wall was almost cool, slick gleaming stone that looked like ice frozen over a myriad of coloured pebbles. She pressed her face and the palms of her hands against the wall, licking off the traces of salty vapour that were left.

From behind her she heard sounds. She sat stock-still, listening; soft pad of feet and adult voices. She flopped to the ground, scrunching her body into the shadows. From under her eyelids she saw Sarah Marion and Esther Marion, Alice's mother and sister. Their heads were high and they approached with slow, sedate steps but as she walked Esther alternately twisted a lock of hair and wiped her hands on the print skirt that hung limply over her gaunt hips.

"Don't be nervous," her mother said.

"I'm not," Esther answered in a high voice.

"Even I," Sarah Marion said, "was a little nervous the first time."

"Really, Mother?"

"But I was proud to become a Producer. Treated like a queen. Lots of food."

"You don't think I'll be too sick to eat?"

"Certainly not."

They passed Nancy who lay like a statue, her thin body part of the shadows. When they had rounded the corner, she crawled along the wall, flattened herself to the ground and peered after them. The door to the Bank opened and a woman in a white robe and turban stepped out. She held the door open and curtsied to Esther who hesitated for a second on the stoop. Sarah Marion put her hand firmly on Esther's back and the two of them entered the Bank. "Oh," Sarah Marion said, "it's so nice and cool I could come here every day."

The woman in the white robe smiled, a thin smile that

flickered and was gone. "I think you're getting too old for our services," she said.

"No," Sarah Marion answered. "Not yet."

The woman stood at the door, her white robe dazzling in the sunlight, scanning the street with bright, piercing eyes. Nancy froze. The woman stepped inside. With a click the door swung shut behind her.

Nancy lingered momentarily in the eddy of coolness that seemed to have emanated from the opened door. Then hugging the meagre shadows she rushed away from the building. She ran toward the Temple whose dome rose like an inverted bowl among a cluster of decaying blocks. The massive doors were locked and looking far down the street she saw that the Temple Goddess was already being taken to her mother's home.

She began to dawdle, shuffling her feet, kicking loose stones. She found a stick propping up a window and took it with her, scraping it along the sides of the buildings as she walked. At the oval tower she stopped and pushed her face against the bars on the windows, peering into the gloomy interior. Pinpoints of light darted to and fro. She tapped her stick on the glass and the lights spun wildly, then disappeared. Her eyes focussed and she saw one fat pale-chested mouse sitting in the middle of the room, its long nose lifted toward her.

"I wish I could get at you," she muttered and banged her stick against the bars. The mouse sprang into the air and bolted through one of the holes that riddled the walls.

"Who's there?" the keeper, Elsa Anita, shouted. "Who's there?"

"None of your business," Nancy muttered, dropping out of sight below the window sill.

"Thief!" Elsa Anita screamed.

"You look fat enough old Elsa." Nancy ran as fast she could to get away before Elsa Anita could set up a hue and cry.

When her apartment block loomed before her she stopped running and began to take small deliberate steps across the heat-softened pavement. First a step forward, then a step sideways so that it looked as if someone with four feet at right angles had been walking there.

With her stick she traced a fissure in the pavement and tried to push her toes into it. A spider running slantwise on filament legs dashed in front of her and she snatched at it but it flattened its fat body under her fingers and slid into the crack.

"Damn!" she exclaimed, dropping to her knees. She stuck her fingers in her mouth and gnawed at the ragged pieces of skin, crouching over the crack, waiting. Finally, she heaved a sigh, got to her feet and walked with big, determined steps to the door of her apartment.

Old Nina Leona opened the door. "I've been watching you," she said. "Fooling around. Today of all days. Why aren't you upstairs, helping your mother?"

"Old fool," Nancy Ann muttered under her breath, turning away. She ran back across the street and flopped down on the curb. Chin in hands, she gazed morosely at the white blur of Nina Leona's face.

Little by little the shadows that had lain in a squat black band along the walls stretched themselves out, reached the middle of the street. The workers from the potato patch, hoes over their shoulders, came strolling along in little bunches, laughing and chattering.

Nancy braced herself.

"I'm going to wear a new robe," Carol was saying. "Mother made it for me out of a piece of cloth that had belonged to her mother. It's just beautiful!"

"Who cares about clothes?" Alice Marion said. "All I care about is sinking my teeth into a piece of that beautiful . . ."

"Ow!" Carol screamed. "You hurt me."

Alice Marion laughed. Seeing Nancy, she went up behind her and prodded her with a foot. "You got off early so that you could go home."

Nancy flinched. "I am home, nearly."

Alice Marion stalked around Nancy, crouched in front of her so that she was looking into her face. "You sat here while the rest of us were working in the garden. And you didn't help your mother like you're supposed to. Can't you live by the Customs?" she asked slyly.

Nancy turned her head away. Alice Marion, still crouching, moved sideways so that they were again face to face. "You don't deserve to eat."

"I don't want to."

Alice Marion's eyes glittered. "Maybe you won't get the chance." She swung on her heel and marched down the sidewalk. The girls fell into step behind her. All except Carol who lingered for a moment at Nancy's side.

"Nancy," she asked. "What's the matter?"

"What's the matter with Nancy Ann Nancy Ann Nancy Ann?"

"I'm not teasing you."

Nancy picked up her stick and began poking holes in the pavement.

"This should be a proud day for you. Your mother giving the Midsummer Feast. Instead, you've been acting like it's the end of the world."

"End of the world? So what does that mean?"

"Who knows what it means? End of the city if you like. 'World'. My mother says it. It's a traditional saying."

"I hate traditonal sayings and I hate your traditions."

"Nancy!" Carol glanced uneasily over her shoulder. "What if Alice Marion heard you say that? She's got it in for you already. You know how powerful her family is."

"Her sister went to the Bank today."

"How do you know?"

"I was there."

"Nancy! You aren't supposed to go there . . . What if . . . ?

"What if?" Nancy said.

Alice Marion's voice, sharp and commanding, came to them. "Carol. Carol Jane."

"I'm coming," Carol called. She pressed Nancy's hand. Looking down Nancy saw a circle of bluish teeth marks on the frail arm. "I have to go get ready."

"Do that," Nancy said.

Nancy placed her hands on her knee and squeezed. A drop of blood oozed out. She licked the blood with the tip of her tongue then put her lips to her knee and sucked. Spat. Spittle fell on the nail of her big toe, a dome of pink bubbles. She flung it off and gently laid her cheek on the sore.

Finally she rose, picked up her stick, and started slowly across the street. The rotunda was vacant. She opened the door to the stairwell and began to climb, haltingly, hunched over, leaning on the stick like an old woman. On the landing she met Nina Leona.

"I was just going down to see if you were still sitting out there."

Nancy grimaced.

"Not a very pleasant expression for a young person," Nina Leona scolded. "On her mother's Feast Day, too." She shook her bony fingers in Nancy's face. Nancy's eyes riveted on the lights that shot from the rings covering her fingers. Following Nancy's gaze, Nina Leona said proudly, "My mother's.

Diamonds, they're called. Not my mother's really. My great-great-great-great-grandmother's . . . maybe even my great-great-great-great-great-grandmother's . . ." The rings slid back and forth and Nancy saw that they were tied to the fingers with bits of dirty string. Nina Leona's dim blue eyes took on a distant, faded expression. ". . . before recorded time. It hasn't always been like this," she whispered.

"What do you mean?"

The eyes suddenly focussed. "You go to the library?"

"Yes."

"See all those empty shelves?" Nina Leona brought her mouth close to Nancy's ear. The words sprayed Nancy's cheek. "There used to be more books. They were destroyed."

"My mother says it's always been like this."

Nina Leona cackled behind her knuckles. "That's because her Mothers never handed anything down to her. It was different with my Mothers. It was all passed down." She pulled out her lips between her thumb and forefinger. "Passed down by word of mouth. No one else can find it. It's all here." She tapped her forehead. "All here," she said sadly, and moisture welled in her eyes, trembled on the swollen lower lids. "I've been accursed."

Nancy waited, chewing on the raw flesh of her little finger. Most of the nail was gone.

"I had no daughters," the old woman said finally. "Not one of them was a girl. It's all here," she tapped her forehead again, "but I have no one to leave it to."

Nancy moved closer. "I'll be your daughter," she said. "You can leave it to me." A bug crawled out of a hole in the corner and began to thread its way along the wall. She grabbed it and popped it into her mouth. Its shell crackled between her teeth.

"You're selfish," Nina Leona said.

Nancy hung her head.

"And you're going to a big feast tonight, too. I'm not invited to your mother's Feast. I'm not invited to any of them. I gave a lot of Feasts in my time but they think they've paid me back and no one invites me anymore." A cunning look came over her face and she grasped Nancy's arm, gripping it so tightly that the girl winced and pulled away.

"If you were my daughter you could invite me to your Feast Days. But if they wouldn't let you," her voice quickened, "you could sneak me a piece." She licked her lips and a dribble of saliva ran down her chin. "You could sneak me something when you had your Feast Days."

Nancy put her hand to her mouth and spat out the chewed bug. "I'm not going to have any," she said. Nina Leona didn't seem to hear. Her eyes were closed and there was almost a smile on her face. The bug lay in Nancy's palm, a gob of sodden brown interspersed with chips of black shell and streaks of red. She flung it on the floor.

"In the olden times they had Feasts every day. . . "

"I hate Feasts," Nancy said.

Nina Leona's head was tilted back and her lips were loose and wet. "Every day, because in those days there were all kinds of savoury creatures." Her eyes popped open and she stared at Nancy. "What did you say?"

"What kind of creatures?"

"All kinds. Big and little and funny shapes. Like we'll never see again. And there were a lot of those kind, too," Nina Leona said, lowering her voice and gesturing toward Nancy's apartment. "You've never seen a grown-up one have you? They keep a few of them in the Bank, but only the Priestess gets to see them. I've got a picture of one," she whispered. "My great-great-great-great-great-great-grandmother tore it out of a book."

"I want to see it," Nancy said eagerly.

"Shh," the old woman said, cocking her head and cupping a hand behind her ear.

Sarah Marion, followed by Esther, appeared in the stairwell. Nina Leona, shrinking against the wall, bowed. The women nodded and passed, their feet rustling on the stairs. Paused.

"Nancy Ann," Nina Leona said suddenly in a loud voice, "why are you dawdling here? You should be home helping your mother."

The footsteps continued up the stairs, out of hearing.

Nancy pressed close, laid her hand on the old woman's arm. "Please," she begged, "can I come to see you tomorrow?"

"Whatever for, Child?" Nina Leona said, opening the door to the hall, passing through and letting the door swing shut in Nancy's face.

Nancy picked up her stick, and cracking it against each step, began to climb the stairs. Outside her door she paused, rattled the doorknob. Listened. She could hear a clatter from the kitchen but the big room was silent. No happy sounds of welcome. She eased the door open and threaded her way among the tables which were set with the precious utensils and covered with the treasured white tablecloths. When she reached the window she raised her eyes to where, among the pots of marjoram and thyme, the white wicker cage was hanging. She tenderly touched the bars on which in play the paint had been worn through to spots of brown like tiny fingerprints. She squeezed shut her eyes and poked a finger into the cage. "Boybee," she whispered. "Boybee."

A savoury brown smell enveloped her. "Nancy!" Her mother's hands were on her shoulders, the bony fingers biting into her flesh. "Nancy, you've shamed me. A daughter must always help her mother on Feast Day. That's the custom."

"I hate your damned Customs," Nancy screamed. "Hate them." She tore from her mother's grasp and flung herself on the cage. "Boybee! Poor Boybee!"

Her mother pulled her away. Slapped her. "Stop it. We must live by the Customs." Her voice rose angrily. "I told you to leave him alone. I told you not to play with him." She grabbed Nancy by the shoulders and began to shake her so violently that her head snapped back and forth. "I told you not to name him."

Suddenly she dropped her hands, stared through the window. "The sun has gone down," she said in her normal voice. "It is time to start the Feast." She rushed from the room.

A gong sounded. They filed through the doorway, taking tiny, measured steps, their full white robes whispering on the floor. First Sarah Marion and Esther, a scarlet ribbon tied across Esther's breast. They halted. Esther stepped forward and drew open the curtains of the alcove where the Temple Goddess stood.

One by one they went forward, knelt, and placed their offerings, bowls of grain, vegetables and fruit at the statue's feet. Then took them up again and placed them on the table and took their places, heads bent. Waiting.

Nancy's mother, triumphant, appeared in the kitchen doorway, the Feast Day crown encircling her head like a ray of sunlight. Carrying in her arms the huge white bowl in which was heaped her offering, she crossed the room and knelt at the Temple Goddess' feet. The statue looked down at her out of painted, calm, blue eyes, cradling in the gilded arms its own offering.

Rising, her mother placed the bowl on the table. Only then did they lift their eyes to Nancy who stood in her dirty gardening clothes, blood oozing from her knee.

Nancy looked into the gleaming eyes, at her mother's averted face and then into Alice Marion's smiling open mouth. She grabbed her stick, flung it at the Temple Goddess and fled.

■

George Bowering

Peter Lord

George Bowering (1935-   ) was born in Kelowna and grew up in the Okanagan Valley. He now lives in Vancouver where he teaches at Simon Fraser University. He is a prolific writer and has published many books of poetry, prose, and literary criticism. He won the Governor General's Award for poetry in 1969 for his two books *Rocky Mountain Foot* and *The Gangs of Kosmos*. His prose fictions include *Mirror on the Floor* (1967), *A Short Sad Book* (1977), and *Protective Footwear* (1978). He believes fiction is made of illusion, and so he frequently makes the problems of fiction-making the subject of his stories. In 1980 he edited the anthology *Fiction of Contemporary Canada* in which "A Short Story" appears; his latest novel, *Burning Water* (1980), won the Governor General's Award that year.

A SHORT STORY

George Bowering

Setting

It was that slightly disappointing moment in the year when the cherry blossoms have been blown off the trees, or shrunken to brown lace out of which little hard green pebbles are beginning to appear. The orchardists were running tractors between the rows of trees, disking the late spring weeds into the precious topsoil left there by the glacier that long ago receded from the desert valley.

Starlings were growing impatient with the season, tired of competing for scraps behind the Safeway store in town, eager for those high blue days when the cherries would be plump & pink, when they could laugh at the sunburnt men in high gum boots, who would again try to deceive them with fake cannons & old shirts stretched between the branches.

High over Dog Lake a jet contrail was widening & drifting south. The orchards on the west bank were in shadow already, & sunlight sparkled off windows of the new housing development on the other shore. The lake was spotted with brown weeds dying underwater, where the newest poison had been dumpt by the government two weeks before.

Evening swallows were already dipping & soaring around the Jacobsen house, nabbing insects in their first minutes of activity after a warm day's sleep. The house was like many of the remodelled orchard homes in the southern part of the valley, its shiplap sides now covered with pastel aluminum, metallic screen doors here & there, a stone chimney marking the outside end of the living room. Fifteen years ago the living room had been used only when relatives from other valley towns came to visit. Now it was panelled with knotty cedar, animal heads looking across at one another from the walls, & the Jacobsens sat there after all the evening chores were done, watching Spokane television in colour, and reading this week's paper, or perhaps having some toast & raspberry jam.

The rug was a pastel shade fairly close to that of the outside surface. The Jacobsens lived with it, though neither of them particularly liked it. One of them had, once, when it was new; the other never thought of offering an opinion, or holding one.

Characters

The Jacobsens did not discuss things. They spoke short sentences to one another in the course of a card game, or while deciding which re-run was more worth watching on the mammoth television set parkt under a deer head on the west wall of the living room.

'We haven't seen this Carol show, have we?' suggested Mrs. Jacobsen. 'I think it must have been on the night we played bridge with Stu & Ronnie.'

'No, we saw it,' said Mr. Jacobsen from behind his sixteen-page newspaper. 'This is the one where her & Harvey are on that jet plane that gets highjackt to South America.'

'Sky-jackt.'

'The same thing. But if you want to watch it again, go ahead.'

'I can't remember a sky-jack one.'

'Go ahead. I'll probably fall asleep in the middle, anyway,' said Mr. Jacobsen.

Art Jacobsen was tired every night. As soon as the after-supper card game was over, & his short legs were up on the aquamarine hassock, his eyes would begin to droop. He was sixty-one years old, & still working eleven hours a day in the orchard. Like most valley orchardists, he wore a shirt only during the early hours of the morning, when the dew was still on every leaf. His body was tanned & muscled, but it was getting more rectangular every year.

Audrey Jacobsen was ten years younger. She had only recently taken to colouring her hair, often a kind of brownish-red she mistakenly remembered from her youth. Her first husband used to tease her about having red hair, though it wasn't true. By the time that Ordie Michaels had died & Art Jacobsen had started courting her on rainy days, her hair was a good plain brown, usually under a kerchief.

She'd taken to wearing the kerchief, as all the women did, while sorting fruit at the Co-op packing house. By the time Donna was five, Audrey had assumed the habit of wearing it all the time, except when she went for drives with Art Jacobsen.

They had been watching Carol on television for five years now, & she didn't know whether she liked the show.

Point of View

It is not that I know all about the Jacobsens & Donna Michaels before I start telling you about them. I am what they call omniscient, all right, but there isn't any Jacobsen family until I commit them to this medium. I have some hazy ideas or images, rather, of their story, a sort of past & a present, I suppose, but really, for me the story is waiting somewhere in the future. Or I should say that I'm waiting for a time in the future when I will have the time to come to it, here. As a matter of fact, you don't have to, now, wait as long for it as I do.

So I am in the position ascribed to the narrator with the totally omniscient point of view. A know-it-all. Don't you believe it! 'God-like.' Don't you believe it!

For instance, I've been thinking about writing this story for two years. Just a month ago I began to imagine a woman visiting her mother & stepfather at their orchard home, & that common emotional violence later on. But I just got the names while I was writing the first parts of the story, & I didn't imagine the Jacobsen house near the lake—I thought it would be forty kilometres farther south.

Do I have to mention that there is something difficult to explain about a third-person omniscient narrative having all these 'I's' in it? Point of view dictates distance. Well, I would like to keep you closer than your usual 'god' will allow (except for people such as yourself, Leda) (no, that's not what I'm trying to do to you, reader: don't be so suspicious).

From up here I can see the Jacobsen house as a little square surrounded by trees that have nearly lost their blossoms & are just producing leaves. I have good eyes; I need them to see all that thru the drifting jet contrail.

By the way, have you noticed that when the narrator speaks in the first person, he makes you the second person? When he speaks of others in the third person, you are perhaps standing beside him, only the parallax preventing your seeing exactly what he is seeing. That makes for a greater distance produced by the first-person narrative. You must have noticed that.

Protagonist

Donna Michaels, an attractive honey-blonde in her early twenties, was about four kilometres from the Jacobsen house, driving along the lakeside road in her dented Morris Minor convertible. She had already gone thru her rite of passage between innocent childhood & knowledgeable maturity, involving strong Freudian implications. Now she was driving thru a warm valley evening, wishing that she had come a week ago, when the cherry blossoms were still at the beginning of their decline.

She had not been home during blossom time for seven years, & perhaps this more than anything else told her that she had really ceast to be a valley kid, that she was a Coast person. Looking to her right she could see, even in the shadows made by the hills over the water, splotches of brown weeds under the surface of the lake. A part of her that still wanted to be a valley person was hurt by that.

She thought about taking a Valium before she got there, only two kilometres to go now. It was not really the time to appear. She should have arrived while Art was still out in the orchard, so she could have a calm talk with her mother. When Art was there, making his blustery remarks or criticisms about her language, her mother could be depended on to remain silent, just has she had always done during family hassles, just as she had done then.

'I love him, Donna. What am I supposed to do?' she had said.

'More than you love me?' That newcomer.

'I *chose* him.'

That was the last time her mother had ever said anything so devastatingly open.

She got out of the car & took a Valium. One gets adept at swallowing them without water. She was mildly surprised that she was walking slowly toward the single little Ponderosa pine that used to be her going-to-be-alone place in the far corner of their orchard. It had perhaps grown four inches taller. Looking further up, she could see Star Bright. She made a trivial wish & walkt slowly back to the dusty car.

What a beautiful sight she was, with her long legs & summer dress, sunglasses percht on top of her short feathery blondish hair.

Symbolism

Donna got back into the dented Morris Minor, & before she let the clutch out, she unaccountably thought about the animal heads protruding from her stepfather's walls. The

first time she had seen one, she had gone to the room next
door, to see whether the elk's body stuck out from that side.
What had ever been done with the bodies, she wondered
now. Were they discarded, left on the forest floor for the
delectation of ants? Did the family eat them? She couldn't
remember eating mountain goat or moose, & she had been a
picky eater as a child.

She decided that whatever had been done with the torso &
legs, Art was only really interested in the trophy. He talkt
about nature a lot, but he was quite comfortable under the
stare of the big glass eyes.

Her dog Bridey passed away after a fit when she was
twelve. Quickly, before he would have a chance to take her to
the taxidermist, Donna put the heavy & limp body along
with an adult's shovel into a wheelbarrow & pusht it for half
an hour thru the crumbling earth, to the Ponderosa. There
she wasted no time looking at Bridey's fur and & tight-closed
eyes. She dug a deep hole & dropt her in & covered her up,
without looking. She left no marker. She knew where Bridey
was, & that was all that was necessary.

Now, she reflected, looking at the sagebrush growing
around her tree, they probably knew too, he probably saw the
wheel tracks the next morning.

She let out the clutch & drove the last kilometre slowly,
having pulled on the lights. Just in time, a mother quail &
her five little ones raced in a line to the safety of the roadside
weeds. She smiled as she imagined the mother there, counting them.

Then she was at the turn just before their driveway, where
the truck & the new Toyota were parkt in a sharp vee. People
here along Rawleigh Road never pulled their drapes. Thru
the window she could see Mr. & Mrs. Jacobsen, an over-
coloured Carol, & a deer she used to call Bambi, first
childishly, then later to needle her stepfather.

Her car's wheels cruncht over the driveway. Before she got
out she did up her two top buttons.

Conflict

Donna had driven four hundred kilometres to be there, but
she didn't want to go inside the house. Of course in a setting
such as this, they would know that somebody had driven up
the gravel driveway, & one of them, probably her mother,
would be walking to the door at this moment.

Donna wanted to be with her mother, & especially because she never wrote letters home. She did not even imagine writing 'Mrs. A. Jacobsen' on an envelope. She felt as if, yes, she still loved her mother, that strange older woman in polyester slacks, though they had not once spoken to each other on the telephone since Jacobsen had mounted her as his casual season's trophy. What ambiguity in the delivery of the thought. When it was accomplisht, & all three knew, what depressing decisions & solitudes.

Donna could not stay in that family where her first love, her first world face, lost all hope & fell in, decided to stay with the bringer of death. What polluted language in the formerly unchallenged eden. Why? How, rather.

'But I chose him. I made my choice.'

'Do you love him? Can you?'

'I chose him.'

She was not a woman then, but she was not a valley girl, either. She left Dog Lake, she had to, & there was no question but the city on the coast, several ruinous jobs, & some very solitary education.

Now the door opened & it was Audrey who was illuminated by the porch light. Donna was momentarily ashamed with disappointment that her mother, Mrs. Michaels, was not the picture of a defeated lustreless farm wife, the sensitive buffeted by life, such as one expected to find in the Canadian novels she had been reading.

'Donna! For the Lord's sake! Why didn't you tell us you were coming? Come in, you rascal,' the woman said, her arms out-stretcht as if offering the red knitting she had been doing while watching television.

Donna held her mother's elbows & kissed her nose as she felt the screen door bat against her rear. Her mother chattered with a little confusion as the pretty blonde deposited her purse & a book & something wrapt in party paper on the telephone table.

'Well, well,' said Art Jacobsen, looking up from his paper, his feet still stretcht out on the hassock.

Dialogue

'I wish I'd gotten here while the blossoms were in full bloom,' said Donna. It was the perfect little bit of business to get thru the awkwardness of their surprise.

'Oh, we had a wonderful year for blossoms,' said her

mother. 'When a breeze came up the whole valley smelled like a garden.'

'It *is* a garden,' said Donna, getting herself a cup of coffee from the pot on the stove. She came back thru the arch into the living room, where her mother was still standing with the knitting in her hands. 'At least that's how we coast people think of it.'

Art shook his paper to a new page.

'It's not blossoms that count. It's the bees.'

'The workers, you mean,' said Donna, a little edge on her voice. She sat down with her coffee, not looking at him.

'Yeah, the queen sits at home, getting fatter & fatter, while the workers bring her the honey,' said Art, his eye looking at a news photo of the local skeet-shooting champs.

'Have you had any supper, Dear?' Audrey piped in.

'Yes, I stopt in at the Princeton bus station cafe, for old times' sake,' said Donna.

That was a nice shot. It was there that she had abandoned Art's truck that night, with the keys in the dash. She'd taken the bus to Vancouver with no baggage, not even clean underwear. Just two apples & her purse.

Art didn't say a word now.

'Well, well,' said Audrey Jacobsen.

There was a silence. Even the knitting needles crost & opened without a sound. It was pitch dark outside. A mirrored deer lookt in from between two young Lombardy poplars.

'How are all your aches & pains, Mom?' Donna askt at last, idly looking at snapshots from a glass bowl on the table beside her chair. Carol was over, & Art raised his remote control & shot the set off.

'Oh, the osteopath in Penticton said I did something to my lower spine when I was a girl, & I can never expect to be a hundred percent.'

'Does that mean you're not all there?' askt Art.

Flashback

When he seemed absolutely ready to give it up, give up on it, to settle for some costly talk then, she offered him a cigarette, which he took politely, & lit one herself. It was the only sort of occasion upon which she smoked, anything. They were always grateful, the talkers, when she by her gestures allowed them a certain comfort, a freedom from embarrassment.

'Thank you.' he said, & lay on his back beside her, carefully sharing the ashtray she kept on her belly.

'You needn't feel badly.' Her voice was soft & sure, caring & casual, it seemed. 'You might be surprised how often it happens. You had a lot to drink, I would imagine, it was only enough to make you think you wanted me. Happens quite a lot.'

'No that's not it. Well, it might be a little, but that's not really it. It's—'

She did not offer the interruption he was waiting for. She just smoked her cigarette. She butted it out in the ashtray, & handed the ashtray to him. So he had something to do with his free hand.

'It's just that you are about exactly the age of my daughter,' he said.

'No kidding,' she said, with a twiggy edge to her voice, & that was his first hint that it was time to go back to his hotel.

Foreshadowing

After he had left, she got the scissors & clipped her toenails. Having done five, she lay back & imagined the john walking back to his hotel. He did not seem like the taxi-taking kind.

She pictured him lying on her, brought by her to the margin of success. Then she yanked the scissors toward her, fetching a jolt as they sank into the flesh of his back. It was not an old movie on midnight television. The points of her scissors were just below the joining of her ribcage, forcing the skin a little.

I wonder whether I could just throw a few clothes into the car & drive to Montreal, she thought.

Maybe you could work your way across the country, she replied.

She clipped five toenails again. They were the same ones.

Plot

The spare bedroom of the Jacobsen house was also a kind of store-room. It contained a gun-rack in which one could find a pump-action shotgun, a .22 calibre repeater rifle, an old .303 that once belonged to the Canadian Army, a .44 handgun in a tooled holster, a thirty-thirty with a scope sight, & a collector's .30 calibre machine-gun with a plugged barrel. This is where Donna was, taking off her light cardigan & shoes, finding the toothbrush & dental floss in the bottom of her big-city street bag, looking at herself, untanned, in the vanity mirror. A severed goat head lookt over her shoulder.

Thru two walls she could hear the Jacobsens disputing. Art's voice rose & rose, & at the end of a declarative sentence fragment it uttered the word 'slut', followed by an exclamation point.

One would expect the ammunition to be lockt up, & it was, in a cabinet with glass-panel doors. Donna shook the pillow out of one of the pillow-cases, wrapt the pillow-case around her fist, & puncht one of the glass panels three times, each time with greater force.

The male voice rose to the word 'hell!' & stopt. A door banged against a wall, & heavy footsteps approacht. Donna threw the pillow case onto the bed beside her sweater. When Art propelled the bedroom door open, Donna was pointing a loaded shotgun at his head.

Art backt out of the bedroom & walkt backward all the way to the living room. There he observed a slight movement of the dark holes he had wiped clean just the night before, & sat down in his favourite chair. He was on top of Audrey's knitting, but he felt convinced that he should not bring attention to such a minor problem.

Audrey Jacobsen, usually a chatterbox, found it hard to find the words she should say.

She said, 'Donna—'

It was very frightening that Donna did not say a word. Art looked depressed. He was a heavy man in his chair. Donna blew out her breath.

'For God's sake, girl, that's my husband!'

Donna did not breathe in.

'He's my husband, he's all I have!'

Donna turned a smooth quick arc, & shot her mother's face off.

Theme

Donna walkt from the house & into the orchard, the shotgun still dangling. She had no shoes on. No one followed her, & she did not look behind. She was walking between two rows of cherry trees, so that when a quick hard breeze came around a rock outface it blew a snow of exhausted blossoms over her head.

Donna walkt down the slope, not flinching when a clacking sprinkler spun slowly & soakt her dress from the waist down. It was really dark out now, & she could see the lights of the retirement village on the far side of the lake.

The gun had made a dreadful noise. But now the night life was speaking again, crickets nearby & frogs from down by the lake. They were calling each other to come & do it.

Donna walkt till she came to the dirt road with the row of couchgrass down the middle, & followed it till she arrived at her Ponderosa. There she sat down with her back to its narrow trunk, & dropt the shotgun to the dry ground. The sky was filled with bright stars that seemed to have edges, & black behind them. One never saw anything like that from the streets in Vancouver. She thought of the universality speaking thru her condition.

Nearby, her dog lay curled, waiting for her to signal something to her. But she ignored her, as she fought to remember what had happened in the last hour, or was it some years? An airline jet with powerful landing lights appeared from the other side of the hills & descended over the lake, heavily pulling back on its fall toward the airstrip at the end.

Now that her eyes were adjusted to the late spring darkness of the valley, she saw a bat flipping from direction to direction above her. She remembered the fear that it might get caught in your hair. Bats don't get caught in your hair.

I'm not very old, Donna thought, I'm not very old & here I am already. She pickt up the shotgun & fired the other barrel, & threw it over the side of the hill.

■

Wilfred Watson

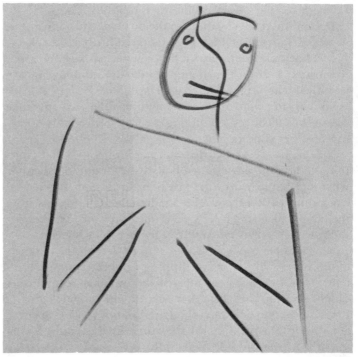

1960 self portrait

Wilfred Watson (1911-) was born in England and came to Canada in 1926, first to Vancouver Island then to the prairies where he taught English literature at the University of Alberta until 1976. Since *Friday's Child* won the Governor General's Award in 1955, he has become widely known as both a poet and a playwright. Among his many plays are *Cockcrow and the Gulls* (1962),*Let's Murder Clytemnestra according to the Principles of Marshall McLuhan* (1969), and *The Woman Taken in Adultery* published in *Prairie Performance* (1981). His two most recent volumes of poetry *I Begin with Counting* (1978) and *Mass on Cowback* (1982) are extended experiments in the use of number grid verse. "The Lice" was first published in *Prism* in 1960.

THE LICE

Wilfred Watson

There was a certain bishop of Edmonton who greatly deplored the behaviour of his congregation and of the people of Edmonton, whom he thought guilty of covetousness and greed, envy, sloth, drunkenness, gluttony and lechery, anger, vanity and pride. He would often talk about this matter with his two priests, especially with the younger, whom he loved. But they preferred to think of their congregation as being materialistic. No, no—said the bishop. He liked to call materialism, he said, by its older names. He would roll off on his tongue the Latin terms for the seven deadly sins: *superbia, invidia, iracundia, accidia,* etc. etc. When the people of Edmonton's actions deserved these labels, he wouldn't neglect to apply them, he told his subordinates. That is what these labels were for.

He preached a good many powerful sermons on the subject of deadly sins. One Lent he preached a series beginning, Pride, and going on through the list of sins till he got to the last. His congregation took these tongue-lashings in a tolerant way. They—the serious people among them—agreed with their bishop about the nature of sin; but though they felt he was right to preach about the utter holiness of God and the deplorable filthiness of sin, they felt that the bishop didn't rightly understand the tenacious nature of sinfulness. How could he? He was a saintly-minded man, and had mastered his passions and appetites. It was easy for him to resist temptation—and besides, he was a priest, and not only that, getting on in years. He couldn't comprehend how difficult it is for the non-clergy, even when they had a mind to, to cure the sinfulness of Adam in our natures—especially with this demon of materialism attacking us from the radios and television sets, from the newspapers and the motion-picture houses, from magazines, advertising mail and shop windows.

Mr. Dobbs, a good Christian, though heretical on the difficult topic of birth control, said as much to the bishop one day. If only, he ended up by exclaiming, the people of this diocese could be made to *see* their sins—in all their ugliness— as you have described it—then, perhaps, father, then, perhaps . . .

The bishop thought deeply about what Mr. Dobbs had said to him . . .

But no way to show his flock the nature of sin came to his mind . . .

If only sin *could* be made visible.

If only . . .

At length, he decided to take his difficulty to God.

If only, he said in his heart, God would make the sin of each sinner in the diocese into a hunchback, why, how many souls would be saved for the New Jerusalem, saved in fact from terrible damnation. If only . . . He shivered a little at the thought. Suppose his own hump were uglier and fatter and more conspicuous than the lump of sin on the backs of his flock? Suppose he himself were, in spiritual pride, uglier and fouler than any of this congregation? It would be for the good of his own soul, he decided, if any condition of sin in him were made manifest.

So the bishop worded an outright prayer, as the spiritual leader of his flock, to God, that the sins of his congregation and of himself, should be made visible to himself and to all of them.

Then he fell asleep.

The next morning was Sunday. It was, the bishop saw when he awoke from dreamless sleep, a glorious clear fresh sunny morning. The sun sang in the sky like an angel. The blue sky sang. The trees seemed to be wearing a fresher green than usual, as if they had been washed with rain during the night—perhaps they had—but no—the ground was dry. It was the sun shining through the marvellously clear air of Edmonton, that made everything so clean and bright.

In church, when the bishop turned round to look over the new clothes and the clean faces of his congregation, the people themselves seemed newer and brighter and more colourful than ever before. The gay hats of the young girls . . . the red dresses . . . the shirts and trousers and jackets of the men . . . even the blacks of those who had come decently garbed in black . . . seemed to glow with the colour of the morning and of the sun outside.

A sombre thought struck the bishop. Perhaps there had been another of those false "sales" at the Westmount shopping centre . . . and this new look . . . this freshness was simply just that. It was then that the bishop remembered his thoughts about hunchbacks and his prayer to God the night before.

343

He glanced at the shoulders of his flock to see if his prayer
had been—but no, and he said a 'Thy will be done' to himself, rather hastily. A terrible fear struck him. He wriggled his
shoulders. They seemed, as he did so, rather odd. He squeezed
his elbows to his side, trying to feel his back. He looked
round, and finally, put his hand to his shoulder, as if—and
this, he realized glumly was a deceit, a hypocrisy—he were
adjusting his clothing. But no . . . his terrible prayer . . . God
in his mercy . . . who sees all issues . . . had . . . in his
wisdom . . . seen fit not to grant. *Non sum dignus* . . .

*Introibo ad Altare Dei—Adjutorium nostrum in nomine
Domini*—I will go into the altar of God—Our help is in the
name of the Lord . . . the bishop had got so far in the saying
of the order of mass. And the confession was over, *Confiteor
Deo omnipotenti, beatae Mariae semper Virgini* . . . I confess
to almighty God, to blessed Mary ever a virgin . . . The
bishop had got as far as the absolution: *Misereatur vestri
omnipotens Deus, et, dimissis peccatis vestris* . . . May
almighty God have mercy upon you, and forgive you your
sins . . .

It was then that the bishop's eyes fell upon the crucifix on
the altar, for at this point he had to turn to the altar and say,
silently,

Take away from us our iniquities, we beseech thee . . .

The words turned to ice in his throat.

For, streaming from the crucifix . . . was . . . terrible thing
to see, a swarm . . . yes, swarm of some sort of insects . . . No,
not streaming from it . . . but drawn to it . . . as if to a
magnet . . . which was sucking them in . . . insects . . .

The bishop didn't know what to think. He wasn't sure
what he ought to do . . . He prostrated himself, burying himself for a time in prayer . . . Then he stood up before the
crucifix . . . and yes . . . it was insects that were hanging in
clusters there . . . as if a swarm of bees had alighted . . . as if
the blessed crucifix were their queen . . . but, *domine misere*,
it was not bees, but some small loathsome insects . . .

Lice . . . said the bishop. *Lice* . . . And then, in an instant
the meaning of the miracle—for it was a miracle that his eyes
were glazed by—dawned on him, as clearly as if an angel had
told him. God had chosen his own way to make the sins of
his congregation (and perhaps the sins of the people of
Edmonton, too) visible to the eye of sense; he had chosen to
turn these foul loathsome wickednesses, evil thoughts, covet-
ousnesses, cupidities of the flesh, into lice polluting the
crucifix.

Even when this realization had punctured its way into his mind, the bishop, like someone who has received a telegram of great importance, understands it, but remains unbelieving, put (or rather pushed) forward his arm, and stretched his finger out to touch one of the hideous things . . . The insect was crushed by the doubting Thomas finger, and a drop of blood smeared—polluted the altar-cloth. Polluted? Ought he, the bishop fearfully checked himself, to conclude, *polluted*? Might not this blood be the blessed blood of the Redeemer of mankind? He sank feebly down upon his knees again, and hid himself in a state between trance and wordless prayer.

Not knowing what they should do, his priests and his acolytes, who had seen almost in the same instant (but with far less comprehension) what he had seen, came towards him, fearing that he had been overcome. But he pulled himself together, and signalled to them to turn to their ritual places.

And he went on, as if instructed by God Himself, in this emergency, with mass. He didn't realize what he was saying. In his mind two ideas were in conflict—swinging backwards and forwards like an irresistible pendulum, which swayed him with its motion. He thought: a miracle, a miracle. But his next thought was: these sins have been turned into *lice*. As far as the glory of the one thought raised him up, the shame of the other sucked him down.

There were hanging to the crucifix, it seemed to him, all sorts of small noxious pestiferous blood-sucking insects. There was the common louse. There were bed-bugs, flat and stupid-looking discs of redness; and every sort of louse. He had seen—once, on the farm he was brought up on, a chicken-house hanging with ropes of chicken fleas; and he thought of the pecked rumps of these sorry infected fowl—their feather-less backs bleeding where other chickens with no less melan-choly backs, had beaked them, pecking at lice, but breaking through the skin. But no sight as horrible as the one before his eyes.

When the *credo* was over, he went down to the commun-ion rail, and stood facing his flock. Casting his eye over them, as a shepherd counts his sheep, or as a father casts his eye over his children, he marvelled at their shining faces, at their shining clothes, at their shining presence—the light seemed to come from within them—they seemed like a churchful of angels, not people. The other swing of the pen-dulum compelled him. He didn't know what to say to them. It certainly wasn't a time for preaching. At last the words came, almost of their own.

"My children, turn round your heads and look at one another."

Surprised, they didn't at once obey him, but stared straight and fixedly at him.

"My children, look at one another."

Shyly, first one and then another turned round to look at his neighbour, and then, catching his neighbour's eye, turned back in a puzzled fashion to the old priest. It seemed to them he stood there in front of them like a shining angel.

"My children," he said over again, with smiling patience, "look at yourselves—turn round and look at yourselves. Take a good look at yourselves. It is a *good* look, isn't it?"

Less shyly this time, they did as they were told, and then turned their eyes back to the priest.

"What is it," he asked them, in the softest voice—in a voice not louder than a whisper—"what is it you see—what do you see?—You see," he told them, "the beauty of holiness adorning each one of you."

He stood silent for a long time.

At length he found words to tell what had happened. "God has performed a wonderful miracle. We think in our hearts that there aren't any more miracles performed in this twentieth century after Christ's birth—we think God has lost the ability to do a miracle. But behold, God has performed one. God has shown each of you the beauty of human beings, even in this shape we stand in—it is a beautiful shape, if it isn't made ugly by sin."

He paused. "Look round you at yourselves again." They still didn't understand him, but they looked around about them, as he told them to.

"And now," he said to them, in a voice sepulchral and low—the voice of one buried in the grave, "look at the crucifix on the altar . . ."

Look at the crucifix on the altar . . . when he said this low-voiced injunction a second time, all their eyes were trained on the crucifix.

None of them could see clearly what it was that had darkened, had clouded over, the shining silver of the cross . . . and the bishop explained to them what had happened. As he spoke, the vision of brightness which he saw resting upon them, vanished.

In thrilling fatherly voice he implored them to gaze on the miracle, and see how God had made visible their sins to them, in the form of lice . . . *lice* which He had caused to infest the crucifix, nasty, loathsome, bloodsucking creatures, lice . . . fleas . . . and *bedbugs* . . . and this was why . . .

His voice trailed away into inaudibility, mere imploration. But everyone in the church understood what he was trying, and unable, to say.

II

When the news of the miracle spread to the world outside—as it very quickly did spread, a nine-day's wonder resulted.

The Edmonton *Journal* gave the miracle front-page headlines, and for several weeks reported daily on the ebb and flow of the swarm of insects to be seen clinging to the cross of the church. *Time* wrote up the miracle in a leading article, honoured the bishop with a cover portrait, and commented on the remarkable reticence he displayed—indeed, complained of it. In truth, he wasn't interested in this sort of fame. *Life* sent photographers to him, but the bishop refused them admittance to the church. Whether they did take photographs surreptitiously, or whether they manufactured them, photographs of the miraculously infested crucifix appeared, in the current issue of *Life*.

Even as far away as Rome, notice was taken of the "miracle of Edmonton," as it was soon called. The Vatican was bound to take an interest in it, for, as may be expected, scientists of a sceptical turn of mind asked to be allowed to test the validity of the alleged miraculous happening. The bishop, however, refused to allow them access to it. They challenged him in the name of truth. There was no lack of witness to the truth, he said. Many eyewitnesses of unimpeachable veracity testified to what had happened—and all that sceptics wanted to do was find some way of throwing doubt on the occurrence.

The editor of the Edmonton *Journal* held the bishop's stand to be right. An editorial appeared which took the bishop's part against the scientists—this editorial pointed out that the saintliness of the bishop had done more for Edmonton in the way of publicity than anything else in the city's history, with the possible exception of the victories of the town's football team, the Eskimos. To this editorial, a University of Alberta classics professor replied caustically, in a letter, that he, for one, didn't want Edmonton to become another home of superstition, like Lourdes, in France.

As for the bishop, he withdrew his skirts with remarkable

dexterity from all these unsavoury arguments about what
had happened.

His heart indeed was set elsewhere.

And the next Sunday after the appearance of the lice, he
rejoiced to notice that the swarm on the crucifix had very
noticeably diminished. He might have attributed this lessen-
ing (or so I am inclined to think) to a waning of the force of
the miracle. But he believed, as a result of their sins being
made visible to them, his congregation had been at some
pains to resist the temptations of sin; and that the crucifix
was a gauge of their success.

When he spoke to them in church, that was what he said.
"My children, I rejoice to see that . . ."

In a low voice, he begged them to try with all their hearts
to continue the improvement of the past week . . . he knew
that a long-settled-in habit of vice couldn't be cured in a few
days . . . but God was helping them . . . and he said he
looked forward to the time when the crucifix would be completely free of lice which still clung to it in swarms . . .

It is difficult, however, for human beings to resist temptation for periods of longer than a few days, even when all the
world has its eye on what is happening; and the second Sunday after the miracle occured showed a marked increase in
the swarming lice.

The bishop in a reproachful voice recalled to his flock
what was happening. They looked at this reproachful figure
sadly, as if they were all signifying to him, we can't help it,
but . . . we are flesh and blood, merely. They received what
he said to them in patience, at least. It was not so on the
third Sunday after the miracle. To the bishop, with anxious
eyes on the crucifix of the church as a true gauge of the sinfulness of his people, it seemed, on this third Sunday after
God had spoken to them with the plague of lice, as if his
flock was more sinful than ever they had been.

His voice, though he tried to modulate it, was petulant. It
bit into the air like an iron rasp. He was not heard in
patience. People in the church stalls fidgeted and squirmed.
It was as if one and all were shrugging their shoulders. When
he called on them to look at their shame, visible as lice on
the crucifix, they didn't raise their eyes, but looked away
almost defiantly. He sensed their hostility.

I must not lose patience with them, he told himself.
Human nature, he reminded himself, is very very weak. It
was natural for his flock to relapse in this way. He must go

out to them, as a father, in loving confidence. He stood at the door of his church, after mass, and tried to give each of them his personal assurance of his belief in them . . .

Person to person, some them relented of their stiff attitude in church. But others openly rebelled. One of them went so far as to ask, how can we be sure, reverend father, that what has happened to the cross is a sign from God, and not an insult from the devil. Another church member said, was it really a good thing to be able to see one's sins in so dramatic a fashion. He wasn't speaking for himself, mind you, father— but wouldn't it tend to harden people's hearts and make them brazen—just as a prostitute is turned into a brazen huzzy by the outward, open wickedness of her life of vice?

The good bishop shook his head. No, no, he said. We must take it as a miracle from God. If it is a miracle, how can it work for evil?

One of his priests ventured to speak to this question. The younger of the two (the one he loved particularly) observed that, if the result of the manifestation of lice on the crucifix did cause *more* sinfulness, then ought we not to conclude that it was, on this very argument of the bishop, one of the works of the devil?

No, no, no, said the bishop in anguish.

The younger priest held his tongue until the bishop had gone, and then observed, to the other priest, that "we must conclude this, mustn't we?"—"I don't know what to think," said the elder of the two.

The bishop however, received instructions from his superior, the archbishop, that it was plain, from the scandal of the "miracle," that the "miracle" must be adjudged "no miracle." He must therefore have the cross cleansed of the "miraculous" lice, which were, in all probability, due to some natural cause, and to be accounted for as some unusual but perfectly *natural* plague.

This intervention of his superior was perhaps brought about because some professors of science at the University had examined specimens of the infestation, as they called it, and had pronounced upon the nature of the insects making up their "sample," obtained with a genuine zeal for truth but in an unlawful way. All were such varieties of bloodsucking vermin as could easily be found in Edmonton. There was no satisfactory explanation forthcoming as to how they occurred where they did in such numbers. However, according to one wag, a rough estimate of the number of insects on the crucifix could be made; and hence, a count of the number of sins committed in Edmonton.

Moreover, an analysis of blood taken from some of the lice was made. The reports about this analysis were conflicting. Not all the samples were said to be human blood; and more than one type of human blood was detected. It could not be maintained then that the blood in the lice was the blood of the Saviour, as the bishop was said to suppose. All in all, these investigations didn't completely prove the miracle to be a fraud, but they left considerable room for speculation.

With a sad heart, the bishop ordered the crucifix to be cleansed of the lice infesting it. What his hopes were, may be expected. He was consequently most despondent when, after vigorous disinfection, the cross was once more free of lice.

He went to his room and prayed, not for another miracle, but simply prayed—wordlessly he opened his heart in passive obedience to God. He remained in prayer for most of the night. When the next morning—it was Wednesday morning— he again went into the church, he didn't dare raise his eyes at once to the cross.

When he did so, he saw it was clean—as clean as the cleaning people had left it. He realized that what had occurred might easily be taken as a defilement of the church—that the church might have to be reconsecrated. The archbishop indeed had gently hinted as much in an exchange of letters.

On Thursday, the crucifix was still free of infestation. And so it was on Friday. And on Saturday.

On Saturday morning, the Edmonton *Journal* reported what had taken place in the church during the week: the cleansing away of the lice infesting the crucifix. Though asserting his belief in the sanctity of the bishop, the editor urged his readers not to draw hasty conclusions from exceptional circumstances. Perhaps, this strange happening might prove to be, not a supernatural event, but one of those many natural miracles that our age has provided, and its solution a feather in the cap, not of religion, but of science.

But when, on Sunday morning, the bishop, about to say mass, raised his eyes to the cross, there, lo and behold, were the lice clinging to it, as if it had not been subject to the activities, on the Tuesday before, of the vermin exterminators.

He wanted to cry out, then and there, Look, O ye of little faith, the lice have returned—your sins and mine have again been made visible. But he made no allusion to the repetition of the miracle, as he thought, or to the re-infestation of the crucifix, as most of this congregation thought. He learned that they thought so, as he spoke to them after mass.

They seemed to be daring him to assert that the crawling insect life on the crucifix was, in fact, a miraculous manifestation of their sins.

He held his peace.

By doing so, he earned the approval of his younger priest (the one he loved), who remarked to his brother priest that he thought the bishop had shown wisdom and discretion in maintaining silence in the face of the return of the plague of lice.

The bishop again ordered the exterminators into the church. But Monday, Tuesday, Wednesday, Thursday, Friday and Saturday—though they exerted all their efforts, the exterminators had no success. They were this time unable to cleanse the cross of its vermin. Nor could they find any natural cause why it should be infested.

They did spray the sanctuary and the body of the church with quantities of an insecticide having deodorant properties. The smell of the lice had become extremely unpleasant—as the younger priest said to his confrere, "God is not only making our sins known to our eyes, but to our noses." The odour of the spray which the vermin-exterminators used rather enforced the stench of the vermin they seemed unable to kill, than eradicated it or covered it up. As one entered the church, a strong suspicion of violets made one's nose quiver. But this scent of violets quickly changed to a strong whiff of carrion. It was as if, in a flower garden, you were hit by an overpowering smell given off, say, by the putrefying body of a dead animal, a dead cat or dog.

Because of this smell, and for other reasons, I should have thought that there would have been no congregation on the following Sunday, but such was not the case. The fact is, an angry congregation makes a full church.

The bishop, for his part, flatly and without emotion (still calling his flock, "my children") re-asserted his belief in the miracle. He said that they were right to be ashamed of what had happened to the crucifix, but, though this shame was a good thing, they were wrong to think there was no way to end the pollution of their church.

The church was polluted by sin.

It could be purified by fighting against sin, and God had helped to make this fight easier, by showing them their sins.

The bishop was nevertheless conscious all through mass of the hostility of the people.

After mass, very few spoke to him, but one forthright, golden-hearted old woman spoke out her mind. "I think it is a miracle, father. But it is a very hard one for human flesh and blood to stomach."

"God will provide us with strength."

"It is a very hard thing, reverend father."

III

All that next week, the bishop reflected on what she said to him. He wondered if he had been too fanatical in his zeal to reform his flock. He recalled to mind how he had asked for the miracle, the wonderful vision he had had of his people, that first morning, when the miracle had come, and the unhappy aftermath. Was God judging *him*? He felt very despondent.

Little by little, however, he began to repair his morale. He chided himself for lacking courage, he blamed himself for lack of faith—he blamed himself, too, for not realizing that he must face a desperate struggle with forces of evil. He also reminded himself that he had an ally in God.

After all, the bishop told himself, he was the shepherd of his flock, and the good shepherd lays down his life for his sheep. He himself must give up his life for his sheep, if need be.

By Saturday, a course of action shaped itself in his brain. That night, he again prayed articulately to God.

Thy will be done, O Lord—but, if possible, let the pollution of the cross with the sins of my flock cease—even if the lice could infest me—yes, yes, the shame of the polluted cross is too great for them—let the lice infest me . . .

So he prayed.

The next morning, Sunday morning, he knew that his prayer had been answered, there was no doubt of that. For he himself was covered with the lice. He was torn between thankfulness to God, and the bodily torment of the plague of vermin.

In church, he saw that the cross was free. As he heard mass being said, he began to wonder if he had the strength to undertake the task he has asked for. After the *credo*, he went to the altar rail, and again stood before his flock.

"By miracle," he told them, "it has pleased God to show us all, my children, how our sins hurt His Son. But here is another miracle. He will now show us, such is His will, how

His priest is hurt by the sins of His people—your sins, my children."

There was neither joy nor reproach in the bishop's voice. He spoke in a factual manner. Having finished speaking, he divested himself of his clothes, down to the waist. Then he held his arms up above his head, so that all in the church could see how the lice which had clung to the crucifix, were now transferred to him.

He walked down the centre aisle of the church and back again, all the time holding his hands above his head.

Then he drew his clothes about him.

He felt, during the rest of that Sunday, and through the other days of the week following, that what God had made happen He had made happen for the best. There was, he believed, a great decrease in the number of lice crawling over his body. He was by no means free from the physical discomfort of them. The comforting thing was, the lice had decreased.

On the following Sunday, he once again experienced the joy he had known, in a surpassing degree, on the day of the first miracle.

It seemed to him that the people in the church were shinning with a new cleanness—especially the faces of some of the girls and young women of the congregation seemed to be lit up with the light that must once have shone in the Garden of Eden, the garden of aboriginal innocence . . .

But, immediately after mass had been said, he sensed a relapse. He knew there must be some retrogression—his experience of human nature told him that. But he suspected from the great increase in the number of lice on his body that the increase had been disappointingly great.

Throughout the following week, the lice on his body increased. In fact, on Sunday, he could hardly bring himself to go to mass.

But he did.

And once again, he stood up before the people, and stripped off his clothes, and showed them his body covered with lice.

"My children," he began, but he got no further.

An unprecedented thing happened.

A woman near him interrupted him. "The smell, father"—this was as far as she got and stopped surprised at herself. "It's the smell of sin—it's your smell, my children," the bishop answered her.

A loud arrogant male voice took up the woman's complaint.

"I'm a Christian, but it's not sanitary for you to appear like this, father . . . you ought not to come into church like it . . ."

A chorus of voices took up the protest, and soon everybody joined the hubbub.

"You ought to be ashamed of yourself, father, coming to mass like this . . ."—"Stay at home, father, until you are fit to be seen in public . . ."—"This isn't any miracle, father, it's just filth . . . How can we expect our kids to keep clean and wash the backs of their ears and comb their hair, father, if you come to church all covered with lice?"—"Be off with you, father, you're lousy . . ."—"Go and wash, father."— "Take a bath, father."—"Wash yourself in Lysol, father."

"Shut up," a girl shouted out hysterically.

The bishop steadied himself on the rail of O'Brien's pew, and wrote with his finger in the dust—for the wind had filled the church with the summer dust, which hung over the city like a cloud, and, sifting into the church, made all the woodwork gritty to touch.

A boy's voice whined from the back of the church, "Go de-louse yourself in the river Jordan, father."

"My children," the bishop began again, "these are your sins . . ."

"No, they are lice, father."

"They look like lice, father."

"My children," the bishop wept . . .

"Off with him."

"Out of the church with him."

"Chase him out."

With the women, girls and children screaming denunciation or encouragement, the male sheep of the bishop's flock pushed out of their stalls, and, approaching their half-naked shepherd, began to butt him out of the church.

His priests ran to help him into the bishop's residence, which was adjacent. Once in, he threw his discarded clothing across a wooden library table, and then searched in the pocket of his jacket for a packet of cigarettes—it was a packet of Player's he had bought as long ago as the week before the *first* miracle. He hadn't smoked a cigarette since then.

He fumbled with trembling fingers at the packet. Approving this indulgence, one of his priests (the younger one he loved), reached into his own pocket for a booklet of matches, tore off a match, and stood waiting to light the bishop's cigarette. But when the bishop got his box of smokes open, he found the half-filled package swarming with lice. They clung to the cigarette he started to extract, and he pushed it back into the contaminated container.

"Have one of mine, father," urged the younger priest, and offered him a cigarette of his own.

"Nō, no—no thank you, my son."

"A smoke will do you good, father."

"I will have one of my own," he told his priest. And he extracted the cigarette he had just rejected, tapped it so that the lice clinging to it dropped back into the box, and put the cigarette to his mouth.

The priest lit the cigarette.

But the lice had crept into the tobacco, and the stench of burning insects made the smoking of the cigarette impossible.

The bishop butted it.

As he did so, an upboiling of emotion, a tide burning hot and freezing cold by turns, seethed through every blood vessel, every artery and vein, every capillary, every fibre of his flesh. His skin contracted under its covering of vermin. What he experienced was a recognition. He knew . . . at this moment . . . with absolute certainty . . . that he was picked out to be a martyr . . . and, too, he knew that his suffering the passion of his martyrdom . . . was now begun.

"Lord," he said, "I am afraid. But let your will be done."

He stood up erect, a sense of glory swelling within him, and pulling at his stiff, slack, aging skin—a sense of glory made trebly delicious to his senses by the itching of the lice which clung to him and were sucking his blood. His skin was aflame. If only the world knew, he thought to himself—it was for nothing so sensually delicious as this, that men lusted after the caresses of harlots, and gave up their immortal souls for the embraces of adultery.

Yet it was an agony.

Embarrassed, awkward, his two priests stood beside him, not knowing what to do, or what to advise. The younger priest was thinking over a course of action. They were both startled when the bishop spoke to them in a voice of command.

"Read to me."

"Read *what* to you, father?"

"Read to me from the scriptures."

"Wouldn't it be better," the younger priest presumed to say, "if you tried taking a shower—I'm thinking of your personal comfort," he added, for he saw the look kindling in the bishop's eye.

"Read to me from the scriptures," the bishop ordered him.

"Yes, father, what shall I read?"

"From the last chapter of the Book of Isaiah," decided the bishop. *Sion deserta facta est. Jerusalem desolata est . . . quomodo si cui mater blandiatur*—but as one who comforts his mother. I will comfort you . . .

He understood now, as the younger priest read to him from Isaiah—he grasped now with the firm-handed grasp of inner comprehension, the meaning of the phrase, *vicarious sacrifice*. He . . . God was going to accept him . . . as a sacrifice for his flock. Because of the shepherd's love for his sheep, the sheep would be saved—what foolish sheep they are! But this, it seemed to the bishop, at this moment, was the most precious of the truths of Christendom. With this imperfect coin of our lives, we can buy the lives of others, and save them from . . . and so perfect ourselves . . . Yet as he thought these words, he realized that he had never loved his congregation. At best, he tolerated them. Indeed, he had *despised* his flock, he had, hadn't he, in trying to purify it— make it what it wasn't? Now he knew the formula. He must offer himself. And God had accepted his pretended love for his people, as *if it had been a real living love*. Or was God showing to him his own worthlessness? No, that was an anthropomorphic idea. Rather, God was taking him at the word of his lips, and overlooking the empty hollowness behind that word—the emptiness of his heart. The bishop recalled the exemplum, the little medieval sermon anecdote, of Pers, the usurer. Pers, the usurer, had never done a charitable deed in all his life. But once he had flung, not *in* but *out* of charity, in anger, a loaf of bread at a starving woman. This act of violence had been reckoned—after the system of accounting of heaven—as a good deed to the credit of Pers, the usurer.

"Now let me be for a little while," the bishop said to them, adding, gently, "my sons." He went up to his room. When the younger of the priests visited him after a short lapse of time, he found the bishop collecting together his belongings.

"You are leaving us, father?"

"You have been making arrangements for me to leave you, haven't you, my son?" The apparent clairvoyance of the bishop disturbed the priest.

"Something must be done soon, father."

"Yes, my son. I'm collecting my personal things together.

But I shan't, I think, have much use for them."
The priest bowed his head, and left.

IV

Later in the day, the bishop agreed, with no fuss, without a single objection, to a proposal of his younger priest. It was that he should leave his see, leave Edmonton, and go into retirement. If he did agree—all the arrangements, said the younger priest, had been made. An unoccupied farmhouse had been put at the bishop's disposal by a member of the congregation, on account of the great scandal the church was suffering. It was provided with a bed, table, chest of drawers, other simple furnishings, and the owner wanted no remuneration for it. Nearby, there lived an old woman who had agreed to look after the bishop—she was unfortunately a Presbyterian, but otherwise of unexceptionable character. The arrangement, the younger priest had admitted to the older priest, seemed almost to be a providence of God. "But will he be persuaded . . ." the older man had wondered. "Ah, yes . . . that's our difficulty," said the priest whom the bishop loved. It had proved, however, to be no difficulty at all.

After all the arrangements had been made, there did occur *some* difficulty in getting the bishop transported out to his new house. No taxicab would agree to accept the lice-ridden churchman as a fare. No one in the bishop's congregation seemed anxious to transport the bishop out there—partly from shame, for no one wanted to be the person chosen to drive the bishop away from the fold; partly, too, there was fear of infesting the car in which the verminous bishop would have to ride.

Put to some pressure, finally one church member offered his car and his services as a driver. It was understood that the car should afterwards be fumigated thoroughly at the church's expense. If the driver of the car picked up any of the vermin on his own person, he too was to be compensated. Some simple precautions were taken. A stout white heavy cotton sheet was draped over the back seat, and another sheet was stretched across between the back seat and the driver's seat— so that the driver would be shielded as much as possible from infestation. Oddly enough, the lice seemed to prefer the bishop to the car or its driver, for none of them (so I was told) were afterwards found either on the driver's person, in the back seat upholstery, in the armrests, in the lining of the car roof, or under the floor-mat. "Isn't that miraculous," the driver said to the younger priest, who had been largely responsible for these arrangements. "Very remarkable," was the answer.

A fairly large crowd gathered at the bishop's house to witness his departure. The police were present, in case of trouble. But there was no demonstration. His farewells were much abbreviated. The elder priest offered to come and live with the bishop. But the bishop, with his eye on the younger priest, whom he loved, wouldn't hear of it. Both priests, he said, were needed in the church. A few intransigents from his congregation assembled a small group of children with fir boughs, which were to have been flung under the car as it drove away. But though the little mites waved their fir boughs faintly at him, no boughs were cast under the front of the car.

The crowd was rather sheepish. They knew the bishop knew they were glad he was leaving. So they merely stood about stupidly. Only one jaundiced teenager called out, with a voice of brass and ashes, "Come back, father, when you've got rid of the lice."

"That will never be," said the bishop, but he spoke to himself merely.

When the bishop had departed, the archbishop from afar caused the church to be reconsecrated, as he had beforehand decided to do.

V

The Presbyterian widow who was to look after the bishop discovered him standing alone in the kitchen of his new house. She had seen his car arrive, and came down "to be of use," she said. She was shocked by the fact that he was unescorted by friends, came, in fact, unaccompanied except for the driver, who, as soon as the bishop had alighted, and his few possessions been put in the house, fled down the road like a juvenile with a stolen car and with a few drinks under his windbreaker. Her good honest Presbyterian heart revolted at what she believed to be the treachery of the bishop's flock. "And they call themselves God's Christians," she exclaimed angrily to herself, "why, I wouldn't treat a dog so. The dirty Catholics . . ."

She tried to make the bishop feel at home and cared for. But the bishop was not responsive. The woman herself felt strange in his presence and supposed he must feel strange in hers. As for his affliction, she resolutely closed her eyes to it. She did, however, take pains to assure him that there was a hot bath for him, whenever he wanted to avail himself of it. (The house had propane gas, and the younger priest had arranged to have a new cylinder of gas attached.)

After the bishop had seen where everything was, came introductions.

"What shall I call you, sir?"

"My flock called me 'father,'" the bishop told her.

"Very well, sir, 'father' it is from now on."

"And what shall I call you?" the bishop asked her.

"M'name is Mrs. McGinis. You can call me that, if y'like, sir. But the lads at the ranch, well they call me mom, or mother . . . guess I am older than you, sir, if'n we took a count of our years."

"Then if you wish it—I will call you . . . mother," said the bishop.

"There's some lovely nice hot water in the tank," were her parting words, to which she added, very self-consciously, "father."

"Thank you, thank you," said the bishop.

She went away muttering curses against the Pope, Cardinal Sheen, monsignor the archbishop, and all Roman traitors—"leaving the old man alone, like this. The dirty Dogans, the dirty Dogans."

VI

All day, the bishop's heart had been anesthetized by inner misery. But as soon as the Presbyterian widow had left, his feelings began to awake. As long as his heart had been numb, he hadn't noticed the torment of the lice. Now that his heart revived, stirred first of all by the solicitude of Mrs. McGinis, and especially by the flowers she had set out for him as his table, desk, and bedroom altar, he could feel the agony of the lice. He tried to school himself not to scratch at his hands, arms, limbs, or trunk. But every now and again he lost control of his fury, and clawed savagely into his flesh, until the futility of scratching wearied his fingers.

He sat down at the table to eat the meal arranged for him by his part-time housekeeper. But as he reached for the potato salad, cold meats and pickles that Mrs. McGinis had left him, lice from his body dropped on to the plate of food,

and though he tried to brush them away, they seemed
viciously intent on getting into his food and contaminating
it. At length, he got up from the table without eating. He
made tea, but he drank none, for it too was spoiled by lice
falling into his cup.

He took off his clothes, because the suffering was less
when he was almost naked. He stood up, because the vermin
were most bearable in that position.

He was almost caught in half-naked state by Mrs. McGinis, when she called later on in the evening to see if all was
well.

After she had gone, he did eat a very little food, and drink
a sip of tea. He lay down on his back on his camp-cot, and at
long last, very late at night, slept a little. He couldn't pray.
All he could do was to keep asking, out of his affliction,
How long, O Lord, how long?

The next day, he tried taking a bath. But though many of
the vermin were drowned in the very hot bath he poured
himself, his suffering wasn't lessened, for the water made his
skin more tender to the biting of the blood-sucking insects.
He couldn't dry himself, because the chafing of the towel set
up an intolerable itching. As he stood dripping onto a towel,
he decided that bathing was a luxury he couldn't repeat.
Anxious not to offend Mrs. McGinis, he was bothered by the
state he left the bathtub in. As much as he tried to wipe it
clean of vermin, fresh ones fell into it. Finally, he abandoned
the task (—an odd fact this, considering that all the reports I
have had of the matter suggest that the lice were attracted to
him as if to a magnet.)

On the night of the second day, he slept early and long.
Next morning, he awoke greatly improved in his mind. He
was able to pray; and he prayed for strength. When he had
finished his prayers, he encouraged himself by thinking how
glorious it was—his terrible fate. He had wanted to cure his
sheep of their sins by showing them how ugly they were. But
he was doing something better. He was actually helping
those who couldn't cleanse themselves. He was taking to
himself their iniquity. Certainly not in love—in wilfulness
. . . but . . . God, he felt sure, was accepting his pitiful effort *as
if* it was a true sacrifice. In desperation, he had said, let the
sins of my flock come to me *as lice.* It was only half a promise, but God had insisted that he keep it. This was the
thought which steadied his heart.

But later that day a relapse occurred. The afternoon was

sunny and hot, the humidity in itself trying. He took off his clothes. He tried to pray, but couldn't. He shut himself up in his bedroom and wouldn't see Mrs. McGinis, who nevertheless called out to him, when she left, about the availability of bathwater . . . And why didn't he take a nice bath? He would feel so much better, she was sure . . .

Finally, his endurance broke.

O God, he prayed, *let me be rid of these accursed lice, so that I can return to my church. Don't punish me with them any more. I've had enough. O God, let me be set free of this torment.*

He fell into a long sleep.

In the morning, all the lice were gone.

VII

He couldn't at first believe either his eyes or his skin, over which he kept running his finger. He immediately threw himself into a great tub of water, and bathed himself with wonderful enjoyment. He was amazed to find that his skin was completely rid of irritation. He gave himself a marvellously revitalizing rub-down with the bath towel. He shaved, a thing he hadn't been able to do. Then, feeling like a new man, he had an excellent breakfast, drank two cups of instant coffee, and smoked three or four cigarettes.

When Mrs. McGinis came about eleven o'clock in the morning, she said to him, "Why, father, you look as if you'd taken on a new lease on life!—I see you've had a bath," she added, glancing in at the damp towels in the bathroom. "I told you it was all that was needed—it's the simple remedies that work. Nothing like soap and water. You see," she told him, "you have another nice hot bath tonight. Keep them at bay it will."

She insited on changing his bedsheets. "But—why, you haven't soiled them at all," she said.

The next morning he took another bath.

He wondered how long he ought to wait before going back to his church. A day—or two days? He seemed so useless, just waiting around in the farmhouse. He smoked cigarettes, given to him by the younger priest as a farewell gift. He ate his meals. He thought of how surprised his congregation would be, to see him again, so quickly. There would be no reproaches. It might be that he would love them better than he had done hitherto, because of the bond of failure between them—he had failed and they had failed. There would be mutual forgiveness. As he conceded his failure, as, putting it on like a new garment, he got somewhat more used to it, his need for the *community* of the church became more insistent. He must get back right away.

But at the end of the day, he discovered one thing: he *could never go back*. It would require just as much courage of him, to think out the new philosophy of life going back would require . . . the excuses . . . the new goals . . . that . . . Ah, just as much . . . as staying.

That night he didn't sleep at all. By morning, he found himself, with his new vitality, hating his cleanness. He bathed himself contemptuously. If only, he said to himself, I still had the lice—better the torment of the lice, than the emptiness of what I am now.

He didn't dare pray.

But, by that evening, he could endure himself no longer. *O God, he prayed, let the lice return to me. Forgive my weakness. Let the lice return, if it is your will, let the lice return . . . non sum dignus, domine, sed . . .*

He fell asleep. When he awoke, it was morning. The lice had returned. They were much worse than before.

VIII

So much worse were they, that before the evening of that day was come, he had again prayed that the lice leave him. In the morning, he was again free of them. He couldn't hesitate now—he mustn't play fast and loose like this. He packed his handbag. He prepared to leave. He would go back and love his flock, this would be the meaning of all that had happened . . . for him and for them, for they in return would love him too.

But when he was ready to leave, his decision wavered again. He unpacked his clothes, he decided to stay. He paced up and down the farmhouse, into and out of all the rooms of it, like a caged tigress, her cubs taken from her and her dugs full of milk. He saw that he couldn't live in this state of irresolution, but it was a long time before he could once again bring himself to pray. But then, a little before two-thirty a.m., he was able to. *Let the lice return to me. Let the lice return to me.* He then slept for an hour or two. When he awoke, they had come back. Back, and much worse than they had been on their second return. He took off his night clothes and lay for a long time naked on his bed.

The lice seemed to be multiplying. They were gnawing in his arm-pits—he tried to clean them out. If he rested on his back, they crawled across his belly. They crawled across the small of his back, if he lay on his belly. They got into his groin, and, into his ears—he had already put wads of cotton wool into his ears, to keep the lice out, but they worked their way past that barrier. Into his ears. What lies, the thought shrieked across his brain, are my people breeding now? The vermin crawled into his anus. They crawled across his scrotum, and got into the folds of the *glans penis*. What sodomy are they now committing, he cried out, as he scratched at his rectum . . . what fornication or prostitution or pimping or adultery am I suffering for now? The lice crawled over his hands—cupidity, cupidity, he told himself . . .

They crawled into his navel—across his teats—into his eyes—into his mouth, even . . .

When Mrs. McGinis called promptly at eleven a.m., she found him completely naked. But it wasn't his nakedness that horrified her, it was the sight of the true deformity of his condition, which, till now, had been more or less hidden from her. Good honest woman that she was, she shrieked with terrified disgust, when she saw *that*. All her fear of him turned into vituperation and reproach. "Why don't you do as I told you?" She threw the bathroom door open.

"Do as I tell you," she screamed. "Get in there and bathe yourself until you are clean again."

He shook his head piteously.

"Look, father. You're going to obey me. Into that bath."

He shook his head.

"Goddam you," she shouted, "do as I say."

When she found that he wouldn't or couldn't do as she ordered him, she banged her fist down on the table. "Very well, father. Very well. If you won't take steps to cure yourself, it's the last you'll see of me. Good-day. Good-day." She slammed the door, and went muttering to herself up the path.

The bishop knelt down to pray. *Lord, have mercy upon me*, he murmured . . . *but, O God, if I pray to be free of the lice . . . and I will pray to be free of them . . . have mercy upon me . . . don't ever listen to my prayer. Don't ever listen to my prayer. Let the lice be with me.* When he had said this prayer, he felt, for a moment of bliss, as if this resolution had carried him up into the seventh heaven of paradise . . . as if his martyrdom was completed.

He was able to say the Lord's Prayer, and to make a brief act of contrition. *My God I love thee.*

But then the torment started again. He kept shrieking, take the lice away, take the lice away, take the lice away. Then he would stop from sheer exhaustion. And then one thought would gnaw in his brain: what is the use of it? Isn't it all entirely useless, like mountain-climbing, aren't I like the mountain-climber, who only keeps on to get to the top, because he has engaged himself to get to the top? Again the bishop would moan, take the lice away, take the lice away. Then again his outcry would exhaust itself, and he would think, I'm like the Anaconda serpent which has swallowed too large a deer and can't let go of it because inward-curving snake-teeth have trapped both the snake and the victim. He was, the bishop told himself, the snake and the victim. He was, the bishop told himself, the snake and God, the deer. He couldn't spit God out, if he wanted to. He also thought, these lice will purify me, but how can they help my flock, how? They continue as they were. Then once again the bishop would begin to keen, take the lice away, take the lice away, take the lice away . . .

Then his mind could think no more. He could only rage. Far across in the McGinis ranchhouse, they could hear him roaring. Mrs. McGinis put in a call to Edmonton, but could get no one at the church. When, however, the next morning, there was complete silence, the good woman again telephoned, and asked that someone be sent to the bishop's assistance . . . because . . . she was afraid of the worst . . .

IX

It was at the eleventh hour that the bishop gave up the ghost. His friends, summoned on the next day, did not arrive at the farmhouse until the next morning after that. They saw then a third miracle, if the lice on the crucifix was considered as one miracle, and the lice on the bishop himself, another. What they saw was, out of the mattress of the camp-cot a thick turf of a marvellously green new grass growing. On, or rather in, this grass, were the remains of the bishop. All the lice were gone, and only his skeleton was seen, at first. There was absolutely no sign of any vermin, no flea, no bedbug, no louse of any kind.

Summoned by the Presbyterian-minded Mrs. McGinis, it was the police who made a second discovery. One was a constable and the other a corporal. The constable *observed* that death couldn't have been recent. The corporal, however, *looking* more closely at the bishop's remains, saw that, within the bony cage of the churchman's ribs, the heart and other chest organs were still fresh and new.

At this, the clergy were filled with fear, for they knew what had happened *must* be a miracle. "I'm afraid," said the constable to the corporal, "there has been foul play."

These policemen were to be present at the performance of yet another miracle.

The first to discover the bones, the younger priest (whom the bishop loved in particular), when he perceived what had happened, drew back. He didn't want to look at the miracle. It was there. He was convinced that it had happened. But there was nothing inside him to receive it. I am like a barren woman, he thought. The bridegroom comes into me, and I don't conceive. He smiled to himself, thinking what would a psychologist make of a celibate Roman Catholic priest using such imagery? He went into the bathroom. When he had made water, he put his hand to the hot water tank. It was, of course, warm. Then he went into the kitchen, and there he saw the carton of cigarettes, which he had given the bishop as a parting gift. He saw how many the bishop had smoked. And thinking of what he had *done* for the bishop (for besides the cigarettes he had out of his own pocket arranged to have the cylinder of gas attached, so that there could be hot water always available for the bishop's use), he was ashamed of *how little* he had done.

Pushing his way through the others who were still wondering at the bishop's remains, and pushing aside the policemen, who speculated as to the possiblity of a crime, he flung himself down before the bishop, seized the bishop's hand, and wept, Forgive me, father.

It was then that the final miracle occurred, before the very eyes of the police. A great swarm of vermin appeared to descend upon the bishop's heart, as if to devour it.

Seeing this, the younger priest fainted away. When he had been carried into the kitchen, laid on the floor, and restoratives given, some one of the party noticed that the lice had consumed the bishop's remaining vitals, and that the skelton was now completely free of the organs inside it.

But when they looked for lice, there were none to be found.

■